ELVIS

A
BIOGRAPHY
BY

JERRY HOPKINS

SIMON AND SCHUSTER · NEW YORK

FOURTH PRINTING

SBN 671-20973-6
LIBRARY OF CONGRESS CATALOG CARD NUMBER: 77-156154
MANUFACTURED IN THE UNITED STATES OF AMERICA

Portions of this book have appeared in
Look *magazine.*

TO
JIM MORRISON FOR THE IDEA,
JANE FOR THE PATIENCE.

CONTENTS

APPENDIXES

"So Elvis Presley came, strumming a weird guitar and wagging his tail across the continent, ripping off fame and fortune as he scrunched his way, and, like a latter-day Johnny Appleseed, sowing seeds of a new rhythm and style in the white souls of the white youth of America, whose inner hunger and need was no longer satisfied with the antiseptic white shoes and whiter songs of Pat Boone. 'You can do anything,' sang Elvis to Pat Boone's white shoes, 'but don't you step on my Blue Suede Shoes!' "

—ELDRIDGE CLEAVER
Soul on Ice

-1-

TUPELO

Tupelo is the seat of Lee County, one of several poor rural counties in the northeastern corner of Mississippi, about halfway between Memphis and Birmingham, where, roughly, the rich farming soil of the Midwestern prairie meets the harsh brick-colored soil of the Southeast. Oldtown and Mud creeks bisect the town and dozens more vein the rolling countryside, many of them carrying Indian names. Euclautubba. Tishomingo. Yonaba. Mantachie. Chiwapa. Little Coonewah.

Legend has it that the Chickasaw Indians settled in the region centuries ago when they fled their enemies in the west. The Great Spirit instructed them to erect a magic pole in the center of camp, and next morning they noticed it had leaned to the east. The migration began, and every night the ritual was repeated, until finally, near where Tupelo stands today, the pole stopped leaning east. More realistically, it probably was the rich broad flood plains of the creeks, coupled with a mild climate, a long growing season, heavy rain (fifty-three inches yearly) and an abundance of timber that brought the Chickasaw east.

The Indians brought seed corn and introduced farming to the area, and the years passed, with only occasional visitors, among them the Spanish explorer Hernando de Soto and the Sieur de Bienville, the French colonial governor who had founded New Orleans and Mobile to the south. Both were run off by the Indians.

In 1801 a treaty was signed between the white man and the Chickasaw, and farmers, mostly Scotch-English, began to till the land. Then in 1832, with the signing of another treaty, the Indians agreed to return to the land of their ancestors, Oklahoma. Now the settlers came in a rush and land prices soared to five dollars an acre.

By 1850 the leading community was Harrisburg, named in honor of a prosperous farmer, but when the Mobile and Ohio laid its tracks through the rich bottom land a few miles away, the citizens of Harrisburg deserted the town and built beside the railroad. The new town was called Gum Pond and then Tupelo, from the Chickasaw word *topala,* meaning "lodging place." The tupelo gum trees provided dense foliage that shed water, their leaves were aromatic and possessed healing qualities, and their trunks yielded a chewing gum.

Soon thereafter came the first of Tupelo's major disasters, when the last Civil War battle fought in Mississippi was staged on the Tupelo slopes. Sherman was marching toward Georgia from Tennessee, and he dispatched General Andrew J. Smith and 14,000 Union troops to confront General Nathan Bedford Forrest and 6000 Confederate cavalry who endangered Sherman's flanks. The Southern forces were beaten three times in two days and then the Yankees burned the town to the ground.

Tupelo was rebuilt slowly after the war. It became the seat of Lee County, which was named for Robert E. Lee and was newly formed from parts of Pontotoc and Itawamba counties. One of those who contributed to its early growth was John Allen, a Tupelo boy who had served the Confederacy as a private and who was elected to Congress when he asked all the ex-privates to vote for him and all the ex-generals to vote for his opponent, who had been a general in the war. The speech made by Private John Allen (and he was never called anything else) to establish a federal fish hatchery in Tupelo is quoted even today: "Why, sir, a fish will travel over land for miles to get into the water we have at Tupelo. Thousands and millions of unborn fish are clamoring to this Congress today for an opportunity to be hatched in Tupelo. While there are larger places than Tupelo, I do not believe there is anyplace just exactly like it. Tupelo is very near if not exactly in the center of the universe. The horizon seems about the same distance in every direction. The sun, when doing business on regular schedule, comes right over town. Come early, gentlemen, and avoid the rush."

Tupelo got its hatchery, and the scramble for progress began. When the town needed jobs, the town's businessmen pledged $150,000 to build a cotton mill. Later they raised money to open a fertilizer plant and another plant to take oil from cotton seed. They built the first paved roads south of the Ohio River. And when disaster struck Tupelo a second time, in 1916 when the boll weevil ravaged the cotton crop, again the small county seat came up with a first—using the $5000 the banks normally spent on Christmas calendars to underwrite a livestock program. Thus Tupelo became one of the first communities in the South to diversify its agricultural base, importing what was the nation's first pure-bred Jersey herd to do so. With this development, Carnation erected a huge plant, its first in the South. This, with three textile plants, gave Tupelo needed industry. A few years later, in 1936, Tupelo became the first city in the nation to acquire electrical power from the Tennessee Valley Authority. Back in 1910 Memory E. Leake, who owned a lumberyard, built some of the first houses in the country to be sold on the long-term installment plan. The city's public library bookmobile was Mississippi's first. In the 1920s Reed's department store held the country's—possibly the world's—first twenty-four-hour-long sale, hiring farmers as salesmen and emptying the store of every item. Tupelo was a city of many firsts.

Then came the Great Depression, and no matter how progressive Tupelo was, it didn't help. A large part of the economy still was rooted in the rich bottom land surrounding the town, and when orders began to fall off at the textile plants, profits declined and workers were forced into what was called the stretch-out system, whereby they would care for several times as many machines as they'd manned before, with only a minimal increase in pay, or sometimes no raise at all. In Lee County, farmers and part-time farmers and their families supplied most of the labor in local industry. Tupelo was (and still is) the principal trading center for a five-county rural area, and when jobs became scarce in town, it meant the income of the farm family was cut. And when the plants didn't have orders for clothes, it meant they wanted to buy less cotton, or pay less for it, so again the farmers were hurt. Fully half of the farm families in the Tupelo area were tenant farmers then, living on someone else's land, or sharecroppers, sometimes living elsewhere—all working the fields for a share of profits. First the profits disappeared and then the jobs.

Tupelo had fewer than six thousand people when the Depression began, the more prosperous of whom lived in white one-story clapboard homes with green roofs and shutters, or two-story homes faced with red brick. South of Main Street, near the textile plants and cotton mill, was another residential neighborhood, a section of yellow and white four- and five-room plank houses that sat behind sagging wire and wood fences, perched on pilings along unpaved streets. This was Mill Town, or South Tupelo, where all the houses were built by the mill owners and rented to their employees.

The town's business section was on Main Street, which was lined with two- and three-story red brick buildings with stores on the street level and small factories or offices in the upper stories.

Beyond the stores and Mill Town were the tracks of the Mobile and Ohio and the St. Louis and San Francisco (Frisco) railroads, and beyond the tracks lay a section called Shakerag. This is where most of Tupelo's Negro cooks, nurses and house servants lived in weathered shacks.

A quarter mile past Shakerag, on a hilly rise the other side of Mud and Oldtown creeks, was the small neighboring community of East Tupelo, then separate from the town from which it took its name. It was cut in two parts by the Birmingham highway, with most of the tiny shotgun-style homes and the schoolhouse south of the highway, and only nine houses, one grocery store and the First Assembly of God Church on the other side.

It was on this side of town, literally the poor side of the Tupelo tracks, that there lived a young farm worker named Vernon Elvis Presley and a teenaged sewing machine operator named Gladys Smith.

-2-

THE CHILD

M RS. FAYE HARRIS was Gladys Presley's closest friend in East Tupelo. She's a widow now and she and her sister, Mrs. Tressie Miller (another widow), are in the same small home on Adams Street they lived in forty-three years ago. The house is directly across from the First Assembly of God Church and backs up to the bottom land, which until recently flooded fairly regularly, sometimes rising so much that Mrs. Harris's furniture sat more than two feet deep in muddy water. She's a thin woman, primly dressed in budget-priced clothing, and when she talks it is with a sense of cheery nostalgia in her voice, a longing for a time when the house was noisy with youngsters and visitors.

"There wasn't one thing I knowed Gladys didn't know it too, and the other way around," she says. "Mr. Presley used to kid us about that. He'd come in and say, 'I got somethin' to tell you, Glad'—he called her Glad—'but you'll have to go tell your buddy down the street, won't you?'

"Gladys's parents farmed some. I never did know what they did, but her mother moved near to me when the kids got grown some. Gladys had five sisters and three brothers. It was a big family. And Gladys was the fifth girl. She only had one younger sister and that was Cletis.

"Gladys didn't meet a stranger. She could meet anybody

and be ready for a big laugh. When things began to get dull, we said we have to go see Gladys and get cheered up.

"Mr. Presley was more distant. I didn't know him so well. He lived the other direction from me, but close by. He had one brother, Vester, and three sisters. After you knew Mr. Presley, he was friendly, but at first he was a little more distant to folks."

In 1956, when reporters first approached the Presley family for interviews, Mr. and Mrs. Presley talked only a little of their origins. When they were told that Presley was a name still prominent in England (although sometimes spelled "Pressley"), Vernon said he'd never heard of his kinfolk coming from anywhere in particular. He said the Presleys always seemed to have lived in northeast Mississippi and it was the same with his wife's family, the Smiths.

"Far as they knew, they always *did* come from hereabouts," says Mrs. Harris. "Some of the Presleys come from down in Itawamba County, I think a few from Alabama. But they'd been here for years and years."

At the time, in the late 1920s and early 1930s, as the Depression was making itself felt, Vernon Presley lived with his family in a two-bedroom house on Old Saltillo Road, one of the two narrow dirt streets that cut north of the highway, winding through rolling farm land for eight miles before it came to another town—Saltillo. It was a single-story home, its white paint peeling and chipped, with a small porch and outside plumbing. It was built on a swampy slope facing west toward the bottom land where Vernon farmed for shares.

Gladys lived with her parents, brothers and sisters in a house just a little larger, on a corner lot on lower land closer to the church, on Berry Street, two and a half blocks away.

"We all knew each other," says Mrs. Harris. "I remember seeing Mr. Presley. He used to run around with my nephews a lot, sometimes spend the night right here in this house. He was going with other girls at the time. Then he and Gladys got to going together, going in to the roller rink in town or having picnics over to the fish hatchery. The hatchery was one of the nicest places we had in those days, with trees to sit under and a nice lake to look at. They didn't go together too long until they got married. They went down in Verona, about five miles from here. They just run off and did it one day. They sure was a handsome couple—him so blond and her so dark—and both of them happy as kids on the day that school lets out."

(A few years later, Gladys's younger sister Cletis married Vernon's brother Vester.)

It was 1933. Vernon was only seventeen and had been working a nearby farm with his father, down on the rich land called East Bottom. They were, like most in East Tupelo, hoeing cotton and corn and peas for a share of whatever profit the landowner might realize at the end of the growing season. The work started at sunup and stretched until the sun set over Tupelo. The land was moist and watering was no problem, but weeds grew like bamboo and it was a continuing back-aching chore to keep them back. Then in late summer and early autumn it was time to harvest the crops and cut the pea vines up and bundle the drying cornstalks for feed for the stock at nearby dairy farms. When all this was finished, there was nothing to do except stretch the meager "share" for a year and look for other work.

In the autumn, when the bottom lands were white with cotton bolls, South Spring Street in Tupelo was blocked with trailers and wagons and trucks piled high with dusty cotton bales. Vernon Presley's farm work would bring him into town and he'd watch buyers and sellers walking around pulling large pinches of fiber from the bales, quickly grading the cotton, dropping it on the dusty street, to begin arguing over the price.

Other days, other seasons, Vernon would walk the dirt roads that wound around the farms and stands of pine or hike into town to look for work. The Presley family, like most families Vernon knew about, was too large to make staying at home comfortable; it was better to get out.

Gladys was four years older than Vernon, twenty-one, and working as a sewing machine operator next to her friend Faye Harris at the Tupelo Garment Company in Mill Town. Each morning at six, the same time her husband began working the fields, she reported for work at her machine. She worked by the piece and she worked twelve hours a day, five or six days a week, and according to Faye Harris, if each of them grossed thirteen dollars for the week, it was a good paycheck. "On top of that," says Mrs. Harris, "the company had a quota you had to meet each day of production, and if you didn't meet it, you were laid off."

On the first floor of the plant a keen-bladed electric knife cut cloth to pattern. The material was then sent upstairs, where it was to be stitched on machines by women operators. Sometimes Gladys moved over to the next most responsible position, that of inspector, and checked all the shirts as they came by for the right number of buttons and buttonholes. Some time later Gladys left the Tupelo Garment Company for Reed's, which occupied the second and third floors of a three-story red brick building nearby and produced women's work dresses, smocks and aprons. There again she ran a sewing machine.

For a time Vernon and Gladys lived with their in-laws, first with the Smiths and then with the Presleys. When Gladys learned she was pregnant, in the summer of 1934, she quit her job at the garment factory. It was, Faye Harris says, "a hard pregnancy and she couldn't work, couldn't work at all." At the time, Vernon was driving a truck, delivering milk from door to door in East Tupelo. His boss was Orville S. Bean, who had a dairy farm a quarter of a mile from where the Presleys lived, and Vernon thought perhaps Mr. Bean could help him get a new house.

"Orville Bean had money and he loant money," says Mrs. Harris. "Mr. Presley went to him and asked him to help him build a house. Him and Gladys wanted a little place of their own now they was raising a family. So he financed the house, then rented it to them. He did that a lot in the neighborhood."

The house was like tens of thousands built in the South in the 1920s and 1930s to house the poor, both black and white. It was in the shotgun-style, oblong with frame sidewalls, a peaked roof and a small covered porch. Inside was a brick fireplace, with a chimney running up the middle of the house. It was thirty feet long—just ten man-sized steps from the front door to the rear—and half that in width, divided equally into two perfectly square rooms.

(Years later Elvis wondered aloud in his twenty-three-room mansion in Memphis if the entire place wouldn't fit in the mansion's living room.)

The front room was the bedroom, where there was an iron bedstead with a lumpy mattress. On one side of the bed was the small iron-grated fireplace, on the other the front door. There were three windows, one at the head of the bed, another across the room at the other side of the house, the third facing the porch. Overhead was a single electric outlet. The floors were bare.

The back room, the kitchen-dining room, was where friends and family were entertained. It was furnished with a stove, table, chairs and a cabinet. Again there were the three windows, one overhead outlet and a rear door. There was no running water. Outside there was a pump, some distance from the outhouse.

There were two fair-sized trees in front of the house, another three to one side, a sixth in the back, offering some shade in summer and places for kids to climb. Nearby was a stand of young long-needled pine, and down Old Saltillo Road were some narrow streams and broad pasture land.

The house sat on ground higher than most in East Tupelo, but like all the one-story homes in the neighborhood it rested on tired stumpy legs made of concrete block and brick—protection against flooding and heavy rain. Below the house and off west toward Tupelo the creeks flooded their banks, and behind the house was a severely eroded clay hillside; when it rained, as it often did, mud slid past and underneath the house to the road below.

The second week of January 1935 County Superintendent W. A. Roper left for the state capital to beg emergency relief financing for the county's schools, because if funds weren't forthcoming, classes would have to shut down six months a year instead of the customary three. . . . It was announced that the cannery operated under President Roosevelt's Federal Emergency Relief Act, which had opened only a month earlier, would close within the week, leaving 160 persons unemployed. . . . J. E. Riley, Lee County's head of the Rural Rehabilitation Division, said 146 farm families would be selected from the relief rolls, provided (on a loan basis) with eighteen acres in cotton, corn, hay, feed and food crops, along with a home, water and wood, to help them toward self-sufficiency. . . . Reed's department store was having a "gigantic sale" offering women's coats for $3.98 and dress oxfords for $1.47. . . . Francis Lederer, Joan Bennett, Charles Ruggles and Mary Boland were featured at the Strand Theatre in *The Pursuit of Happiness*. . . . And Elvis Aron Presley was born.

He was born shortly after noon on January 8, one of identical twins.

For those who place some credence in astrology it meant Elvis was a Capricorn, a cardinal earthy sign whose key words were ambitious, persevering, diplomatic and reserved —the sign of the priest, ambassador or scientist.* Among those sharing this sign with Elvis: Gary Grant, then almost thirty-one and starring in *Sylvia Scarlet;* Joan of Arc; Richard Nixon, a twenty-two-year-old law student at Duke University; Martin Luther King, who was only six; Mao Tse-tung, Humphrey Bogart, Pablo Casals, Carl Sandburg, Albert Schweitzer and Edgar Allan Poe. Fairly heavy company.

* For a detailed astrological reading and chart see Appendix A.

For others, the fact that Elvis was a "mirror" twin meant he had psychic strength beyond the norm but was only "half a person"; he needed his twin for total strength.

"They didn't have insurance and the doctor didn't believe in carrying his expectant mothers to the hospital, so Gladys stayed at home," says Mrs. Harris. "All along Gladys told everybody she was going to have twins, but the doctor wasn't having any of it. Elvis was borned, they had done washed him and she said she was still in labor. The doctor said he didn't think so.

"Gladys said, 'Well, it's the same pain.'

"Finally a neighbor said, 'Doctor, there's another baby got to come out of there.'"

The second child was born dead. ("We matched their names," Mrs. Presley said years later. "Jesse Garon and Elvis Aron.") They were born in the early afternoon and by six, when Faye Harris came rushing up to the Presley home from work at the garment plant, little Jesse Garon was laid out in a tiny coffin in the front room.

The baby was buried the next day in an unmarked grave on a hillside in the Priceville Cemetery a few miles to the north and east.

Elvis was to be an only child, and he was as spoiled as the meager family budget could afford.

"Sometimes he was a little overbearing," says Mrs. Harris. "Gladys thought he was the greatest thing that ever happened and she treated him that way. She worshiped that child from the day he was borned to the day she died. She'd always keep him at home, or when she let him go play, she always was out seeing about him, making sure he was all right. And wherever she went, visiting family or down to Roy Martin's grocery store, she always had Elvis with her. She wouldn't go nowheres without Elvis. Elvis'd get out of her sight and you could hear her hollerin' and cryin' and carryin' on to plumb down here, afraid he'd got lost or something."

If Mrs. Presley treated Elvis as a mother bear cossets her only cub, spoiling him, she also gave him a means of earning respect from others, feeding him something that seemed a cross between Emily Post and a rigid sort of Christianity.

"One time he found a Coca-Cola bottle on my porch and he carried it home with him," says Mrs. Harris. "She spanked him and sent him back. He said, 'Miz Harris, I done wrong and my mama whipped me for it, so here's your Coca-Cola bottle back.' I gave it back to him and gave him some cookies besides. He told Gladys, 'Mother, I told you she didn't care if I took it.' And she told Elvis, 'But you didn't ask her first.'"

Elvis himself once said, "My mama never let me out of her sight. I couldn't go down to the creek with the other kids. Sometimes when I was little I used to run off. Mama would whip me, and I thought she didn't love me."

Mrs. Presley was once quoted as saying she tried to teach Elvis and his little friends not to fight but to be happy. She said that once in a while a bully came along and then Elvis's daddy would have to show him how to stand up for himself. She said that Elvis did, of course, winning most of the fights.

The Presleys also taught their son to say "sir" and "ma'am," to stand when an elder (Grandma, Uncle Vester, Aunt Delta Mae) entered the room. Not to interrupt or argue. And if you don't have nothing nice to say, don't say nothing at all. So well did they impress the young Elvis with these simple rules that years later, even after he had worked with movie directors and recording executives only a few years older than he, and they insisted he use their first names, he continued to call them Mr. or Mrs. and to say "yes, sir" and "yes, ma'am," and "please." Elvis was, if nothing else, polite.

And as his parents loved him, he returned their love. Both his parents told stories about how upset he'd get when his father plunged into a lake to swim or rushed into a burning building to help save a neighbor's furniture. (The home of his Uncle Noah, Aunt Christine and his playmate and cousin

Bobby was one of several that burned in East Tupelo, and another fire gutted the church.) His parents said Elvis was afraid of losing his father, that's why he cried so much.

In the 1930s and early 1940s the First Assembly of God Church in Tupelo was a small one-story structure on Adams Street, just a block and a half from where the Presleys lived. It was there Elvis heard his first music.

In later years Mrs. Presley liked telling a story about Elvis's behavior in church: "When Elvis was just a little fellow, he would slide off my lap, run down the aisle and scramble up to the platform of the church. He would stand looking up at the choir and try to sing with them. He was too little to know the words, of course, but he could carry the tune."

As Elvis grew, he and his parents would sing together at camp meetings, revivals and church conventions, but only as part of the congregation, never as a "popular trio" or in the church choir, as has been reported in several magazines and "biographies." Nor, apparently, were the Presleys quite the churchgoers legend has it they were. Mrs. Harris, who says she never missed a service (and it's difficult to doubt anything she says), claims the Presleys were "regular but not fanatical; they'd miss a service ever' now and then."

The Assemblies of God churches, founded only twenty-five years earlier, in 1914, were at the time part of the evangelical movement that swept most of the South and Midwest during the roaring twenties and depressing thirties. Like other white pentecostal church groups (many shared the same basic beliefs but adhered to different founders and names), those who took their prayers to the Assembly of God held a conservative interpretation of the Bible, believing among other things that the wicked would be judged and on dying be consigned to everlasting punishment in the lake which burneth with fire and brimstone. The simple message: Be good or go to hell.

The Sunday services usually opened with song, the Presley family joining the congregation and choir. Behind the altar would be the pastor and his lay associates, dressed much as the congregation in inexpensive but "decent" dress. Later one of the laymen would lead the congregation in silent prayer and likely as not the pastor, sitting quietly to one side, his hands folded in his lap, would begin to speak "in tongues," a phenomenon that purportedly represented direct contact with God as God speaks through the individual in a language unknown to him. Among white pentecostals the speaking-in-tongues experience has virtually no high emotional content. In contrast with Negro churches of similar stripe, the white congregation remains calm; it is taken as matter-of-factly as the condemnation to hell for wickedness.

Which is not to say the Presley congregation was lethargic. Anything but. During much of the service the mood was formed by the minister, who when not speaking in tongues was praying fervently—providing a noisy lead for those others present who wished to cry aloud, "Praise God . . . thank you, Lord . . . I love you, Lord!"—and stalking the aisle of the church delivering a fire-and-brimstone sermon. During the sermon the pastor's voice rumbled and shook, carrying equal parts of threat and hope. Filling the small plank church in East Tupelo were a flood of words that coiled and uncoiled in measured cadence, exhortations and chastisements that came in a rush, followed by whispers of spiritual ecstasy.

"They was good revivals," says Mrs. Faye Harris. "Lots of people was saved."

Years later, when asked where he got his wiggle, Elvis said, "We used to go to these religious singin's all the time. There were these singers, perfectly fine singers, but nobody responded to them. Then there was the preachers and they cut up all over the place, jumpin' on the piano, movin' ever' which way. The audience liked 'em. I guess I learned from them."

Elvis was not a handsome boy. What is probably the

earliest photograph shows him at two or three—huge eyes looking off to the left, a twisted, flattened nose, drooping lips, all round and soft and looking rather like an infant doing an impression of Edward G. Robinson; there's even a hat with a brim, worn a little cockeyed, leaning to Elvis's right.

In another early photograph, taken when he was six, there is no hat and his platinum blond hair is parted as if with a garden hoe, cut close at the sides, a few strands falling over his prominent forehead. His eyes are outsized and heavily lidded, his nose flat and off-center, his thick lips even then twisted in the lopsided leer that later would become world famous.

In both these pictures it was as if his head hadn't yet grown enough to match the prominent features. Dressed in a loose sweater pulled over a cotton shirt, one collar-point in, one out, Elvis looks in the second photograph almost as much the perfect waif as he seemed in the earlier one.

A later picture, taken outside his home with his parents, shows Elvis wearing a white long-sleeved shirt open at the neck, the sleeves about two inches too short, white and brown shoes, suspenders yanking his trousers halfway up his chest. His father is wearing a white shirt, a leather jacket and loose-fitting slacks, his mother a dotted print dress, belted at the waist.

In none of the photographs is anyone smiling.

When Elvis was five, his mother began walking him to class (a practice she would continue through part of his high school days in Memphis) across Highway 78 into the main section of the little town to the simple wooden frame buildings that served as the East Tupelo Consolidated School. All twelve grades were being taught and the school had a high school accreditation, the first high school graduation having been held six years earlier, in 1934, when there were nine teachers with four students in the senior class. By the time Elvis was in fourth grade there were seven hundred students at East Tupelo and twenty-six teachers.

No one associated with the school system remembers much about Elvis before he was in the fifth grade, when Mrs. J. C. Grimes was his homeroom teacher. She lived less than a hundred yards from the Presleys on Old Saltillo Road and had introduced herself to Gladys when she'd been told they were related distantly.

"He was a good student," Mrs. Grimes says today. "You remember if they're not. I knew him that well, I'd remember that. Sweet, that's the word. And average. Sweet and average.

"There were about thirty in each of the homerooms and each morning we'd have chapel," she says. "Devotions. Well, two mornings in a row I asked my children if anybody could say prayer. No one said anything. Then on the third day Elvis put up his hand. He said he could say prayer. And he said prayer and he sang several songs he knew. I remember one of them and it wasn't really right for chapel, but Elvis sang it so sweetly, it liked to make me cry. That was 'Old Shep.' Mr. J. D. Cole was the principal at the time and I asked him to listen to Elvis sing. And Mr. Cole was so impressed he carried Elvis to the Mississippi-Alabama Fair and entered him in the annual contest."

The Mississippi-Alabama Fair and Dairy Show was organized in 1904 as the Lee County Fair and was municipally owned and operated as a non-profit event for the farmers of the area. There were horse shows and cattle auctions and, later, beauty contests at which Miss Mississippi and Miss Alabama were selected for the Miss America Pageant in Atlantic City. In the 1940s talent contests were held, with local winners coming from the two states to compete for an annual prize. Elvis was ten when Mr. Cole entered him to represent East Tupelo, which was only half a mile from the fairgrounds.

Elvis sang "Old Shep" at that fair, standing on a chair and reaching for the microphone, unaccompanied, because the guitar players present were reluctant to give help to any of the competition. Elvis won second prize—five dollars and free admission to all the amusement rides.

"My husband Clint had a furniture store at the time," says Mrs. Grimes, "and I had Elvis to come by and sing 'Old Shep' for him, because he couldn't get away to see him at the fair. Elvis sang his song and Clint gave him a nickel for a soda."

Says Mr. Grimes today: "I didn't think Elvis'd ever amount to anything, of course."

As Elvis was growing up, his father moved from job to job, leaving the milk delivery route when there weren't customers enough to continue it, working crops in the bottom, sorting lumber and hiring out as an apprentice carpenter at the Leake and Goodlett Lumberyard in Tupelo. Tupelo served as headquarters for eighteen counties in the administration of President Roosevelt's New Deal projects, and so Vernon also found himself doing carpentry for the Works Progress Administration (WPA), eventually becoming a foreman. Whatever he could get he took—like other men during the Depression.

"They lost their house and moved several times," says Mrs. Harris. "They lived in several houses this side of the highway, on Kelly Street, then on Berry. Later the house on Berry was condemned. They was real poor. They just got by."

At least they ate regularly. The food may not have been the most nutritious, but it was regular. Mrs. Harris says there wasn't much meat, though. "You had to buy your meat," she says. "A few had hogs in the yard, but most had to buy their meat and that was expensive. So we mostly relied on vegetables. Peas, cornbread, okra, tomatoes, lettuce, radishes, boiled corn when we had it, and in the wintertime we'd have dried stuff and canned peaches and apples. We never went real hungry, but we worked at it sometimes."

Times were equally tough on Tupelo. The year Elvis was

born cotton growers were predicting the South's first billion-dollar crop, but if this represented prosperity for some, little of it reached the common man. And the weather, always unpredictable in northern Mississippi, only made matters worse. Often the creeks would flood the bottom land and many of the small homes in East Tupelo. And in 1936 one of history's most killing tornadoes came whirling out of neighboring Harrisburg into Tupelo, killing two hundred and sixteen, injuring another thousand and some, and destroying nine hundred homes—all in just thirty-two seconds. In East Tupelo, where damage was by contrast minimal, the Presleys watched roofs torn off and walls warped so they'd never settle straight up and down again and there'd always be cracks and leaks.

There were no tornado cellars in East Tupelo. The land was too low and water would have seeped into them. So on the hot dry days when the sky suddenly went black and the woolly stillness of the afternoon air was torn by the cry of wind, Elvis was rushed some distance by his mother to a storm shelter cut in a distant hillside, to wait hours before it seemed safe to leave.

One of those days Vernon was at work and Elvis and his mother were in the shelter alone, singing at first to keep from being so frightened, then talking about the singing Elvis'd been doing and how well he had done at the fair. Elvis told his mother he wanted a bicycle. Mrs. Presley knew this and Mr. Presley had priced bicycles and the fifty-five-dollar tag was too high. So Mrs. Presley asked her son wouldn't he rather have the ($12.95) guitar in the same window with the bike; after all, it would help him with his singing, and maybe later he could have the bike. The way the story goes, Elvis said if he got the guitar, he wouldn't ask for the bicycle again for a year.

In the months following, Elvis taught himself how to play the guitar—with a little help from his uncles, Johnny Smith and Vester Presley, who showed him several chords—and began listening to the radio, trying to copy the sounds he heard. He listened to the popular country music vocalists—Roy Acuff, Ernest Tubb, Ted Daffan, Bob Wills and Jimmie Davis, along with the records of the man generally recognized as the Father of Country Music, Jimmie Rodgers, who had been from Meridian, Mississippi, a hundred or so miles from Tupelo. He also listened to the blues singers who were from the same neighborhood, Mississippi's cotton bottom, stretching west to the Mississippi River and south to New Orleans—people like Booker (Bukka) White, Big Bill Broonzy, Otis Spann, B. B. King, John Lee Hooker (who wrote a song called "Tupelo Mississippi Flood"), Chester (The Howlin' Wolf) Burnett, Jimmy Reed, Earl Hooker, and McKinley (Muddy Waters) Morganfield. And on Sundays and Wednesdays—Wednesdays being revival days at the First Assembly of God Church—Elvis learned to sing spirituals.

Slowly the style was being formed.

"In the afternoons we'd bunch up, go to one house, talk, listen to the radio and entertain ourselves," says Mrs. Harris. "In the spring we went to the woods out behind his house. Me and Gladys would sit and gossip while the kids rolled down the hill. They loved to gather the wild flowers—the dogwood and the honeysuckle. Gladys liked to have flowers in the house."

Just as often Elvis's friends would come over to the Presley house to sit on the hill behind it and listen to Elvis slowly pick out the songs he knew.

Elvis never wanted for friends, company at the house, or people to visit nearby. Besides his school chums there were the large Presley and Smith families, and elsewhere in the county were *more* relatives—cousins of cousins of cousins and such. Buck Presley was first cousin to Elvis's grandfather, for one example, and he and his wife Alice and their seven sons lived and farmed in Richmond, eight miles away. Today Buck and his wife and two of his boys, Hershell and J. W., live in small sparsely furnished homes in Nettleton. Buck is in his seventies, usually wears bib overalls and sits in a worn chair, a small jar on the floor at one side to collect the spittings of the tobacco he chews. Hershell is a muscular black-haired six-footer who wears loose-fitting citified garb— slacks and a sport shirt open at the collar.

"I was born in Richmond," says Buck. "Been living within fifteen miles of Tupelo all my life, except for two years in Arkansas. Farming mostly. That's what all the Presleys do. Raise cotton and corn."

Buck doesn't say much. He's taciturn, a little suspicious of strangers—but cordial, *extremely* cordial—and likes to size a man up before he tells him anything. Hershell is much the same.

"We would ride over to Tupelo on the school bus," he says. "Go to visit Elvis and all—go to shows, fight, everything else. I remember a lot of times we used to jump that fence to go to the fair. We got caught one time and that broke it up. Those guys with the clubs they had around the fence like to scare us to death."

Hershell sits back, silent again. He crosses his legs awkwardly. He thinks of something else to say.

"I remember Elvis used to carry that ol' gi-tar around. He loved that gi-tar. It didn't have but three strings on it most of the time, but he sure could beat the dickens outa it."

When strangers leave the Buck and Hershell Presley house in farmland outside Nettleton, the last thing they hear is "Y'all come back."

It was when Elvis was in his first years of school, before he won the fair contest and got his guitar, that his father began to seek work in Memphis, a hundred miles to the northwest. Wartime plants had mushroomed in the city and work was easier to find there. He came home every weekend he could, and when the war ended he moved back. He had hoped to take his family to Memphis, but the housing was inadequate or unavailable and when the war ended there was no job.

In 1946 the East Tupelo Consolidated School was merged with the Tupelo School District. (The two towns merged in 1948.) This meant that in June 1947 Elvis's school held its last high school graduation ceremonies. From then on the eleventh and twelfth grades were bussed to class in Tupelo.

About the same time, the Presleys moved into town, settling near Shakerag, Tupelo's black ghetto, and Elvis was enrolled at Milam Junior High School at the corner of Gloster and Jefferson, a much larger school in a much nicer neighborhood. Soon after, in 1948, when Elvis was thirteen, the Presleys left town.

"We were broke, man, broke, and we left Tupelo overnight," Elvis said years later. "Dad packed all our belongings in boxes and put them on the top and in the trunk of a 1939 Plymouth. We just headed to Memphis.

"Things had to be better."

-3-

HIGH SCHOOL

THINGS WEREN'T ANY BETTER in Memphis, not at first. If anything they were worse. The living quarters in East Tupelo and Tupelo had never been spacious or especially comfortable, but compared to what they found in Tennessee's largest city (population then about 300,000) they seemed almost palatial.

At first they packed themselves into one room of a large boxlike home at 572 Poplar Avenue, a mile from where the Mississippi River flanked the city's business center. It was a once-exclusive neighborhood considered part of North Memphis and, like many just outside the city's commercial core, it was inhabited almost exclusively by the poor. At one time the house may have been elegant, but in 1948 it was cut up into greasy one-room apartments. There were no kitchen facilities and the Presleys shared a bath with three other families. There were sixteen high-ceilinged rooms in the building, providing shelter for no less than sixty individuals. The electrical wiring was a daily threat. Heating was totally inadequate. There were holes in the walls, and wherever there wasn't a hole there was dirt. The Presleys slept, cooked (hauling water from the bathroom, to prepare meals over a hotplate) and ate in the one room. It was not the sort of home you invited your friends to see.

Initially Elvis had no friends. Largely this was because of

his reticence, his shyness. A new boy in any neighborhood undergoes a period of painful adaptation, and when it is a thin, polite country boy from a small village in Mississippi moving to Memphis, a city he'd only heard about (and might have feared because his father hadn't found work all that easily), the pain becomes acute, the strangeness and bigness nearly overwhelming. The L. C. Humes High School Elvis was taken to his first week in Memphis, for instance, had more than 1600 students in its six classes (seventh through twelfth), more pupils than there were people in East Tupelo.

Years later Vernon Presley talked about that first day of school, when he took Elvis to class, left him outside the principal's office, and no sooner was he back home than Elvis was back home too. Vernon said Elvis was so nervous he was bug-eyed, and when he asked what was wrong, Elvis said he wasn't sure about where things were and there were so many kids . . . he was afraid the kids would laugh at him.

Elvis returned the following day and slowly he found his way, while his father worked in a tool company and drove a truck for a wholesale grocer and his mother sometimes worked in a curtain factory or as a waitress in a downtown cafeteria. The combined Presley family income came to about thirty-five dollars a week.

No one outside the Presley family recalls much about that first year in Memphis. Elsie Marmann remembers Elvis was in her eighth-grade music class and says he really didn't show much promise. "He wasn't in my glee club," she says, "he didn't have the kind of voice I could use in a glee club." Mrs. Tressie Miller, who'd followed the Presleys to Memphis from Mississippi to live in the same house on Poplar Avenue, says there was a big yard in front of the house and after school Elvis sometimes would entertain friends, picking and singing the songs he knew. Others comment on how serious Elvis was, or how quiet, or how polite. Everyone says he loved his mother—no, worshiped her. And that's about it. It would be a year before any of his teachers or classmates knew Elvis well enough to talk about. And even then most at Humes seldom if ever really recognized Elvis. All high schools have students who go nearly unnoticed. Elvis was one of those.

In February 1949 Vernon Presley began working as a laborer at the United Paint Company, packing cans of house paint into boxes for shipment. United's factory, in a five-story brick building that had been a brewery in pre-Prohibition times, a cotton warehouse after that, was located at the corner of Winchester and Concord, only a few blocks from where the Presleys lived. Vernon was paid 83 cents an hour, grossing $38.50 on the good weeks, when he picked up five hours of overtime. It wasn't a fortune, but it was a job Mr. Presley would hold for five years. However minimal the pay and status attached to the job, at least the pay was regular.

On June 17 the same year, Elvis and his mother had a caller at their one room—Mrs. Jane Richardson, who was one of two home service advisers working for the Memphis Housing Authority. The Presleys had applied for assistance, and Mrs. Richardson was there to determine whether or not they were qualified.

"They were just poor people," says Mrs. Richardson, a kindly, confident woman who's just retired from the Housing Authority after thirty-two years. "I interviewed Mrs. Presley and Elvis and at that time I said he was a very nice boy. They seemed nice and deserving. Those were my remarks from my investigation of their living conditions before they moved into the project."

Her report, which described the Poplar Avenue residence as "infested" and "in need of major repairs," was submitted. Vernon's salary at United Paint was checked; it was determined he sent ten dollars a month to his mother in West Point, Mississippi; it was noted he had a 1937 Pontiac that operated rather fitfully; and it was suggested the Presleys be accepted for residence at the Lauderdale Courts, the federally funded housing project in the same neighborhood and near Vernon's work.

Three months later, in May, as Elvis was completing his first year at Humes High, the Presleys moved into a two-bedroom ground-floor apartment in the Lauderdale Courts at 185 Winchester Street.

The red brick project was one of several constructed in the mid-thirties by the federal government, and it had been operated since that time by the city. It was designed for low-income families, and rent traditionally had been adjusted to how much the individual family could afford to pay. The Presleys were asked to pay thirty-five dollars a month initially.

"Most of the people who lived here came from slum areas, substandard housing," says Mrs. Richardson. "That was the requirement then that we'd move them in here. Our slogan was 'From slums to public housing to private ownership.' And we have had a number of people who have lived here who have saved enough to make a down payment on a small home."

There was a quiet anguish hovering over the dry grass lawns, the harsh symmetrical walks and anonymous brick buildings. The 433 units in the project—some in one-story structures with wrought iron trim, others in three-story monoliths—were kept as neatly as the housing authority insisted, but money for individual comfort and decoration was scarce. The Presleys lived in one of the monoliths, and across the street were gray leaning shacks housing some of the city's poorest blacks, a drugstore and a beer parlor, and beyond that the United Paint Company and St. Joseph's Hospital. A half mile to the south was dark and scabrous Beale Street, the legendary home of the blues. The Lauderdale Courts had been open just eleven years and the housing was better than adequate, but the neighborhood was not a good one.

The first day in the apartment Vernon filled out a report describing the condition of the living room, two bedrooms, and (hallelujah!) separate kitchen and private bath. Carefully making check marks on the form and adding his comment in a neat, legible hand in pencil, he wrote, "Wall around

bath tub need repair . . . apartment in need of paint job . . .
1 shade will not roll in bed room . . . light in front hall will
not stay on . . . oven door will not shut tight . . . one leg [of
dresser] broke off . . . bathroom sink stopped up . . . faucet
in kitchen sink needs repairs."

There were things wrong. But it was a decided step up
from the place on Poplar. From slum to public housing. Next
stop private ownership. At the time it seemed quite unlikely.

The form that Vernon submitted on the apartment's condition is one of dozens remaining in the Presley file still being
kept in Mrs. Richardson's old office.* When you live in public
housing, it is like being in the armed forces; there are regular
reports and inspections, and the paperwork turns into a dos-
sier. The Presleys lived in the project apartment three and
a half years, and during that time Mrs. Richardson or someone else from the Housing Authority came through two or
three times a year to see how the linoleum and woodwork
were holding up, as well as to check on income and other
meager facts of life. Mrs. Richardson was (and is) a friendly
woman, genuinely concerned about her tenants, but still
there was that crushing anonymity, the cold metallic feel
that goes with life on the dole.

It was noted by Mrs. Richardson in the first home service
report, made Thanksgiving week of 1949, that the Presley
car had given out, that there was no telephone in the apartment, and that Vernon remained at United Paint with an
estimated annual income of $2080.

Even with Elvis in high school now, his parents continued
to coddle him, to worry even more than most parents of an

---

* Like so much of Elvis's past, the file has been visited by his ardent fans
and is worn (and torn) with use. Elvis's fans—about whom more later—are
fanatical in their devotion and larcenous in their souvenir hunting. They'll
go anywhere to see, feel, talk to, photograph (or take) any object, building,
person or gimcrack that's crossed their idol's path. Several major newspapers
and magazines have had their entire clipping and photo files stolen. At
Graceland, Elvis's Memphis estate, the grass along the highway has been
plucked regularly for the fifteen years Elvis has lived there.

only child. "They treated him like he was two years old," says Mrs. Ruby Black, who still lives in the Lauderdale Courts. (She is the mother of the late Bill Black, who played bass for Elvis's first records and concerts.) "Mrs. Presley talked about her twin babies and she just lived for Elvis. Years later he called her every night when he was touring and Mrs. Presley couldn't go to sleep until she'd heard from him." Elvis himself once recalled that his mother walked him to school until he was fifteen.

"That only happened some of the time," says Evan (Buzzie) Forbess, one of Elvis's closest friends at Humes. "Most of the time he went with us."

Buzzie lived with his sisters and mother in the same building the Presleys lived in. His father had run off with a waitress soon after he was born, and since that time his mother had been working in a curtain factory. It was, in fact, Mrs. Forbess who got Gladys her job sewing curtains. Buzzie was a year behind Elvis, but for four years they were practically inseparable.

"It was a lower poverty-type school, one of the lowest in Memphis," says Buzzie today. "I wouldn't have taken much for that school and I don't think Elvis would've, either. He said so several times. In that neighborhood the fact that Elvis got through without getting into serious trouble was an accomplishment."

Buzzie looks like a stocky Peter Falk—even smokes cigars —and he works for the city's water, power and light department today. He grins somewhat sardonically and talks about the fights Elvis was in. He tells about how there was a scrap after a football game and Elvis was one who "jumped a rope and joined right in." He tells about when Elvis was in the tenth grade and someone from the opposing team cussed out Humes's coach from a parked school bus, and Elvis "threw his bony ol' arm up there, right through the open window of the bus, and clipped that boy on the nose, and that ended it."

Buzzie says football was Elvis's consuming interest, and he

goes right into a story about the time he and Elvis and some others went over to the waterworks to play ball with a bunch of "nigras." "Man, they had the craziest way of snapping the ball," Buzzie says. "We were used to numbers, like four, thirty, eighteen, five, snap! And the center would hike the ball to the quarterback. With this colored team the center would bend over the ball and the quarterback would start shouting something like 'Beans, maters, taters . . .' They'd be hollering vegetables and we'd be falling down laughing. We'd still be on our fannies laughing and they'd've scored a touchdown."

For a year Elvis played ball for the Humes High Tigers. "He went out in the eleventh grade and made the team all right," says Buzzie. "He didn't play in twelfth grade, but eleventh, junior year, he did. He was a little small and not used to organized ball, but he never shied away from sticking his nose in. He played end. He played a few games of the ten or so we had that year. He didn't score any touchdowns. He usually played defense. He did score a lot in sandlot games. He had real good hands and he was fast. But he was just too small for organized ball games."

Bobby (Red) West was also a high school friend. He lived in another, nearby government housing project, Hurt Village, and he was a year ahead of Elvis at Humes. Like Buzzie, Red was a varsity regular on the football team. He doesn't look much different today from what he did in the early 1950s, perhaps a little softer in the midsection and a little older, but still his shoulders are broad and muscular, his wiry red hair cut bristle-short.

"Elvis had his hair real long in those days," Red says. "He was the only guy. The rest of us had crew cuts. I remember once when all the guys were gonna get him and cut his hair. I helped him escape from that. He had trouble with his hair when he was playing ball. He just played one year and the coach told him to cut his hair or get off the team. That's about what it boiled down to. He wore the loud clothes, the pink

and black. He was just different. It gave the people something to do, to bother him."

Elvis once said he had to let his hair and sideburns grow to
look like a truckdriver, to make him seem older. He's never
really talked much about why he dressed so loudly; it was
merely something he did.

"I would see them to leave every Sunday morning for
church," says Buzzie Forbess's mother, a large soft woman
in her sixties who still lives in the project. "He was so cute.
One Sunday he'd have a pink pair of pants on and a dark
coat. Next Sunday it'd be the dark pants and the pink coat."

Down on Beale Street, at the corner of Second Street, there
was a men's clothing store owned by the Lansky Brothers,
who specialized in selling vibrant yellow suits and pink sport
coats with black lightning streaks, white shoes, and glittery
men's accessories. Whenever the country musicians came to
Memphis from Nashville, this was one of the stops they
made. It also was a favorite of the blacks who lived in the
neighborhood. Elvis seldom had much money to spend on
clothing, but whenever he did, it was spent there.

Through football, his hair style and manner of dress, Elvis
was developing an identity, slowly building a confidence, a
sense of personal security. Yet he remained shy, and oddly
enough it was his music about which he was most reticent.

Elvis wasn't reluctant to sing for his friends, picking out
the few basic chords he knew on the guitar, but when it came
to performing in front of anyone else, he backed down. Buzzie
Forbess says, "He and I had biology together and it came
time for a Christmas party. Elvis was in the tenth grade and
we wanted to get Elvis to sing. He was scared to death and
he left his guitar behind on purpose, so he could say he
couldn't sing. And he *didn't* sing."

Another classmate, Mona Raburn Finley, once said that
when Elvis did bring his guitar to school, she and her friends
sometimes would beg him for an hour to sing, then when he

started, the bell would ring and class would be over.

Not until Mildred Scrivener, a history teacher at Humes High, put Elvis in the school's variety show did he begin to walk away from his timidity.

"I never knew Elvis could sing until someone in my class said Elvis should bring his guitar to our homeroom picnic," she says today. "Elvis did bring his guitar, and while everybody else was running around doing what young people do, Elvis sat quietly by himself playing and singing to the few who gathered around him. Slowly, other students began to come to him. There was something about his plaintive singing which drew them like a magnet."

Miss Scrivener was Elvis's homeroom teacher his senior year, and when the school's 1600 students crammed the auditorium for the variety show, Elvis was on the program. The show was held to raise money for a special school fund and no one would dare miss it. Most pupils at Humes were from poor homes, and if ever a boy or girl couldn't afford to attend a dance, or lacked money enough for lunch or clothing, he or she had a quiet talk with Tom Brindley, the school's principal, who would pull enough money from the fund, and no one was the wiser.

"There were three teachers in charge of the show," Miss Scrivener says today, "and I was the one appointed to be producer. That meant I was the one to make up the program. This year, when Elvis performed, I remember there were more than thirty acts—nearly more acts than there was time to show them properly. And what about encores? When a student did well, he or she was entitled to an encore. I solved that problem by calling everyone together and saying we just didn't have as many minutes, so there would be only one encore—the person who got the most applause could go out again at the end of the show.

"The tension was there that night, more than ever before. As the students finished their little act—singing or dancing or playing the piano or doing a recitation—they'd come off stage and say, 'Boy, was I lousy!' and another student would say, 'No, you were the most.' But a teacher knows her students and I could tell—every one of them was hoping to be the one to get the encore. You know who got it. Elvis was standing at the edge of the stage, half hidden by the curtain, when I told him, 'It's you, Elvis. Go on out there and sing another song.'

"I'll never forget the look on his face when he came off the stage from doing the encore. 'They really liked me, Miss Scrivener,' he said. 'They really liked me.' "

"One of my sisters had given me a red flannel shirt and he liked it, so I let him wear it for the show," says his friend Buzzie. "He sang a love song first and the teachers started to cry. Really. They just started to boo-hooing. He sang a couple of songs more and about the third one he dedicated it to me. I wondered why. Afterward he gave me my shirt back and he showed me where he had made a little tear in it, closing it in a car door. He was buttering me up by dedicating the song to me."

Buzzie says the only other times Elvis performed "publicly" for strangers was when he joined the Odd Fellows' local boys' club, which urged its members to participate in charitable activities in exchange for the use of game and meeting rooms. Buzzie was a member, he says, and he would do a little improvisational dancing and fooling around while Elvis played his guitar and sang when they visited the patients at the Memphis Veterans Hospital.

In November 1950 one of the home service reports shows that Elvis was working as an usher at Loew's State Theater downtown from five to ten each night at $12.75 a week. It was a job he quit soon thereafter because he was falling behind in his studies. He resumed it the following summer, only to be fired. Arthur Groom, the theater manager, says it's a long story, but what happened was the girl who sold candy and popcorn in the lobby was slipping Elvis some stuff on the side and the other usher snitched on Elvis, so Elvis took a punch at him and Elvis was canned.

His next job was working a full shift, from three in the afternoon until eleven-thirty at night, at the Marl Metal Products Company. He began to fall asleep in class—something Miss Scrivener says she overlooked, knowing the circumstances—and his mother worried. "That's too much for any young boy," Gladys said a few years later. "It got so hard on him—he was so beat all the time—we made him quit, and I went to work at St. Joseph's Hospital."

The home service report of June 19, 1951, shows Vernon had received a $10-a-week raise to $48.50, counting the five hours of overtime. And the rent was bumped accordingly, seven more dollars to forty-three. It was the next report, filed in December, that included Mrs. Presley's income as a nurse's aide, and although this was only four dollars a day, it proved to be a problem. The Housing Authority worked on annual income figures, not daily or weekly figures, so when her projected yearly income came to $1248 and this was added to her husband's yearly sum, the total exceeded the maximum permitted by the city.

"Have had illness in family, wife is working to help pay out of debt. Bills pressing—and don't want to be sued," were the words on another report filed in December in an attempt to explain why Mrs. Presley had taken a job. The illness was Vernon's; he'd hurt his back at work and the medical costs were piling up. It didn't matter. Still the projected family income was beyond the $3000 ceiling. That meant the Presleys had to be evicted.

Dear Tenant:

The Memphis Housing Authority is obligated by law and contract to house only the low-income families, with the result that leases with families have incomes above our ceiling for continued occupancy must be notified to find housing elsewhere.

Information now available to us indicates you are ineligible for continued occupancy for the reason that your net annual income of $3,770.00 exceeds the maximum. We are therefore required to send you this notice of ineligibility to put you on notice to move.

A notice similar to this is sent to all ineligible project families. In normal times we require possession in 30 days, however we are still permitted to adopt a more liberal policy because the housing supply is still below normal.

Complying with our obligation, you are officially notified of cancellation of your lease effective not later than February 29, 1952. We are obligated to take steps to obtain possession of your apartment unless it is surrendered to us by that date. If your circumstances change at any time before you move, please notify the manager. If the change is of such a nature you are no longer ineligible, removal from the project will not be required.

A short time later Mrs. Presley quit work at the hospital, the Presley income was re-examined and the eviction notice was withdrawn.

However strapped the Presleys were economically, still there seemed to be enough in the family budget to keep Elvis reasonably content. "His parents gave him money for a push lawn mower," says Buzzie, "and Elvis paid them back out of his earnings. We usually mowed just enough to get the money for what we wanted—movies, carnivals and so on. Except for those two jobs he had, he didn't work too much. His parents provided well enough, considering how poor they were." Buzzie scoffs at the story about Elvis once selling a pint of his blood. "He didn't need to," he says. "He never had a need for money. He didn't need much and if he did, his parents took care of him. Any story you hear like that, stack it up against the Lincoln coupe they bought him. It was an old car, but that's how good his parents were to him. His father used the car too, of course, but really it was bought for him."

Mr. Presley once told a story about Elvis and that car, which was then more than ten years old. It was a hot summer night and, as is the custom even today, residents of the project gathered outside to sit on porches and under the scattered trees, looking for some cool breeze and friendly gossip. "That ol' car sure could eat gas and I suppose Elvis was worried I'd not have enough to get to work," Vernon said. "So he come running up yelling, 'Hi, Dad. I put fifteen cents' worth of gasoline into the car.' Everyone laughed and he like to died of embarrassment."

The Presleys were like family to Buzzie. "One time I hurt my arm," he says. "I fell on concrete playing basketball and a little later I was at Elvis's house, my arm all bruised. Tears come to Mrs. Presley's eyes when she saw my arm. She was a softhearted woman, that's all she was."

Sometimes, Buzzie says, usually on Friday or Saturday nights, the Presleys would walk to a movie theater in the neighborhood, the Suzore No. 2, turning the apartment over to Elvis and Buzzie for a party. "They weren't noisy parties, nothing like that," says Buzzie. "Instead of records, Elvis would play and sing, but it wasn't noisy." (Mrs. Richardson says that only once did someone have to run over and tell Elvis that the tenants were beginning to complain, so he'd have to play and sing more quietly.) "Elvis was always doing that at parties and so we learned to dance before he did. We were conforming to the dances of the time. The bop was big —and slow dances. This was right after the jitterbug went out. Elvis had his own movements, of course, and eventually we all came around to his way. I remember seeing him in front of a jukebox one time, listening to the record and imitating playing a guitar and doing those moves. Another time we went to a party and there was a piano there. He started fooling around and the first thing you know he was beating out a song. He never had any training, on the piano *or* the guitar, so far as I know. He picked it up by ear. He had the feel for it."

Buzzie sat back, relighted his cigar. It had been a long speech for him and he said he thought it was because he hadn't talked about Elvis in several years. He continued: "He dated pretty good. He liked to date. He wasn't the sort to just walk up and ask for dates right off, though. And the girls he did go out with, they were pretty affectionate; they really cared for him. At parties he'd be there. He wasn't that shy. And if we talked him into being the life of the party, he'd be that. He wouldn't let a party drag on."

On most dates, Buzzie says, they doubled and went to movies or to local carnivals to throw balls at milk bottles and ride the rides. "I remember one time we were gonna rent a truck for a hayride," he says. "We all chipped in fifty cents apiece but we were a little short. So Elvis went down to the record store next to the Suzore and made an announcement that we were having a hayride and we had a truck outside. Pretty soon we had a truck full and enough money to pay for it."

Friday and Saturday nights when Elvis didn't have a date, usually he'd see a movie with some of the guys from the neighborhood. The Suzore No. 2 was one of those big old theaters found in poorer Southern neighborhoods in the fifties —two ancient heaters huffing and puffing to keep things barely tolerable in winter, two creaky fans for the blistering summer heat, and the roof leaked. Buzzie says Elvis tried to see at least one movie a week and that he liked Tony Curtis best. At the time, Curtis was becoming a favorite with the teenagers, usually appearing in swashbucklers and adventure flicks.

In school Elvis liked shop and ROTC the best, although that was where Red West says he suffered some of the roughest harassment concerning his clothes and hair. In shop Elvis made a cutting board and a salad bowl for his mother. And so much did he like ROTC, that after he had made some money from his first records, he returned to Humes High (something he did often the first few years) and spent $900 on uniforms for the school's ROTC drill team. One of the few pictures taken at the time, in fact, shows him standing proudly in his khaki uniform, overseas cap at a cocky angle on his blond head, and under that a lopsided grin.

In the Humes High yearbook, *The Herald*, for 1953, there is only one picture of Elvis, showing him in a dark coat, a white shirt, a light tie, acne, prominent sideburns, hair long at the sides and slicked back into a classic ducktail, the top pompadoured and swirled and stacked just so, a spit curl hanging over his forehead. Next to the picture it says:

> PRESLEY, ELVIS ARON
> Major: Shop, History, English
> Activities: R.O.T.C., Biology Club,
> English Club, History Club, Speech
> Club.

The only other mention of Elvis in the book is in the class will, where it says, "Donald Williams, Raymond McCraig and Elvis Presley leave hoping there will be some one to take their places as 'teachers' pets'??????" (Buzzie says he has no idea what that means, unless it's a reference to Elvis's making the teachers cry when he sang.) He was not voted most popular, most talented, most charming, most outstanding, or most likely to succeed. He was not voted most anything.

"He was like the rest of us," says Buzzie. "He wasn't an A student because he didn't want to be. He was plenty smart enough, but I don't remember many times where we'd carry books home. We all passed with Bs and Cs, that's all."

Vernon's salary continued to creep upward, but it never was enough. In the spring of 1952 the Presleys fell behind in their rent and utilities and they received a notice from the Housing Authority that they were delinquent in the amount of $43.74, and a fine of a dollar a day was being imposed, effective immediately.

In August the same year a report filed by United Paint Company showed Vernon was earning an average of $53.22 a week, and a week after that Vernon filed a report with the Housing Authority saying it wasn't true, he didn't average that much.

In November Gladys returned to St. Joseph's Hospital as a nurse's aide, the family income again passed the maximum allowed, and once more the Presleys received a letter of eviction. They were told they had until February 28, 1953, to get out.

The Presleys spent the Christmas and New Year's holidays in the project and on January 7 moved to a small apartment at 398 Cypress Street, closer to the center of the city. It was a seven-room house that had been cut into four apartments. It didn't look a whole hell of a lot better than the one-room slum they lived in on Poplar Avenue. And it cost them fifty-two dollars a month.

Elvis graduated from Humes in June and began looking for something to do.

wo years old, a sharecropper's son in
upelo

Senior picture at Humes High School,
age 18

vis Presley Birthplace and Community Center, now a public park and recreation
cility, Tupelo

Lauderdale Courts neighborhood in Memphis; Presleys lived in center, ground floor apartment, 1949–53

Sam Phillips of Sun Records, 1954

From left to right: Bill Black, Elvis and Scotty Moore in their first publicity photograph, in the Sun studio, 1954

OPPOSITE: *A picture from Elvis's personal publicity file, taken in the Speer studio, Memphis, 1954*

RIGHT: *The $10,000 diamond-studded gold lamé suit, Hollywood, 1957*

BELOW: *Colonel Parker keeps the fans happy, selling 50-cent photographs before a concert*

ABOVE: *Sun Records' "million-dollar quartet"—Elvis at the piano with (from left to right) Jerry Lee Lewis, Carl Perkins and Johnny Cash joining him in an informal gospel sing, 1956*

OPPOSITE: *Elvis rides his favorite, the Dodgem, at the Memphis Fairgrounds, 1957*

Backstage in 1956, looking blond-er than usual

Explaining how he defends him-self if necessary

Hysteria in a Miami movie house, 1956

Singing with his parents at home, 1956

With Richard Egan in his first film, Love Me Tender, *1956*

"If I stand still when I sing, I'm dead . . ."

The idol at Graceland, Memphis, 1957

-4-

SUNRISE

In the summer of 1953 Elvis went to work for the Precision Tool Company—a factory job—and then applied for and got a job at the Crown Electric Company, an electrical contracting firm that wired churches, schools, industrial plants, shops and residences. There were forty-five electricians on the payroll then and Elvis was one of two truckdrivers who ran materials out to the jobs and sometimes helped keep stock in the warehouse. He made $1.25 an hour. After taxes it worked out to forty-one dollars and some change each week.

The job was a good one for Elvis, for then Crown was situated in a two-story stucco building at 353 Poplar Avenue, hiking distance from the apartment on Cypress where the Presleys lived—only a block from their original Memphis home and three from the Lauderdale Courts, so Elvis was close to friends. Elvis usually *did* walk to Crown, checking in about eight in the morning. The working owners, James and Gladys Tipler, remember how he first came to them.

"We called Tennessee unemployment," says Mrs. Tipler, "and when I talked to the lady, she told me she had a very nice boy, but not to be—these were exactly the words she used—don't be fooled by his appearance. And when he walked in and I seen him, if she hadn't-a said that, I think I would-a told him to take to the door. Because I mean his hair was long! Even though he was a clean-cut-lookin' kid, I just wasn't used to that."

Mr. Tipler jumps in: "Elvis used to like that hair. He'd wear it way back there! He'd come back from a run in the truck, and he'd go right to a mirror to comb his hair. Wouldn't be a time when he didn't do that, combing the hair just so."

"He was neat in appearance," says Mrs. Tipler. "Even if I wasn't used to that long hair, you know. Now it wouldn't make any difference."

Mr. Tipler's turn again: "You made his appointments for him to go to the beauty shop!" Then, confidentially, joshing her: "She made *all* his appointments for him to get his hair fixed. He went to the beautician, you know, to get his hair trimmed. He didn't go to a reg'lar barber. He was way ahead of those other fellas, even way back yonder. He used to go up to the place at Poplar and Lauderdale. What was the name of that beauty shop, Gladys?"

Mrs. Tipler is a matronly woman who wears modest dresses, has black neck-length hair neatly coifed, beneath it eyes that shine like bituminous coal, and in her loving dialogue with her husband she sounds precisely like Molly McGee going for Fibber's funny bone. Mr. Tipler is a hefty suntanned man in his middle fifties who, because of his wide grin and the part in his teeth, looks rather like a pixyish Ernest Borgnine.

Elvis was Crown's youngest employee, and as such he came in for some good-natured kidding from some of the older electricians. "They used to play jokes on him," says Mrs. Tipler. "He came in from a job one day, I'll never forget it. He came in and he said, 'Miz Tipler, I have to have some sky hooks.' Him and I both looked in that warehouse I don't know how long for some sky hooks, until Tip come in and I said, 'Tip, they need some sky hooks out at East School,' and Tip laughed at us both and he said, 'How crazy can you be? You don't put any hooks in the sky.'"

Not too long ago Mrs. Tipler assigned herself the task of rooting through fifteen years of papers and canceled checks, looking for some material proof of the young truckdriver's employment at Crown. There were some checks back there, she said, because she used to give them away to anyone who asked. Finally, she found two of them. The checks had been made out to "Alvis Presley"—dated in mid-July 1954, for $41.35 and $41.71, each representing a week's pay—and were endorsed in pencil in the signature familiar to the millions who have since received "autographed" Elvis Presley Easter and Christmas cards and pocket calendars and photographs.

She turned the checks over in her hand, rubbed the fading signatures and said, "Sometimes when he'd come in, he was supposed to be here earlier. This one day he had already blew a tire out on the truck. Instead of stoppin', he drove on in with it like that. And he had that ol' gi-tar of his and I said, 'Elvis, put down that gi-tar.' I said, 'It's gonna be the ruination of you. You better make up your mind what you're gonna do.'

"And he laughed at me."

The truck Elvis drove was a Ford pickup with a carry-back for equipment, and sometimes on his way to pick up or deliver supplies he'd pass the Memphis Recording Service, a small but lucrative sideline to the Sun Record Company, both of which had been founded and were being operated by Sam Phillips. At the time, Sun was being run as an independent production company, and Sam was selling and leasing his tapes to other companies, operating on a profit margin thinner than the aluminum discs he used to make the master records. The Memphis Recording Service provided added income by recording bar mitzvahs and weddings and making off-the-air transcriptions for local radio stations and personal records for the walk-in trade. Elvis had known about this service—make your own record, two songs for four dollars—and when he had the money saved, he parked the truck in the neighborhood during a lunch hour and went in. Running the office that day was Marion Keisker, a gregarious woman in her thirties who had been a radio personality since childhood. She recently had retired as "Miss Radio of Memphis" to serve as Sam's office manager. Today Marion regards Elvis with the warmth a woman has for a son.

"It was a Saturday afternoon, a busy, busy afternoon, and for some reason I happened to be alone in the office," she says. "The office was full of people wanting to make personal records. It was a stand-and-wait-your-turn sort of thing. He came in, said he wanted to make a record. I told him he'd have to wait and he said okay. He sat down. Of course he had his guitar. They *all* had their guitars in those days.

"While he was waiting his turn, we had a conversation I had reason to remember for many years afterward, because later I had to tell the story so often. He said he was a singer. I said, 'What kind of a singer are you?' He said, 'I sing all kinds.' I said, 'Who do you sound like?' He said, 'I don't sound like nobody.' I thought, Oh yeah, one of those. I said, 'Hill-billy?' He said, 'Yeah, I sing hillbilly.' I said, 'Who do you sound like in hillbilly?' He said, 'I don't sound like nobody.'"

The Ink Spots were among Elvis's favorite singers in 1953 and it was one of their songs, "My Happiness," that Elvis had decided he wanted on a record as a present for his mother. The second song was "That's When Your Heartaches Begin," a weepy ballad that was part recitation. On both songs he accompanied himself on his battered guitar, sounding, he said years later, like "somebody beating on a bucket lid."

Says Marion Keisker. "When we went back to make the record, a ten-inch acetate, he got about halfway through the first side and I thought, I want to tape this.

"Now this is something we never did, but I wanted Sam to hear this. He was out at the time and the only thing I could find was a crumply piece of tape and by the time I got it set up, I'd missed part of the first song. I got maybe the last third of it and all the second song. I don't even know if Elvis knew I was taping it."

In explaining why she made a tape copy, Marion tells

something about Sam Phillips that Sam himself never tells—and explains part of the motivation for Sun Records. First, she says, you have to understand Sam's background.

Sam had been raised on his father's Alabama plantation, she says, where Uncle Silas Payne, a black, held him on his knee and sang the blues to him. In school Sam learned how to play the sousaphone and drums, and following college he became a radio announcer, moving to Memphis, where he coordinated the broadcast of orchestra music from one of the city's hotels. He was making $150 a week and had a wife and two young sons when he quit to open his own studio. Marion says the music Sam had been programming bored him.

"It seemed to me that the Negroes were the only ones who had any freshness left in their music," Sam himself once said, "and there was no place in the South they could go to record. The nearest place where they made so-called 'race' records—which was soon to be called 'rhythm and blues'—was Chicago, and most of them didn't have the money or time to make the trip to Chicago."

Memphis long had been of major importance in the history of the blues. It was the world's leading cotton marketplace, serving the rich broad Mississippi delta country to the south, and for years had been a magnet to the bluesmen of the cotton country. Many blacks settled on and around Beale Street—only a few blocks from Sam's studio—to pick and sing in back rooms and tawdry beer parlors.

In the first years of Sam's independence, from 1951 to 1953, he recorded several of the finest singers in Memphis—Bobby Bland, Jackie Brenston (whose "Rocket 88" was a hit in the Negro market and was covered a year later by Bill Haley and the Comets), Chester (The Howlin' Wolf) Burnett, and Doc Ross—peddling the aluminum masters to Chess and Checker Records in Chicago. He recorded Joe Hill Louis, B. B. King and Big Walter Horton and sold their songs to Modern and RPM Records, blues labels in Los Angeles. Then in 1953, before Elvis walked in to make his four-dollar record,

Sam began issuing the first 78-rpm records to carry the bright yellow and orange Sun label. He released two regional hits, "Love My Baby," by Little Junior Parker and "Just Walking in the Rain," by the Prisonaires, the latter being a group formed when its members were in the Tennessee State Penitentiary. (The song was a hit for Johnny Ray.) None of the artists Sam recorded ever had been recorded before; he took pride in being first.

All of which brings us back to Marion Keisker and Elvis Presley. She says, "The reason I taped Elvis was this: Over and over I remember Sam saying, 'If I could find a white man who had the Negro sound and the Negro feel, I could make a billion dollars.' This is what I heard in Elvis, this . . . what I guess they now call 'soul,' this Negro sound. So I taped it. I wanted Sam to know."

Marion says that when Sam returned, she fed the crumpled tape through the studio's one-track recording system. Sam said he was impressed, but the boy needed a lot of work. He asked her if she'd written down his name and address. She said yes and showed him the slip of paper on which she'd written "Elvis Pressley[sic]. Good ballad singer. Hold." The address showed he was living at 462 Alabama Street, a modest two-story brick home set back from the street and flanking the Lauderdale Courts. The telephone number was that of a friend on the same block who'd come and get him if anyone ever called.

Says Marion: "Funny thing is I came home and was telling about him and my mother said, 'Oh, I've seen that kid on the streetcar. The kid with the sideburns.'

"Those days, nobody had sideburns."

Several months passed and on January 4, 1954, a Friday, Elvis visited the Memphis Recording Service a second time, when Marion was out and Sam was in. Elvis told Sam his name and asked if Marion had mentioned him. Sam said yes, Marion had spoken highly of him and yes, he liked the tape she had made and he hoped Elvis was getting along tolerably, but no matter how much he wanted to do something, he just couldn't, not right away. Smiling. Sam was then, as now, a gentle, charming man, somewhat absent-minded but usually sensitive in his contact with the public. Elvis shuffled nervously, ran his hands through his hair and said he wanted to cut another four-dollar record. Sam nodded and Elvis made his second "demo," pairing "Casual Love," a ballad, and "I'll Never Stand in Your Way," another country song. According to Marion, Sam was equally impressed by Elvis and he, too, noted his name and a phone number in the cluttered files. And he told Elvis he'd call.

Often during his lunch break while at Crown, Elvis would run past one of the local radio stations, WMPS, to watch the live broadcast of the *High Noon Roundup*. Country artists were featured on the first half of the hour-long program, the Blackwood Brothers Quartet and other gospel groups on the second half. The show's master of ceremonies was Bob Neal, a disc jockey with a deep, deep voice who would become Elvis's personal manager; but that was more than a year away.

About the same time, Elvis almost joined one of the Blackwood family's vocal groups. The leader of the quartet, James Blackwood, tells the story: "When Elvis was eighteen, when he was driving the truck, my nephew Cecil and three other boys had a gospel quartet they called the Songfellows. They thought one of the boys was gonna leave, and so Elvis auditioned and he would-a joined them in singing around the Memphis area, except the other boy changed his mind. That finished it, and I think Elvis was disappointed, but he still sang with the boys from time to time, during rehearsals. And he often came to our all-night gospel sings at the auditorium."

At the all-night sings, a tradition in the South, Elvis sometimes got up and sang spirituals as a solo vocalist. With the Blackwoods backing him harmonically, and singing the songs he loved best, he seemed to find unusual confidence. James Blackwood says Elvis kept his eyes closed most of the time when he sang. He also says Elvis moved his hips in a manner not totally suited to spirituals, but he wrote it off to enthusiasm.

"Elvis liked to sing, you could see that," he says today. "Singing came natural to Elvis, all right."

Elvis wanted a musical career, there seemed to be no doubt. But he wasn't counting on one. Besides driving the truck by day, he began to study at night, learning how to be an electrician. He knew that he was making far less than those to whom he delivered supplies in the old Ford pickup, that good electricians never went looking for work, work came looking for them. So life remained little changed for Elvis. His father continued to pack cans of paint in cardboard boxes. His mother took occasional jobs and battled with occasional illnesses.

Says Marion Keisker of this period: "Every time a song came up, I'd say to Sam, 'How about the kid with the sideburns? Why don't we give him a chance?' And Sam'd say, 'I'm afraid he's not ready yet' or 'How do we get in touch with him?' and by the time I'd say, 'Here's the number,' Sam'd be into something else again. Well, this little game went on and on."

Then one day—in 1954, approximately eight months after Elvis had first visited the Memphis Recording Service—Sam got a demonstration record he liked, a dub that had been made in Nashville. For most of a day Sam had been on the telephone trying to learn who the singer was, because he wanted to get permission to release the dub as is.

"It was a single voice with a single guitar, a simple lovely ballad," says Marion. "Sam couldn't find out who the singer was, he was told it was just a Negro kid hanging around the studio when the song came in, and so he said, 'If I can't find him, I'll have to find somebody else, because I want to release the song.' I told Sam. 'What about the kid with the sideburns?'

"Sam said, 'Oh, I don't know how to get in touch with him.

I've even forgotten his name.' I said, 'I just have the card right here.' I pulled out my little piece of paper. Again it was a Saturday afternoon, and Sam said, 'If you can get him over here . . .' So I called and they went up the street and called Elvis to the phone. It was like 'Mr. DeMille will see you now.' I was still standing there with the telephone in my hand and here comes Elvis, panting. I think he ran all the way."

Sam played the dub for Elvis. It was called "Without You." Elvis tried it and was awful. He tried it again and again, and there was minimal, if any, improvement.

"We were taking a break," says Marion, "and Sam said, 'What can you do?' Elvis said, 'I can do anything.' Sam said, 'Do it.' So he started playing, just snatches of anything he knew—religious, gospel, western, everything. Real heavy on the Dean Martin stuff. Apparently he'd decided, if he was going to sound like anybody, it was gonna be Dean Martin. We stayed there I don't know how many hours, talking and playing. Elvis said he was looking for a band. Sam said maybe he could help him, he wasn't sure."

What Sam did next was call Scotty Moore, a twenty-one-year-old guitar player who'd come to Memphis from the armed forces two years earlier to work in his brother's cleaning plant and organize a hillbilly band called the Starlight Wranglers. Scotty was thin, boyish and enthusiastic, willing to fit in almost any slot offered him, so long as he could play his guitar and be with people he liked. In later years Sam Phillips, and many others, would say it was Scotty more than anyone who provided and/or influenced much of the "Elvis Presley sound," that Scotty was the Great Unsung Hero in Elvis Presley's life.

Scotty says today, "We were playing several honky-tonks around town and I went in to see Sam, realizing that anybody had to have a record to get anywhere. We became close. In fact, Sam was lookin' for somebody that was willing to work, so we more or less donated the band. He did put out a record on ourselves, I guess he probably pressed fifty, maybe a hundred copies. We sure didn't sell any more than that."

Scotty laughs when he recalls his inauspicious start. Today he and his three business partners have their own recording studio in Nashville (Music City Recorders) and the hungry days of the early fifties seem distant. "We tried backing up different people," he says. "I can't remember any names now. Everybody in the band had daytime jobs and were doing this on the side. The job I had got through about two in the afternoon and I'd go down and Sam and I would go next door to Miss Taylor's restaurant, sit there and drink coffee for a couple hours, you know . . . discuss what could we do, do this, do that, and so forth. Finally he mentioned Elvis's name."

Sam told Scotty who Elvis was and said he might have some potential. "I said, 'Well, call him. Let's get him in and work with him,'" says Scotty. "Every day for two solid weeks I'd go down there in the afternoon and talk with Sam. I'd say, 'Did you call this guy? Did you call Elvis?' Because Elvis sounded like a name outa science fiction.* And he'd say, 'No, no, I haven't done it yet.' I think Marion heard us talking and she finally went and dug through the files, pulled out his card and said, 'Here, call!'"

Sam said no, he didn't want to make a big thing of it and suggested Scotty telephone, maybe make a date for the weekend, listen to the kid on his own ground, or maybe at Scotty's house, and report back with what he thought. Scotty said okay and he called Elvis early Saturday night, identifying himself as "Scotty Moore of Sun Records." Elvis was at a movie, his mother said, but she'd go get him. Elvis then called Scotty and they made plans to get together at Scotty's house the following afternoon.

Elvis was wearing pink slacks, a pink shirt and white buck shoes, the way Scotty remembers it, and after the initial awkwardness had passed, Elvis and Scotty began playing their

---

* Elvis is an ancient Norse name, originally "Alviss" and meaning "all wise." If Scotty had come from northeast Mississippi, the name wouldn't have seemed so unusual. In Tupelo, Elvis, Goble, Quay, Arlon, Ferrell, Olena, Bedie, Elford, Loye, Ruble, Bethel, Ora and Flaunt all appear in relative profusion in the 1970 telephone book.

guitars, with Elvis singing several songs recently popularized by Eddy Arnold and Hank Snow, two established country artists, and Billy Eckstine, one of Elvis's favorite popular black artists. Bill Black, a bass player who lived just three doors away from Scotty, wandered in about halfway through the two-hour session and after listening for a short time wandered out again, returning after Elvis had left.

Says Scotty: "I said, 'Well, what did you think?' Bill said, 'Well, he didn't impress me too damned much.' You know—snotty-nosed kid come in here with the wild clothes. We didn't think much about it at all. So I called Sam Sunday afternoon, I told him, 'Well, the boy's got a good voice . . .' I told him the songs that Elvis did and I said, 'He didn't do them any better than the originals did.' And so forth. Sam said, 'Well, tell you what. I'll call him and we'll set up an audition for tomorrow night, Monday night. We won't bring the whole band in, the hillybilly group with the steel guitar, the whole thing.' He said, 'Just you and Bill come over, something for a little rhythm. We'll put down a few things and we'll see what he sounds like coming back off the tape recorder.' I said okay."

What followed was not a simple audition but several months of hard work. No one seems to remember precisely how many months. Almost every day, after they'd finish work, Bill and Scotty and Elvis would meet in the small Sun studio to rehearse, to (quoting Marion) "develop a style." Elvis appeared with Scotty's band in a local club a few times, but Sam said he didn't sound right with that much instrumentation behind him.

"Mostly I think they were coming in every afternoon to please Sam," says Marion today. "He kept saying, 'Keep it simple, keep it simple.' Sam was listening while doing other things. They were trying to evolve something that was different and unique. Finally one night—I don't know whether Sam decided *he* was ready or he had finally heard something —he said, 'Okay, this is the session.'"

"The first thing that was put on tape was 'I Love You Because,'" says Scotty. "Then he did a couple of those country-orientated things. They were all right. Little while later we were sitting there drinking a Coke, shooting the bull, Sam back in the control room. So Elvis picked up his guitar and started banging on it and singing 'That's All Right, Mama.' Jumping around tthe studio, just acting the fool. And Bill started beating on his bass and I joined in. Just making a bunch of racket, we thought. The door to the control room was open, and when we was halfway through the thing, Sam come running out and said, 'What in the devil are you doing?' We said, 'We don't know.' He said, 'Well, find out real quick and don't lose it. Run through it again and let's put it on tape.' So to the best of our knowledge we repeated what we just done and went through the whole thing."

"That's All Right [Mama]" was a song written and originally recorded for RCA Victor's Bluebird subsidiary in the 1940s by Arthur (Big Boy) Crudup, a black country blues singer who was one of Elvis's vocal influences. (Years later Elvis would finance some recording sessions for Crudup, although in 1969 Crudup said he still had never met Elvis.)

"We spent three or four nights trying to get a back side in the same vein," says Scotty. "We finally did 'Blue Moon of Kentucky' and this came about the same way. We'd gone through this song, that song, and I don't think any of them were on tape. Then Bill jumped up, started clowning with his bass and singing 'Blue Moon of Kentucky' in falsetto, mimicking Bill Monroe [the bluegrass musician who wrote the song]. And Elvis started banging on his guitar. And the rhythm thing jelled again.

"That was the first record."

What had been cut in the tiny studio was in many ways historic. Not only were Elvis and his two backup musicians combining the sounds of white country and black blues to form what would be called "rockabilly," but on "That's All Right [Mama]," the blues song, the instrumentation gave the version a country sound, and on Bill Monroe's bluegrass hit Elvis was singing the blues.

Scotty says he and Bill shook their heads as they listened to the songs played back through Sam's recording system, agreeing that, yes, the sound was exciting enough, "But, good God, they'll run us outa town when they hear it."

Sam said he was going to take the record to Dewey Phillips, a white disc jockey who talked like a hick and devoted his radio show *Red Hot and Blue* on station WHBQ to records by black blues artists. It seemed the only place to go. At the time, mixing black and white music wasn't as acceptable as it would be just a few years later.

Dewey Phillips is dead now, one of those classic "good ol' boys" who followed the broken trail so many country singers blazed, marked by amphetamines and alcohol. In August 1954, when "That's All Right [Mama]" was released, he was one of the top disc jockeys in Memphis. He was a tall wavy-haired man with a soft voice, a bit of a paunch, a ready grin, and sitting in his shirtsleeves listening to his friend Sam, and then to Elvis's record, he said yes, he liked it too, and he'd sure give it a spin. Dewey was not related to Sam, but as Sam became better known, Dewey seldom denied it if someone said he was. Deep down, he said, they must-a been cousins at least.

The night Dewey played the record, Elvis tuned the family radio to WHBQ and ran to his favorite escape, the Suzore No. 2 theater. His parents said later he was too nervous, or shy, to be where he might hear his own record. Elvis probably doesn't remember which film he was watching that night, because his parents walked the aisles to find him before the movie was over. Dewey had played the record, the listeners had begun to call in their enthusiastic reaction. Dewey played it again and again, and now he wanted to interview Elvis on the air.

Not long before he died, Dewey told what happened during that interview. Elvis arrived out of breath and Dewey said, "Sit down, I'm gone interview you." And according to Dewey, Elvis said, "Mr. Phillips, I don't know nothing about being interviewed."

"Just don't say nothing dirty," Dewey said back.

"He sat down and I said I'd let him know when we were ready to start," Dewey recalled. "I had a couple of records cued up, and while they played, we talked. I asked him where he went to high school and he said Humes. I wanted to get that out, because a lot of people listening had thought he was colored. Finally I said, 'All right, Elvis, thank you very much.' 'Aren't you gone interview me?' he asked. 'I already have,' I said. 'The mike's been open the whole time.' He broke out in a cold sweat."

Within a few days, there were orders for five thousand records sitting on Marion Keisker's desk. "We hadn't even cut a master when he took the dub to Dewey," Marion says. "We were back-ordered on a brand new artist with a brand new type of thing before we could get our mastering done and get some pressings from Plastic Products. It was that immediate."

It was not all that immediate for Elvis. Next day he reported for work at Crown Electric same as the day before, and he began appearing at local night clubs, not for a star's wages but for whatever he could get.

One of Elvis's first jobs was singing at the Eagle's Nest, a spacious ballroom on Lamar Avenue that featured country swing bands and was tied in with a motel and swimming pool. An early Sun recording artist named Malcolm Yelvington had a band playing weekends in the club, and Marion says Sam persuaded Malcolm to let Elvis sing with him a couple of times. And then Elvis appeared in the club with another band, one headed by Jack Clement. Clement was the band's vocalist and Elvis was what Clement calls "the floor show," singing between regular sets. A local disc jockey called Sleepy Eyed John (Lepley) was booking the place and Elvis was earning ten dollars a night.

In time, of course, Elvis appeared more often with his friends Scotty Moore and Bill Black, who were having trouble with the rest of their band. Scotty says, "Bill and I still had the Starlight Wranglers and we were playing two or three clubs around town. You can imagine the jealousy factor that jumped real quick as soon as that record popped out—from a rehearsal. The whole band would-a been on it had it been a regular record session. Elvis played the Bel Air Club with us a couple of weeks. He was the guest artist and there was a conflict right away."

Scotty says audience reaction to Elvis at the Bel Air was minimal. "There was a little response, but it was more like What's he doing? Show time, folks, it's show time!" But when Elvis, Scotty and Bill helped open the Katz family's first drugstore on Lamar, Scotty says an entire parking lot full of teenagers "just went crazy."

About the same time, the Starlight Wranglers finally broke up, and Elvis and Scotty and Bill agreed to split whatever they earned three ways—25 per cent for Bill, the same share for Scotty, 50 per cent for Elvis.

It was the end of July 1954 and "That's All Right [Mama]" was in the number three position on the Memphis country and western sales chart, where it remained for two weeks, then bounced in and out of first position for a while, hovered around the fifth and sixth places for a longer period, and finally disappeared in December. It also appeared briefly on charts in Nashville and in New Orleans, but total sales were well under twenty thousand. *Billboard*, the country's leading music publication, praised the record, calling Elvis, in the magazine's quaint vocabulary, a "potent new chanter who can sock over a tune for either the country or the r&b markets." Still, the record was only a hit regionally. It was an encouraging beginning but not an exceptional one.

Says Marion Keisker: "On that first record of Elvis's we sent a thousand copies to disc jockeys and I bet nine hundred went into the trash can, because if a rhythm and blues man got it and heard 'Blue Moon of Kentucky' [the bluegrass number], he tossed it away . . . same thing if the country man heard 'That's All Right.' Later, of course, they all wrote back and wanted second copies. All Sam ever said was 'Play it once, just play it once.' Trouble was, nobody listened."

One of Sam's brothers, Tom Phillips, was working for the Scott Paper Company in Mobile, Alabama, and carrying Sam's records around from radio station to radio station, traveling an area that covered much of his own state, southeastern Louisiana (including New Orleans) and the southern half of Mississippi. "Everybody told me to take them back," says Tom laconically. "All I could do was leave my number."

And so it went nearly everywhere.

"You can't believe how much criticism I got from my friends in the disc jockey business," says Sam Phillips today. "I recall one jockey telling me that Elvis Presley was so country he shouldn't be played after five A.M. And others said he was too black for them."

In the South in July 1954, just two months after the U.S. Supreme Court banned racial segregation in public schools, it was not easy to sell a singer whose voice was "integrated."

Still, the record did accomplish more than most first records. It sold well in Memphis, where the public was given a chance to hear it and thereby decide for itself whether or not it was worth buying, and this provided the Presleys with some needed money. Sun wasn't a rich company and Elvis hadn't received any advance against future royalties when he'd signed a contract, but when the record began to sell, he was given a hundred dollars here, two hundred there when he needed it. The record also helped get him on two of the nation's most revered country radio programs, Nashville's *Grand Ole Opry* and Shreveport's *Louisiana Hayride*.

Sam Phillips arranged the *Opry* booking, calling friends he had known in Nashville when he was in radio. (The *Opry* is an official function of radio and television station WSM.) Marion Keisker says she and Sam closed the Sun office and drove the winding two-lane highway, four hours to Nashville, for the show, with Elvis, Scotty and Bill in another car behind then.

"For al of me Marion says, "the *Grand Ole Opry* was the summit th   you hoped you'd get eventually —not v.   ae record out."

Almo   eption in 1925 the *Opry* had been a   for every hopeful in the country and western field. Over the years the Saturday night show had been broadcast from a number of locations, ranging in size from a crowded neighborhood movie house (the Hillsboro Theater) to the huge Greek-columned War Memorial Auditorium, which seated 2200, to the present location, the Ryman Auditorium, which is the largest hall in central Tennessee and has seats for over 3500. No matter where the *Opry* was staged, there were long lines waiting to get in and hundreds, sometimes thousands, were turned away each night. Payment to musicians appearing on the show traditionally has been union scale—about thirty dollars for a star the year Elvis was there, a third that for sidemen—but the Ryman Auditorium, better known as the Opry House, was no less than country music's Carnegie.

The way Marion Keisker tells it, Elvis wandered around the afternoon of the show, amazed at how shabby the building was. It had been built in 1892—same year as Carnegie Hall— and didn't look as if it'd been painted since. Marion says Elvis kept saying, "You mean this is what I've been dreaming about all these years?"

They were greeted by Jim Denny, who headed the *Opry* talent office, booking all the acts for the show. Says Marion: "He was very incensed. He said, 'I wanted the full band that's on the record. Our agreement was we were gonna have the performance just like it's on the record.' What he was objecting to was the only musicians he saw were Scotty and Bill and he thought there should be more. This was one of the great mysteries that perplexed everyone—how Sam got that sound. He made such a big sound, everybody thought there was a big band on the records. Jim Denny thought he was getting at least four or five people besides Elvis."

The *Opry* was divided into half-hour segments, each with a different host, and the star who introduced Elvis in 1954 was Hank Snow, who'd recently had a number one hit on all the country charts ("I Don't Hurt Anymore") and who asked Elvis as he was going on, "What's your name again?"

"Elvis Presley, sir."

"No," said Hank, "not that. I mean what name do you sing under?"

"Elvis Presley, sir."

And then he went out there and sang "That's All Right [Mama]" and "Blue Moon of Kentucky."

When it was all over, Jim Denny went up to Elvis and told him he might consider trying driving a truck again. Marion says they were so upset at this, they drove off and left a suitcase full of Elvis's clothing in a gas station on the way out of town. And according to Gordon Stoker of the Jordanaires, a gospel quartet then appearing on the *Opry* every week, "Elvis cried all the way home. It took him days, weeks, to get over it. Much later Jim Denny threw his arm around Elvis at a social occasion and said to the people present, 'I always knew this boy had it in him to make it.' Elvis said, 'Yes, sir, thank you, sir,' then said out of the side of his mouth to friends, 'The sumbitch don't remember when he broke my heart.' Elvis wasn't being a hypocrite saying 'yes, sir, thank you, sir.' He was first of all a gentleman. But his heart was broken in Nashville that night."

(Marion offers a footnote: "That same day we went over to the *Opry*, Sam had a piano player he wanted to check out in a little bistro over there. Elvis came in with us, turned around, was very uncomfortable, finally said he'd wait for us outside. Sam said, 'Why?' He said, 'Cause my mama wouldn't want me in a place like this.' That was reason enough for Elvis not to be there. So he went outside and waited on the sidewalk. People said it was just publicity about how he felt about his mother and all. Elvis's reaction to this was: Well, doesn't everyone do like this? It was unthinkable to him that everyone didn't love his parents, didn't want to do everything for his parents. Here's a young man so pure, so sweet, so wonderful, that he's unbelievable.")

The second radio booking, on the *Louisiana Hayride*, was more successful. This too had been arranged by Sam, and early the day of the appearance in October Scotty, Elvis and Bill set out for Shreveport in Scotty's Chevrolet, the vehicle they used for most of their early out-of-town dates. (Neither Bill nor Elvis owned a car.) The *Hayride* was only six years old when Elvis sang the songs from his first record on it, but the program already figured significantly in the careers of several country personalities (Hank Williams among them), and so this booking too was considered a plum.

Frank Page, one of the *Hayride's* two announcers, introduced Elvis effusively: "Just a few weeks ago a young man from Memphis, Tennessee, recorded a song on the Sun label and in just a matter of a few weeks that record has skyrocketed right up the charts. It's really doing well all over the country. He is only nineteen years old. He has a new, distinctive style—Elvis Presley!"

One of several people Elvis met at KWKH, the powerful station that broadcast the *Hayride* over much of the middle South and then bicycled it to others in the Southwest, was D. J. Fontana, the program's staff drummer. He remembers the Saturday night when Elvis appeared: "He was purty hot in the area anyway and he tore the house down. He was the kingpin. Horace Logan was program director for the station and when Horace heard Elvis that first time, he did fourteen back flips."

Elvis was invited back and then was given a year's contract to appear on the show each week. He became so much a regular, he even warbled one of the show's commercial spots, a practice that was fairly common for country singers on the jamboree type of show: "You can get 'em pipin' hot after four P.M. / You can get 'em pipin' hot / Southern Made Doughnuts hits the spot / You can get 'em pipin' hot after four P.M."

"We would do the show in segments," says Frank Page today, now the *Hayride*'s producer. "One half hour would be sponsored by Lucky Strike, another half hour by Jax Beer, and so on. They wanted different commercial voices, so that's why there were two of us announcers. It ran eight to eleven —three hours long. Most of the acts appeared twice, early in the show and late.

"Elvis was popular on the *Hayride*. We filled it up every Saturday night. We had filled it up with Hank Williams before, we filled it up with Johnny Cash later on. Usually some of the 3500 seats were empty, but not when Elvis was there.

"He was very mild-mannered. He said 'yes, sir' and 'no, sir' and 'what do you want me to do, sir?' Then as he became more popular, he developed that double-talk that he had, that mumbling and bowing of his head and talking through his beard. Sort of chewing up his words, y'know. He'd come on, say, 'Ah'm gonna do somethin' for ya now, little thang that ah got out heyah, ah'm gonna . . .' He just rattled on and you had to listen carefully or you'd miss half of what he said. He adopted a style. I guess he thought it was suave.

"For the record, we never had one minute's trouble with Elvis. I recall only one time he had a fight with a boy who was jealous. It was a non-performer, backstage. And Elvis laid him out."

Another new friend was Pappy Covington, who had a country swing band and ran the *Hayride*'s artist service bureau, booking small country shows throughout what was called the "Ark-La-Tex area," which included the seventy-some counties in southwestern Arkansas, northern Louisiana and east Texas covered by KWKH. Elvis and Scotty and Bill worked several of these package tours, with Elvis often appearing as the "Hillbilly Cat" or "The King of Western Bop," obvious reference to his voice. In Texas rhythm and blues was called "cat music," and the phrase "western bop" combined the two sounds he had mixed.

In time D. J. Fontana joined Elvis's backup band, at first when Elvis worked the Shreveport area, later wherever Elvis went. He remembers one of the early jobs: "For years they were used to havin' a country band at this place on weekends. Friday and Saturday night you couldn't stir 'em with a stick, that's how crowded it was. This was at the Lakecliff, a combination night club and motel shack-up place. So we went on and I guess they thought their regular band was comin' on after us and they looked at us, wonderin' what we were gonna do. So we started hooting and hollering and jumping and I have to say it thinned out sharply. Those people looked at us and said, 'That's not Hoot and Curly.' And they left. By the time we got through, there wasn't five or six people left. They wasn't ready for it, man. They never did book us back in there again. Said we ruint the place. Nooooo way! Get out! Wouldn't even let us stay in the motel."

Another in the list of all-time Elvis shows—depressing then, funny now—is described by Cecil Scaife, now an executive with Columbia Records in Nashville, then a disc jockey in Helena, Arkansas. He remembers when Elvis and Scotty and Bill worked in Helena on a twelve-dollar guarantee, performing on a flat-bed truck.

"We had two shows planned," Cecil says, "one at two-thirty in the afternoon, the other at seven or eight. Elvis came by to look at the radio station on his way to the first show and then he stopped at the drugstore next to the station and bought some Havana sweets . . . smoked one . . . had two chocolate milkshakes . . . and smoked a second cigar. Then he started turning green and after he finished vomiting and so on, we didn't know if we had an act or not. Scotty found an extra pair of pink pants that'd been on a coat hanger in the car, 'cause Elvis had ruined the first pair. And they'd been hanging down at one end of the hanger, so when Elvis put them on, they looked like they were gathered at the knees. He looked just awful, but he went on and did the show."

By now Elvis had quit his job at Crown Electric. Says his old boss, James Tipler: "He come to us finally and he said he didn't think he could keep on working nights, playing his music and singing, and still give us a good day's work, too, so he left us."

It was about the time he left Crown that he appeared at the Overton Park Shell in Memphis at an all-country music show. Marion Keisker says, "This was the first time Elvis had ever come on a stage before a big audience on a commercial show. And there was such a stage presence, such fantastic ease, what's called charisma today. I remember talking with a woman and I asked her, 'Who'd you come to hear?' She said, 'Marty Robbins, I never miss Marty Robbins. Who'd you come to see?' I said, 'Elvis Presley.' She said, 'Who?' I said, 'After this show, you won't ask me again.'

"By this time the union had heard of Elvis and he was not a union member, because Sun wasn't a union company. They refused to let him go on stage. So there was a great scrambling around, everybody taking up money, trying to get enough to make the initiation fee so he could go on and sing. He finally made it and one of the songs he sang was 'I'll Never Let You Go, Little Darling.' He'd sung that in the studio and looked at me. Now I'm a restrained person, in public anyway, and I heard somebody screaming, just keening, and I discovered it was me, the staid mother of a son. I was standing out there screeching like I'd lost my total stupid mind."

Dewey Phillips was another who was there that day and the way he told the story, Elvis sang country ballads during the afternoon show and the audience didn't react. So Elvis went to Dewey, who had spent part of the afternoon with Sam, and they told Elvis to forget the country songs that night and sing "Good Rockin' Tonight," one of the faster songs in his repertoire. Dewey said that when Elvis sang that song, and started to shake, the place came apart. Dewey said he was standing at one end of the stage watching it and went out to walk Elvis off. When they passed Webb Pierce, an established country headliner who was waiting in the wings to go on, Dewey said he smiled at Webb and Webb snarled back at him, "You sonofabitch!"

A few months later the nation's country music disc jockeys were getting a questionnaire from *Billboard* asking them, among other things, "Whom do you consider the most promising new hillbilly or country and western artists coming up at the present time?" The vote was to be based on the period from the first of the year (1954) through the first week of October. Elvis finished eighth, an exceptional showing for someone who'd never been heard of in July and who had but one record release at the time the poll was taken.

Even with acceptance like this, Elvis's income was minimal. Screaming crowds, a favorable vote from disc jockeys and a contract with the *Louisiana Hayride* notwithstanding, things were rough. The bookings had been few and, literally, far between, with Scotty, Elvis and Bill (and sometimes D. J.) pushing their car all over the South, working for little more than would get them a starchy meal and gasoline enough to reach the next village. And in time, they couldn't even count on the transportation, the 1954 Chevrolet Bel Air they'd bought on the credit Scotty's wife had by working at Sears back home in Memphis. The car worked well enough at first, of course, but the back roads and long-distance driving pointed it toward one of those Southern automobile graveyards long before its time.

Says Scotty: "My wife was working to pay the car and we were sleeping in the back of it starving to death. It finally said floooooomph and fell all to pieces."

It was time to find a manager.

Although few know it, Elvis actually has had three managers, the first being his guitar player, Scotty Moore. "Sleepy

Eyed John Lepley was after him," Scotty says today, "and two, three other—I can't say crooked, but, well—people we didn't know, that really were jumpin' up and down trying to get him. It was Sam's suggestion: Sign him to a management contact and this will squelch all this activity. Then, if somebody asks, you can say he's got a manager and you won't be lying or anything. So I did. I signed him to a year contract."

The contract was a one-page document drawn up after consultation with a local attorney and identified W. S. Moore III as a "band leader and booking agent" and Elvis as a "singer of reputation and renown [who] possesses bright promises of large success." Scotty was to receive 10 per cent of all earnings from any appearance Elvis made, so long as Scotty had made the booking. The contract was signed by Scotty, Elvis and both his parents July 12, 1954, nearly a month before "That's All Right [Mama]" was released.

Scotty doesn't regret giving the contract away six months later. He says that when the right man came along, he happily filed the contract with his souvenirs.

"I was interested in playing, not booking show dates and telling anybody how to sing," he says.

The manager who got Elvis next was Bob Neal (born Robert Neal Hobgood), a disc jockey in his middle thirties who had an early morning country music show on station WMPS in Memphis. Bob was raised in Kentucky but had been in Memphis since 1942. In the years following he served in every capacity except station manager at WMPS, then one of the leading hillbilly broadcast operations in the mid-South. He had the five to eight A.M. show starting in 1948, spinning records, playing a ukelele and telling corny jokes to help the farmers and factory people off to work. Bob also began staging small concerts, using his program to promote them. He was married and had five sons, some of them teenagers.

Today Bob remains beefy, has added a spadelike salt-and-pepper beard, and runs a small management office in Nashville. He smokes cigars and speaks in the same articulate rumbling baritone: "We worked out just a simple thing without consulting attorneys, just a simple management-type contract. Of course he was under age, so his mother and Vernon approved the thing when we started."

In return for 15 per cent of Elvis's earnings, off the top, before taxes (if anybody bothered to take them out) and expenses, Bob was to handle all the bookings. Another 10 per cent was put into a fund for promotional expenses. And Scotty went back to picking guitar.

Actually, Bob and Elvis had met years before, when Bob had the afternoon gospel show on WMPS that featured Elvis's friends the Blackwoods. And they met again when Bob staged the country music show at the Overton Park Shell. So in a way it was like going into business with an old, respected friend. Indeed, Bob Neal and his wife Helen speak today of Elvis as a son.

Elvis's second record had been released by the time he had signed with Bob, in January 1955. This was a song the blues singer Wynonie Harris released in 1949 and the song he had used to get the crowd moving at the Shell, "Good Rockin' Tonight." On the back side of the record was "I Don't Care if the Sun Don't Shine," one verse of which was written by Marion Keisker because Elvis didn't know the rest. The original composer, Mack David, agreed to the record's release when it was promised Marion's name would be left off the label and she wouldn't share in royalties. It earned one of *Billboard*'s spotlight positions and Elvis was called "a sock new singer." More important, *Billboard* said Elvis could appeal to both country and rhythm and blues and pop. All three. Few records before had earned that distinction. Elvis was now being recognized as a man in a special category.

Strangely, the record didn't sell as well as the first, rising no higher than number three in Memphis, appearing not at all on the country music charts in other cities.

Even this early in his career a pattern had formed in Elvis's recording sessions that would continue with only minor variations throughout his career. "Every session came hard," says Marion. "He never had anything prepared, and the sessions always went on and on and on. First thing, he'd always want to cover some record he'd heard on the jukebox. And Sam would have to persuade him he couldn't do that. He'd have to do something new and different and let the people try to cover *him*. Elvis was different from the other Sun artists who came later. He did not write his own songs. We had to create them on the spot or take somebody else's song from our stable of writers. And he'd never rehearse. The others would get back from shows on the road and rehearse until they thought they had something presentable, and *then* go to Sam. Not Elvis. Elvis never had *anything* ready. It was always a case of the same thing we did when we first called him in—sitting down and letting him go through everything he knew or he would like to do, and we'd pick things to concentrate on."

With Bob Neal in charge, it began to build. Elvis and Scotty and Bill—now being billed as the Blue Moon Boys— were playing essentially the same type of show, but they were playing more often. Bob Neal explains that most of the bookings followed the format he had set in the past: "Going out and working shows in the territory. Having a good following on WMPS," Bob says, "I could cover a range of a hundred and fifty to two hundred miles around town, and I would simply set a date for a schoolhouse, basically do all the advertising on my radio show, sometimes buy a few window cards, and that was it. We'd do three or four shows a week. My wife Helen'd go along and stand at the door with a cigar box and sell the tickets, and I'd get up and tell a few of my jokes, M.C. the show. Usually we took in about three hundred dollars. And if we sold dates outright to other promoters, maybe farther away from Memphis than I thought I could handle, we'd ask two, three, four hundred dollars, whatever we thought we could get."

Schoolhouse shows were a tradition in Southern rural America, and Scotty remembers that with Elvis they differed from those that came before only slightly or not at all. "We'd drive way off out into the country to a little schoolhouse in a place you never heard of," Scotty says. "It was thirty, forty minutes ahead of time and you wouldn't see a car around. We'd go in and get things set up. Fifteen minutes before the show it was like an avalanche. Woooooomp! They'd be hanging from the rafters."

Some of the early attraction was Bob Neal, not Elvis, but in a short time the number of Presley fans increased to a point where Elvis began to command enough money for his manager to re-evaluate the financial arrangement Elvis had with Scotty and Bill. So far, Elvis had been pocketing 50 per cent, but Bob apparently felt that was unfair and that Elvis should be getting more. Sam Phillips says Elvis owes as much to Scotty Moore for his musical style as he owes to anyone— and it was generally acknowledged that Bill Black's clowning, his riding that battered standup bass around the stage as if it were a horse, had been a large part of the show Elvis had to offer an audience—yet Elvis was the star, and as such, Bob believed he deserved a larger cut. Slowly, then more quickly and noticeably, it was Elvis and his contribution, musical and physical, that pulled the audiences into the school gymnasiums and auditoriums, and it was Elvis's voice, not Scotty and Bill's music, that made Horace Logan extend the *Hayride* contract from a year to eighteen months. So Bob had a talk with Elvis and it was decided that Scotty and Bill would have to take a cut in pay.

"I remember there was quite a bit of unhappiness about this at that time," says Bob today. "That they would quit and so on. But they stayed on. The same thing happened later with Johnny Cash and the Tennessee Two. It was impossible to say to the musicians in the beginning, 'I'll pay you such and such,' because no one had any money. Then when success began to come, it had to be changed.

"The eventual basic decision to change from a percentage to a salary was Elvis's. We talked about it, he and I, and we talked about it with his parents and decided it had to be done. It was my job to carry the word [to Scotty and Bill]."

It didn't come as a surprise to them. Says Scotty today: "One day we were sitting on the front steps talkin' about it all, and he wanted to draw up contracts saying we'd always get twenty-five per cent and he'd take fifty, and I told him it wouldn't work out, because if it keeps goin' like it is, you got records and a lot of other things that possibly we wouldn't be involved in. It wouldn't be right. So we ended up he was gonna give us—only off the records, which was at my suggestion—Bill and I were gonna take one-fourth of one per cent each, outa record royalties. I believe this was right about the time we were talkin' about goin' on salary, gettin' so much per week whether we played or not. Anyway, the percentage deal never did get put on paper and I doubt very seriously if he'd ever remember it."*

Between weekend appearances on the *Hayride*—and to make some of them, Elvis and the boys had to race across much of Texas, driving all night and all day—and well-scattered schoolhouse shows, Elvis returned to the cramped twelve-by-twelve-foot Sun studio at 706 Union Street. Sun was a small company, so poor that when they'd run low they'd take the unsolicited tapes they received from hopeful singers in the Louisiana bayou country or the Georgia farm lands or wherever else they came from in the morning mail, splice them together and record Sun releases over them. There was a shipping room toward the rear, and the back room was being subleased to an auto upholstery firm. The walls were covered with acoustic tile (Carl Perkins later would call it the "pokey-dot room"), painted institutional

---

* If anyone did remember and cared to compute the moneys owed, they would, on the basis of a penny a record (the rough equivalent of ¼ of 1 per cent) and RCA Victor's claimed total sales of 250 million records, be worth nearly $1,250,000 apiece to Scotty and the late Bill Black's estate.

green and all the woodwork was white. Marion Keisker says she papered the bathroom herself.

Elvis was here to cut his third record, one side of which started out as one of those smooth, shuffling blues ballads, and then Elvis said, "Hold it, fellas. That don't move me. Let's get real, real gone." And then the song, "Milkcow Blues Boogie," began to rock. It had been recorded originally in 1930 by blues singer Sleepy John Estes, again in 1938 by another blues vocalist, Joe Williams. On the other side of Elvis's record was "You're a Heartbreaker," a typical hillybilly weeper given a rocking beat.

This record wasn't even mentioned in *Billboard* and, according to Marion, it sold poorly.

Even so, Elvis was building a following of sufficient size and ardor to warrant a fan club and attract the first of what would be a long series of paternity suits. Paternity suits are a hazard faced by almost all male performers and the first to hit Elvis came in 1954, when a teenager in Mississippi said Elvis had done her wrong. The suit was dismissed.

Elvis had a steady girl during this period—Dixie Locke, a shapely brunette he had dated his last year at Humes High. Elvis carried Dixie's picture in a compartment in his wrist watch and announced he wanted to marry her, but was discouraged from taking that step by his mother. When it came time to form the first Elvis Presley fan club, a contest was held, with the presidency going to the fan who wrote the best letter explaining why he or she wanted that honor. Marion says there was no question but what Dixie's was the most convincing letter of the hundreds received.

Sometime during the winter of 1954–55, before Bob Neal signed Elvis—the principals involved don't have any more specific remembrance than that—a man named Oscar (the Baron) Davis came to Memphis to promote an Eddy Arnold Show for his boss, Colonel Tom Parker, a flashy personal manager who reminded most of his friends of something between W. C. Fields and P. T. Barnum. In those days Oscar was nearly as colorful as the Colonel. He was a thin white-haired dude who, if you believed the stories, had earned a million dollars in country music and spent a million and a half.

Oscar was working as Tom Parker's "advance agent," handling Eddy Arnold's publicity. "I was in Memphis to cut my spots, the transcriptions for selling the show, at WMPS, and Bob Neal was the big disc jockey there," Oscar says today. "I had heard much about Elvis. I asked Bob if he had the Elvis records and he said he did. He played them for me. He said, 'I can't play them on this station because they're barred here.' Bob was playing sweet country, good listening music, and Elvis was too raucous.

"Then he said, 'Incidentally, he's playing at the Airport Inn if you'd like to see him.' I said I'd be glad to. We went out to the airport and he just had the two boys with him, a guitar player and a bass player. The place was full of women. It seated only around sixty people, but they were screamin' their heads off. I said, 'Bob, this guy is sensational. I'd like to meet him. Introduce me to him.' He said, 'I can't. He hates my guts because I can't play his records.' I said, 'Well, I'm going to meet him.' And I brought him over to the table. Now, Scotty Moore, the guitar player, was acting as the manager at that time. So we made a tentative deal and they were somewhat excited about getting me in the picture with them. We agreed to meet the following Sunday when Eddy Arnold would be in town and I would be back."

Oscar is a thin dapper man in his seventies now, partially paralyzed by a stroke in 1963 but livelier than most men his age. "It was a rather cold day and around eleven o'clock in the morning they showed up," he says. "I steered them to the coffee shop across the street from the auditorium, not telling Colonel Parker anything about Elvis. Then, after I got through setting up the box office, everything ready, I started across the street. The Colonel followed me.

"I didn't want him to know about Presley. I was working for him. I was doing the exploitation for him. But I didn't want him to know. He said, 'Where you going?' I couldn't say, 'I'm going nowhere,' so I said, 'I'm going over to have a cup of coffee.' So we went over there, and Elvis and Judd Phillips and Bill Black and Scotty Moore were in the restaurant, waiting for me to come and make a deal. So Tom entered into the negotiations and the first thing he said was 'Well, the guy will get nowhere on Sun records. This is the first thing.' And Judd Phillips, who is Sam's brother, said, 'Well, he's not going off Sun records and that's for sure.' Because they were beginning to get a little action. So Tom brought up a lot of other objections to handling Elvis, and I proceeded almost at that time to be discouraged about the whole thing. We went back and we had a few arguments about Elvis, Tom and I. Finally I was riding with him, we were coming back to Nashville, and Roy Acuff called me up. He wanted me to exploit him and Kitty Wells and Johnny and Jack as a package. So I proceeded to forget about Elvis."

The Colonel apparently did not forget. First he wanted to see how well Elvis would do on the record charts and then he waited for reports from the field. The *Billboard* award— eighth place in the "most promising" category—made Elvis a "possible." The Memphis sales charts designated him a "local hero." The reports from the field, and personal observation of the audience reaction, tagged him a "potential smash." (In even the most rural corners of show business there are well-defined categories of success and near success.) Elvis was big on the *Louisiana Hayride,* but they hated him on the *Grand Ole Opry.* You could pay your money or take your choice. The Colonel split it down the middle. He made no move of commitment but started to get involved in a small way by helping Bob Neal make a deal for a concert in Carlsbad, New Mexico. This was in February 1955, just one month after Neal got involved.

-5-

THE COLONEL [1]

ONCE UPON A TIME (the way the Colonel tells the story) a younger, thinner Tom Parker was working the foot-long-hot-dog concession on a carnival runway. The buns were a foot long but there was no more than a little piece of wiener sticking out of each end, while the rest was filled with the cheaper condiments. If anyone complained about being gyped (the Colonel says), why he'd just point to the piece of hot dog he'd dropped in the sawdust that morning and say, "You dropped your meat, boy. Now move along, you dropped your meat." One can see W. C. Fields, as Larsen E. Whipsnade in *You Can't Cheat an Honest Man*, contriving the same stunt.

Once upon a second time (the way the Colonel boasts) the same younger, thinner Tom Parker filled a barrel with hose water, added a packet of citric acid and a lot of cheap white sugar, cut up a single lemon to float on the top, and sold the swill as lemonade.

Once upon a third time he caught sparrows, painted them yellow and sold them as canaries.

And if that weren't enough to knock your hat in the creek, when Tom Parker was booking country singers across much of the South and Southwest (he says), he was scheduling them "round robin" style, meaning the same bill of acts would play two shows simultaneously in cities as far apart as a hundred miles. The way it worked was as soon as the first act in

one town finished, he'd drive like hell to the second town opening the show there and all the other acts would follow. Thus,
in a single night, the Colonel and his musical minions made
double the money. Now (the Colonel says), he always scheduled an intermission in these shows. That was so that if in
shuttling the acts from one town to the next something unforeseen happened (flat tire, whatever), there'd be that half-
hour break to serve as a cushion. And it was during that
intermission that the Colonel peddled his glossy eight-by-ten
photographs as the audience left the tent or schoolhouse for
a smoke and a stretch—and then he sent a small boy inside
to pick up the souvenir books the people'd left on or under
their seats, books they'd purchased on entering. Parker (says
Parker) figured they could be sold again in the next town if
people were dumb enough to leave them behind.

In 1955 Colonel Tom Parker already was something of a
legend. Not only had he managed two of the top country
singers, Eddy Arnold and Hank Snow, he'd left that stack of
amazing stories behind him, piling up like jokes in Henny
Youngman's night-club act. Or, more accurately, like the
anecdotes in a book that certainly must have been one of the
Colonel's then-recent favorites, H. Allen Smith's *The Com-
pleat Practical Joker.*
Tom Parker came by his prankishness "honestly," being
born the twenty-sixth of June in 1910 in West Virginia, where
his parents were traveling with a carnival. The elder Parkers
died before Tom reached the fifth grade, and he went to work
for his uncle's outfit, the Great Parker Pony Circus. At seventeen he struck out on his own with a pony and monkey act,
touring the "cherry soda circuit," which meant soft drink
companies paid him three dollars a day to accept bottle caps
as the price of admission.
Says the Colonel's close friend Oscar Davis: "He was later
with the Royal American, which was the granddaddy of all
the traveling shows—a railroad show, as opposed to a truck
show. It was headquartered in Tampa. He handled the food—

what they call the 'pie car' on the train, where all the carnival people ate as they went from town to town. He also ran a 'mitt camp' for reading palms. He was almost psychic, that man. Upon occasion he would do the palm reading himself. All in a humorous spirit, of course."

In a sense it was a wonderful world for Tom Parker, for nowhere else could his imagination be so rapidly expanded, so readily applied. On all sides he was surrounded by super-salesmen and easily exploitable freaks. The voluptuous snake charmer slept with her pet python, the sword swallower was one of the few in the world who swallowed fluorescent light bulbs and then turned them on so you could see his chest glow, geeks bit heads off live chickens, the tattooed lady invited you to examine almost all of her body, midgets ran between the barker's legs, and dozens of fast-talking con men invited thousands of passers-by to step right up and pitch pennies, throw baseballs, shoot rifles, have their fortunes told, watch kootch dancers and buy canaries, lemonade and foot-long hot dogs.

Which makes it sound exciting and glamorous. Which it wasn't most of the time. The cast of characters may have been such that schoolboys and bored families were drawn to it, but for those in the carnival themselves, more often than not it was anything *but* attractive. Carnival life never has been quite as glamorous as it is supposed to be, and although Colonel Parker's imagination may have been fired by exposure to so many outlandish characters, just as often it was pushed by hunger. He was clever not so much because it was amusing but because he had to be. When traveling with smaller, poorer carnivals, often there weren't even tires enough to move all the trucks from one town to the next. If there were tires enough to move two trucks, they'd do that and then return to the first carnival site in one truck, carrying the four tires from the other, to be used to move a third. Then, once arrived in a new location and with everything set up, sometimes it was difficult to attract customers.

Says one of the Colonel's friends: "There was one time when everybody called a meeting in the cookhouse. They'd been charging fifty cents admission and the meeting was to discuss lowering the price to twenty-five. The Colonel said no and they fought him. But he said he had a better idea, if they'd just let him try it one day. What he did was have a sign painted that said, 'Admission $1.00. If not satisfied, half your money back.' Of course no one admitted to being satisfied and they all asked for, and got, half their money back. But the gimmick worked. There were crowds and they hadn't lowered their price."

To milk a final nickel from his customers, the Colonel also improved on the old P. T. Barnum "Egress" stunt. (Barnum had trouble getting people to leave his exhibits and posted a huge sign over a door that said, "Egress this way." People thought it was another freak or weird animal, not knowing "egress" was just another word for "exit.") The Colonel's improvement came in charging his customers to leave. He had rented a cow pasture and kept cows on the only road through the pasture all the preceding night, so that by the time the carnival opened its tent flaps, the road was knee-deep in manure. After the show the customers were led to the road, the only exit. They could then walk a quarter mile through soft fresh cow manure or pay the Colonel a nickel to ride a pony through.

"It was day-to-day living," says the Colonel's friend. "Sometimes he didn't have food for he and his wife. He smoked cigars even then and did most of his shopping in the gutters of the cities he visited. When he found a cigar butt more than an inch long, it was a good day."

Tom Parker began to pull back from this ugly yet fascinating world in the mid-1930s, first to hire out as a press agent for carnivals, circuses and showboats. He and his wife and her son by an earlier marriage settled in Tampa, Florida, not far from where most of his clients spent the winter.

In the late 1930s Tom was working for Tampa's humane

society and promoting anything that crossed his path he
liked. One month it might be sending feature stories about a
circus to newspapers, the next promoting a series of concerts
for Gene Austin, the popular singer who'd had such a big
hit with "My Blue Heaven," the next raising money for a
new kennel or dog catcher's truck. And when some of the
headline country artists came through Florida from Nashville, he'd help them. Says Minnie Pearl, the country comedi-
enne, who met Parker when she played Tampa with Roy
Acuff in the early forties: "We went down there and he tied
our show in with some chain, like Kroger, and it was smart
promotion because it filled the house several times. It was a
point-of-purchase thing, where you clip the coupon and go
to the store to get tickets at a discount. The store paid for the
newspaper advertising that way, and many more tickets were
sold, because every Kroger cashier in a three-county area was
working what amounted to a box office. The man was thinking even then."

(Similarly, the Colonel later would take Eddy Arnold's
first radio sponsor, the Ralston Purina Company, and book
Eddy and his band to play at dozens of mill openings and
Purina feed and seed dealers' conventions. He had a genuine
fondness for involving commercial enterprises outside show
business, knowing it always broadened the record market
while diminishing immediate costs and boosting the take at
the till. There was, however, one product to which his name
is often linked that he did not have anything to do with:
Hadacol, the twenty-four-proof patent medicine that swept
the South in the late forties. Even today he occasionally
meets someone who swears he met the Colonel during the
Hadacol days. The Colonel is cordial, never denies the relationship, but never had it either. Says Oscar Davis: "I don't
know how they got started, but I can tell you the Hadacol
stories are a fallacy. I was very close to the Hadacol deal
because I had Hank Williams at that time and we were the
very first act Hadacol put on the road in caravan to sell the

stuff. I made the transcriptions, the fast-talking minute-long radio spots, to sell Hadacol. And Tom was never involved.")

Says Minnie Pearl: "Shortly after that we went on a tent show with Eddy Arnold and his band and Jam-Up and Honey [a blackface team] and Uncle Dave Macon. And Tom became connected with the tent show as an advance agent. Instead of working auditoriums, we took a tent along with us and played all these little tiny towns. The tent seated three thousand. We couldn't do twenty miles a day, because we'd 'strike the rag' at night after the show and then have to put it back up again in the next town. We all traveled in cars. Tom stayed ahead of us, but every now and then he'd jump back and travel with us for a while."

What the portly cigar-smoking advance agent was doing this summer was lining up the radio and newspaper advertising, placing posters on walls and in store windows, and trying for some local publicity, a radio interview or a news story in the local weekly. He may not have admitted it then, but he was preparing himself for a move to Nashville and a full-time commitment to the country music field, while getting to know Eddy Arnold, the man he would serve as personal manager.

Says Roy Acuff, now the patriarch of the multimillion-dollar Acuff-Rose complex of record companies, talent agencies and music publishing firms: "I presume I was the first one ever to invite Tom to Nashville. He had helped me sell a flour company I had behind me then, helpin' to advertise it in the state of Florida. I suggested he come to Nashville, meet the boys."

Acuff says Parker wanted to manage him, but "he wouldn't take anyone who just wanted to stay with the *Grand Ole Opry*, and I wanted to stay with the *Opry*. He wanted to manage them completely, to have complete control. That's his style and he's been very successful. You can't argue with success, but I wanted to go on as I was doin'."

So Tom looked around Nashville and finally signed Eddy

Arnold, who then was making his first feature appearance on the *Opry* as a soloist. Eddy had been born on a farm near Henderson, Tennessee, in 1918, the son of a onetime country fiddler who encouraged him to learn the guitar when he was ten. He dropped out of school in the 1930s to help on his family farm, and for years all he played for were local dances, usually traveling to and from the jobs on a mule. He made his living on the farm and as an assistant in a Henderson mortuary. He made his radio debut in 1936 on a radio station in nearby Jackson and then joined Pee Wee King's Golden West Cowboys Band, singing in a style reminiscent of Gene Autry. He was calling himself the "Tennessee Plowboy" when Tom persuaded Eddy to leave the *Opry* and go with him.

Up to and after World War Two most country and western talent scheduling was handled by radio station talent bureaus which were designed to use the talent on the station's programs while booking it over that area covered by the station's transmitter. At the end of the war, however, several individuals like Tom Parker came along who ignored the radio station stranglehold on talent and announced themselves as "independent bookers and promoters." Now it was possible for talent to work the entire South through one office, rather than jump from station to station, and to avoid working for any one station in an area to the exclusion of all others. In this way Tom Parker became one of the true pioneers in country music.

According to Eddy Arnold, he was a good manager in other ways. "When he managed me, it was always exclusive management by Thomas A. Parker," he says in his autobiography, *It's a Long Way from Chester County*. "When Tom's your manager, he's all you. He lives and breathes his artist. I once said to him when he was managing me, 'Tom, why don't you get yourself a hobby—play golf, go boating, or something?' He looked me straight in the eye and said, 'You're my hobby.'"

Parker managed Eddy for most of a decade, taking him to

a point where he eclipsed Roy Acuff's record on the top of what *Billboard* called "the h.b. [for hillbilly] talent heap." In 1944 he took Eddy to RCA Victor to record, and Eddy began to crank out hits, reaching the first of a series of peaks in 1947, when Victor released the million-selling "Bouquet of Roses." He also kept Eddy on the road, knowing that one of the best ways to build, and keep, a record audience was through saturation "personals," appearing everywhere there was a schoolhouse or room to pitch a tent.

Says Hubert Long, now one of Nashville's top talent manipulators but then apprenticed to Parker as an advance agent: "I'd go out alone in front of a tour a week or ten days to see everything was in order—the interviews, the accommodations and so on. I'd talk to him on the phone or I'd leave an envelope with all the information in it—who'd be stopping by to see him, that sort of thing. Besides Eddy, he had the Willis Brothers, then called the Oklahoma Wranglers, Guy, Chuck and Skeeter Willis—those three musicians along with Roy Wiggins on steel guitar—a girl singer or a comedian, or maybe a girl comedian. A well-rounded country show. He put the package together and I will say this: He left no stone unturned. When Eddy came to a town, whether it had five thousand or five million people, everyone knew he was coming. I think if there's any one thing that led to his success, it's the promotion."

It also was an ability to wheel and deal, making outrageous demands. When Eddy Arnold first appeared in Las Vegas, for example, Parker went to the William Morris Agency, which was handling the deal, and insisted on getting the two weeks' pay in advance. Says Oscar Davis, "They tried to argue him out of it. He said, 'I don't know these people; they might go outa business.' And they said, 'But, Tom, they buy the biggest acts in the nation. They won't go out of business.' He said, 'Well, if they don't want to okay it, you okay it and you'll be responsible for the money.' William Morris said it couldn't do that, something about policy. And Tom said,

'Well, if you can't be responsible, there must be an element of doubt.' Tom got his money."

It was during the day-to-day touring that Tom put his carnival background to work. It was Eddy Arnold he booked "round robin" style, so he could collect double the box office, peddle those eight-by-tens and sell souvenir books two and three times apiece. It also was with Eddy he introduced one of the more incredible acts in all show business history, what he called Colonel Parker's Dancing Chickens.

Country singers long have performed at rodeos and live-stock shows and in those days there was a twenty-dollar entertainment tax charged per performance unless you had a livestock exhibit, so the Colonel would carry a hog or a couple of chickens in the back of his car, put them in a box outside where Eddy sang and mark it "Livestock Exhibit," thereby saving the twenty bucks. The Colonel was traveling with two chickens when Eddy was too sick to appear and so he went to the stock show's producer and said he had a sub-stitute act, Colonel Parker's Dancing Chickens. As the Colo-nel tells the story, he sent his assistant to the nearest general store to buy a two-dollar hotplate and an extension cord, which he placed in the chicken cage and covered with straw. The hotplate was plugged in, Bob Wills and the Texas Plow-boys went into "Turkey in the Straw," the curtain went up and a bewildered audience saw two chickens high-stepping around the cage, trying to keep from burning their feet. The Colonel says he got away with this for two days, two shows per day, until Eddy was able to sing again.

Eddy Arnold wasn't the only act Tom Parker booked in the 1940s and 1950s. There were, for example, three nameless country singers the Colonel had traveling in tandem—two of them (according to the Colonel) being miserable louts who did little but complain, while the third singer was a joy to work with. Matter of fact, the poor ol' Colonel (which is how the Colonel sometimes addresses himself) wasn't doing so well in those days, and it was only this third vocalist who came to him and volunteered to take a cut in salary. Then one spectacular Friday night the three acts proved to be a singing gold mine, drawing a turnaway crowd. Immediately following the show the two louts went to the Colonel and demanded a larger piece of the action. (So far they'd been on salary.) That did it. The Colonel called all three acts together and told them, "Tomorrow I'm gonna give *you* fifty per cent of the box office and I'm gonna give *you* fifty per cent of the box office and I'm gonna give *you* fifty per cent of the box office. How's that?" The three country boys, better singers than they were mathematicians, said it was more than generous. And the following night the Colonel put three box offices outside the school auditorium. Each of the acts had his own box office and the people were told to buy their tickets at the box office of the singer they were there to see. So at the evening's end, the singers got half of *their own* box office take, instead of the customary day's salary. The way it worked out (the Colonel says) the two louts didn't come up to salary, the good guy singer did a little better than usual and the Colonel pocketed a greater share than he ever had.

In the early 1950s the Colonel and Eddy Arnold split up. Oscar Davis intimates there were a number of incidents leading to the break, but says it was an argument in Las Vegas that made the relationship collapse. Parker had been laying out a two-page newspaper advertisement as a surprise to Eddy, he says, and when Eddy walked into the Colonel's room unexpectedly, Parker quickly hid the layout, Eddy accused him of doing something behind his back, one thing led to another and pretty soon Eddy was without a manager, Parker was without a star.

Bill Williams, then a newsman for the *Grand Ole Opry*'s radio station, WSM, and now *Billboard*'s man in Nashville as well as an officer in the Country Music Association, remembers what happened to the Colonel next. "It was very hard for a man like the Colonel to make any headway then," he says. "There was a time when independent promoters had influence and the time would come again, but in the early fifties the *Opry* was the thing and no one functioned much without reaching the *Opry* or being booked by the Artists Service Bureau, which was run by Jim Denny right there in the *Opry* office. Sometimes if an artist felt the Service Bureau was slighting him, he'd latch onto one of the loose promoters and managers, who'd get them a few bookings and then they'd find it wasn't the way they thought it was, so they'd run right back to the *Opry* again." Williams says it was during this time that Parker, along with Oscar Davis and others, operated from WSM's lobby, using the lobby telephone. "The Colonel and the others would report in each morning at nine, shortly after the work staff came in, sit down on the sofas, and start calling all over the South booking their acts. When the phone rang, by agreement whoever was closest answered it by the number, fearing they might lose a booking if someone calling Tom got Charley Brown on the phone instead and Charley said it was Brown Productions instead of Tom's company. It was quite complicated, but they had it all worked out. And between them they lined up more clients and did more business than the *Opry*'s Service Bureau, which was directly across the hall . . . while WSM blithely picked up the tab—for years!"

The time came, of course, when the free phone was cut off, when an aggressive new assistant to the president was brought in to cut costs and he discovered all those hundreds of dollars being charged each month to the telephone in the lobby. This forced the Colonel and his pals into the station announcer's booth, where there was another telephone, and then into the studios themselves. Finally a system was installed whereby no one could call out unless he went through a newly installed switchboard. It came as such a shock, two of the promoters quit show business altogether, went home to Missouri and entered politics. (One was elected to Congress.)

Bill Williams remembers Parker vividly from this period. "I always knew when he was in the lobby, even when I was in the newsroom forty feet away," he says. "He had an early reputation, not necessarily one of love, but admiration. He was noted even then as a man with the remarkable ability to recognize talent. I remember some of the old timers saying, 'If Tom Parker says they're good, they're good and you better listen.' He stood out there in the lobby, noisy, telling stories, wearing that old battered five-gallon hat of his and smoking those cigars, grabbing many acts that others passed up. He had that knack. He was something special among those who were something special."

After he left the WSM lobby, it was from his one-story eleven-room flagstone home on the Gallatin Road north of Nashville in Madison that Parker ran his company, Jamboree Attractions. The house was (and is) situated on former grazing land and in a few years would be worth an enormous sum, just as the land across the highway would rise in price fast enough to convince its owner, Eddy Arnold, to sell it to Sears. The actual business the Colonel ran from the basement and then the garage he converted into offices—all of which were (and are) covered with posters, photographs and souvenirs, including the certification of his honorary colonelcy, presented by Tennessee's Governor Frank G. Clement in 1953.

Working with Parker was a small, cordial, almost penguin-like man with sandy hair, Tom Diskin. He had come to the Colonel from Chicago when Parker had Eddy Arnold, and the Colonel put Diskin's sisters—who sang and called themselves the Dickens Sisters—on several of his shows. Diskin joined Parker as his right-hand man, handling most of the dirtier office work at first and then taking over management of the tours, which meant he accompanied the acts and was responsible for much of the menial back-breaking work that goes with being on the road. *

* For a time, Diskin ran an office for Jamboree Attractions in Chicago and it was to that office that Scotty Moore once had addressed a letter, seeking work for Elvis. Apparently Diskin wasn't impressed by the record Scotty enclosed, as he sent Scotty a one-paragraph reply saying Jamboree wasn't looking for that kind of act. Scotty keeps the letter framed today.

In 1954 one of the artists the Colonel represented from Madison was Hank Snow, a short, almost scrawny forty-year-old who had been on his own since he was fourteen, singing in his native Nova Scotia, Canada, where he built a following that attracted the attention of RCA Victor. At first his records were available only in Canada, but after 1949 Hank began to sell in the United States—which brought him to Nashville to appear on the *Opry*. Among the big hits that followed was "I Don't Hurt Anymore," the number one country and western song of 1954, the song that was in the number one position in Memphis the week Elvis's first record made its first appearance (as number three). Less than two months later Hank signed with the Colonel, giving him exclusive rights to booking him for all personals. A month later Parker had taken over administration of Hank Snow Enterprises, the loosely organized business umbrella over Hank and all his publishing, recording, radio, television and film activities. Once again Tom Parker was in control of the South's leading country and western singing star.

It was shortly after that the Colonel began helping Bob Neal with Elvis's bookings in the South and Southwest.

-6-

SUNSET

IMMEDIATELY FOLLOWING THE SHOW in Carlsbad, New Mexico, Elvis and Scotty and Bill joined Hank Snow, touring the Southwest, closing ten days later in Bastrop, Louisiana. Elvis was billed beneath Snow, Hank's son Jimmy, the Duke of Paducah, Mother Maybelle and the Carter Sisters, and the Jimmie Rodgers Show. Then he went to Cleveland with Bob Neal to appear at the Circle Theater, one of three houses competing for the city's Saturday night country music market. The same week Bob began advertising in the music trade publications, asking night club and concert promoters to call him for bookings, urging disc jockeys to get in touch if they wanted records. (Sun's distribution setup left much to be desired and this was the only way some jockeys could get Elvis's records.) and Mike Michael of KDMS in El Dorado, Arkansas, reported in *Billboard* that Elvis was "just about the hottest thing around these parts. His style really pleases the teenagers." In Dallas, where Elvis was putting in a return appearance at the Big D Jamboree, the press agent for the Sportatorium, home of the Big D, said Elvis was just terrific, they wanted him back again.

The only rejection Elvis received during this time came when Bob Neal flew the boys to New York to audition for Arthur Godfrey's *Talent Scouts*, then the most popular, and

therefore important, new talent showcase on television. It
was Elvis's first airplane flight and his first time in New York.
Elvis didn't like New York and Godfrey didn't like Elvis; the
Talent Scouts said no.

In May Elvis went on what Bob Neal calls "his first big
tour," a three-week sweep through the South, again with
Hank Snow's Jamboree, starting in New Orleans May 1, jumping from city to city in Louisiana, Alabama, Florida, Georgia,
Virginia and Tennessee, closing in Chattanooga on the twentieth. Snow was the headliner. Others were Faron Young, the
Wilburn Brothers, Slim Whitman, Martha Carson, the Davis
Sisters, Mother Maybelle and the Carter Sisters, Onie Wheeler
and the Jimmie Rodgers Show. All country. Except for Elvis.
Booked and promoted by the general manager of Hank Snow's
production company, Tom Parker.

It was while Elvis was on this tour that his fourth record
from Sun was released. This was "Baby, Let's Play House,"
a blues song that introduced the hiccuping glottis strokes for
which Elvis would become famous, backed by "I'm Left,
You're Right, She's Gone," a country song written a few weeks
earlier by a Memphis steel guitar player named Stan Kesler.

It would be nearly two months before the songs appeared
on the record charts, and in the meantime Elvis made another week's sweep in another direction with Hank Snow and
Ferlin Husky, the Carlisles, Maxine and Jim Ed Brown, and
Onie Wheeler. The third week in the month he slid into
Meridian, Mississippi, for the Jimmie Rodgers Memorial Celebration. In connection with this performance Bob Neal took
out a quarter-page advertisement in the trade magazines
calling Elvis "the freshest, newest voice in country music."
There was a picture of Elvis in a white shirt, dark coat and
necktie, a mention of his new Sun record, a mention of his
weekly *Hayride* appearances, and Elvis said, "Howdy to all
my friends at the Jimmie Rodgers Memorial." The same week,
"Baby, Let's Play House" and "I'm Left, You're Right, She's
Gone" got a seventy-seven (good) rating from *Billboard*, a

B (very good) from *Cash Box*. The next week "I'm Left . . ." appeared in the number eight position in Memphis, and Elvis began touring Texas and Oklahoma again.

Elvis was buying Cadillacs now, in pink and pink and black. Country musicians loved Cadillacs and Elvis was no exception. A year or so later when Sun Records had added Johnny Cash, Carl Perkins and Jerry Lee Lewis, among others, to its impressive roster, someone would say you could find Sun by looking for the chicken coop nested in Cadillacs.

Then Elvis began to have trouble with his cars. "When the Chevy finally give out, Elvis went and bought a 1951 Lincoln Continental," says Scotty Moore. "Bill wrecked that one. We were doing a date in Arkansas and a truck pulled out and he run it under the truck and totaled the thing out. That's when Elvis bought the '54 Cadillac. That's the one that burned up, near Texarkana, Arkansas. What happened was the wheel bearing went out. His chick was with him. They were comin' behind us. He wasn't payin' no damn attention to the car and all of a sudden he realized the damn thing was on fire. He couldn't put it out. All he could do was open the trunk and throw our clothes and instruments out all over the road."

Scotty laughs and then sighs, perhaps over the loss of the vehicle, even if fifteen years have passed. "So we rented a small plane," he says, "loaded all the instruments in it and barely got off the ground the next day, going to Sweetwater, Texas. Elvis had bought his folks a '54 pink and white Ford at the same time he bought the Cadillac, and somebody brought it to us in Sweetwater so we could finish the tour."

Elvis was energetic, almost to a nervous fault, often keeping his closest friends—in those days, Scotty and Bill and D. J. —awake all night talking and clowning. Says Scotty: "We'd have to throw him outa the car practically. He'd catch me or Bill or D. asleep and he'd take off one of our shoes and toss it out the window. We'd have to stop and go back and find it. Another time he threw out the car keys. At night! He had so

much nervous energy we'd have to sit up nights to wear him
out so we could go to sleep. There'd be pillow fights. We'd
wrestle. Anything we could think of. It like to wore us out,
and every day, every night was the same."

He chewed his fingernails, drummed his hands against his
thighs, tapped his feet, and every chance he got he ran a
comb through blond hair that, quoting Marion Keisker, "had
so much goop in it, it looked dark."

It seemed somehow that all this energy was but a prelude
to what came on stage. Just as there is today—in Las Vegas,
primarily—little introduction to Elvis's performance, there
was little then. It was possible someone would introduce him,
but likely as not Scotty and Bill and D. J. would be set up,
having provided the backup music for another singer on the
show. Then Elvis would come out and go right into one of his
ballads. Draped in black slacks with a pink stripe down the
sides, a pink shirt with the collar turned up catching the ends
of his longish hair, and a pink sport jacket with big black
teardrops on the front and back, he *was* the Hillbilly Cat,
he *was* the King of Western Bop. He leaned forward, legs
braced, guitar hung around his neck, hands clutching the
stand microphone. He looked at the girls in the front row
with lidded eyes, eyebrows forming a loving and woeful arch.
During the song's instrumental break he gave them that lopsided grin and maybe twitched one leg. Once.

The next song might be a rocker, giving Elvis a chance to
show the folks what they'd come to see. Now both legs were
twitching—jerking and snapping back into that original braced
position. It's not likely Elvis was thinking of the pentecostal
preachers of his Tupelo childhood at moments like this, but
it was apparent he hadn't forgotten them. All he'd done was
translate hellfire and damnation into "Good Rockin' Tonight."
His arms flailed the inexpensive guitar, pounding the wood
on the afterbeat and snapping strings as if they were made
of cooked spaghetti. From one song right into another, most
of them already recorded for Sun or soon to be released.

Country songs. With a beat. The girls began to squirm and move; it was music that made their behinds itch.

"You'd see this frenzied reaction, particularly from the young girls," says Bob Neal today. "We hadn't gone out and arranged for anybody to squeal and scream. Not like Frank Sinatra did in the forties. These girls screamed spontaneously. Nowadays it seems to be fashionable for the teenyboppers when they see the act, they know they're supposed to squeal and quiver and so forth. Back in that time there'd been a long period when nobody'd done that—not since Sinatra . . . and that was fifteen years earlier. For Elvis they just did it automatically.

"Plus," Elvis's former manager adds, "it was almost frightening, the reaction that came to Elvis from the teenaged boys. So many of them, through some sort of jealousy, would practically hate him. There were occasions in some towns in Texas when we'd have to be sure to have a police guard because somebody'd always try to take a crack at him. They'd get a gang and try to waylay him or something. Of course, Elvis wasn't afraid of them and was quite willing to defend himself—and did on occasion.

"I remember one night in Lubbock, Texas, we were on a series of one-nighters out there and we worked this deal with the radio station where they said they could get us four or five hundred extra dollars for doing a deal at some club in town. So Elvis thought that was fine. At that time picking up an extra four or five hundred was very helpful. The day before we got there, though, the station people called me, out on the road somewhere, and said they'd had an awful lot of threats from guys about what they were going to do to Presley. So they'd arranged for police protection for Elvis all day long. I explained this to Elvis and he said, 'Oh, I don't need that.' I told him he better listen. So sure enough, all day, all afternoon, all night, they were there—policemen and plainclothesmen. We got in about three in the afternoon, spent a little time at the motel and then went to the auditorium.

Then later he went to the club. The sheriff's deputies took over out there. Along about twelve or twelve-thirty, everything had been very peaceful so far, and the deputies said, 'I guess we can leave.' And I said, 'Go ahead. Everything's okay.' We were walking out to the car in the parking lot when somebody called, 'Hey, Elvis, come here.' Friendly. Elvis walked over, grinning, figuring somebody just wanted an autograph. It was somebody waiting for him. And the guy sitting there in the car just reached out and hit him in the face as hard as he could and drove off. Elvis ran back and got in our car and said he'd recognize him and made us drive around Lubbock until five o'clock in the morning. He was determined he was going to find somebody and fix him up.

"He was naturally pleased to get a reaction from an audience," Bob says today. "He got a real kick from it. He really enjoyed the reaction from the girls, but he asked me, 'Why do those guys want to be like that?' He considered himself a regular fella, just as much an ordinary-type stud as any of them, but they were mad at him. I explained and others explained, but he just didn't seem to understand. He said it didn't seem logical."

Bob Neal sits back behind his tidy desk, lights the stub of a thick cigar and says, "On the little shows in the area Elvis was getting top billing. We'd just say we're bringing the Elvis Presley Show to you. But naturally when we were working some of the big packages—the things Colonel Parker was putting together—he'd get more or less minor billing. One thing that always happened, though, after the first night of a tour, Presley would always close the show. No matter what, nobody wanted to follow him.

"I remember one time we had a package playing six or eight days out in Texas and I'd set the show with Elvis on last. After the first show Ferlin Husky approached me and said he thought he should close the show, being the headliner and all. I said if he wants to take the chance, okay, so the next night I switched it around. I told Elvis and he just laughed, said it didn't make any difference to him. Sure enough, Ferlin followed Elvis. It was pitiful. Ferlin did everything he could. He was a fine performer. But the audience was screaming bring back Presley, where's Elvis! Plus: leaving. So the next morning Ferlin conceded there was no way to follow Elvis. He came to me and said, 'I think we better go back to the way you had the show set up the first time.'"

Bob says Elvis couldn't stand to see an audience sit on its hands. "He threw everything into it, trying to break that audience down, trying to get it with him. He'd always react to audience reaction and in the rare instances when he'd be placed on the show early, I always felt he kind of outdid himself, making it tough for the guy to follow. He was a very competitive showman. He was greatly anxious for success. Helen used to talk with him on the way back from one-nighters in the Memphis area, and she says he talked not in terms of being a moderate success. No—his ambition and desire was to be big in movies and so forth. He'd ask her did she think he could make it. She said he could go as far as he wanted to. From the very first he had ambition to be nothing in the ordinary but to go all the way. He was impatient. He would say, 'We got to figure out how to do this, we got to get ahead.'"

At the beginning of the third week of June Elvis was in Beaumont, Texas, playing a police benefit with Marty Robbins, the Maddox Brothers and Rose and Retta (Maddox), Sonny James, the Belew Twins and the Texas Stompers. Twenty-four hundred seats were sold five times in two days, with the top ticket price at one dollar. On June 26 he was in Biloxi, Mississippi, the next two days at Keesler Air Force Base nearby, the next two at Curtis Gordon's Club in Mobile, Alabama. On July first he was playing Baton Rouge, Louisiana's capital, and on the third he was in Texas, at Corpus Christi. He was singing at a picnic in De Leon, Texas, on

July 4, along with his old friends the Blackwood Brothers
and the Statesmen, and a bunch of the usual country acts.

There seemed to be no end to it.

It was when Elvis first appeared in Jacksonville that he experienced his first "riot." It was here that teenagers tore his
clothes off, shredded his pink shirt and white jacket, and
ripped his shoes from his feet, actually putting Elvis himself
in physical danger, although at the time he laughed it off.

Previews of coming attractions.

"They loved him in Florida," says Oscar Davis, who promoted the concert for the Colonel. "I guess we put more
emphasis on Florida, because Tom was acquainted with the
state and he wanted to show him off down there. So we
devoted more time in Tampa and Orlando and Jacksonville."

The same week *Billboard* again reviewed Elvis's fourth
record, saying, "In the past few weeks, various Southern
territories have been seeing nice action with this disk. After
a strong kick-off in the Memphis area, it has begun to sell
well in Houston, Dallas, New Orleans and Nashville and is
moving out now in Richmond, St. Louis and the Carolinas."

In the middle of July another important mark was made,
when "Baby, Let's Play House" became Elvis's first record to
appear on one of the national best-seller charts. Previously
he had been on regional charts only, but now he was on the
chart drawn on the basis of dealer reports throughout the
nation with a high volume in country and western sales. And
the next week the record was on *two* national charts—number
fifteen on the best-selling country list, number eleven on the
list of country records that got the most air play by country
disc jockeys.

As this record worked its way up the charts, Elvis's fifth, and
last, for Sun Records was released. This was "Mystery Train"—
a song that was written by Sam Phillips and a black blues
singer named Little Junior Parker and had been a rhythm and
and blues hit by Parker on Sun a few years earlier—backed
with "I Forgot to Remember to Forget," a country song writ-

ten by Stan Kesler, who'd also written "I'm Left, You're Right, She's Gone."

As the record was being shipped to record stores, Colonel Parker and his assistant, Tom Diskin, began meeting with Bob Neal, Elvis and Elvis's father to discuss their fall and winter plans. At these meetings, the first that would be talked about publicly as "policy meetings," it was agreed that Elvis probably would do very well in all the polls to be announced during November's disc jockey convention in Nashville and that it would be announced soon that Elvis would leave Sun Records for a larger company.

"In practically all of 1955 there were negotiations of one sort or another going on," says Bob Neal. "Some people thought I had an interest in Sun, and I'd get a call from some company asking can we buy the Presley contract, how much is it? I'd say, 'Let me see, I'll check with Sam Phillips and let you know.' I know when it started off it would have taken only four or five thousands dollars, but I recall one time later when Mitch Miller, who was with Columbia, called me. We were out on a tour in Texas and he said how much is the contract? I said I'd check. By that time Sam was asking eighteen or twenty thousand. I called Mitch back and he said, 'Forget it. No artist is worth that kind of money.'"

The bidding continued. Ahmet Ertegun, president of Atlantic Records, essentially a rhythm and blues and jazz label, offered $25,000. "That was everything we had, including my desk," Ahmet says today. "I figured we'd get Elvis, we'd have a star and we'd take off in the country field. But going from Sun to Atlantic was like trading an Austin for a Morris. Besides, the Colonel said he had to have forty-five thousand, which at the time was not only outrageous but silly."

Arnold Shaw, now a writer, in 1955 was associated with the Edward B. Marks Music Corporation, a song publishing outfit in New York, and he claims he was the cause of some of the Presley excitement. He says he first heard Elvis's records in the summer when he visited Colonel Parker in Madison. Then he returned to New York, where he played them for Bill Randle, a disc jockey whose program was broadcast there and in Cleveland. He says Randle was afraid to break the records in New York but was willing to give them a try in Ohio. And the response to *this* was enough to cause Randle —who'd discovered the Crew Cuts and therefore commanded a lot of respect in the cash-register if not the creative end of the record business—to start hyping Elvis to record companies in New York. That, says Arnold Shaw, had damned near every label in the city wondering how much to spend on Elvis's Sun contract.

The Colonel went to New York and took a small suite in the Hotel Warwick. With him he had an enormously long telegram, signed by Elvis's parents, which said the poor ol' Colonel was empowered by them to find a buyer. Among the many he met were his old friends at RCA Victor, Steve Sholes, who was head of the company's artist and repertoire department in Nashville, and Frank Folsom, Victor's president. The Colonel had known these men for years, largely through his dealings with Eddy Arnold and Hank Snow, both RCA recording artists. He also met with Jean and Julian Aberbach, the German-born brothers who operated Hill and Range Music, Inc., the young, aggressive music publishing company then taking over much of the country and western market.

Sam Phillips flew to New York to hear Victor's final offer: $35,000 in cash for Elvis's contract (which had about a year to run) and rights to all his released and unreleased material —with another $5000 going to Elvis as a bonus for signing. In today's highly competitive record market $40,000 isn't much, but in 1955 it was regarded as something decidedly larger than a king's ransom. Sun was to retain the rights to press records to fill all orders until the first of the year, after which Victor had exclusive rights to everything Elvis had recorded or would record—for a period of three years. Sam said it seemed fair, contracts should be drawn up and probably they would be signed during the disc jockey convention in Nashville, then only a few weeks away.

It had been determined a short time earlier that Hill and Range would publish the Elvis Presley song folio, and during these later negotiations the Aberbachs bought the rights to Hi Lo Music, a subsidiary of Sun Records Sam had formed to publish several of the songs his artists recorded. These included three of Elvis's: "Mystery Train," "I'm Left, You're Right, She's Gone" and "You're a Heartbreaker." Hill and Range also agreed to set up Elvis Presley Music, Inc., to publish songs Elvis would record, sharing the publisher's royalties with Elvis on a fifty-fifty partnership for a period of five years.

RCA said it hoped to have the first Presley record—a reissue of one of Sun's records—out by early December, and that the company would promote Elvis not just in the country market but in the three existing fields simultaneously—country, rhythm and blues, and pop.

Hill and Range said it was going to have the first Presley song folio—words and music to Elvis's recorded songs—ready for release by December 10.

Back in Memphis, Bob Neal continued to serve as Elvis's "official" manager, and he opened a small record shop on Main Street, using it as a ticket location for the occasional concerts he was staging locally. The Elvis Presley Fan Club (answering all letters on black and pink stationery) and out-of-town bookings were run from an office on Union Street not far from Sun Records. And, of course, he still had that early morning show on WMPS.

There was another accident on September 2, as Elvis and Scotty and Bill and D. J. were driving from New Orleans to Texarkana, which caused a thousand dollars in damage to one of their Cadillacs, but no one was hurt. Elvis then worked his way through Arkansas, parts of Missouri, much of Mississippi (beating it back to Shreveport each week for his *Hayride* appearances), then made one of his rare airplane trips to Norfolk, where he joined Hank Snow's All-Star Jamboree for a tour that took him to Asheville in the western North Carolina mountains and to Roanoke, Virginia. After that Elvis headlined a smaller unit—with the Louvin Brothers and Cowboy Copas—that crisscrossed the same two states, closing in Kingsport, Tennessee, a twelve-hour drive from home.

All the audience records were being broken now and by mid-September Elvis had three songs on the national country music charts. "Mystery Train," "Baby, Let's Play House" and "I Forgot to Remember to Forget." And a month after that, in mid-October, Elvis went out with his own jamboree, head-lining over Jimmy Newman, Jean Shepard, Wanda Jackson, Bobby Lord, Floyd Cramer (who also played piano for Elvis) and his new pal from Sun Records, Johnny Cash. The tour started in Abilene and closed two weeks later in St. Louis. Then, in mid-November, Elvis interrupted his touring to attend the country and western disc jockeys' convention in Nashville.

"They had him on display," says Minnie Pearl. "That was the first time I ever saw Elvis, although I had heard about him before that. Believe me, they had him on display."

They also held him up for considerable praise. "Baby, Let's Play House" ranked sixteenth in the year's country and western song category, the same position Elvis himself occupied in the disc jockey's favorite artists list. He was named the thirteenth most played artist on radio and—now, this is the important one—whereas he had been eighth most promising country artist in 1954, now he was number one.

And it was announced that Elvis was leaving Sun Records for RCA Victor.

A lot of thought had gone into Sam Phillips's decision to sell, much of it prompted by Tom Parker, who apparently had been weaning Elvis away from Sun (and Bob Neal) for some time.

"Colonel Tom had been working on Mr. and Mrs. Presley for about a year, in the most polished and Machiavellian way," says someone who was in a position to watch. "You wouldn't believe it. You just couldn't believe it. Mrs. Presley, God rest her soul, she was just a mother, that's what she was.

And the Colonel'd go to her and say, 'You got the finest boy in the world, Miz Presley, and it's terrible the way they're makin' him work.' He'd go to them and sweet-talk them. Mrs. Presley, she didn't know. Colonel Tom knew they were"— and here the voice drops, sadly—"poor white trash, and he told them her son was working too hard and Elvis was entitled to *some* leisure after all. He had a farm up in Madison, he said, with horses and all, and he gave the Presleys two hundred dollars, told them to send Elvis up there to relax, ride the horses."

Says the observer: "Colonel Tom was a salesman. I'll give him that. He sure knew how to sell."

Marion Keisker's observations mesh with these. "The Colonel had completely won Vernon Presley over to his side," she says. "And, of course, Colonel Parker didn't think he could continue with Sam, that they could do business together. He envisioned bigger things, more money."

Having won Elvis's father, Marion says, Elvis's father changed. "Mr. Presley had become very antagonistic, and whereas a year earlier Elvis had stood there with tears streaming down his face, saying, 'This is what I've always wanted, my very own record with my very own name on it,' all of a sudden, under the suggestion of the Colonel, *we* had become totally dependent upon Elvis . . . *we* had no studio without Elvis . . . and so on and so on. He became quite demanding. Very difficult. And, of course, Elvis wanting to do what his parents wanted, this put him under a strain too."

Still another factor, Marion says, was the trouble involved in recording Elvis. "We knew his potential," she says today, "but each record was sweated out with hours of do it again and hold onto that little thing there. Every session came so hard. He didn't have anything prepared. He wasn't like Johnny [Cash] and the ones who came later, like Jerry Lee [Lewis] and Carl [Perkins], who always had material prepared, who always were ready to record.

"Elvis was out for fun. He never rehearsed. He was nineteen and he had a motorcycle and he liked to ride the streets, looking for excitement. So often I'd see him zipping along Union Street, a new girl on the back of that motorcycle, or walking with two or three girls at once. Later he'd tell me, 'I'm sorry I didn't introduce you, Marion. I didn't know their names.'

"One day we had him and one day we didn't. He'd left us. And *I* had written the original contract."

Obviously, Marion is emotional about Elvis's departure from Sun. But she seems equally realistic. "By this time we'd have had to go out and spend more money and be a big company, or we had to fall back to being a nothing company," she says. "It was a moment of decision. Sam decided, and I think wisely, that he could use the money. He could make other stars just as he made Elvis. And it wasn't six weeks later we came out with 'Blue Suede Shoes.' Of course a lot of disc jockeys then said it wasn't Carl Perkins, but Elvis. They said we were just calling him something else and trying to put something over on Victor.

"I can tell you this, it was Carl Perkins, all right. Victor got every one of our tapes. That's my only regret: Sam gave Victor all the out-takes. There must have been—easy!—fifty or seventy-five cuts, different versions of the same song in many cases, dozens and dozens of tapes. They were songs we wouldn't release—because we didn't think they were good enough or fresh enough, or Scotty broke a string or Elvis flatted or something. We never intended to release them. By George, Victor released them. All of them. I'd have destroyed them. Sam just gave them to Victor. He didn't have to. It was a gesture."

-7-

HYSTERIA

RCA RELEASED THE FIVE SUN RECORDS on its label within a few weeks of the contract signing, so in the winter of 1955 Elvis was in a unique position—that of having two record companies behind him, both selling the same product. And then advertisements began appearing in the music trade publications listing Bob Neal as Elvis's manager—"under the direction of Hank Snow Jamboree Attractions . . . Col. Tom Parker, General Manager." So in a way Elvis now had two managers working for him as well.

Actually it was the Colonel, not Neal, who now was guiding Elvis's career. Neal had been active in the negotiations with Victor, helping to make final arrangements for the contract signing in Nashville, but it was the Colonel who had done all the bargaining. And it was the Colonel who had eased Elvis out of his *Louisiana Hayride* contract, trading the remaining six months for a free concert appearance, held December 17 as a benefit for the Shreveport YMCA. The *Hayride*, helpful in the early days, had too parochial an audience and it committed Elvis every Saturday night, the biggest night of the week for personals as well as a popular network television night; the Colonel wanted Saturdays free.

"The Colonel was setting bookings and he'd send the papers to me for the Presleys' signatures," says Bob Neal.

"So I wasn't really devoting full time to it by any means. It was a partial-type thing. I still did the morning show and ran the record shop. The Colonel did all the basic negotiation. I stayed away from that."

As was Elvis's custom, he returned home to Memphis for the Christmas and New Year's holidays, then on January 5, 1956, he went into the studio that RCA shared with the Methodist Church in Nashville to cut some new material. The facilities at 1525 McGavock Street were owned by the Methodist TV, Radio and Film Commission and were so primitive the stairwell in the rear of the building doubled as an echo chamber and whenever anyone pulled a Coke from the soft drink machine at the foot of the stairs, that sound was included on the recording.

The Elvis session went smoothly and seemed, on the surface at least, to be little different from most country sessions: three hours, in and out, with a minimum of fooling around. But if anyone had taken a picture—and no one did, apparently—it would have been not only a historical one but one which clearly showed the brain trust that was forming around Elvis, an efficient mix of flashy hard-nosed salesmanship and musical and professional expertise that would help make Elvis king.

One of those sitting in the cramped control room was Steve Sholes, the bulky and somewhat rumpled forty-five-year-old father figure and head of Victor's artist and repertoire department in Nashville. He had begun what was to be a forty-year association with RCA when he was in high school in New Jersey. He was one of the first record producers to see the potential in Nashville and more than anyone else had built the label's enviable country and western roster—finding, signing, recording and/or promoting Chet Atkins, Elton Britt, Jim Ed and Maxine Brown, Hank Locklin, Hank Snow, Homer and Jethro, Jim Reeves, Pee Wee King, Roy Rogers, and the Sons of the Pioneers before Elvis had come along.

Even with his enviable track record, Sholes said later that over Elvis he practically had put his job on the line.

"We had never bought up any contracts before, or masters or anything like that," he said a year before he died in 1968.* "The money we paid which seems like peanuts today, was pretty big, and they called me in and wanted me to assure them that they would make their money back in the first year. I gulped a little and said I thought we would. How the heck was I to know? A story was going around Nashville that I was the biggest fool that ever came down the pike, because we would never be able to make the kind of records he made for Sam Phillips over in Memphis. The truth of the matter is we didn't. By the time we got around to making 'Heartbreak Hotel' for Victor, his style had evolved a lot. We were making a new sound that was different even from the very original sound that Elvis had put together."

Also in the control room were Colonel Parker and his assistant, Tom Diskin, and an engineer. And in the small studio were Elvis and the musicians—Scotty and Bill and D. J. and a group of hand-picked studio men, including guitarist Chet Atkins and the Jordanaires, one of the top vocal groups in the gospel and country fields, the quartet serving as regulars on the *Grand Ole Opry* when Elvis appeared on that show a year earlier. The Jordanaires had been formed in 1948 in Missouri with Gordon Stoker, a first tenor, and Hoyt Hawkins, baritone, joining two years later. They then lost their founders and in 1953 Neal Matthews, second tenor, and Hugh Jarrett, bass, made it four again. All had studied music in college and although they had begun singing barbershop songs as well as spirituals, it was for the latter they became regular performers on the *Grand Ole Opry* and then were asked by Elvis to become a part of his recording team. The Jordanaires also were noted for their ability—largely Neal's —to create "head arrangements" (arrangements written dur-

* From an unpublished interview conducted in New York in 1967 by David Dalton.

ing the session itself rather than in advance), which were
part of Elvis's recording style.

The first of three songs completed at that session was
"Heartbreak Hotel," which had been written by Mae Boren
Axton (mother of folk singer Hoyt Axton), who had worked
for Hank Snow as a publicist a year earlier and then was
teaching school in Florida. The building's bizarre echo
chamber came in for heavy use on this song, so much in fact,
at times it almost sounded as if Elvis were hollering from
the bottom of a well, with the rest of the ballad coming in a
deeper, slurring, nearly hiccuping tone. All of which was
punctuated by assertive guitar chords, an occasional tinkle
from a piano and a barely discernible bass. The second and
third songs were "I Want You, I Need You, I Love You,"
Elvis's second Victor release (to be dropped on the market
after "Hotel" had peaked), and "I Was the One," to be released as the back side of "Hotel." On both of these the
Jordanaires contributed a series of "wah-wah's" or "oooooh's"
and "aaaaaaaah's," giving the songs a fuller, softer sound.

Steve Sholes said Elvis's style had evolved in the months
since he'd recorded in Memphis and if these songs were any
criterion, it was true. Much of the biting edge of Scotty's
country guitar and nearly all the pelvic boogie beat had
been neatly removed. All the songs were ballads. A piano
had been added, an instrument Elvis himself played on later
recording dates, but which made this one sound almost cock-
tail-partyish—if you could forget, for a moment, the voice.
Elvis's solo voice had been augmented, giving the two songs
on which the Jordanaires sang a "group" sound. Elvis's rhythmic, fluid tenor—dipping toward baritone—voice and the
amazing vocal gimmickry remained distinctly his own, but
the over-all impression was he had abandoned rockabilly for
pop.

Says Gordon Stoker today: "After the session, Elvis said if
any of the songs went big, he wanted us to record all his stuff
with him. We didn't think they'd go big. We didn't think

much about it at all. We didn't even remember Elvis's name, really. It was just another job for us."

Elvis was back on the road with Scotty and Bill and D. J. and his buddies Red West and Bitsy Mott, still plugging away in the South, when it was announced that Elvis had been booked for a series of six Saturday night appearances (at $1,250 apiece) on the Tommy and Jimmy Dorsey *Stage Show,* a half-hour program produced by Jackie Gleason and carried by CBS-TV preceding Gleason's *Honeymooners* and opposite the first half of *The Perry Como Show.* The Dorseys had been having rating troubles and Gleason's executive producer, Jack Philbin, said at the time that he and Gleason had been on a somewhat desperate search for something to help the show when he was shown a picture of Elvis and decided "this kid is the guitar-playing Marlon Brando." (There were many comparisons of this sort being made in early 1956; besides Brando, the other names most mentioned were the late James Dean and Robert Mitchum.) Gleason himself never has said more than "If I booked only the people I like, I'd have nothing but trumpet players on my show. It was and is our opinion that Elvis would appeal to the majority of the people."

It was rainy and cold on January 28, the date of Elvis's first appearance, and in the otherwise puffy liner notes on Elvis's first album—released three months later—"very few braved the storm. The theater was sparsely filled with shivering servicemen and Saturday nighters, mostly eager for the refuge from the weather. Outside, groups of teenagers rushed past the marquee to a roller-skating rink nearby. Just before show time, a weary promoter returned to the box office with dozens of tickets, unable even to give them away on the streets of Times Square." The theater was in mid-Manhattan's West Fifties, New York's theatrical district, and although Elvis's name was on the marquee, it attracted little attention. He may have been causing riots in the deep South, but in New York only a few in tthe music business had heard of him.*

He was introduced with the same professional enthusiasm given all television guest stars, and in living rooms all over the country the small-screen television sets went dark for a second and when the picture returned, Elvis was standing center stage, gazing into the camera with his dark lidded eyes. He moved his shoulders slightly, adjusting the draped sport jacket he was wearing, relaxed his wide-spread legs, snapping his right knee almost imperceptibly. "Wellllll, since mah beh-bee left me / Ah've found a new place to dwell / It's down at the end of Lonely Street / It's Heartbreak Hotel . . ." As Scotty came in on guitar, Elvis's legs jerked and twisted. He thumped his own guitar on the afterbeat, using it as a prop and almost never playing it now. He bumped his hips. He moved his legs in something that seemed a cross between a fast shuffle and a Charleston step. He sneered, dropped his eyelids and smiled out of the left side of his mouth. He used every physical trick that had come to him in the sixteen months since his first record was released, tricks which were polished by repeated use, but still natural and spontaneous. The television audience had never seen anything like it. After all, the most popular programs of the period were Ed Sulli-van's *Toast of the Town, $64,000 Question, I Love Lucy* and *You Bet Your Life,* none of which did much to affect, or mirror, the American libido. And now Elvis Presley was "do-ing it." On television. Coast to coast.

Mail for that Dorsey show far surpassed anything in the program's experience.

"Heartbreak Hotel" was released the same week and *Bill-board* noted, wisely, that "Presley is riding high right now with network TV appearances and the disk should benefit from all

* One barometer of his popularity was sheet music and songbook sales, and people who were at Hill and Range at the time say Elvis's first song folio was doing very well in Memphis and Texas; everywhere else they couldn't *give* it away.

the special plugging." A week later *Billboard* noted that sales of the record had "snowballed," and in listing some of the top markets for the record, showed that Elvis now was a smash on the West Coast as well as throughout the South. By February the record was in *Billboard*'s Top 100, the major national tabulation of record hits. And the following week it jumped forty places to number twenty-eight—on its way to number one.

Elvis was a national hit, but it appears he was one of the last to know. Says Scotty Moore: "We were working near every day. We'd pull into some town, go to the hotel room and get washed up or go right to the auditorium or movie house, and after we played our shows, we'd get back in the cars and start driving to the next town. We never saw any newspapers. We didn't know we were getting big write-ups. They told us the record was going good, but we'd heard that before and even if it was, we weren't seeing any money from it. And we didn't hear much radio, because it was drive all night, sleep all day, and there wasn't much radio at night. There was a lot of crowd reaction, but we'd been seeing that for a year. How were we to know? All we knew was drive, drive, drive."

Red West says the schedule was so tight at the time, Elvis and the boys usually used somebody else's instruments on the Dorsey shows while he drove with their instruments to the city where the Sunday concert was to be. Then Elvis and Scotty and Bill and D. J. would fly to that city as soon as the Saturday Dorsey show ended.

"The next weekend it'd be the same thing all over again," Red says today. "We'd be in some city somewhere and they'd go off to New York and I'd start driving to where they'd meet me the next day. I remember one show we were in Virginia somewhere and they flew from there to the show and drove all the way to West Palm Beach, Florida. I was by myself. I drove straight through because we didn't have that much time. There was a show the next night. I took No Doz and kept going. I'll never forget it. I was really fightin' it to stay awake. But the TV shows was what did it. That's what sent him on his way."

The worst was yet to come, in March, when following the last Dorsey show, Scotty and Bill and D. J. and Elvis left New York in a snowstorm, drove to Los Angeles to play the Coliseum and then drove to San Diego to appear with Milton Berle on an aircraft carrier, and from there drove straight to Denver for another concert. So demanding was the pace Elvis finally collapsed and was taken to a Jacksonville, Florida hospital. Although he had a fever and doctors said he should rest for at least a week, Elvis got dressed and walked out of the hospital the following morning, to resume the current tour.

During this same period Elvis went back into the studio usually in New York, where RCA had its most modern facilities. It was there he recorded most of the material that went into his first album. There were twelve songs on the album, several of them already familiar in the rock and rhythm and blues markets. He sang Carl Perkins's song "Blue Suede Shoes" (released as a single in Canada and England, where it became a hit nearly equal to "Heartbreak Hotel" in the U. S.); "I Got a Woman," a song Ray Charles recorded in 1955; "Tutti Frutti," which had been a hit for its author Little Richard Penniman, as well as for Pat Boone; "Money Honey," the first song recorded by the Drifters, featuring Clyde McPhatter (in 1954); and "I'm Counting on You," a song written by Don Robertson, who soon would record a national hit of his own ("Happy Whistler") and later would crank out dozens of songs for Elvis's movies. There was also an old standard, "Blue Moon," by Richard Rodgers and Lorenz Hart, one of four songs on the album from those RCA had inherited from Sun. The other three—all considered inappropriate for release by Sam Phillips because Elvis or Scotty or Bill had flatted or blown a note—were "Just Because," "I'll Never Let You Go" and "I Love You Because." However weak Phillips may have thought the Sun leftovers were, they did still have the recognizable rockabilly beat that made Elvis, and Sun, so famous and, in fact, still were stronger than some of the newer songs. Thus it seemed Elvis had at least partially returned to the sound that had established him. But it never was mentioned publicly that anything on the album wasn't new.

The cover of the album showed Elvis (in a black and white photograph) playing his guitar, his thin, boyish face twisted in the pain of screaming a gutty blues. Running down the side of the album was Elvis's first name in large pink letters, across the bottom his last name in large green letters. It was released in mid-March and went immediately into the eleven spot on *Billboard*'s best-selling album chart.

"When we first started recording," Steve Sholes said of this period, "the way he held the guitar was pretty close to where his mouth was, and we were trying to record him vocally at the same time because we didn't do tracking in those days. The guitar was so loud you couldn't hear his voice. We moved the mike around and so forth, and we finally ended up using a ukulele pick, a felt pick. He played the guitar so hard that every two or three takes he would break a string. And even after we got the ukulele pick, he was still breaking strings. I remember one take we were doing, he dropped the ukulele pick in the middle of a take, but he kept on banging the thing with his fingers. Jesus, when we got done with the take, his fingers were bleeding, so I said to him, 'Why didn't you quit?' 'Oh,' he said, 'it was going so good, I didn't want to break it up.'

"In the early days we would make a lot of takes and we would get to the point where I thought we had a pretty good one. And I'd say, 'I think we got it pretty good there, Elvis.' And he would say, 'I think I can do a little better.' He never criticized anybody else. If anyone made a mistake on a number, he would never point it out to them. He'd just say, 'Let's try it again, I think I was a little flat on that one,' until the musician picked up on it himself. A lot of artists are the reverse. You have to keep driving them—'Make one more take, I think you can get this a little better.' Some of them are so gosh-darned big-headed that you can't even say that to them, you have to say, 'The third trumpet player was flat,' or something like that. It's a lie, just to get him to sing a little more, because if you told him he was flat, he'd get hysterical and walk out. When you get an artist of Elvis's caliber, one who analyzes himself as closely as Elvis does, and is willing to keep working as hard as Elvis, you know that all these things added together are what made him successful."

Of course there was that voice. "Bill Haley and the people who preceded Elvis had a very primitive sound, comparatively," Sholes said. "Elvis has a fine musical ear and a great voice, a much better voice than people really think he has. He has a feel for popular music much greater than other people at that time had. That's why he was able to groove it in a direction that the kids liked, because that was the way *he* liked it."

At the same time that Elvis's first album was released, RCA spat out a couple of what were called "extended play" records, which were the size of 45-rpm records but had two or more songs per side. These EPs also went to the top of the best-seller charts.

There was another development in March, when half-page advertisements began appearing in the trade press. The ads included two photographs proving Elvis was alive and well and putting on weight, and five lines of headline type:

> The New Singing Rage!!! ELVIS PRESLEY
> Exclusive RCA Victor Recording Star
> Currently on Record-Breaking Tour
> Direction: William Morris Agency, Inc.
> Personal Management: Col. Tom Parker.

Bob Neal's contract had expired and the Colonel had taken control, signing Elvis, who now was twenty-one, to what is generally thought to have been a five-year contract. In return for guiding the Presley career it is believed that the Colonel was to get 25 per cent of Elvis's total earnings—before taxes and other deductions, as was usual.

Many think the figure was, and is, as high as 50 per cent, some even say 51, and although this is one of those guarded secrets, one close friend of the Colonel's reacts to the 51 figure by saying, "It's nowhere near that." Still, 25 is a hefty slice, somewhat grander than most personal managers get. Most settle for 15 per cent—although Brian Epstein held a quarter interest in the Beatles.

Bob Neal was not left like a beached whale in this transfer of "property." He still had his morning radio show, the record store, the occasional concerts in the area; and a short time later he became president of Stars, Inc., a management company he formed with Sam Phillips to handle all of Sun's still-impressive roster of artists: Carl Perkins, Johnny Cash, Warren Smith (then being described as a possible successor to the Presley crown), Eddie Bond, Jack Earls, Roy Orbison and his band, the Teen-Kings.

"My contract with Elvis was to expire and I simply let it go," Bob says today. "The only further thing: I received some small amount of commissions and royalties from the initial period. There wasn't anything involved in a continuing commission or share. I hadn't asked for anything and hadn't tried to negotiate anything. I could have. But I didn't try to."

In April Elvis went to Hollywood for a screen test at Paramount Studios, flying there at the invitation of Hal Wallis, a producer of films that ranged all over the creative map from *Casablanca* to the Martin and Lewis quickies. He had called the Colonel about the screen test after seeing Elvis on one of the Dorsey shows and getting reports from the Paramount-controlled movie theaters where Elvis had been appearing recently.

"Tom wanted to pursue a career in motion pictures for

Elvis," says Oscar Davis, "so he played the Florida State theaters and the various theater chains on the East Coast, with Elvis singing between movie showings—starting at two and working until about eleven at night. I exploited the dates and we packed the theaters everywhere. Hollywood became aware of Elvis this way. These were all Paramount-controlled theaters, so Paramount became interested. Hal Wallis entered the picture and made the deal with Tom."

Elvis played a scene with veteran character actor Frank Faylen in the test. He was wearing jeans and a work shirt and was told to run through a few emotions, which he did—gesturing wildly and fervently, shouting at Faylen at one moment, poking a cigar in his mouth the next moment as he tapped the older actor on the chest to emphasize a point he'd just made. Faylen, knowing he shouldn't attempt to upstage Elvis—for the singer was an amateur, no matter how assured he seemed—did little more than react.

Wallis reviewed the test and offered the Colonel a three-film contract, the first to be made in the fall, possibly in early winter, depending upon how rapidly a script, director and supporting cast could be arranged. For his services, Elvis was to be paid $100,000 and for subsequent films this figure was to be increased, to $150,000 for the second and $200,000 for the third.

While in California for the screen test, Elvis made another network appearance, on the *Milton Berle Show*.

"You know how he moves around all the time," says Neal Matthews, one of the Jordanaires. "He's hard to contain, hard to keep in one position. And Milton and the producer and director kept telling Elvis to stay on the chalk line. And Milton said, 'You or me, one, is gonna be outa the camera and it's not gonna be me.'"

The show was aired April 3, with an estimated 40 million in the audience, a figure that represented one out of every four people in the U. S.

His records continued to dominate the charts, making it

seem as if someone had taken a rubber stamp to all the music trades: no matter where you looked, it said ELVIS PRESLEY. The first album passed the 100,000 mark and went to the number three position the second week—behind Belafonte's first album and the sound track from *The Man with the Golden Arm*. By month's end both the album and "Heartbreak Hotel" were on top. "A Howling Hillbilly Success" was the way the headline read in *Life*, Elvis's first national magazine spread, "Young Elvis Presley's Complaint Becomes Nation's Top Pop Tune."

In Amarillo, Texas, where Elvis had been interviewed by *Life*, fans kicked through a plate glass door to offer him bits of underwear to autograph. In San Diego it was necessary to call out the Shore Patrol to bolster local police security.

"From then on it became a battle," says D. J. Fontana. "Hard to get into the auditorium, hard to get out. The Colonel had it set up security-wise. Nobody got in anywhere. Lotta times we'd go in two or three hours ahead of time to set up and they wouldn't let us in. So we'd set there and wait until somebody came out that knew us. Same way getting out. Soon as he'd get through his act, they'd have a police car or something there and he was gone. We'd pack up and two or three hours later they'd let us out. We'd stick our heads out of the door and the kids would say, 'Is he in there?' We'd say, 'No, he's gone.' They'd say, 'You're lying.' They just didn't believe us. We had a heck of a time getting out of those buildings."

By now the touring conformed to a pattern shaped by the Colonel years earlier. Oscar Davis described the pattern: "First we had the country music acts. And then we had a different format, more in the pop field. But we never had any names. Frankie Conners, an Irish tenor . . . Phil Maraquin, a comic from Detroit . . . various acts out of Chicago. It was a hodgepodge show, but it made Elvis look good. When he came out, it was dynamite.

"We had trouble," Oscar says. "It was hard for the early

acts, because the audience'd yell for Presley. This caused a lot of confusion. So I got out in the beginning and I explained that we had policemen and firemen there and in the event anyone left their chairs, we would stop the show immediately, so if you want to see Elvis, stay in your chairs. And I said all acts on the first part of the bill, you're gonna see these, and they're all friends of Elvis and Elvis asked that you treat them as kindly as you would treat him. And any outburst, we stop the show and you don't see Elvis.

"Sometimes it worked, sometimes it didn't, and when it didn't, that's when the newspapers wrote it up big, made it seem a riot. Of course sometimes it *was* a riot, but not as often as most people think."

On April 23 Elvis went into Las Vegas for two weeks at the Frontier Hotel. It was, in retrospect, a mistake; the bunch that kept Las Vegas alive was not Elvis's crowd. The middle-aged marrieds from middle America celebrating twentieth wedding anniversaries, the Eisenhower Republicans, the rich vacationers and gamblers and tourists—these weren't the ones who swooned when they heard the first words of "Heartbreak Hotel" or kicked through a door to offer Elvis a well-filled teenaged brassiere and a ball-point pen for an autograph. Only curiosity kept the Venus Room open where Elvis was appearing—with the Freddie Martin Orchestra and comedian Shecky Greene. Thanks to the publicity or to their own kids, these people knew about Elvis, but that didn't mean they liked him. Elvis never played to an empty house, and there were *some* matrons who went for Elvis in a manner that rivaled the pubescent attacks from their daughters: jaws slack, saliva flowing freely, hearts pounding. But most entered the huge showroom hating Elvis, and no matter how hard he tried, he couldn't get them off their hands. Curious, they'd come to see what he was all about and they'd paid the sums asked by the hotel, but that didn't mean they'd scream, applaud or faint. From what Bill

Black said afterward, according to friends today, it was so quiet at the Frontier when they performed, for the first time they heard the musical clinkers. Prior to that time the noise of the audience had drowned out any mistakes.

When Elvis opened, it was his name that appeared at the top of the marquee outside the hotel. A few days later Shecky Greene's name was on top and Elvis had been put on the bottom, beneath the name of the orchestra leader.

The Colonel and the people at the Frontier had a meeting and agreed the best thing to do was to tear up the $8500-a-week contract and forget about the whole thing. The Vegas booking seemed like a good idea a week earlier, but now it was a bomb.

"Heartbreak Hotel" was in the number one spot—where it stayed for eight weeks—when Elvis's second RCA single was released in early May. This was one of the songs he'd recorded in that first Victor session in January, "I Want You, I Need You, I Love You," backed with "My Baby Left Me," an up-tempo blues written by Arthur Crudup, the black blues singer who'd written "That's All Right [Mama]."

That same week both *Time* and *Newsweek* greeted Elvis with columns of hesitant praise. *Time* called him the "teeners' hero," said his voice was rich and round, his diction poor, his movements sexy. Tenaged girls went wild when they saw him, the magazine said, and as a result Elvis was pocketing $7500 in profits each week. *Newsweek* put Elvis on its "Music" page, a subdivision of "The Arts" (he shared the page with a review of a Broaway play, *Most Happy Fella*), and offered a number of "typical female comments," all making some reference to Elvis either being a dope peddler or a jailbird, or looking like a snake. Both magazines had him owning three Cadillacs and a three-wheeled Messerschmitt.

With all these vehicles, Elvis also had bought a new home in Memphis, a $40,000 one-story green-and-white-trimmed ranch house at 1034 Audubon Drive in one of the city's better neighborhoods, not far from Audubon Park. The house sat in the center of a wide plot, with a thick stand of trees in the rear giving privacy to the swimming pool Elvis had built. There were three bedrooms, a game room, a sitting room, dining room and living room, furnished in what generally is called "borax"—large cheap pieces of elusive period and taste. On the walls were scattered some of Elvis's early publicity photographs and souvenirs he bought on his tour trips.

The Audubon neighborhood hasn't changed much over the years. Today there are the same wide curving streets and spacious lawns broken by groups of trees. Most of the homes, like Elvis's (he lived there about a year), are one-story structures; but never in the neighborhood—before or since—has so much attention been paid to one of them. In 1956 the home was a target for Memphis teenagers, so much so, in fact, that Elvis had a brick wall built to separate the house from the street and then added tall metal spikes—none of which did any good. The girls only trespassed more aggressively, pulling up blades of grass from the lawn, pressing their noses against the windows, even scraping dust from the Cadillacs into small envelopes.

Says Buzzie Forbess, Elvis's friend from his project and high school days: "I remember so many teenagers were coming by, the neighbors began to complain, and then when Mrs. Presley began hanging the wash out on the line . . . whooooeee, boy, they really howled. They said it wasn't that kind of neighborhood. People just don't hang their wash out on Audubon Drive. Well, Elvis just told them what for. Said it was his house and his parents could do anything they wanted. And the way it came out in the papers, it was the only house on the block that was paid for. Elvis had paid cash and his neighbors was still making payments, or renting."

Mr. and Mrs. Presley seemed little changed by this. They kept their old friends in the Lauderdale Courts; the only difference was when they got together, the Presleys would sometimes drive to the project in one Cadillac, bring friends to the house for a visit, then return them in a second car.

Elvis, meanwhile, still was visiting *his* old friends, stopping by at Sun—once joining Carl Perkins, Johnny Cash and Jerry Lee Lewis (all of whom were on the label then) in an impromptu gospel sing around the studio piano—or revisiting his teachers at Humes High. On one of these visits he performed at the annual talent show, the same show he had sung at during his senior year.

For recreation he'd visit the amusement park at the fairgrounds. Because of his popularity, it was impossible for him to attend during the park's normal hours, so he'd rent the park after it closed, inviting friends to accompany him. When Elvis had a date, this is where he usually took her. His touring had ended an eighteen-month-long relationship with Dixie Locke, his high school sweetheart, and Elvis didn't date any one girl regularly.

Elvis behaved at the time like most males of his own age and marital status: He was free, white and twenty-one, there were a lot of girls around, and he got while the gettin' was good, changing girl friends and dates the way some people change socks.

Most of these girls he met on the road. Says Ralph Gleason, critic for the San Francisco *Chronicle,* of Elvis's visit to Oakland in 1956: "Before he made the run to the car, an occasional chick would get past the cops and bust all the way through to the dressing room door. He was sweet to them as earlier he had baited them as they hung over the railing or, when he was onstage, they ran up to the line of cops. He'd slap his crotch and give a couple of bumps and grinds and half grin at the insane reaction it produced each time.

"It was the first show I'd seen that had the true element of sexual hysteria in it."

Elvis was bouncing all over the country now. His appearances early in the year had been in the South, even during the months when "Heartbreak Hotel" was becoming a national hit, but now instead of moving from city to city he was jumping from state to state. In mid-May he was headlined over Hank Snow and the Jordanaires at the Cotton Pickin' Jamboree in Memphis, part of the annual Cotton Carnival, a show promoted by Bob Neal and one which required both sides of the city's Ellis Auditorium be opened to accommodate the crowd. The first week of June he was back in California, making his second appearance on the *Milton Berle Show*. Then he was in Colorado and then he was signed to appear on Steve Allen's new Sunday night show being broadcast live from New York.

It was after he'd appeared on the Berle show again on June 6 that Elvis collected some more of the criticism that now seemed as much a part of the act as the wiggle and the voice. It was Jack Gould, television critic for the New York *Times*, who delivered the longest and most virulent blast.

Mr. Presley made another television appearance last night on the Milton Berle show over Channel 4. Indeed, the entire program revolved around the boy. Attired in the familiar oversize jacket and open shirt which are almost the uniform of the contemporary youth who fancies himself as terribly sharp, he might possibly be classified as an entertainer. Or, perhaps quite as easily, as an assignment for a sociologist.

Mr. Presley has no discernible singing ability. His specialty is rhythm songs which he renders in an undistinguished whine; his phrasing, if it can be called that, consists of the stereotyped variations that go with a beginner's aria in a bathtub. For the ear he is an unutterable bore, not nearly so talented as Frankie Sinatra back in the latter's rather hysterical days at the Paramount Theater. Nor does he convey the emotional fury of a Johnnie Ray.

From watching Mr. Presley it is wholly evident that his skill lies in another direction. He is a rock-and-roll variation of one of the most standard acts in show business: the virtuoso of the hootchy-kootchy. His one specialty is an accented movement of the body that heretofore has been primarily identified with the repertoire of the blonde bombshells of the burlesque runway. The gyration never had anything to do with the world of popular music and still doesn't.

Certainly Mr. Presley cannot be blamed for accepting the adulation and economic rewards that are his. But that's hardly any reason why he should be billed as a vocalist. The reason for his success is not that complicated.

The man second to Gould in television criticism was Jack O'Brien of the New York *Journal-American,* and it seemed as if he had written his review while looking over Gould's shoulder: "Elvis Presley wiggled and wriggled with such abdominal gyrations that burlesque bombshell Georgia Sothern really deserves equal time to reply in gyrating kind. He can't sing a lick, makes up for vocal shortcomings with the weirdest and plainly planned, suggestive animation short of an aborigine's mating dance."

Nor was this the end of it. During the next few months Elvis appeared on television again and again, and each time the reviews were more anatomical than musical.

It was the first of July when Elvis was in New York for the second show of Steve Allen's new series, initiated by NBC-TV in a futile attempt to bump off the CBS opposition, Ed Sullivan. Steve had opened his series a week earlier with Kim Novak, Vincent Price, Wally Cox, Dane Clark, Sammy Davis and the Will Masten Trio among the notables, and in this show Elvis was to share the music and laughs with Imogene Coca and Andy Griffith. Steve admits today he was going for names—at the network's insistence—to assure some impressive ratings. It worked. Steve got more than 55 per cent of the audience, while Sullivan was left stumbling around with a miserable 15 per cent.

What Steve did to earn this astonishing figure was to put Elvis in a comedy sketch that had been inspired by his background, a silly satire of deep South country and western shows, such as Elvis had played for years. It opened with "your old partner, Big Steve," a six-gun strapped around his

waist, making a speech to all his friends and neighbors, with
Elvis and Imogene Coca and Andy Griffith standing behind
him in western clothing. The set itself looked much like the
Louisiana Hayride set. For most of the sketch Elvis, designated as a part of the "gang," did little more than contribute
a few "yahoos." Finally he was introduced as Tumbleweed.

"Tumbleweed is a trick rider," said Steve. "Yes, sir, you
ain't seen trick ridin' till you've seen Tumbleweed. Yesterday
he went across the range at a full gallop, blindfolded . . . he
picked up a rattlesnake with his teeth, jumped four fences,
and dropped that snake in a gopher hole—all at a full gallop.
Tell 'em why it was so tough, Tumbleweed."

Elvis stepped forward and said, deadpan, "I don't use no
horse!"

It went on like that for a while, Steve delivering set-up
lines, his guests coming in with the punch lines, and the skit
closed with Big Steve introducing a cowboy song, with each
of the guests taking a verse. When it came Elvis's turn, he
blinked his eyes, plunked his guitar and sang:

> "I got a horse, I got a gun.
> I'm goin' out and have some fun,
> But I'm a-warnin' you galoots,
> Don't step on my blue suede boots."

A little later in the show Elvis sang "Hound Dog," a
rhythm and blues hit from 1952 that he had picked for his
next single release. The way Steve tells it today, "We'd recognized the controversy that was building around Elvis and so
we took advantage of it, putting him in a tuxedo—white tie
and tails—and taking away his guitar. We thought putting
Elvis in formal wardrobe to sing the song was humorous. We
also asked him to stand perfectly still, and we positioned a
real hound dog on a stool next to him—a dog that had been
trained to do nothing but sit and look droopy. I must say
Elvis took it quite naturally, and good-naturedly."

The fans did not take it so well. They began picketing the

Steve Allen theater the following morning, carrying signs that said "We want the real Presley."

Said John Lardner in *Newsweek:* "Allen was nervous, like a man trying to embalm a firecracker. Presley was distraught, like Huckleberry Finn when the widow put him in a store suit and told him not to gape or scratch."

The same week Ed Sullivan began negotiating with the Colonel for Elvis. He previously had said he wouldn't touch Elvis with a long stick, but when he saw Steve's ratings, there was a certain amount of hemming and hawing and before it was over, he'd promised Elvis $50,000 for three performances, the first in September, the others at eight-week intervals. Per show, this more than tripled the previous high Sullivan had ever paid—$5000—and more than doubled Steve Allen's fee of $7500.

Says Steve: "We could have engaged in bidding against Ed, but it wouldn't have proved anything. It would have given our show a higher rating, but it would have been Elvis's rating, not ours."

Elvis's first appearance on Sullivan's *Toast of the Town* was on September 9, when he helped Ed corner 82.6 per cent of the audience, equal to about 54 million people, a record that stood until 1964, when Sullivan coaxed the Beatles onto his show. Elvis's portion of the show—two songs—was broadcast from the CBS studios in Hollywood as an insert, and Elvis was shown on the home screen from the waist *up*. The only way anybody at home could tell his hips were moving was to listen to the screams from the girls in the studio audience.

That must have made Jack Gould of the *Times* happy, right? Wrong.

The following day Gould wrote, "Elvis Presley made his appearance on the Ed Sullivan Show over Channel 2 and the National Broadcasting Company didn't even bother to compete. It gave Steve Allen the night off and ran an English film. From his extensive repertoire of assaults on the Ameri-

can ear, Mr. Presley included 'Hound Dog.' The maidens in
the West Coast studio audience squealed appreciatively over
their idol's mobility. On the East Coast, Charles Laughton,
substituting for Mr. Sullivan, patiently waited until it was all
over." That was the complete review.

And if that weren't enough, Gould then wrote a much
longer article, which appeared in the *Times* the following
Sunday. He first recalled Elvis's "strip tease behavior" on
Milton Berle's show, applauded a "much more sedate" appearance on the Allen program, but then said that when
Elvis "injected movements of the tongue and indulged in
wordless singing that was singularly distasteful" on the Sullivan show, enough was enough.

Quite possibly Presley just happened to move in where society
has failed the teen-ager. Certainly, modern youngsters have been
subjected to a great deal of censure and perhaps too little understanding. Greater in their numbers than ever before, they may
have found in Presley a rallying point, a nationally prominent figure who seems to be on their side.

Family counselors have wisely noted that ours is still a culture
in a stage of frantic and tense transition. With even sixteen-year-
olds capable of commanding $20 or $30 a week in their spare
time, with access to automobiles at an early age, with communica-
tions media of all kinds exposing them to new thoughts very early
in life, theirs indeed is a high degree of independence. Inevitably
it has been accomplished by a lessening of parental control.

Small wonder, therefore, that the teenager is susceptible to
overstimulation from the outside. It is at an age when the aware-
ness of sex is both thoroughly natural and normal, when latent
rebellion is to be expected. But what is new and a little discour-
aging is the willingness and indeed eagerness of reputable businessmen to exploit these critical factors beyond all reasonable
grounds.

When Presley executes his bumps and grinds, it must be remembered by the Columbia Broadcasting System that even the twelve-
year-old's curiosity may be overstimulated.

In the long run, perhaps Presley will do everyone a favor by pointing up the need for early sex education so that neither his successors nor TV can capitalize on the idea that his type of routine is somehow highly tempting yet forbidden fruit.

A perennial weakness in the executive echelons of the networks is their opportunistic rationalization of television's function. The industry lives fundamentally by the code of giving the public what it wants. This is not the place to argue the artistic foolishness of such a standard; in the case of situation comedies and other escapist diversions it is relatively unimportant.

But when this code is applied to teenagers just becoming conscious of life's processes, not only is it manifestly without validity but also it is perilous. Catering to the interests of the younger generation is one of television's main jobs; because those interests do not always coincide with parental tastes should not deter the broadcaster. But selfish exploitation and commercialized overstimulation of youth's physical impulses is certainly a gross national disservice.

What Gould was saying, once all the verbiage had been thinned, was he thought Ed Sullivan and CBS were going too damned far in putting Elvis on television at eight o'clock, when impressionable youngsters might have their libidos stroked unnecessarily. More simply, the television industry was presenting something definitely obscene and thereby forgetting it was, after all, a public trust.

Earlier the "Threat" had been Frank Sinatra and bubble gum and Communists writing film scripts in Hollywood and flying saucers and television itself and, going back, the horseless carriage and the flying machine and jazz and the Charleston and Roosevelt and the WPA and rumble seats. Later it would be beatniks and peaceniks and the Beatles and the twist and hippies and all of San Francisco and marijuana. Always there was something or someone, real or fictional, responsible for the imminent destruction of Society As We Know It. In 1956 it was Elvis and rock 'n' roll.

All across America the edicts were posted. In San Antonio, Texas, rock 'n' roll was banished from city swimming pool jukeboxes because, according to the city council, the music "attracted undesirable elements given to practicing their spastic gyrations in abbreviated bathing suits." In Asbury Park, New Jersey, newspapers reported that twenty-five "vibrating teenagers" had been hospitalized following a record hop, prompting Mayor Roland Hines to prohibit all future rock concerts in the city's dance halls. Which in turn spurred officials in nearby Jersey City to cancel a rock show at the 24,000-seat Roosevelt Stadium. In San Jose, California, it was said teenagers routed seventy-three policemen, injured eleven and caused $3000 in damage to the auditorium—which caused neighboring Santa Cruz to ban all concerts from its civic buildings. In Boston, following a riot by students at the Massachusetts Institute of Technology, a specially appointed committee organized to study the music branded disc jockeys "social pariahs" and banned them from participating in record dances and other public entertainment. In two other Massachusetts towns, Somerville and Medford, there were stabbings, and a local district attorney, Garret Byrne, said, "Tin Pan Alley has unleashed a new monster, a sort of nightmare of rhythm. Some of our disc jockeys have put emotional TNT on their turntables. Rock 'n' roll gives young hoodlums an excuse to get together. It inflames teenagers and is obscenely suggestive." The New York *Daily News* said the rioting stretched from "puritanical Boston to julep-loving Georgia" and accused record makers and disc jockeys of "pandering to the worst juvenile taste." The paper then recommended a "crackdown on riotous rock 'n' roll"—describing the music as a "barrage of primitive jungle-beat rhythm set to lyrics which few adults would care to hear"—and advocated banning all teenagers from dancing in public without the written consent of their parents, along with a midnight curfew for everyone under twenty-one.*

---

* As all this righteous indignation was being hurled around in the newspaper's editorial department, the boys in promotion were, oddly enough, sponsoring a rock 'n' roll contest.

Concentrating their attack on Elvis specifically, in Syracuse, New York, a group of women circulated petitions demanding that Elvis be barred from television and sent them to the three networks. In Romeo, Michigan, a sixteen-year-old high school student was expelled for refusing to have a local barber cut his sideburns and Elvis ducktail, while in Knoxville, Tennessee, three crew-cropped football players set up their own barbership and trimmed all the Elvis hair styles in sight, whether or not the owners liked it. Elvis was hung in effigy in Nashville and burned in absentia in St. Louis. In Ottawa, Canada, eight students of the Notre Dame Convent were expelled for disobeying a school edict to stay away from one of Elvis's local concerts. At Yale University two students formed the national I Like Ludwig [Beethoven] Fan Club and started handing out "I Like Ludwig" buttons to counter all the "I Like Elvis" buttons; three of the Ludwig buttons eventually found their way onto the lapels of violinist Isaac Stern, Philadelphia's conductor Eugene Ormandy and cellist Pablo Casals.

Nor was radio totally behind Elvis. In Halifax, Nova Scotia, station CJCH said his records weren't up to station standards and forbade their broadcast. In Nashville a disc jockey who called himself the Great Scott burned six hundred Presley records in a public park. In Wildwood, New Jersey, another disc jockey said he could not morally justify playing Elvis's records and offered to begin an organization to help "eliminate certain wreck and ruin artists." And in Uvalde, Texas, radio station KVOU auctioned its collection of Presley records, and the top bidder was an anti-Elvis group.

Although men from every professional walk of life joined the massive assault, it was the religious fraternity that seemed the most incensed. Said the Reverend William Shannon in the *Catholic Sun:* "Presley and his voodoo of frustration and defiance have become symbols in our country, and we are sorry to come upon Ed Sullivan in the role of promoter. Your Catholic viewers, Mr. Sullivan, are angry; and you cannot compensate for a moral injury, not even by sticking 'the Little Gaelic Singers of County Derry' on the same bill with Elvis Presley." Evangelist Billy Graham said he'd never met Elvis and didn't know much about him, but "From what I've heard, I'm not so sure I'd want my children to see him." Cardinal Spellman, in a sermon in New York during a "Pageant of Prayer" marking the close of the Tenth National Confraternity of Christian Doctrine, quoted at length from one of Jack Gould's articles. Downtown in Greenwich Village— where you'd think there'd be some liberalism—the Reverend Charles Howard Graff of St. John's Episcopal Church called Elvis a "whirling dervish of sex."

Of course, it shouldn't have surprised anyone that this sort of reaction to popular music occurred. Thirty years earlier public reaction to jazz was, as in 1956 with rock 'n' roll, more "violent" than the music itself. At that time, in the 1920s, the *Ladies' Home Journal* said jazz was Bolshevik-inspired and constituted a replacement for sex and marriage that would reduce the birth rate. Articles of the period were titled "The Jazz Path of Degradation," "It Is Worse Than Saloon and Scarlet Vice," "Unspeakable Jazz Must Go" and "Does Jazz Put the Sin in Syncopation?" Said the *Journal* in one of its more acerbic onslaughts: "Jazz originally was the accompaniment of the voodoo dancer, stimulating the half-crazed barbarian to the vilest deeds. The weird chants, accompanied by the syncopated rhythm of the voodoo invokers, have also been employed by other barbaric people to stimulate brutality and sensuality. That it has a demoralizing effect on the human brain has been demonstrated by many scientists."

In 1956 much the same sort of public hysteria prevailed.

Elvis was granting occasional interviews in those days, and invariably this criticism would crop up during the questioning. One of those interviews was released as a 45-rpm record, in cooperation with *TV Guide*. First he was asked what he thought about the nickname he'd been given, "Elvis the Pelvis."

"I don't like to be called 'Elvis the Pelvis,' but, uh . . . I mean, it's one of the most childish expressions I ever heard comin' from an adult. 'Elvis the Pelvis.' But, uh, if they want-a call me that, I mean there's nothing I can do about it, so I just have to accept it. You have to accept the good with the bad, the bad with the good."

Elvis next was asked about the predominantly adult criticism he'd been getting.

"As a rule, most of the adults are real nice," Elvis said. "They're understanding. They . . . they . . . uh, I've had 'em to come round to me by the hundreds and say, 'I don't personally like your kind-a music, but, uh, uh, my children like it and so on, and, and if they like it, well I ain't got any kick about it, 'cause when I was young I liked the Charleston. I liked the fox trot. I liked this and that.' They, uh, they're adults with a little intelligence. I mean, you know, they don't run people into the ground for havin' a nice time."

Elvis's voice came rolling out like syrup on an autumn day: thick and smooth and sweet, with a soft bite. He sounded like a hillbilly James Stewart, with a slur that ran into a twang. He was asked, "When you hear rock 'n' roll, it just gets you on fire?"

"Oh, I, uh . . . not when I just hear it on the radio. When I do it on a stage, you have to put on a show for the people. In other words, people can buy your records and hear you sing, 'cause they don't have to come out to hear you sing, you have to put on a show to draw a crowd. If I just stood out there and sang and never moved, people would say, 'Well, my goodness, I can stay home and listen to his records. But you have to give 'em a show, somethin' to talk about."

And finally: "How did that rockin' motion get started?"

"The very first appearance after I started to record, I was on a show in Memphis where I started doin' that," he said, referring to the concert in the Overton Park Shell. "I was on the show as an extra added single . . . a big jamboree in an outdoor theater . . . uh . . . outdoor auditorium. And, uh, and

I came out on stage and, uh, uh, I was scared stiff. My first
big appearance, in front of an audience. And I came out and
I was doin' a fast-type tune, uh, one of my first records, and
ever'body was hollerin' and I didn't know what they was
hollerin' at. Ever'body was screamin' and ever'thing, and, uh,
I came off stage and my manager told me they was hollerin'
because I was wigglin'. Well, I went back out for an encore
and I, I, I kind-a did a little more. And the more I did, the
wilder they went."

Elvis certainly wasn't naïve. He had many things going for
him in 1956—timing, good looks, a rich and versatile singing
talent, a crafty manager—but he also was quick enough to
know when he'd (however naturally) stumbled onto a good
thing, a show business gimmick that might win him an enthusiastic following. He was too modest when he told a
writer, "I'm not kiddin' myself. My voice alone is just an
ordinary voice. What people come to see is how I use it. If
I stand still while I'm singin', I'm dead, man. I might as well
go back to drivin' a truck." But there was some truth in what
he said, just as there was truth in the advertising slogan "It's
the sizzle that sells the steak."

Still, Elvis was not a pushy or cocky young man. He was
many things, but he was not overly aggresive; he was not
the raving egotist many with sudden wealth and fame become. He owned a fleet of Cadillacs and a small parking lot
full of other assorted vehicles, he had a wardrobe that included thirty sport coats and forty sport shirts, and his fingers
and wrists were hung with enough diamonds and star sapphires to ransom an Arabian oil prince; but this wasn't ostentation, not in the usual sense. It was just his way of conforming
to the customs of that peculiar cultural group from which he
recently had graduated, the country and western singer. Back
home in Tennessee, soon as any of those good ol' boys got a
few dollars together, they bought Cadillacs and fancy duds
and flashy jewelry; that didn't mean they gave up grits. And
in Elvis's case, the *first* thing he bought was a house for his
parents.

"When you come right down to it," says Bob Neal, "I think it was a matter of his wanting to accomplish a great deal of this for his mother, to make her comfortable and happy."

"That's right," says Mrs. Gladys Tipler, Elvis's old boss at Crown Electric. "Before he ever knew he was going to make a nickel, one day he set here in our office and he said to Tip, 'If I ever get my hands on any money, Mr. Tipler, I'm gonna buy my mother a home.' He stated that, he sure did. And that was the first thing he did when he did get some money. That's no come-on stuff."

When you put it together, it made perfect newspaper copy —and Elvis had been cast in the perfect mold. He was six feet tall and quick to punch a boy out if he got out-a line. His hair was worn long and slicked back and his sideburns came all the way down to the bottom of his ears. He rolled the sleeves on his short-sleeved sport shirts three times to show the biceps, wore his collar pulled up in back, and slipped a half-inch leather belt into two-inch loops and shoved the buckle over one hip. He liked to drive flashy cars, race motor-cycles, shoot pool and lay girls. (Says Johnny Cash: "He had a project to see how many girls he could make. He did okay.") He was what "good girls" called a hood. But he was Southern, dripping manners and charm. He loved—no, worshiped—his mother; he wouldn't do anything that would embarrass her. He addressed everyone as Mr. or Mrs.; his sentences were punctuated with "sir" and "ma'am." It was as if a scrap of teenage doggerel of the period had come to life: Slam, bam. Thank you, ma'am.

Within a week of Elvis's first Sullivan show, RCA released seven of his records simultaneously, all of them 45s. No one had done anything like this before. (One could imagine the Colonel shouting in a carnival bally: "Seven—count 'em, folks! —seven amazing singles at once!") It was considered foolish, even suicidal; the public would be confused, and no one record could ever rise above the massive choice facing the radio programmer and record buyer. Sure, RCA had reissued all five of Elvis's Sun records less than a year earlier, but that had been regarded as a move executed to take advantage of Sun's final sales push and to fill the time between Elvis's signing and the recording and release of new material.

Said *Billboard:* "Fourteen tunes, formerly available on Presleys' LPs or EPs, now available on seven singles, within reach of any kid with eighty-nine cents." And that's where it was at. Saturation marketing. So what if none of the seven rushed to the top of the charts, every one of them sold at least 100,000 copies—which, multiplied by six or seven cents per record (Elvis's cut, including performance fees and publishing or writing royalties), adds up to an impressive figure.

Besides that, one of the two songs Elvis sang on the Sullivan show was "Love Me Tender." In introducing this song, he said it was the title tune from his first picture—then two months from release—and he hoped everybody liked it. This and this alone created such a demand—orders for 856,327 copies a week *before* shipping—that RCA had to put it out earlier than originally planned. This gave Elvis *eight* new singles.

The bizarre thing about all this was that "Hound Dog" was, in early September, in the number one spot for the sixth week in a row, and it was abundantly clear that the next week it would be succeeded by "Don't Be Cruel," the song on the other side of the same record. And chances were good that "Cruel" would stay on top for several more weeks. So who needed "Love Me Tender?"

What happened, of course, was Elvis had three number one hits in a row. Two million kids bought "Hound Dog" and then *another* two million went in and bought "Don't Be Cruel." (Even if it was the same record.) And after that more than a million went back and bought "Love Me Tender." From August, when the run started, until December nobody but Elvis was going to be at the head of the charts. No one. In the autumn of 1956, as teenagers returned to school, the saturation gamble paid off.

During the past few years Bones Howe has been producing number one records with the regularity and apparent ease most men display in knotting neckties and shoelaces. Since 1965 he has produced more hits than most producers have in a lifetime—"It Ain't Me, Babe" and "You Baby" for the Turtles, "Windy" for the Association, "Stoned Soul Picnic" and "Aquarius / Let the Sunshine In" for the Fifth Dimension, Diana Ross's solo records, to name a few. In the late summer of 1956 he was a $72-a-week recording apprentice and serving, he says today, as bottom-rung engineer for Elvis's first recording sessions in Hollywood.

"They would come to town and take an entire floor at the Roosevelt Hotel on Hollywood Boulevard, or the Plaza near Hollywood and Vine, and later the Knickerbocker on Ivar, just north of the boulevard," he says. "They had to take a whole floor because they couldn't guard his room otherwise. Girls would be crawling up the fire escapes. And Elvis would encourage them. Finally I think they threw him out of one of the hotels. Anyway, they'd come to Hollywood, traveling in one of those Cadillacs with an extra section in the middle —you know the kind, four doors on each side—driving here from Memphis—Scotty and Bill and D. J. and Elvis and a few of the other guys, his bodyguards. And in the morning, from the time they got up, they'd drive up and down Hollywood Boulevard. They'd pull up to a stop light and just before the light changed, if there were girls standing on the corner, Elvis would roll the window down, take his sunglasses off and say hello. And then the light would change and they'd take off, leaving hundreds of people wandering around in the intersection screaming and jumping up and down and chasing the Cadillac down the street. Elvis just loved it."

Bones says afternoons were spent in the large funky room that was Studio B in Radio Recorders at 7000 Santa Monica Boulevard, a few blocks from Hollywood High School. At the time it was one of the most popular recording facilities in Los Angeles. Henry Mancini had cut his *Peter Gunn* album in that room. Norman Granz took Ella Fitzgerald and Stan Getz and Gerry Mulligan there. Columbia Records used the studio to record most of its artists. But when Elvis came to town, says Bones, no one else got near the place. For Elvis, it was booked not by the hour but by the week.

"Everything had to be left alone," says Bones today. "They'd come in the first day and they didn't move the drums or anything for two weeks sometimes. Fifteen hours a day, seven days a week. It was all up to Elvis how long the sessions ran. They'd run all night if he felt like it. He was the barometer. If he felt good, we'd get things done. If he didn't feel good, or couldn't get into it in an hour or so, that's all."

Those in the control room with Bones included most of the regulars—the Colonel, Steve Sholes, some of Elvis's pals— along with Thorne Nogar, whose studio it was, usually somebody from RCA and either Jean or Julian Aberbach or their right hand in running Hill and Range Songs and the manager of Elvis's music publishing company, Freddie Bienstock. Bienstock, a cousin of the Aberbachs, had joined the Elvis team during his second recording session for RCA in New York the preceding spring, and by summer his role was clearly defined. It was Freddie Bienstock who would for the next twelve years collect all the material from which Elvis would select songs for his records; Bienstock was then the equivalent of Elvis's A&R (artist and repertoire) man.*

"We had a number of writers under contract," Freddie says today, his Swiss childhood still coloring his speech. "We would suggest they write some material for Elvis. People like Otis Blackwell, Doc Pomus, Mort Shuman, Joy Byars in Nashville, Sid Tepper and Roy Bennett. And more would

* Ordinarily this responsibility should have gone to Steve Sholes, who was head of A&R for Victor, but by now Sholes was becoming less and less involved. His presence at recording sessions continued, of course, and he still was Victor's "representative," but he seldom had much, or anything, to say about how the session was conducted. In time he would even talk to Elvis not directly but through the Jordanaires.

arrive unsolicited, naturally, hundreds of songs each week. I was like a clearing house for Elvis, so that after a while even RCA was sending me songs."

Bones says that all of this material was brought to the sessions by Bienstock or one of the Aberbachs on "dubs" or demonstration records, which are precisely what they are purported to be: records made to demonstrate a song's values, or lack of them. Almost all of them had been semiprofessionally produced (at worst) and many could have been released commercially as is, if anyone wished. The instrumentation was seldom changed, and usually Elvis would sing the song the way the singer on the demo sang it—largely because *that* singer was doing it the way he thought Elvis would.

Says Bones: "They'd come in with these stacks of dubs, stacks that were twenty inches high sometimes. Elvis hadn't heard them before arriving at the studio. He'd come in with his entourage. Usually they'd all be dressed alike: dark pants and a loud sport shirt. Sometimes all the guys would be wearing 'I Like Elvis' buttons. It was a carnival. Then when it finally settled down, my job was to play disc jockey . . . to play these dubs out into the studio, where there were big speakers, and Elvis and the guys would be. I'd put a record on and Elvis would listen and at some point or other he'd signal take it off and I'd stick it on the 'out' pile. If he liked it, he'd tap the top of his head, meaning play it again from the top. He'd listen to it two or three times, and if it was something he really thought he wanted to record, we'd play it over and over again until everybody knew the song. And then Elvis would sing it as the group played behind him.

"He might make thirteen or fourteen takes and he'd go back and listen to the early ones. He'd say, 'I think we had one back there that was better . . .' And we'd go back and listen. And when he listened, he'd dance, work out, with the tape playing real loud . . . the same way he usually performed when he was singing. With Elvis every take was a performance. The same way as on stage."

According to Steve Sholes, when Elvis danced in the studio it created a problem. "In the session I'd say, 'Elvis, can't you stand still?' And he'd say, 'No, I can't. I'm sorry. I start playing and the movements are involuntary.' The reason I wanted him to stand still was because he kept getting off-mike."

In time Elvis stopped playing the guitar and merely thumped it on the side or back on the afterbeat. This often was added as an "overdub," in another session, which made it easier for Sholes and the others to record his voice.

"Fantastic thing about Elvis was that after one playing of the record he would have the thing in mind, the melody perfect, the chords all down. This isn't too amazing for a country singer," Sholes says, "but the thing that killed me was that he generally had most of the lyrics too, sometimes all of them. The second time through he'd have all the lyrics. Sometimes we'd be making a take and I'd say, 'Gee, Elvis, I think you made a mistake in the lyrics there.' And he'd say, 'I don't think I did, Mr. Sholes.' And I'd look at the damn sheet and I'd find he was right. He has something close to photographic memory."

Says Bones Howe: "So what it really boiled down to was Elvis produced his own records. He came to the session, picked the songs, and if something in the arrangement was changed, he was the one to change it. Everything was worked out spontaneously. Nothing was really rehearsed. Many of the important decisions normally made previous to a recording session were made *during* the session.

"What it was," says Bones, "was a look at the future. Today everybody makes records this way. Back then Elvis was the only one. He was the forerunner of everything that's record production *these* days. Consciously or unconsciously, everyone imitated him. People started doing what Elvis did."

In many ways people started doing what Elvis did. Popular culture hasn't been the same since.

For years things would be in disarray in Nashville, thanks to Elvis. The regulars on the *Grand Ole Opry* didn't just dislike Elvis's music, they disliked him. It was bad enough he'd bastardized country music, they said, but then he went and made the goddam stuff popular, which meant their own records weren't selling as well as they had. Before Elvis a hit for Hank Snow sold maybe half a million copies, but now Hank, and most others, couldn't get half that. This caused a split in the country ranks. In rejecting rock 'n' roll, some went even more "country" than they had in the past. Others jumped aboard the rockabilly bandwagon rolling through town, so many that by 1957 the record charts were nearly dominated by former good ol' country boys—Jerry Lee Lewis, Johnny Cash, Sonny James, Marty Robbins, George Hamilton IV, Conway Twitty and the Everly Brothers among them. In the meantime about a hundred country radio stations changed formats and went rock. And so did a lot of the fans. Never before had there been so much pickin' and grinnin' on the best-seller charts, and at the same time never before had the source of this sound taken such a beating.

Things also changed regarding black music. Early in his career Elvis had displayed an open respect for black music and black musicians. He wasn't the first to record songs written or originally recorded by Negroes, but most of *that* action in the middle fifties came when somebody like Bill Haley "covered" Big Joe Turner's "Shake, Rattle and Roll" or Georgia Gibbs took "Jim Dandy" from LaVern Baker. Those singers were taking established rhythm and blues hits and cleaning them up for the white pop market. Elvis may have wanted to cover some rhythm and blues songs he heard while at Sun, but he never did. And when he included songs by Little Richard and Ray Charles and others on his RCA albums, it was long after the originals had been hits. Elvis wasn't snagging songs from the black for gain, but because he honestly dug the music. And so others began to show respect.

Sort of parallel to this was the increased respect the black market began to manifest for the white artist. Elvis wasn't the first Caucasian to appear on the rigidly segregated rhythm and blues chart, but he was the first to appear there consistently and his presence made it simpler for others to follow. Country music and the blues never had been so far apart, really, and all Elvis was doing was bringing them together in a way that might be palatable to both sides. Said Paul Ackerman, *Billboard*'s music editor and one of rock's earliest chroniclers: "Often the difference between a country side and an r&b side is merely the use of strings as against the use of horns. The Presley sound—it is pointed out—might be called r&b without horns, but with strings."

Additionally, thanks to Elvis, there was an obvious, healthy, good-natured sexuality added to the popular music stage. It is too easy to say that what he did was in a direct line from burlesque; certainly it appealed to young people for reasons other than that one. Until rock 'n' roll (and Elvis) came along, "popular music" was 100 per cent White Bread America—starch with no nutriments but lots of added preservatives. There had been a total embargo on sex in pop music. Teenagers were worrying about saltpeter in their school cafeteria lunch and whether or not the rubber was going to come off at the crucial moment. Could Rosemary Clooney and Eddie Fisher mean anything to them? So along came rock 'n' roll, dealing with sex point-blank. And along came Elvis, putting action to the words he sang.

There were also many other ways in which Elvis changed the shape of popular tastes. Guitar sales climbed astronomically. There had been guitars in popular music for many years, but there really hadn't been any guitarists—none who had stepped forward to become "personalities." (Bill Haley didn't count, because he was old—twenty-nine!) When Elvis came along thumping his guitar, it changed; now it was "cool" to play the guitar, now it was manly, something a stud did. And, of course, the sale of records increased. As *Billboard* noted, "The attendant publicity concerning Presley, bad as it may be in some cases, has cued national tongue-wagging beyond all imagination, and fortunately for record dealers, produced brisk sales. When there are a number of big hits to which the public has taken a fancy, all records sell better."

Elvis also changed the style of stardom, making it—among other things—more commercial than it previously had been, while establishing once and for all the enormous weight and power of what is now called the "youth market."*

The man responsible for all this, of course, was the poor ol' Colonel of carnival fame. He wasn't quiet all these months while Elvis was becoming the biggest single attraction in the history of popular music. He was, in fact, standing in the wings at every turn—the hard-nosed, fast-talking, at once flamboyant and deceptively homespun, totally honest and extremely likable man who (as they say) made the whole thing possible. It is idle to discuss whether or not Elvis would have been as big without the Colonel's help, but there is no doubting that the poor ol' Colonel must get much of the credit for making him a superstar so fast. Just as Gladys Presley had held her son close to her ample bosom, so did the Colonel—guiding him, advising him and protecting him.

"Elvis trusted the Colonel explicitly," says Oscar Davis. "He was a young man and he flared up a little bit, but Tom was a strong man and he'd lay the law down and that's the

---

* And we haven't even talked about what was to happen in the late fifties and early to middle sixties, when all of Elvis's musical fans were old enough or experienced enough to begin recording themselves. People like Ricky Nelson, who at sixteen was driving over Laurel Canyon in Los Angeles taking his date home when a Presley record came on the radio, and the girl said she thought Elvis was the smoothest ever, and Ricky said, "Well, he's not so much, I'm making a record too." And although he'd never thought about it before then, Ricky had to do it to save face. Other people, like John Lennon, who told Hunter Davies in *The Beatles*, "Nothing really affected me until Elvis"; and Alvin Lee, who named his group Ten Years After because they started that many years after Elvis did; and Tony Joe White and Tom Jones and several hundred more.

way Elvis went. He trusted Tom to do what was right for him."

First he saw that Elvis was comfortable, that he had everything he wanted—cars, clothes, jewelry, a new home each year.

Then he had some of Elvis's pals put on the payroll—people like Red West and Lamar Fike and Bitsy Mott and his cousin Gene Smith, who'd been tagging along as company anyway. Now they were being paid to continue to keep Elvis company and to serve as personal security guards.

He continued to shove Elvis's concert price up. Says Oscar Davis, still doing the Colonel's advance promotion during this period: "It jumped to $25,000 a night. That's not phenomenal in these days to pay for Tom Jones, Barbra Streisand, people like that. But before Elvis probably the top money paid to artists was to Martin and Lewis, who were getting $10,000 a night against a sixty [per cent of the box office]. Al Jolson was *asking* $12,500. But $25,000 was unheard of. And Tom Parker turned it down from New York City and Chicago.

"What did he need it for?" Oscar says. "As Elvis got larger, we discontinued the use of radio and used only newspapers to promote the concerts. When we played Chicago, Fort Wayne and St. Louis, Toronto, Ottawa and Philadelphia, we used nothing but newspapers . . . and the disc jockeys. We'd take the leading teenage disc jockey in every market and let him M.C. the show. He'd love it, he'd talk about it all the time. We'd also arrange a dinner date for a girl, which they'd select, running a contest and things like that. It became very easy to sell him.

"There was never a time when Tom sold Elvis or any of his acts when the promoter made more money than the act did," Oscar says today, leaning forward as if to reveal a secret. "Oftentimes you buy an act and it'll be a sleeper, and you'll do $10,000 and the act only costs you $200. I had that experience with Roy Acuff. I used to pay him $500 a day and do $10,000, $15,000 a day. But the Colonel always adjusted the costs so the promoter didn't get away with anything. It's uncanny. He'd figure the capacity of the auditorium and the popularity of his artist in that particular area, and he priced him right, so the artist made more money than the promoter. The promoter wouldn't lose any money, mind you, but he wouldn't make very much either."

And he promoted Elvis as no singer had been promoted before. Sometimes this was as simple a thing as tipping the radio and press whenever Elvis made a move, so that they would notify the teenagers Elvis was going to make that move and then would go out and report on how many teenagers were there. Steve Sholes's secretary, Juanita Jones, says today, "Whenever Elvis came to town, we had to promise complete security, not to tell anyone. Then Colonel Parker would tip the press and the kids would tear the place apart. Elvis'd live in a railroad car or in a trailer bus or have a room at the Anchor Motel and it was supposed to be a big secret, but later we'd find out the Colonel had told everybody." Falling back on his carnival habits, he rented elephants and advertised Elvis with posters hanging from their flanks. He wore shirts that had Elvis's name stitched across the back and front. And in a stroke of bizarre genius, he hired all the midgets in Hollywood—most of them Munchkins left over from *The Wizard of Oz*—to parade through town as the Elvis Presley *Midget* Fan Club.

It was in August that the Colonel announced what would be one of his more extravagant—and profitable—schemes. That was when he said he had engaged Howard Bell and Hank Saperstein of Special Projects, Inc., in Beverly Hills to handle all his product merchandising. Saperstein, through his own company, H. G. Saperstein and Associates, previously had licensed and promoted merchandising for several television shows, *Super Circus, Ding Dong School, Lassie, The Lone Ranger, Jim Bowie* and *Wyatt Earp* among them. While Howard Bell brought with him experience in merchandising Peter Pan, Mickey Mouse and Davy Crockett, all for Walt Disney.

In 1851 the Swedish Nightingale, Jenny Lind, was the vocalist who caused merchants' and manufacturers' palms to itch. There were Jenny Lind bonnets, gloves, coats, hats, parasols, combs, shawls and jewelry. Butchers sold Jenny Lind sausages, and hardware stores carried a line of Jenny Lind teakettles. The phrase "à la Jenny Lind" was affixed to a restaurant's special of the day, and Jenny Lind pancakes became well known. For a while there was even a Jenny Lind billiard table being advertised. It is not surprising to learn that her first U.S. tour was produced by P. T. Barnum, a Tom Parker think-alike.

One hundred and five years later the marketing theory remained the same. Only the products had changed. And, of course, the market was larger now, but before it was all over, there were no less than seventy-eight different Elvis Presley products being sold—and sales were reported in the millions of dollars each month.

So pervasive was the marketing, if one of Elvis's fans bought one of everything, she could, upon arising in the morning, pull on some Elvis Presley bobbysocks, Elvis Presley shoes, an Elvis Presley skirt and Elvis Presley blouse, an Elvis Presley sweater, hang an Elvis Presley charm bracelet from one wrist, put an Elvis Presley handkerchief in her Elvis Presley purse and head for school where she might swap some Elvis Presley bubble gum cards before class, where she would take notes with an Elvis Presley pencil. After school she might change into Elvis Presley Bermuda shorts, Elvis Presley blue jeans (which were not blue but black, trimmed in white and carried Elvis's face on a pocket tag) or Elvis Presley toreador pants and either write an Elvis Presley pen pal (whose address she got from an Elvis Presley magazine) or play an Elvis Presley game, while drinking an Elvis Presley soft drink. And before going to bed in her Elvis Presley knit pajamas she might write in her Elvis Presley diary, using an Elvis Presley ball-point pen, listen to "Hound Dog" a final ten times, then switch out the light to watch the Elvis Presley picture that glowed in the dark.

That wasn't all. There were Elvis Presley photographs (glossy eight-by-tens and wallet size), belts, bolo ties, gloves, mittens, novelty hats, T-shirts, neckerchiefs, necklaces, statues and plaster-of-paris busts, bookends, guitars, lipstick (in Hound Dog Orange, Heartbreak Hotel Pink and Tutti Frutti Red), colognes, stuffed hound dogs, dancing dolls, greeting cards, pins, sneakers, buttons, photograph albums, phonographs, Ivy League pants, Ivy League girls' shirts, pillows, combs, hairbrushes and twenty-nine other things. It boggled the mind.

Not only was there a wide selection, it was practically impossible to avoid the stuff. Among the places where this Elvis Presley stuff was sold: Sears, Roebuck, Montgomery Ward, W. T. Grant, Woolworth's, Kresge, AMC Stores, Macy's, Allied Department Stores, H. L. Green, Rexall and Whelan drugstores. Or you could buy any of it by mail.

For every item in the Presley line, Elvis and the Colonel collected a royalty of 4 to 11 per cent of the manufacturer's wholesale price. This probably didn't come to more than two to five cents for each dollar item, but when that was multiplied by several million, it was like having another number one record. By the end of 1957, Saperstein said, he thought the gross would be about $55 million.

Saperstein also agreed to take over administration of the Elvis Presley National Fan Club, which had been operating at a loss for several months. There were 250,000 members in the U. S., another 150,000 elsewhere, and until now the 3–4000 letters that arrived daily were being answered from Madison, Tennessee, where the Colonel kept his office. Anyone who wrote got a free membership card and was offered three different Elvis Presley souvenir packages, costing a quarter, fifty cents or a dollar. The cheapest

package included two small photographs and a button, the
next size a couple of larger pictures and a button, the
largest package even larger photographs and a button, plus
a songbook and a picture book.

Mrs. Presley was beginning to feel the pressure. Says
her close friend Mrs. Faye Harris: "They'd take little
pieces of brick and pull up the grass and swarm all over
the house, peeking in windows. She was so glad when we
come for a visit. She said, 'Thank God you're here to answer the doorbell.' We had to stay under lock all the time
we was there. We couldn't walk in the yard and if we went
for a ride, they followed us.

"Gladys tol' me one day, she was settin' there, the checks
was comin' in, 'I wish Elvis would quit right now and
marry a girl and have a child. That'd make me so happy.
He's got enough comin' in from his hits and his cosmetics
and things, he could retire right now. He could put himself in a furniture store and really mop up. If he did that,
I'd be so happy, I don't know whether Memphis could
hold me or not.'"

Apparently Mrs. Presley never told her son how she
felt.

Elvis was back in Tupelo. It was a model homecoming,
so clichéd as to defy credibility. Already Elvis represented
the all-American prototype, the Horatio Alger hero of the
South: the son of a dirt-poor sharecropper who sang in his
mama's church and went on to massive wealth and fame.
Providing the irony that is so much a part of so many
clichés was the fact that Elvis would be appearing at the
Mississippi-Alabama Fair and Dairy Show, where he'd
sung his first public song, "Old Shep," a decade earlier as a
ten-year-old. And now he was getting $5000, or 60 per cent
of the gate, whichever was more. (A special low price for Tupelo.)

The fact that only a few individuals honestly remembered the thin flat-nosed towhead with the lidded eyes from the wrong side of the G.M.&O. and Frisco tracks did not in any way deter anyone in Tupelo from turning out or in some way contributing to the day's events. September 26 was declared Elvis Presley Day and a banner was hung across Main Street. The merchants decorated their shopwindows in what the local boosters called an "Elvis Presley Theme," with most of the displays taking their direction from the titles of Elvis's records. A parade was planned. And just before the afternoon show Mayor Jim Ballard, who began his political career as a restaurateur and ran for city clerk the year the Presley family moved to Memphis, gave Elvis a three-foot-long guitar-shaped key to the city. "This town's proud to call you its son," he said. And Mississippi Governor James P. Coleman had come up from Jackson to tell him, "This state and the nation admire you."

J. M. (Ikey) Savery, head of the oldest insurance agency in Mississippi and president of the fair the past twenty years, says he'd never seen anything like what Tupelo was that day. "It was unbelievable," he says today. "Buses came from Atlanta, Birmingham, Jackson. There were girls who'd been here two or three days, from Philadelphia and Boston and New York. I guess there were fifteen or twenty thousand. We had to put out chairs and bleachers in front of the grandstand. We had the local police, county sheriffs and the highway patrol there in the afternoon, and the girls went right over them. That night we had the National Guard, and the girls went over *them*."

On his way back out of town, Elvis autographed the $10,000 check he got for his performance and gave it back to Tupelo.

Elvis had begun work on his first film, *Love Me Tender*, on August 22. He was away from Hollywood for the Tupelo

concerts in September but returned to stay at the Knickerbocker Hotel through mid-October. Originally the film
was titled *The Reno Brothers* and there were no songs, but
when it became apparent even to the most cynical Hollywood producer that Elvis represented enormous box office
potential, four tunes were hurriedly shoved between the
pages of an already shaky script and the title of the film
was changed to *Love Me Tender*—so the film would get a
free plug whenever the record was played. None of this
endeared Elvis to anyone in Hollywood—Hedda Hopper
led the attack—but almost everyone ended up loving him.
In part this was because Elvis went out of his way to make
friends. For instance, the first day of shooting he let it slip
to the director that he knew not only his own part in the
film but everyone's. Elvis had memorized the entire script!

Elvis had two brothers in the film, the oldest played by
Richard Egan, and the way the story went, everybody but
Elvis went off to fight the damn Yankees in the Civil War,
leaving Elvis back home on the farm to look after Mother
(Mildred Dunnock). Word comes that Egan is dead, and
Elvis and Debra Paget get married. Debra had been Egan's
fiancée before he was "killed," although Elvis doesn't
know that. Then Egan returns and it gets complicated for
a while, but Elvis solves the problem by dying dramatically. The film ends with Elvis's face superimposed against
the sky singing the title song again. It was a terrific film
debut.

The producer of *Love Me Tender* was David Weisbart,
who had been producer of James Dean's most popular
film, *Rebel Without a Cause*, in 1955. Because Dean was
the only other true teen idol to emerge in the 1950s, numerous comparisons were made. On Elvis's first day on the
set, in fact, part of the talk between Elvis and his producer
was devoted to whether he might not be right for the leading role when Hollywood got around to producing *The
James Dean Story*, a film concept much discussed in 1956,

the year following Dean's death. Elvis said he thought he could handle the assignment, said he'd be flattered to get it.* Then Weisbart was asked by Joe Hyams of the New York *Herald Tribune* to compare the two.

"So far as teenagers are concerned, Elvis is what I call a safety valve," Weisbart said. "By that I mean they scream, holler, articulate, and let go of their emotions when they see him perform. But when they watched Jimmy perform they bottled their emotions and were sort of sullen and brooding. Elvis is completely outgoing, whereas Jimmy was the direct opposite. Basically, Jimmy was a loner, whereas Elvis is gregarious.

"Both boys were immature, but it was not as easy to spot in Jimmy, who was introverted. Part of Elvis's great charm lies in his immaturity . . . I never got an uneasy feeling about Elvis, because on the surface he seemed to be open and impulsive, but Jimmy was never open, never did anything impulsively.

"Elvis was by far the most healthy. Jimmy was apparently the typical confused teenager, but Elvis is something every kid would like to be—a phenomenal success without having to work hard for it. He's up there enjoying himself and getting millions of dollars. According to a child's logic, what could be better?"

There was another connection with James Dean during this period. This was Elvis's friendship with Nick Adams, who had been one of Dean's close pals. Nick and Elvis met when Nick was trying to get himself cast as one of Elvis's brothers in *Love Me Tender*. Nick had asked Elvis to help him and Elvis did (although Nick was rejected ultimately because he was too young for the part) and they became friendly.

"Nick and Elvis complemented each other just right," says a mutual friend. "On the surface Nick was aggresssive

* *The James Dean Story* never was dramatized but was released instead as a documentary.

as hell. He'd scratch and push his way anywhere. And Elvis was shy, retiring. And deep down Nick was shy and Elvis had the strength. It sounds like they were opposites, but they weren't, not really. They had a lot in common—their age, a mutual desire to be fine actors, football, girls, all the other things young men share. And where they weren't alike, they were the two sides of the coin, making the whole. Elvis was very close to Nick. Elvis got closer to him than anybody else in Hollywood."

Elvis was enjoying Hollywood. He had his guys around for jokes and any errands he wanted taken care of. The studio gave him a secretary. And the writers and photographers stood in line. One of these was a little girl named Patricia Vernon, who wrote for the New York *Herald Tribune:* "A press agent came by to tell me I had had enough time with Elvis. I started to leave and Elvis, who was still sprawled on the couch, darted out his hand and caught my foot. 'Maybe she's shy; maybe she'd like to be alone with me,' he said. The press agent shrugged and left. I asked Elvis to take his hand off my foot. 'Okay,' he said, looking up under heavy lids. 'Ah'm just spoofing you.' I asked Elvis how he felt about girls who threw themselves at him. Again the heavy-lidded look. 'Ah usually take them,' he said, watching my face for the shock value of his words. He grinned. 'Hell,' he said, 'you know, Ah'm kind of having fun with you because you're so smart.'" And when she asked Elvis if he thought he was a sex symbol to kids, as some psychiatrists were saying, he said something that would be quoted for years: "They all think I'm a sex maniac. They're just frustrated old types, anyway. I'm just natural." It was apparent in nearly every way that Elvis was having fun.

By the time Elvis was making *Love Me Tender*, the Army had become a part of his life. On October 24 his draft board in Memphis said yes, it was true that he had been sent a questionnaire to "bring his status up to date." Lots of boys don't report address changes, marital status and other such facts, a draft board spokesman said, so occasionally what is called a Selective Service Dependency Questionnaire is sent to all registrants. But there was nothing to worry about, the board's chairman, Milton Bowers, told newsmen. Elvis was 1-A but there were several hundred 1-As ahead of him.

It was then, in October, that *Billboard* published a front-page story of Elvis's draft call in such detail it was generally regarded as true. It said that he was going into the Special Services, or entertainment branch, of the Army, that he would be reporting for duty at Fort Dix, New Jersey, and that he would be allowed to continue his television and recording dates and probably would be granted an early six-week furlough to make another film. The story was totally inaccurate, but before it could be denied, a former *Billboard* staff writer, Steve Schickel, then with radio station WGN in Chicago, recorded a song that was inspired by this premature call: "Leave My Sideburns Be."

Songs like this were one of the stranger phenomena associated with Elvis's hysterical success. In 1956 and 1957 there were dozens about Elvis or inspired by him. Humorist Stan Freberg had the first and most successful, his satiric version of "Heartbreak Hotel." The others were more flattering. Janis Martin, a South African vocalist, recorded "My Boy, Elvis," a song whose lyric contained the titles of Elvis's first six or seven singles. "Dear Elvis" was sung by somebody identified only as Audry and took the form of a gushy fan letter using lines from current hit records. "To me, Elvis, you are the dreamiest," said Audry. "Ohhhhh, you've got the magic touch," sang the Platters from their hit "Magic Touch." Billy Boyle contributed a plaintive wail whose message was in its title, "My Baby's Crazy 'Bout Elvis." Peter de Bree and his Dutch backup band, the Wanderers, shouted a biographical thank-you called "Hey, Mr. Presley." Lou Monte provided "Elvis Presley for President," which sounded like a cross between a high school football cheer and a chewing gum commercial. Jerry Reed sang about "The Tupelo Mississippi Flash," a song about Beauregard Rippy, who came from Tupelo, Mississippi, wrote songs and sang like a bird, played licks on his gi-tar like you ain't never heard. A Jerry Lee Lewis type piano accompanied Ivan Gregory's "Elvis Presley Blues," a song that said Elvis had affected not only his girl friend but him as well. And for Christmas, Mary Kaye told a moving tale of a little girl who promised to brush her teeth and pick up her clothing without reminder if she found Elvis under the tree ("I Don't Want a Bracelet or Diamonds, I Just Want Elvis Instead"); and Little Lambie Penn and Marlene Paula sang slightly different versions of "I Wanna Spend Xmas with Elvis."

Most of the songs offered the same rockabilly beat established by Elvis, but only a few were popular enough to appear on any of the best-seller lists.

Elvis's second album came out in October, carrying his first name as its title and a collection of twelve songs rather like those included in the first LP. Again Elvis paid his respects to his roots, recording "So Glad You're Mine," another Arthur (Big Boy) Crudup song; "How's the World Treating You," a country ballad by Chet Atkins and Boudleaux Bryant; and the song he'd sung at the Mississippi-Alabama Fair when he was ten years old, Red Foley's song about a boy and his dog, "Old Shep." Others included three of Little ·Richard's biggest hit songs—"Ready Teddy," "Rip It Up" and "Long Tall Sally"—"Love Me" by Jerry Leiber and Mike Stoller, who'd written "Hound Dog"; and "Paralyzed" by Otis Blackwell, who'd written "Don't Be Cruel."

Within a couple of weeks the album was number one, meaning Elvis Presley again was the only name at the top of every important chart—also making it laughable when in the same month *Colliers* magazine, among others, intimated Elvis might be slipping and that another singer was gaining on him. This was Pat Boone, who had been a winner on Arthur Godfrey's *Talent Scouts* in 1954, shortly before Elvis was turned away by the same program. Like Elvis, Pat was a religious man; they'd both have sacred records on the best-seller lists within a few months. The differences were rather more noticeable. Pat was married and the father of three, while Elvis was a polite but enthusiastic womanizer who was quoted as saying about marriage, "Why buy a cow when you can get milk under the fence?" Pat had juggled his personal appearances to permit a straight A average at Columbia University (he would get his degree the following June), and Elvis considered himself lucky to squeak through Humes High. Their choice of material was different too, as Elvis generally picked guttier songs than those Pat recorded, remaining more respectful of the material's origins. Both Elvis and Pat recorded rhythm and blues hits, but Pat's "covers" did little more than homogenize or neutralize the power of the original. Elvis himself once said he thought Pat was a fine ballad singer, and that's where Pat was at. Elvis was versatile—he could sing rock or country or pop or blues, up tempo or down—and so his audience was bigger than Pat's.

On October 18 there was an incident in a Memphis gas station. Witnesses said Elvis—just returned from Hollywood—had pulled into the station in his $10,000 white Continental Mark II and asked the station manager, Edd Hopper, to check the gas tank for leaks. Elvis was recognized by passers-by, and a crowd formed. Traffic was blocked and Hopper asked Elvis to move on. Elvis said he would but apparently delayed long enough to sign a few more autographs, at which point, witnesses told police, Hopper slapped Elvis on the back of the head and said, "I said move on!" And so Elvis got out of his car and slammed Hopper with a right cross that cut a half-inch gash at the corner of his left eye. A nearby cop and a bystander moved in and broke it up just as one of the station attendants entered the fight and Elvis took a punch at *him*.

In court a few days later Hopper appeared with one eye swollen almost shut, the left side of his face puffed, bandages covering the cut. He said he had asked Elvis to leave three times and pushed him only when Elvis made a move to get out of the car and go for him. Then Elvis was called to the stand to give his side of the story, which was confirmed by the police officer present. He said Hopper had swung at Elvis before Elvis'd done anything and then had pulled a knife on him.

Acting City Judge Sam Friedman listened patiently— fans in the courtroom had disrupted testimony with groans and cheers—and after suggesting that Elvis take into consideration the fact that he had a large following and should cooperate fully with businessmen in order to avoid "disruptions," he fined Hopper twenty-five dollars and lectured him about "taking the law into your own hands." Next day the service station's owner fired Hopper. Elvis intervened, telling newsmen later, "I asked him not to fire him. The man has a family. It was one of those things that happens in life. We regret it, but it's too late." The station owner wasn't listening. Business had fallen off drastically and he was afraid if he hired Hopper back the kids would boycott him for sure.

A month later, on November 23, nineteen-year-old Louis John Balint took a swing at Elvis in the Shalimar Room of the Commodore Perry Hotel in Toledo, Ohio. Balint was an unemployed sheet metal worker and he said, when questioned by police, that he was recently separated from his wife and he resented her carrying a picture of Elvis in her wallet instead of a picture of him.

Balint was hauled into court, and after pleading guilty to a charge of disturbing the peace he was fined ten dollars, plus nine dollars and sixty cents in court costs. He couldn't come up with it and went to jail, where he said the whole thing was staged—he had been paid two hundred dollars to start the fight. It was a lie, of course. In 1956 Elvis was doing what he could to avoid fights, not paying for their initiation.

Other fights were breaking out among songwriters and publishers over songs Elvis had recorded. The first battle had been over who wrote "Heartbreak Hotel." The next was over who wrote, and who published, "Hound Dog." And then there was a fight over "Don't Be Cruel." It was as if someone had declared open season on Elvis's hits.

It's obvious why so many were willing to take expensive legal shots at Elvis and his empire and those who surrounded him. Writers' and publishers' royalty percentages are small, usually a penny apiece per 45-rpm record sold. When you're talking about an Elvis Presley record, though, this penny could represent a small fortune.

And a twenty-year-old telephone operator in Memphis named Robbie Moore threatened to sue Elvis when a picture appeared in a fan magazine showing Elvis's head on her shoulder. She said Elvis had come into a cafe and after clowning with her for a while ate part of her hamburger, drank some of her milk and then the picture was taken. It embarrassed her, she said. Elvis paid her $5500 to keep it from going to court.

When you're a star, you become a target in many ways.

Back in Memphis during this time, Elvis and a Hollywood starlet named Natalie Wood were having what the newspapers called a "motorcycle romance." Everything Elvis did was watched closely by newsmen hungry for the latest gossipy tidbit, and so when Elvis bought a new motorcycle on October 31, the United Press knew about it, and when the "Big E" from Tennessee (the "Chief" was another nickname he picked up in 1956) took Natalie for a three-hour ride on that motorcycle that night, the United Press knew about that too. And the United Press knew about it when Elvis's buddy Nick Adams went along on a second bike the next day. One newspaper, the Nashville *Tennessean,* headlined the U.P. story, "Natalie's Jeans Grip Tight As Cycle Romance Deepens." Sometimes the adults —in this case newsmen—were as silly as the teenagers. Sometimes sillier. And for Elvis it merely became tougher to find freedom and privacy.

Says Neal Matthews, one of the Jordanaires: "The only time he could get out, really, was at night, if he had the night off. He'd rent a skating rink or a movie house and rent it for the whole night and he and whoever'd be around would go to the skating rink and skate all night until they'd just drop over. Or they'd see two, three movies, after the movie theater had closed. That's the only kind of entertainment he had. He couldn't go out.

"One time I was talking to him about playing golf. I told him how relaxing it was. I said, 'You ought-a come play golf with me one day.' He said, 'Man, I sure wish I could. I just can't.' Or tennis, or anything. Anybody else I could say, 'Hey, come out to the house, play some tennis.' I got a tennis court out the house. But if he did that, it wouldn't be fifteen minutes until everybody in the neighborhood was over there.

"Even today I'd be willing to bet a thousand dollars he could draw a hundred people in five minutes anywhere he went. And he knows this. It's bound to make him unhappy. He'd like to be able to walk down the street like a normal human being. He can't be a person like anybody else. It's bound to have an effect."

Usually two to three hundred prints of a film are released at one time, but when *Love Me Tender* was ready for the nation's theaters, no less than five hundred and fifty prints were ordered. Saturation marketing. In New York they called out thirty-five cops, hired twenty extra ushers and notified the city's truancy department when three thousand teenagers—mostly girls—were lined up outside the Paramount Theater by eight A.M. It had been advertised that the first two thousand in line would get their choice of an Elvis Presley scarf, hat, lapel button or charm bracelet—items among those on sale inside for the latecomers. In New Orleans there was a girl who sat through forty-two showings of the film, just as she had sat through forty-two showings of the previous week's movie to see Elvis in the previews of coming attractions.

Within three weeks the million dollars that had been sunk into the movie had been recovered. Never before had any Hollywood film got its money back so rapidly.

The critics welcomed Elvis less ecstatically. The New York *Times* credited him for his enthusiasm, but used words like "turgid" and "juicy" to describe his characterization and, noting the film was a horse opera, said Elvis's "dramatic contribution is not a great deal more impressive than that of one of the slavering nags." The Los Angeles *Times* said, "He pales by comparison when pitted against the resonant inflections of Egan, of course, but who came to watch Elvis act?" Certainly not *Time* magazine, whose critic apparently *ran* all the way back to his typewriter to write one of the great put-downs of all time:

Is it a sausage? It is certainly smooth and damp looking, but who ever heard of a 172-lb. sausage 6 ft. tall? Is it a Walt Disney goldfish? It has the same sort of big, soft, beautiful eyes and long, curly lashes, but who ever heard of a goldfish with sideburns? Is it a corpse? The face just hangs there, limp and white with its little drop-seat mouth, rather like Lord Byron in the wax museum.

But suddenly the figure comes to life. The lips part, the eyes half close, the clutched guitar begins to undulate back and forth in an uncomfortably suggestive manner. And wham! The midsection of the body jolts forward to bump and grind and beat out a low-down rhythm that takes its pace from boogie and hillbilly, rock 'n' roll and something known only to Elvis and his Pelvis. As the belly dance gets wilder, a peculiar sound emerges. A rusty foghorn? A voice? Or merely a noise produced, like the voice of a cricket, by the violent stridulation of the legs? Words occasionally can be made out, like raisins in cornmeal mush. "Goan . . . git . . . luhhv . . ." And then all at once everything stops, and a big trembly tender half smile, half sneer smears slowly across the CinemaScope screen. The message that millions of U.S. teen-age girls love to receive has just been delivered.

Most other critics felt the same about Elvis's debut. For someone who wanted to be an actor it was difficult stuff to take.

On the Christmas cards mailed from Memphis that year—and received by film critics all over the country, as well as by disc jockeys and fans—it said, "To wish you all a Cool Yule and a Frantic First and a billion thanks to everyone."

Signed: "Elvis"—in big letters—"and the Colonel"—in smaller letters.

Elvis started work on his second movie role during the holiday season, in *Loving You* at Paramount. This was Hal Wallis's first film with Elvis (the first of nine) and the first of several which were especially written for Elvis and based rather loosely on his own rags-to-riches story. In this one Elvis was Deke Rivers, a small-town boy who became an overnight sensation when he was signed by a lady press agent (Lizabeth Scott) to sing with her ex-husband's (Wendell Corey's) country music band. At first Miss Scott and Corey show little more than greed in their interest in young Deke, but when they learn of his life as an orphan, they tear up the early contract to dedicate themselves to seeing Deke is happy as well as successful.

It was in the preparation of this film that it became evident that the Colonel, acting through Hill and Range Songs, had been constructing an enormous music machine that would guarantee Elvis a broad selection of material. For this was the first film whose script was distributed to Hill and Range songwriters like morning papers on a surburban street.*

"We would give out dozens of scripts to writers we had under contract or I thought would do well," says Freddie Bienstock. "All the spots where songs went were marked. We asked the writers to submit songs for as many of those spots as they wished. That way, we would always have three or four different songs for each spot in the movie."

There was no guarantee the song or songs submitted by any writer would be used. The songwriters were told other composers had scripts too and that everything was to be sent to Elvis in the form of demonstration records and that he would select which ones would go into the film and, subsequently, on an album.

There were seven songs in *Loving You,* enough to fill up one side of what would be Elvis's first album for 1957 (to be released with the picture in July), and it was presumed that this album would sell at least as well as the first two, so the songwriters didn't balk at the unusual arrangements. Writing for a Hollywood film produced by a major studio never was done on speculation; some of the composers' guilds and unions even forbade it. In the past, composers who wrote for Hollywood musicals not only did so on assignment rather than on speculation, they also did so on salary. Not so with Elvis Presley flicks. When you wrote for Elvis, it was write now, pay later. Maybe.

Still, it was rare when a songwriter didn't submit some material once given the opportunity. Says Mike Stoller: "The writer felt that if the song was done, the royalty that would come from the record would be great enough compensation, and actually that's the way it worked. If there are, say, twelve songs in a film and you prorate each song, on a flat fee it might come out to, I don't know, fifteen hun-

* In recognition of his contribution to the film, the Colonel was included in the credits as technical adviser, a role he has played many times since.

dred or two thousand dollars a song in terms of the budget, the going rate at the time. But if Presley recorded a song and it came out in an album, it was good for a lot more than that."

Asking writers to produce on speculation was one thing. Asking them to share their royalties with Elvis and the poor ol' Colonel was another. Almost always the songs were published by one of Elvis's companies, which meant if the writer had his own publishing company (often the case), he couldn't use it and sacrificed any publisher's royalties. Worse, there were several instances when Elvis was given partial writer's credit and so the composer gave up another bite.

It is not difficult to get writers to talk about these practices, but few will do so "on the record." They will tell which songs were and which were not co-written by Elvis and explain how ownership and authorship were changed, but generally they don't want it known they were the ones who blabbed. Songwriters also will talk about each other's songs, and song publishers provide still more information, so slowly a reasonable picture forms.

It is abundantly clear, for example, that the authorship was changed on the four songs Elvis sang in *Love Me Tender*. Composers credited for these songs are Vera Matson and Elvis Presley, neither of whom had anything to do with any of the four. They were, instead, written by Vera's husband, Ken Darby, who served as the film's musical director and had a trio that backed Elvis when he recorded them. They were put in his wife's name because Darby was an ASCAP (American Society of Composers, Authors and Publishers) writer, and at that time Elvis had but one publishing company and it was a member of rival BMI (Broadcast Music, Inc.); although soon after, an ASCAP company, named for Elvis's mother, was formed—Gladys Music, Inc. Elvis was listed as co-author with Darby's wife, an insider says, "at the Colonel's suggestion."

This sort of arrangement, however unethical, was common practice in the 1950s. Disc jockey Alan Freed claimed half authorship of Chuck Berry's "Maybelline," and Norfolk promoter Sheriff Tex Davis put his name on Gene Vincent's "Be Bop A Lula." Just as payola was rampant in the industry, so was sharing royalties. But no one ever complained.

Says one composer: "When you're dealing with the Colonel, it's an either-or situation. Either you join the team or you don't play. And it's their ball game so they can make the rules. It was a matter of fifty per cent of something or a hundred per cent of nothing."

These are words echoed by Robert (Bumps) Blackwell, who was co-author of several of Little Richard's hits. Two of these, "Rip It Up" and "Ready Teddy," originally were published by Venice Music, Inc., a Los Angeles-based company, but before Elvis included them in his second album, half the publishing rights (meaning, ultimately, half the publishing royalties) were transferred to Elvis Presley Music, Inc.

"Either we agreed to that or they said they wouldn't release the songs, Elvis wouldn't record the material," says Bumps today. "It didn't bother us. Why should it? Do you know how many records Elvis sold? Ffty per cent of several million records is much tastier than a hundred per cent of zero. We weren't upset. We were happy."

Friends say Elvis wasn't aware that any advantage may have been taken. They say that when he asked why his name was listed as an occasional composer, he was told his contribution in the studio in terms of arrangements and the occasional word changes he made entitled him to royalties and writer's credit. In fact, this is an arguable point, although Elvis once said he didn't think he could write a song if his life depended on it.

All Freddie Bienstock says today for Hill and Range is "Elvis wrote only a handful of songs. In those days if he was dissatisfied with certain lines, he would make some changes. Later on he made suggestions to writers rather than get involved."

Friends (again) say that once Elvis learned what was going on, he ordered an end to the practice.

Hill and Range was further fattening the Elvis calf in the winter of 1956–57 by buying other music publishing companies for Elvis. The first of these was American Music, one of the stalwarts in the country music field, now listed as the American Division of Elvis Presley Music, Inc. Among the copyrights acquired were "Divorce Me C.O.D.," "Smoke, Smoke, Smoke [That Cigarette]" and "So Round, So Firm, So Fully Packed," all three being big country hits written by Merle Travis in the mid-forties. Others were "The Cry of the Wild Goose," a country hit in 1950; "A Dear John Letter," a hit in 1953; and one of the biggest country music copyrights of all time, "Sixteen Tons." Although long past their peak in sales before Elvis bought them, these songs, along with many others, were well worth picking up. As country standards, they were included in dozens of albums subsequently, and when those albums sold, of course Elvis (and Hill and Range) got the publisher's slice of the pie.

On January 4, 1957, four days before his twenty-second birthday, Elvis reported at Kennedy Veterans Hospital in Memphis a few blocks from his home for his preinduction physical. Elvis went to the examination center with friends, Dotty Harmony, a show girl from Las Vegas, then staying with the Presley family as a house guest, and Cliff Gleaves, one of his salaried sidekicks. Gleaves drove the Cadillac, and Elvis and Dotty rode in the back.

When he might be drafted depended on several factors, Army hospital spokesmen said, ranging from the local draft board's quota to the number of volunteers. In any case, newsmen and fans were assured the call probably would not come for at least six months, perhaps for as long as a year, and during that time Elvis could enlist in any branch he chose.

Elvis was the only potential recruit to be poked and prodded that day. Normally the Army moved men through in groups of forty or more, but given two days to ponder what might happen, the Army decided that forty men plus Elvis plus all the newsmen and curious employees would be a bit much. As it was, doctors had to chase photographers who were trying to snap Elvis in the raw.

A few hours after the examination Dotty boarded a plane for Nevada and Elvis and his gang boarded a train for New York, where he was to make his third and final appearance on Ed Sullivan's show.

The scene in New York was typical.

"They had the streets blocked off for seven or eight blocks around the theater," says Neal Matthews. "The side street by the theater was packed. I'd say five thousand kids standing around screaming. They had policemen on horses directing, trying to keep crowds from getting out of control."

Neal says he thinks that was the time they used a decoy to get Elvis inside. "They'd use decoys a lot," he says. "Send a big black limousine up to the stage door, have somebody that sort of looked like him and dressed like him. All the kids would come over there and Elvis'd slip in the side door."

Elvis appeared in a gold lamé vest with a black satin lining and a velvet shirt and he introduced a religious song that was to be on his next EP record, *Peace in the Valley*. It was his last television appearance for more than three years.

The following week, on the eighth, Elvis's birthday, the Army recruiters in Memphis held a press conference, during which Captain Elwyn P. Rowan said, "Physically he's an A-profile and that's as high as you can go." Mentally? "Can't give you the exact score," the Captain said, "but Presley's score was about average."

Of course it couldn't remain as simple and uncluttered as

all that. There had to be published accounts hinting that Elvis might be given preferential treatment if and when he was inducted—that, specifically, he might not have to get his hair and sideburns clipped. "Relax, girls," was the way the Associated Press started such a story, quoting an unnamed Army spokesman as saying Elvis probably would go into the Special Services branch and could, as someone who would entertain troops and perhaps serve in a publicity-recruiting capacity, wear khaki but forgo the GI haircut required of the ordinary soldier.

As might be expected, there were those who objected to the thought of such favoritism. So much so, in fact, that several veterans in Miami wrote blistering letters to their Senator, George Smathers, who kicked the complaints over to the Pentagon with a request that he be informed whether the published reports were accurate. Said the Pentagon: "Many were present [when Elvis took his physical] and it is possible that numerous conjecturable remarks and off-the-cuff comments were expressed by military personnel, cameramen and reporters. It must be emphasized that these remarks, if made, do not represent the official position of the Department of the Army."

It was added that if Elvis was drafted, he would receive his basic training at Fort Chaffee, Arkansas—where the press went to Captain John Mawn, the post's public information officer, who said, "No one gets preferential treatment at Chaffee. All recruits get a military haircut the day they arrive." Asked what that meant, the Captain said it bore a striking resemblance to a "peeled onion."

Of such things were headlines made in 1957.

That same week RCA released "Too Much," another in the long line of lurching rockabilly songs recorded months earlier in Hollywood. The back side was "Playing for Keeps," a country ballad. By mid-February it was number one and became Elvis's eighth million-selling record in under a year.

The Colonel called a small press conference in his cluttered office in Madison to say that his boy would be making his third movie beginning the first of May. It was also to be filmed at Elvis's third studio, M-G-M, he said, and it was called *Jailhouse Rock*. The only other thing he had to announce was Elvis's price tag: $250,000 plus 50 per cent of all profits, unheard of for someone who'd had but one film released.

And then another single was released. This was "All Shook Up," another hard rocker written by Otis Blackwell, who'd written "Don't Be Cruel." It was backed by one of the few real country-style weepers Elvis ever cut, "That's When Your Heartaches Begin." The song's title became a part of the teenage vocabulary about the same time it sold its millionth copy.

Despite this continued success, Eugene Gilbert, head of the then-influential Gilbert Youth Research Institute in New York, said a national survey he had conducted showed Elvis's popularity had taken a serious drop. Not true, the Colonel squealed, calling another little get-together with the boys in the Nashville press corps.

"All right," he told Red O'Donnell, the music writer for the Nashville *Banner*, "so I'm prejudiced. I also got facts and figures to back my argument in favor of Elvis. Lookee here: Elvis starts a personal appearance tour in Chicago March twenty-eighth. He also is booked for one-nighters in Fort Wayne, Indiana, St. Louis, Philadelphia, Buffalo, Toronto and Ottawa. Five of those towns already are sellouts [this at least a week before the first date] and he's playing auditoriums which seat ten thousand people. Does that look like the boy is losing favor?"

Red asked the Colonel, How about that tour through the Midwest the Colonel'd promoted starring Hugh O'Brien, who was then playing the title role in the *Wyatt Earp* television series? Only fair, the Colonel said, only fair. And he leaned forward, as if to share a closely guarded secret, tapped the ash from his cigar and said, "O'Brien was a nice guy, but maybe he's been overexposed." Red said, "What the hell you talking about, Colonel? That was Earp's first tour."

"It's like this," the Colonel said. "I go on the assumption that an artist who is red hot shouldn't be seen too much by the public. Make the fans clamor for a view of the product, so to speak. I handled Eddy Arnold that way. I am using the same system, if you can call it that, with Presley. It works, I do believe. A typical local example is Hank Snow. Snow isn't overexposed. You don't see him on the TV too much. The result is that when Hank makes a personal appearance tour, people show up at the box office and pay to see Hank sing."

Same thing with his present boy, of course. Make 'em pay to see Elvis. Make 'em go to the movie theater or the local civic auditorium or baseball stadium. Don't give him away free on the television set.

Usually the Colonel went on Elvis's tours. There weren't that many now and the Colonel enjoyed them. They gave him a chance to get out there and sell stuff, just like the old carney days, back when he was selling foot-long hot dogs. Moe Weise tells a story. Moe and his partner, Dave Barnett, were selling pictures of movie stars by mail in those days and on the side they had a license to advertise Elvis Presley statues and Elvis Presley lipsticks in the magazines. Moe says they did very well selling statues and lipsticks, but it is a story about photographs he tells.

"I got a call from the Colonel one day," he says. "He wanted five thousands prints of Elvis in a hurry. That sonofabitch. He chiseled me down and chiseled me down. I finally let him have them for five and a half cents a piece. Somebody else had said six cents, right? And I agree to five and a half, so I get the order. And I get them out in time, all five thousand, delivered like I promised.*

---

* In fairness to the Colonel, five and a half cents a print for eight-by-tens in orders of five thousand or more was low, but no lower than most cut-rate photo houses charged. Moe didn't make much money on the order, but he did make a little.

"The next week I go to Long Beach for an Elvis concert with my sixteen-year-old daughter and there's the Colonel at the door, selling my eight-by-tens for fifty cents. I said, 'Not this . . . you don't need *this!*' Elvis had just had his sixth or eighth or tenth gold record and he'd signed a contract with RCA guaranteeing him a thousand dollars a week even if he goes fishing that week, and the Colonel's out there hustling eight-by-tens. He said, 'I'm only filling a need. These people want autographed pictures and I'm providing them. I'm not cheating them, am I? I'm giving them what they want and I'm asking a fair price. I could charge a dollar, you know."

Inside the auditorium it was even more bizarre.

"The real shows were in the audience, not on the stage," says Gordon Stoker. "I can't express that experience, being on a stage with as many as thirty thousand people screaming and hollering. He had a way of crooking his little finger and wiggling it. He'd do that and they'd scream. He didn't really understand the audience reaction to him and so he'd have fun, he'd put them on. He'd burp and they'd scream. He'd burp or wiggle his finger, then look at us and grin.

"We'd get so engrossed in what he was doing, we'd forget to come in vocally," Gordon says today. "He never planned any of his moves and they fascinated us. You never knew what was coming. He didn't do the same thing at the same place in a song. So we'd be watching, and we'd be watching so hard we'd blow the part, we'd forget to come in with the 'ooooowahhhh' and he'd turn around and give us the lip—you know the way he moves the left side of his mouth in a cocky sneer—or he'd say something like 'oh yeah?' or 'sumbitch.'

"He always wanted us in as close to him as possible. Scotty and Bill too. He wanted the protection. Those kids broke through police lines in Kansas City, Missouri, once and he said, 'Run for your lives.' We ran. We got into a car just as the kids reached us. They stole our instruments, our music, everything. He never could do any curtain calls or encores. This is what saved him. He'd disappear as the last notes were hit.

Those kids would think he'd come back and he'd be gone.

"It was always a large show—with a dancer, a soloist, a juggling act, a comedian and a full orchestra. There'd be five to eight specialty acts. An hour and a half would pass before Elvis came on. By that time the audience was out of its mind.

"Elvis'd do 'Hound Dog' as his grand finale. The girls were in a fever pitch by the time he got through that. They were to a climax. And they wouldn't dare leave as long as he was on the stage. Sometimes he'd do sixteen choruses of that song, and all the time it kept building.

"One concert they were begging for something he owned and he threw his coat into the audience. It was like throwing a pound of meat to a pack of hungry dogs. They tore it to shreds."

On May 1 Elvis showed up at the M-G-M- studio in Culver City, outside Los Angeles, to begin the recording sessions for *Jailhouse Rock*. Gordon Stoker remembers what the day was like.

"I don't remember what time it was, but it was morning," he says today, "and Elvis went to the piano and began to play spirituals, his first love. We all fell in with him, all the Jordan-aires and Bill and Scotty and D. J. We sang all morning with Elvis, probably not even thinking about the songs for the film, certainly not rehearsing or recording them. And then we broke for lunch.

"That was when one of the studio officials called me over and said it was costing the studio a fortune and not to fall in with him in the afternoon if he tried to sing spirituals again. He said we had to get down to work.

"So we came back from an hour-and-a-half lunch break and Elvis went right to the piano again, starting right where he left off. I had talked with Hugh and Neal and Hoyt and we didn't join him. We refused to sing along. When that happened, Elvis stopped playing and looked at us. He called me over and asked me what was happening. I told him, 'Elvis, they told us not to sing spirituals. They told us we have to cut the songs for the film.'

"That did it," Gordon says. "Elvis blew up. He didn't make a scene. When he blew up, he blew up inside. And he walked out, taking his six or seven cronies with him. The day was canceled. Elvis didn't come back.

"It was really unfortunate. What the studio didn't realize was that Elvis hadn't sung in a studio in some while and this was his way of warming up, getting in the mood . . . that he might have done all seven songs that afternoon, or perhaps by the end of the following day. In that way he still would have finished the tracking in far less time than most singers would. They should have given Elvis his head, let him do what he wanted. Most singers have taken at least two weeks."

It was easy at the time to say Elvis was on some unpleasant selfish star trip, but apparently this wasn't true. As Gordon says, Elvis knew what he was doing and he knew how he worked best. His schedule and style may have been unorthodox, but apparently Elvis thought everyone understood. Certainly there were enough of the regulars there—Freddie Bienstock, Steve Sholes, the Colonel, all his own musicians and backup singers. Someone should have said something. But no one did and Elvis blew up and walked out.

He returned the following morning and everything ran smoothly.

The film is one of his best and worthy of some detailed attention. *Jailhouse Rock* told the story of a young hothead (Elvis) named Vince Everett who got one to ten years for fatally slugging a bum who got fresh with a waitress. While in prison Elvis's cellmate (Mickey Shaughnessy), an old-time country singer, teaches Vince to play the guitar, and when he hears Vince sing, he has him sign a contract that gives him 50 per cent of everything, if and when.

When Vince is released, he auditions for a job at a bar, where he meets a record company promotion gal (Judy Tyler), who is impressed enough to get him a recording session. In this and several subsequent scenes the band playing behind Elvis on-camera is Scotty and Bill and D. J., with Mike Stoller making his acting debut on piano, and all four of them lip-syncing the harmony provided on a prerecorded transcription by the Jordanaires. Peggy (Judy Tyler) takes the record from office to office, and what follows is a lot of dialogue that either begins "Thanks, Peg, for lettin' me hear it" or "I'm afraid I have bad news . . ."

There were many now-classic lines in *Jailhouse Rock.* Back when Vince and Peg meet, for instance, he says to her, "Okay, you're used to the top talent. What are you wasting your time working me over for?" And she says in what can be described only as a slinky voice, "I like the way you swing a guitar." And later, after Vince insults her parents, she says, "I think I'm gonna just hate you." And he looks at her, lids drooping, eyebrows leaning in like the two sides of a sagging barn roof, and says, "Uh-uh . . . you ain' gone hate me. I ain' gone let you hate me." And he grabs her and kisses her. She pulls away and says (mock angry): "How dare you think such cheap tactics would work with me?" He looks back at her, eyebrows leaning some more, kisses her again and says, "That ain' tactics, honey. It's just the beast in me."

Eventually Vince Everett connects and becomes an over-night sensation, and just as the money is coming in in buckets, who should appear but Vince's old prison buddy, who puts in his claim for 50 per cent. Vince says he's consulted his attorney (who appears periodically—thin, balding and fidgety—to handle the wheeling and dealing) and the contract isn't worth anything. The ex-con says he thought it was made in good faith. Vince settles out of court for 10 per cent and his buddy says to him, "You're gonna have the most expensive flunky in show business."

Nor is the ex-con the only flunky soon seen with Vince. Just like Elvis in real life, he begins to acquire an entourage. He goes to Las Vegas and all his records are smasheroos and then he goes to Hollywood, where he starts necking with his leading lady, off-camera as well as on. Finally Mick tells Vince he's being a louse, that he's walking on people who love him. Vince ignores the good advice. Then Peggy talks to Vince about isn't it time you cut some more records? Vince tells her to flake off. And then the fidgety lawyer tells Vince they've been made a good offer for Laurel Records, which is the company Vince and Peggy started together way back when. Vince tells the lawyer to sell, without consulting Peg.

Things come to a head when he tells Peggy about the sale. She breaks into tears and leaves, and Mick, who was a witness to this touching scene, proceeds to beat up our hero—punching him in the throat, causing Vince to lose his voice. Two scenes later a doctor is saying Vince may never sing again.

Oddly enough, On May 14, just two weeks into the shooting schedule, Elvis swallowed a porcelain cap from one of his front teeth during a dance sequence, and when he experienced some pain in his chest the next day, he was rushed to the Cedars of Lebanon Hospital. There, X rays showed he'd not swallowed the cap but inhaled it and it was lodged in one of his lungs. Thus the pain in his chest. The cap was removed with forceps and bronchoscope and after resting for a couple of days he returned to *Jailhouse Rock*.

To hasten this epic of brilliant cliché to its logical end, Peggy and the ex-con visit Vince in the hospital, everybody tells everybody else how much they love each other, some time passes and a doctor says Vince's throat is healed, and there is a dramatic scene with Vince's pal playing the piano and Vince a-c-t-u-a-l-l-y, m-i-r-a-c-u-l-o-u-s-l-y singing again. Of course it's a love song and Peggy is listening from the next room.

The end.

In June another single was released, combining the two best songs from *Loving You*, the film about to go into the nation's neighborhoods and drive-ins—the title song, backed with "Teddy Bear." "Loving You" was another Leiber-Stoller song; "Teddy Bear" was written by two Philadelphians, Kal Mann and Bernie Lowe, who'd later give the world such terrific acts as the Dovells, the Orlons, Dee Dee Sharp and Chubby Checker. They claim they wrote the song because of Elvis's well-publicized fondness for teddy bears, as demonstrated by his ability to win so many by tossing baseballs in amusements parks. It occupied the number one position in July and August.

As for the film, Jim Powers of the *Hollywood Reporter*, who didn't like Elvis in *Love Me Tender*, actually thought he wasn't bad in *Loving You*. Even if he did have to see the picture along with several hundred fan club members—invited by the Colonel—who screamed every time Elvis appeared on screen. "Presley . . . acts naturally and with appeal," Powers wrote. "He would be attractive to a member of the older generation if the picture could be seen without the maddening female chorus. Kanter [Hal Kanter, the director] has anticipated some of this by ingeniously using the massed feminine juvenile effects on screen so that at times you are not sure if it is the on-screen or off-screen females who are creating the din. Wendell Corey and Lizabeth Scott are handicapped by speaking their lines into the teeth of a hurricane . . ." The appraisal was typical.

And Elvis Presley teddy bears with Elvis's autograph began appearing in dime stores and supermarkets all across America.

Elvis took a three-week summer vacation, beginning in July when he finished *Jailhouse Rock*. Part of the vacation was spent supervising the remodeling of the new home he'd bought in March, using the house on Audubon Drive as a down payment. Named Graceland, the new place was a $100,000 estate in what was then a Memphis suburb, a small town called Whitehaven a couple of miles north of the Mississippi state line. (Whitehaven was absorbed by Memphis in 1969.) The basement was dirt and there was no pool outside but it didn't lack much else. The house was two stories tall with a high-ceilinged attic under a pitched roof. It was built of tan Tennessee limestone, with tall white Colonial pillars outside, and had five bedrooms—some of which were occupied almost immediately by Elvis's parents and his grandmother—and almost as many baths. Twenty-three rooms in all. And it was situated on a hilltop in the middle of thirteen acres of land, which in turn was surrounded by rolling grazing land. In 1957 the only neighbors Elvis had were cows.

"It was just an old mansion he made into a home," says Alan Fortas, a stocky ex-guard from Central High who had met Elvis a year earlier and by the end of 1957 would be on his payroll. "Every year he does somethin' different to it. When he originally bought it, it was just a reg'lar old house. He put a floor in the basement, paneled the walls, all his gold records are hanging there. He's got a pool table, a record player, used to have a slot car track there, any kind of entertainment you want. It's two big rooms. Got a projection screen that comes down. Got his own sixteen-millimeter projector and we rent any movies we want."

When Elvis wasn't renting movies, he still was renting roller rinks and amusement parks.

"We'd rent a roller rink and play football on skates," Alan says. "That was out at the Rainbow. We used to rent the fairgrounds here, the amusement park, ride these rides till we were sick. You know when you're a kid, you ride a ride and the ride ends and you have to get off, buy another ticket. So we'd just ride these things till we got tired and say, 'Okay, stop the ride,' and we'd get off.

"There'd be one favorite that we always ended up on. This'd be the last treat, the bumper cars. Here in Memphis they call 'em the 'dodge-'ems.' We'd choose up sides, ten to a side, and we'd have a war. It got so we had to have pillows around our waist, gloves . . . we'd really actually wear blisters on our hands from these dodge-'em cars, from ridin' 'em so long.

"We'd have a ball. The people who came didn't have to

pay for anything. I mean, hot dogs, pronto pups, hamburgers, popcorn, candied apples, anything you want. Elvis being from Memphis, it was a special favor to him through the Park Commission, I'm sure. They would keep four or five operators there who could operate the different rides. They would stay open and they'd charge Elvis so much per ride or for the operators on an hourly rate.

"Elvis wouldn't turn anyone away. If they were people who just wanted a good time, he didn't care. Sometimes a friend would bring a friend or somebody would drive by and stop and say, 'Can I come in?' He wouldn't refuse anybody."

He added a swimming pool to the house and told friends he wanted to make his bedroom the "darkest blue there is, with a mirror that will cover one entire wall." He said he was going to decorate the entrance hall with a facsimile sky—clouds painted on the ceiling for daytime, little lights that blinked for stars at night. Over the mild objections of his mother—it was said—he ordered purple walls with gold trim for the living room, dining room and sun room, with white corduroy drapes. And the whole house outside was lighted with soft blue spots, making the limestone seem to have a life of its own, glowing in the dark like a phosphorescent birthday cake.

Down from the house, at the ten-foot wrought-iron Graceland gates that had larger-than-life-size metal figures of Elvis playing the guitar, the fans were in constant attendance. Some youngsters in a car with Arkansas plates had tried to steal Elvis's lawn furniture once and Elvis had to chase them several miles in one of his Cadillacs before he forced them to the side of the road. The same month that happened, two other fans, Helen Magyar and Alice Steinhauer, both nineteen, spent $250 each to get to Memphis from St. Paul, Minnesota; it was worth it, because Elvis saw them and, as they put it to the newspapermen afterward, "He let us run our fingers through his sideburns."

No matter where Elvis was, there were fans—in hotel lobbies, outside studio gates, backstage, at his home, anywhere he went. All over the United States, whenever a youthful runaway was reported by parents to police, if the missing teenager was female the police checked the mob of girls outside Elvis's house in Memphis before doing anything else. In Hollywood, outside the Knickerbocker Hotel, when Elvis was registered, there was a group called the Hotel Hounds. To be a member you had to have been kissed by Elvis and sing "Heartbreak Hotel" backward. Once when Elvis had tried to take a girl to the movies in Memphis, he was spotted by fans, and although he ducked inside the theater to the safety of a reserved booth, the fans found his Cadillac and in their worshipful enthusiasm jumped up and down on the hood and fenders, shredded the upholstery for souvenirs and wrote pledges of undying love all over the white paint with lipsticks and nail files.

It got crazier farther away from him. In Boston a disc jockey named Norm Prescott offered seven strands of Elvis's sideburns for the seven most absurd reasons for wanting one—and in one week received 18,400 entries. In Forth Worth, Texas, high school students carved his name on their forearms with pocket knives. In Russia Elvis recordings cut on discarded hospital X-ray plates were selling for fifty rubles, the equivalent of $12.50.

In Memphis the fans began to arrive each day—whether or not Elvis was there wasn't important—about dawn, taking pictures of each other standing in front of the gates, then driving on into Memphis and maybe coming back later to see if anything was happening. Sometimes they'd talk with his uncles, Travis Smith and Vester Presley. Other times they'd chat among themselves, talking about the times they saw Elvis close up, the times he actually spoke to them. Occasionally Elvis would wander down the hill and give autographs for an hour or so. That'd keep things stirred up for a week.

"Those fans were somethin' else," says Alan Fortas. "We used to stand up there on the porch of the house and watch 'em. Every one of 'em was convinced that if only she got a few minutes with him, he'd know she was the one for him. That's all it took, just a few minutes—and what they were doing, a lot of them, was scheming and telling Travis and Vester lies. Occasionally Elvis's uncles, who worked as guards, they'd let some of the girls inside the gates. But not often. Usually they'd just take their cameras and run up to the house in the jeep and take a nice picture for them.

"Those fans were something else all right."

When Elvis finished his vacation, he went back on the road again, this time to make his first appearances in the Pacific Northwest. On September 1 he was in Vancouver, British Columbia. First there was a noisy, bordering-on-inane twenty-six-minute-long press conference in a dressing room normally frequented by football players, and then Elvis went out to meet his fans.

"We had the stage set up at the end of this huge, huge stadium," says Scotty Moore, "and the people that were on the field were at the twenty-yard line and we were at the other end. It was impossible to see, so they started moving forward."

"We were all scared," says Neal Matthews. "They turned all the lights on. They warned the crowd over the loudspeaker: If you close in any more, we're stopping the show. It didn't do a bit of good. They kept closing in, moving in. They were wild-eyed. Elvis said, 'I'm cuttin' out, man,' and he quit right in the middle of a song and he took off. He left us all stranded there. We just barely got out. They turned the stage over, they turned over the instruments. It was pretty bad."

Says Scotty: "It took us an hour or two to get away. They'd ask us where he was and we'd point over that way and they'd take off running. Then they'd come back and we'd point off in another way, and they'd take off screaming again."

Elvis broke all records in the Pacific Northwest, grossing $147,000 for five half-hour performances. The biggest date was Vancouver, where $44,000 was taken in at the box office; other stops were in Spokane, Tacoma, Seattle and Portland.

The same weekend Elvis was making this brief tour, posters went up all over northern Mississippi and Alabama announcing his return later that month to Tupelo: "Miss.-Ala. Fair & Dairy Show Welcomes Tupelo's Own—in Person—Elvis Presley with His Own Show. Fairgrounds 8:00 P.M. Friday Sep. 27. All Seats $2.00. Get Your Tickets Early. Don't Miss It." And in a box at the bottom of the posters was the note: "Benefit Elvis Presley's Youth Recreation Center to be Built in Tupelo."

Tupelo Mayor Jim Ballard explained that the city wanted to make a memorial of the birthplace—then still sitting on the same sumpy snake-infested hillside—and a park of the surrounding property, with a swimming pool and community building. It was stipulated in the agreement with Elvis, when he said he would appear, that none of the money would go toward purchase of land. The city would cover that. The benefit money was to go to development of the property once the city owned it. Tupelo passed a bond issue to raise money of its own, bought thirteen acres and commissioned an architect to draw up some plans.

Scotty Moore and Bill Black didn't appear with Elvis in Tupelo that year. They'd quit working with Elvis less than a week earlier, telling newsmen they weren't being paid enough.

"Elvis is the star and we know it," Scotty was quoted as saying then. "I didn't expect to get rich on this, and I certainly don't begrudge him any of the success he has had or what it's brought him, but I did expect to do better than I have and to make a good living for my family."

Scotty said he and Bill had been getting a hundred dollars a week at home and two hundred a week while on the road, plus a thousand-dollar Christmas bonus. The hundred dollars came in every week, whether or not they worked, but they also were responsible for paying all their own traveling expenses. Scotty said he told Elvis he wanted a raise of fifty dollars a week, plus ten thousand in cash, "so I could clean up my debts and have something to show for these four years."

("Scotty and Bill really got a going over," says Gordon Stoker today. "Nobody ever will know how bad.")

Although friends say there was quite a blow-up at the time —Elvis finally told Scotty he wanted a few days to think it over—Scotty doesn't make much of the resignations today: "It wasn't a good salary, you have to admit that, and like any group that lives together you build up these little things . . . so Bill and I quit. We weren't away but a month or so and he wasn't touring that much anyway. He had one recording session during the period, but he was using a lot of Nashville musicians in addition to our own group at the time, so that was no problem. We never did go back on the payroll. We just booked it by the day. We'd just hire on and then go do somethin' else until he needed us again."

The touring continued sporadically the next six weeks as Elvis concentrated again on recording and making movies. Scotty and Bill rejoined him for two appearances at the Pan Pacific Auditorium in Los Angeles. The shows were like most others: Elvis was accompanied by a full carnival of novelty acts,* nine thousand girls screamed continuously and wet their pants and fainted and mauled themselves, the local vice squad told Elvis he'd better clean up his act or he wasn't doing a second show, and Elvis pocketed about $56,000. Even the press had to pay for tickets; by now the Colonel was giving *nothing* away.

---

* Hollywood serves as a vast repository of novelty acts, and the line-up here was a classic one, including Jerry Rosen's band, the Burns Twins and Evelyn (a trio of tap dancers), Howard Hardin (doubling as M.C. and juggler), Joe Termini (a comedy violinist), Wells and Four Fays (a fast acrobatic act), Paul Desmond (an impressionist) and the good old Jordanaires.

Then Elvis made his first visit to Hawaii, to perform twice in one day in the Honolulu Stadium. The Colonel flew to Hawaii first to supervise arrangements, which included rehearsing an American Legion band, which would provide the accompaniment to Elvis's arrival at the airport. The Colonel positioned the band in a fenced enclosure not much larger than the band itself, and when the plane landed, he began barking his marching orders. Within moments the musicians were hopelessly snarled—trombone players slamming trumpeters in the neck; drummers on their knees, feet and hands stuck through their drum heads; the entire woodwind section rammed up against a fence, bleating for help. And the Colonel stood proudly at attention—suppressing a smile—saluting the King of Rock 'n' Roll.

"Jailhouse Rock" had been released by now—first the song, and then the film. "Teddy Bear" was still in the top ten. His third album, *Loving You*, which carried the seven songs from the film and five others, including Fats Domino's hit "Blueberry Hill," was number one in album sales. There were three records ("All Shook Up," "Teddy Bear" and "Paralyzed") on the British charts, and his 45 EP of religious songs was the best-selling record in that category. When "Jailhouse Rock" was released, it was, quoting *Billboard*, "a smash in all markets"; and by November 1 *it* was number one.

As for the film, it was greeted about the same way the first two were—with critical reservation and audience adoration. In many cities it was released as the top half of a double feature—over *Action of the Tiger*, a slow-moving adventure starring Van Johnson. Probably there was no actor on earth who could deliver a line like "That ain' tactics, honey, it's just the beast in me" and get away with it.

Elvis played football between recording sessions, concerts and films. It was one of his favorite means of escaping from the pressures of his career, and usually those he played with were old high school pals and friends he'd made in Hollywood.

"He'd rent the football stadium at Whitehaven High School, have 'em turn the lights on if it was at night, and get an official to call the game," says Buzzie Forbess. "He'd bring his limousine full of Cokes and stuff for everyone who showed up. He played these games four or five years. He'd come home to Memphis, buy the equipment, the balls and so on. And then he'd start putting teams together—usually fifteen, maybe twenty men to a side, eight for offense, eight for defense and some extras. Sometimes he had about thirty players. He had the team he sponsored here in one of the amateur leagues, plus Red West and some of the guys from Rick Nelson's team in Hollywood, people he'd bring back with him."

When he wasn't actually playing ball—as an end—he was watching the big games on television. It was impossible for him to attend in person. He tried once, showing up at the annual charity game between the two top high school teams in Memphis in 1956, and nearly caused a riot. Rather than try that in 1957, he spent about a thousand dollars for tickets to send all fourteen hundred Humes High School students in his place.

Growing up and being a football hero was what he dreamed about as a kid, Elvis said at the time, and even if things didn't work out that way, he still liked it better than any other game.

Back in October, Milton Bowers, the draft board chairman in Memphis, said that because of reduced draft quotas, probably it would be another year before Elvis got his call. But it was only two months later, on December 20, when the government's greetings were delivered in person, by Bowers, to Elvis at Graceland, where he had returned for the Christmas holidays.

Rumors had been circulating despite the October announcement, so much so that earlier in the week Army and Navy

recruiters visited Elvis to offer him special enlistment oppor-
tunities. The idea was that if he enlisted instead of waiting
for the draft, he could pick the branch and probably the specific job he was to have the next two years. The Navy, through
Chief Petty Officer D. U. Stanley, even went so far as to say
the Navy would form an "Elvis Presley Company" with boys
from Memphis if Elvis would sign Navy enlistment papers.
Elvis thanked everybody and said he'd take his chances.

After all this—every bit of it covered in depth by the press
—it was almost anticlimactic when the notice finally arrived,
ordering him to report to the Memphis draft board office
January 20, 1958. Most of the controversy had come a year
earlier, when veterans, fans and senators alike all reacted
so noisily to the no-haircut rumor. Now not even Elvis was
ruffled. He was going to miss his mother and father, he told
newsmen, but "I'm kind-a proud of it. It's a duty I've got to
fill and I'm gonna do it."

Elvis then added, "My induction notice says for me to
leave my car at home. Transportation will be provided. They
tell me just to bring a razor, toothbrush, toothpaste, a comb
and enough money to hold me two weeks."

So saying, Elvis climbed into a surplus set of Army fatigues
a photographer had brought along, supervised the unloading
of an $1800 Isetta sports car he'd ordered and gave it to the
Colonel, and then began taking telephone calls from Martha
Raye and Milton Berle and others he'd met in Hollywood.

If Elvis was treating everything matter-of-factly, Paramount Pictures and Hall Wallis in Hollywood were not. Elvis
had been scheduled to report for his next film the same week
the Army wanted him, and between $300,000 and $350,000
already had been committed to the project, all of which would
be lost, they said, if Elvis went into the Army before March.
In making this announcement, studio production chief Frank
Freeman said he had sent a letter to Elvis's draft board asking an eight-week delay.

That was December 21. The letter arrived two days later,

and the draft board bumped it back, saying such a request would have to come from Elvis not Paramount. So on the day before Christmas, Elvis wrote his letter. He said he hoped they understood that he was acting not in his own interest but in behalf of the studio; Paramount had helped him at the start of his career, he said, and now he felt it only fair to go along with the studio's request, "so these folks will not lose so much money, with everything they have done so far." Elvis closed his note with a Merry Christmas wish to the board.

The three members held a special meeting December 27 and voted unanimously to grant Elvis a sixty-day deferment, meaning induction would be delayed from January 20 to March 20. Elvis said he was grateful—"for the studio's sake"—and the Colonel described the deferment as "very kind."

Of course there were others who felt differently. In the last days of 1957 Milton Bowers and his two compadres on the board were among the most unpopular men in all America; for a while there, in fact, it seemed no one liked them. First there were Elvis's fans, who began writing letters and calling to complain about Elvis being drafted at all. And then there were those who didn't like Elvis much to start with, calling to complain about giving the no-good greasy-haired hip-wig-glin' singer a deferment. It was the Christmas season, a time of peace on earth and good will toward men, but not at the Bowers house.

Bowers was one of the city's civic leaders, a former Democratic state legislator and onetime president of the Memphis School Board, as well as the head of a family-owned welding shop and metalworks. He said he had expected some criticism for his board's actions—after all, what draft board *isn't* disliked by an individual or two occasionally?—but nothing like what he got. Sometimes the calls were humorous, as when one fan called to shout, "You didn't put Beethoven in the Army, did you?" Bowers calmly told the caller that Beethoven wasn't American and wouldn't have been eligible if he had been, because he was deaf—and dead. More often there was real hatred in the letters and calls. They wished Bowers all the bad luck in the world, said they were hoping for illness and death in his family; some even threatened to come down to Memphis and kill the whole damned board.

At the same time there were others charging Bowers with giving Elvis preferential treatment because he was a celebrity. Up in Harlan, Kentucky, a state representative, Nick Johnson, resigned from his draft board, saying, "I cannot conscientiously ask any mountain boy to serve the same country unless afforded the same treatment as Presley." Once the lines had been drawn, Veterans of Foreign Wars and American Legionnaires all over the country began making their pro-Army, anti-deferment voices heard. Some even carried their complaints to Lewis Hershey, the director of the Selective Service System in Washington.

"I'm fed to the teeth," said Bowers as 1958 began. "I eat, sleep and drink Elvis Presley. In fact, I talk Elvis Presley more than I sleep. With all due respect to Elvis, who's a nice boy, we've drafted people who are far, far more important than he is. After all, when you take him out of the entertainment business, what have you got left? A truckdriver."

A comment that caused cheers from one side, boos and hisses from the other. And the controversy staggered on.

Elvis' Christmas Album had been released in mid-November, along with a Christmas EP, and both soon appeared at the top of all the popularity charts. The selection of songs was reasonably broad, including Gene Autry's "Here Comes Santa Claus," Irving Berlin's "White Christmas," a number of sacred songs that had appeared earlier on the *Peace in the Valley* EP, a couple of songs by writers Elvis had used previously ("Santa Claus Is Back in Town" by Jerry Leiber and Mike Stoller, "Santa Brings My Baby Back to Me" by Aaron Schroeder and Claude Demetrius), and some carols. It was the carols "O Little Town of Bethlehem" and "Silent Night" that caused the second peculiar controversy of Elvis's holidays.

In Los Angeles disc jockey Dick Wittinghill of KMPC said he had been getting requests to play songs from the album, but he refused, saying, "That's like having Tempest Storm give Christmas gifts to my kids." And when Al Priddy of KEX in Portland, Oregon, did play one cut, he was fired. According to station management, the album was in "extremely bad taste." The album was similarly banned at almost all Canadian stations—even after a jockey in Kingston, Ontario, Allen Brooks of CKWS, started playing the album and asking listeners to call in their opinion, and 93 per cent (including several who identified themselves as clergymen) heartily endorsed it.

Then during Christmas week Victor released another single, still another song by Leiber and Stoller, "Don't." Once again advance orders exceeded a million.

Elvis returned to Hollywood in January to begin work on *King Creole*, taking almost a dozen people with him, including his new "employee" Alan Fortas.

"I went to work for him and we left within two days," Alan says. "We took a train. Myself, Gene Smith, Cliff Gleaves, Freddie Bienstock, Tom Diskin, a few others. It was exciting, very exciting. Every town we passed through, no matter what time of morning or night, the whole station was jam-packed. These people knew as soon as Elvis finished this movie, he was going in the Army, so most of them considered it the last time to see him. As soon as he got on the train here in Memphis, it hit the wire, it got in the papers and on radio. People knew and they were lined up along the tracks all the way across America."

Elvis's fourth film was based loosely on the Harold Robbins novel *A Stone for Danny Fisher*. In the book the hero was a prize fighter, in the film a singer. The story also was moved from New York to New Orleans, where Elvis worked as a busboy in the King Creole, a honky-tonk on Bourbon Street.

It was in this club that he met a prostitute (Carolyn Jones) and three bush league hoodlums (Walter Matthau, Vic Morrow and Brian Hutton), who swept Elvis into their miserable little underworld, eventually to plan a robbery of a store owned by Elvis's father. With the help of a demure, virginal dime-store clerk (Dolores Hart), Elvis extracts himself, is reunited with his father, and sings eleven songs, enough to fill out another album. *King Creole* was at that time, and remains today, Elvis's favorite film. Thanks in large part to the director, Michael Curtiz, and flashes of brilliance by Miss Jones and a few others, it also is Elvis's best.

It was Hal Wallis's second film with Elvis and the first to utilize location shooting. Once Elvis had completed recording sessions and all the studio work in Hollywood, he and his gang—augmented by some of the cast and crew, producer Aaron Spelling (then Carolyn Jones's husband) and Nick Adams—took another train cross country. Alan Fortas says that once again the tracks were lined with fans. As, of course, were the streets of New Orleans.

"We left the French Quarter one day and there were so many people they almost turned the taxicab over," Alan says. "There were thousands of people. Hal Wallis couldn't believe it. The Colonel told him before we went down there, 'You're gonna need a whole lot of security.' And Hal Wallis said, 'Oh no, we can handle it. I had Dean Martin and Jerry Lewis at their peak and nobody ever bothered them.' The Colonel said, 'Okay, but you never had Elvis Presley. You watch!' I got news for you," says Alan, "I never saw so many people in my life. They declared it Elvis Presley Day and let the kids out of school and it took us two hours to get back to the hotel no matter where we were, even from across the street."

As when Elvis stayed in Hollywood, he had taken an entire floor of a hotel—the Roosevelt, situated half a block from the French Quarter—and elevators were not permitted to stop at that level. "Once we got to the hotel, security was good," Alan says. "One time after we finished filming we got on the elevator and we said, 'Tenth floor, please.' The elevator operator said, 'No, sir, I can't stop on the tenth floor. Mr. Presley is up there and we just can't stop.' Elvis was on the elevator with us and he said, 'Yeah, I know. I'm Elvis.' The elevator operator looked straight at him and said, 'I'm sorry, sir, I can't stop on that floor for anybody.' We had to go to the eleventh floor and walk down."

Then when the film company moved to Lake Pontchartrain for a scene in a house on stilts over the water, the crowd on the adjoining beach got so huge and unruly, Elvis was forced to exit through a rear door in the structure, board a motorboat and travel several miles down the lake to a waiting car.

Elvis returned to Hollywood at the end of February.

"Here we were, only four hundred miles from Memphis," says Alan. "But we had to go back to California to get a release. They had to run the picture, make sure there was nothing they had to do over again, because once they give you a release they can't call you back. So we went back to Hollywood by train, Elvis got his release and we got back on the train to come to Memphis. Now this was our fourth train ride in a month and it was getting pretty boring. All you can do is sleep and eat and after a while you get tired of sleeping and eating. We were young and we didn't drink. We'd just sit and talk, try to write songs, try to sing. You know, just typical ol' boys. But it got to us by the time we got to Dallas. We couldn't take it any longer. So we got off that train and rented some Cadillacs and drove the rest of the way home."

-8-

THE ARMY

ON THE COLD, RAINY MONDAY MORNING of March 24 Elvis arrived at Local Board 86. It was 6:35 A.M., and although he was nearly half an hour early, already dozens of newsmen and photographers were there. He looked a little sleepy-eyed from an all-night open house at Graceland but was filled with cheerful wisecracks. He was accompanied by his parents and Judy Spreckels, the blond former wife of a sugar millionaire, who said she was not a girl friend but "like a sister," and Lamar Fike, who tried to enlist but was rejected because his 270 pounds were considered more than the Army could handle in a single recruit. The Colonel was there too, of course, handing out balloons that advertised Elvis's upcoming film, *King Creole*. And although several Army spokesmen kept saying Elvis's induction was "routine," it was clearly anything but. Elvis Presley in the Army? The contrast was so right for press exploitation that much of what followed was to be covered in detail normally reserved for coronations and medical journals.

Elvis and his fellow recruits boarded a bus for Kennedy Hospital, where blood tests, mental examinations, the signing of loyalty oaths and the like took much of the rest of the day. Photographers trailed along, popping flash bulbs every time he stepped before another examining officer. Then Elvis was sworn in, designated US53310761, and at five o'clock boarded a chartered Greyhound bus for Fort Chaffee, Arkansas.

The bus crossed the Mississippi River and stopped in West Memphis, Arkansas, at the Coffee Cup, a small restaurant where the Army had hoped to feed its small band of new privates. They hadn't counted on the dozens of fans who soon arrived, and as Elvis began working his way through a plate of spaghetti, they stormed the cafe. In the rush to get back to the bus, Elvis lost a fountain pen, had his clothing torn, and behind him waitresses were arguing over who'd keep the chair he'd used.

Said Tennessee's Governor Frank Clement in a telegram to the recruit: "You have shown that you are an American citizen first, a Tennessee volunteer, and a young man willing to serve his country when called upon to do so."

Much thought, and newspaper space, had been given to Elvis's entrance into the service and what it meant to his career.

On one side were those who said it was the end of his reign as pop music king. They said that not only would he take a rather noticeable cut in pay—from over $100,000 to $78 a month—he also would be unable to defend his position against other singers who were not so rigidly restricted. He would be unable to make any movies and it was unlikely he could do any concerts. And when dealing in the vagaries of popular culture, two years is a long, long time. Elvis was dead, the critics and skeptics said. All that was missing was a proper funeral.

Not so, said the Colonel. Certainly Elvis wasn't going to miss any payments on anything he was buying, and if he wanted to buy something new during his two-year hitch, the loss of income wasn't going to be so great he'd notice it. There was that thousand dollars a week coming in from RCA. Paramount owed him 50 per cent of all profits from *King Creole,* as yet unreleased, and it was regarded as a sure thing that that film would make millions, it being the only way Elvis was going to be seen until 1960. And not only were there several songs already recorded and ready for release as singles, but it was believed several more could be cut if necessary. Army regulations regarding off-duty activities by military personnel were broad enough to make it fairly easy for Elvis to churn out more product.

One rule said GIs could engage in private activities while on pass only if those activities were essential to the national welfare—an arguable point when discussing the necessity of making rock 'n' roll records—but others said off-duty pursuits of any sort were acceptable, so long as the uniform wasn't degraded and the soldier wasn't depriving the local talent where he was stationed of work. Said the Army, not wishing to step on any toes, whether they were clad in blue suedes or combat boots: "Each case of this sort is handled separately. Each case is different."

Besides, the lipstick and T-shirts and other novelties continued to sell, and now that Elvis was in the Army, that only increased the already broad range of product possibilities. When a group called the Three Teens released a song called "Dear 53310761" and Trinity Music, the publisher, made up fifty thousand Elvis Presley dog tags as giveaways to disc jockeys, for instance, the Colonel immediately claimed proprietary rights, licensed someone to merchandise the tags and took a juicy royalty. They were available in gold or silver plate, were stamped with Elvis's name, rank and serial number, along with his blood type (O), a facsimile signature and an etched-out picture. They cost one dollar.

By now there were several new novelty songs about Elvis: "Bye Bye, Elvis" by Gennie Harris ("I know I'll cry the day you go / My friends and I will miss you so"), "All American Boy" by Bill Parsons ("And then one day my Uncle Sam / Said —thump thump—here Ah am"), "Marchin' Elvis" by the Greats, and "I'll Wait Forever" sung by Elvis's latest sweetie-pie, Anita Wood (on the Sun label, of all places). The Colonel couldn't claim a penny of royalties from these records—Elvis was, after all, a public figure and therefore open to public comment—but the records did help strengthen the Elvis market.

The new Elvis "image" was being accepted. Adults began to accept him because he was going to get his hair cut, start dressing like a human being (in uniform), said he was going to serve like any other boy, and stopped shaking publicly. The kids were taking the soppy farewell equally well; it wasn't all that unpopular to be in the Army in 1958, remember.

As for that massive drop in income—which some said would cost the United States $400,000 in taxes alone—the Colonel said, "I consider it my patriotic duty to keep Elvis in the ninety per cent tax bracket." The Colonel's first order of business, of course, was to coordinate all the hooplah that was to accompany Elvis's reception and indoctrination at Fort Chaffee.

Private Presley was dressed and making his bed by the time a sergeant flipped on the lights in the barracks to wake the men at five-thirty the morning of March 25, Elvis's first full day in the Army. He and his fellow recruits had arrived at Chaffee late the night before and it meant he had had little sleep. (He'd also been greeted by a crowd of at least three hundred girls when the bus drove past the camp entrance.) He then marched to the mess hall for breakfast, where he was met by Colonel Parker, who seemed to be using his honorary title to pull rank on Captain Arlie Metheny, the post public information officer.

"Let the boys take all the pictures they want," the Colonel said, pointing to no less than fifty-five reporters and photographers, exceeding by five the number of recruits being fed. And before the Captain could react, the boys moved in, preserving on film Elvis's every forkful of egg and sausage, every chew of toast and every swallow of coffee. Finally one of the reporters asked the Colonel what he was doing there and he said he was hanging around to "look after the boy . . . see that he gets everything he needs." Captain Metheny stood by, perhaps remembering with some peculiar sense of nostalgia one of his earlier assignments—handling the press when troops were brought into Little Rock during the crisis over integration.

Following breakfast Elvis and the other inductees were marched off for five hours of aptitude testing, the results to be used in determining what assignment they'd be given once past basic training, also whether or not they were eligible to take another test for Officers Candidate School. (Next day Elvis said he didn't take the officers' examination, indicating he hadn't scored high enough in the preliminary tests to qualify. "I never was good at arithmetic," he said.) As Elvis passed a barracks on the way to take these tests, several soldiers standing on the steps greeted him with catcalls.

At lunch it was the same thing all over again. The reporters and photographers swarmed around Elvis so much, Captain Metheny resumed command and ordered a five-minute reprieve so Elvis and the others could eat in peace.

One of the recruits sitting next to Elvis, Benny St. Clair of Texarkana, Arkansas, looked at Elvis and said, "Is it always like this?"

"Yep," said Elvis, stuffing his mouth with mashed potatoes.

"Doesn't it bother you?" the private asked.

"No," said Elvis. "I figure I better start worrying when they don't bother me any more."

The Colonel stood to one side beaming.

Next the rookies and newsmen trooped over to a post theater, where the chaplain welcomed Elvis and his buddies to their new home. And from there it was right into the main event—the haircut that had been making headlines for so long.

As it happened, Elvis had had his hair trimmed twice before this, removing an inch of sideburns in Hollywood for *King Creole* and some from the top and sides during his final week as a civilian in Memphis. It's not likely he expected it was enough, but if he did, he was mistaken.

Elvis sat down in the chair and barber James Peterson of Gans, Oklahoma—himself a lean, smiling crew-cutter—threw a towel around Elvis's neck. He plugged in his electric clippers and taking careful aim, holding for the photographers momentarily, neatly peeled one sideburn off with one swipe. Then he took the other. He threw the sideburns into the air, went up the back of Elvis's head with the clippers and then started leveling the top.

Elvis caught some of the falling hair in one palm and blew it toward the cameras. "Hair today, gone tomorrow," he said, grinning a little woodenly.

Elvis paid sixty-five cents—the Army's going rate for a clipping—and walked away as the barber shook the smock and let the hair mix on the floor with that of the other recruits. The Colonel explained how much that hair was worth and how many thousands of letters they'd received from fans wanting a little of it. And then Elvis went into a telephone booth to call his parents. He hadn't talked with them yet that day.

One more meal and his first day was done. Elvis returned to his barracks and the press returned to nearby motels.

Wednesday, the second day, began with the issue of seventy-five pounds of uniforms and other gear. It was the usual noisy, crowded affair, with recruits stepping gingerly over a carpet of flash bulbs and around the post commander, a brigadier general who said he wouldn't have missed it for anything.

Elvis was given a shiny new pair of size twelve combat boots. (He was then wearing some low-cut motorcycle boots, along with the same plaid jacket and dark pants he'd worn the past two days.) He said thank you, sir. Then he was given his fatigues. Again he said thank you, sir. Before he was through, he had sirred one private first class, one corporal and one sergeant.

The Colonel stood there, still beaming, and tried to sneak a Southern string tie into the pile of clothing in Elvis's arms.

That afternoon a press conference was called, during which the General announced to the anxious world that Elvis would be going to Fort Hood in Texas for basic combat training with the Second Armored Division.

Elvis had been vaccinated against tetanus, typhoid and Asian flu only minutes before the announcement and was rushed from the infirmary to the hall where all the newsmen were. Asked what he thought of the assignment, he said he was happy about it.

"You name it, I been all over Texas," he said. "I got my start in music around Houston."

He was asked next about his barracks buddies. "They've been swell to me," he said. "The only GIs I've seen are the ones in the barracks. They treat me like anyone else, though. They consider themselves for what they are—just GIs—the same as me. That's the way I want it."

Apparently running out of inspiration, the reporters then expressed interest in what Elvis was going to do for girls in Texas. Elvis patiently told them, "I suppose it's the natural thing when a fella goes to a strange place to try to find a girl friend."

The press conference limped along in this way for a while and then the General stepped forward to make his contribution: "I feel the Army has shown that it is trying to make an ordinary soldier out of Mr. Presley, the same as all the other fine young men who are with us, and that he has been afforded no special privileges. I believe Presley should make a tremendous success in his Army operation. At least in my opinion, he has conducted himself in a marvelous manner."

After that the press was cleared out. Enough was enough,

Captain Metheny said. After all, the boy did have to have some time to acclimate himself to his new environment. And so the fifty-five reporters and photographers scattered, moving through the camp slowly, interviewing anybody and everybody who had anything to say about Elvis. Damned near every one of them said something nice. One even called him "wholesome."

And then on Friday, March 28, Elvis and eighteen other buck privates boarded a bus at dawn for the 425-mile trip to the middle of Texas. No, the Army was sorry. It couldn't release the names of towns and restaurants where the bus would stop. Security, you know. Security against the "enemy"—teenagers.

The public information officer at Fort Hood was a woman, Lieutenant Colonel Marjorie Schulten, and she, along with several other high-ranking officers at the post, had received mysterious calls from the Commanding General, who said only that "I have information that would be of interest to you." They hurried to his office and were told Elvis was on the way.

The WAC officer didn't quite know what to say and in the hours that followed she met first with her fellow officers and then with Colonel Parker. Newspaper writers and photographers, television cameramen, magazine writers, editors from New York—the press was as thick as the dust in the area. She called a brief press conference the afternoon of Elvis's arrival.

"He has a mission and we have a mission," she said, standing on a table. "We expect to perform them mutually. Hereafter there will be no more interviews or picture taking during his training."

Elvis arrived at 4:34 P.M. (newsmen still were chronicling the operation minute by minute) and was assigned to A Company, Second Medium Tank Battalion, Second Armored Division. Reporters were thanked for their attention and concern and gently told to leave; it was now time to make a soldier of this rock 'n' roll star.

This didn't make Marjorie Schulten's job simple, however. Even if no interviews were granted, still there were the mail and the telephone calls. Elvis received two thousand fan letters at Fort Hood the first week and no one ever tabulated the hundreds of calls. Each, the WAC colonel said, deserved a personal response.

Then, of course, when it became apparent the lady wasn't kidding about interviews, the press wanted to interview her. That's right, she said patiently, Elvis is a prompt riser. Yes indeed, he was standing up well under the strain. Why just the other day Elvis's drill instructor, Sergeant William Fraley, *and* his superior, Master Sergeant Henry Coley, *both* said they were impressed.

In actual fact Elvis *was* behaving himself; he *was* being an exemplary recruit. Much of Army training is based on a philosophy of competitive gung-hoism, whereby trainee is pitted against trainee, company against company, battalion against battalion, in a constant quest for medals, ribbons, citations and grades. This was a philosophy that appealed to Elvis anyway, and recognizing his vulnerability, knowing there were millions of adults waiting for his first show of impatience, Elvis probably tried harder than the others.

Removal of the press was a help certainly, but that represented only slight relief. Still Elvis had to contend with his fans, who swarmed over the post on weekends, hoping for a glimpse of their hero. And he had to live with his fellow soldiers, who rode him good-naturedly but endlessly. If he wasn't ducking back into a barracks to escape being seen by girls zipping up the company street in convertibles, he was forcing grins at comments like "Maybe you'd like some rock 'n' roll instead of reveille" and "Miss your teddy bears?" and "By the right wiggle—march!"

Elvis went through the standard indoctrination program —orientation to Army life, history of the service, military courtesy and justice—and then into basic instruction in equipment maintenance and small arms. In most courses he was as adept as any in his class, and when he failed to qualify on the pistol range, he signed up for additional instruction, given during his off-duty time.

Outside, back in the civilian world, many who'd once criticized Elvis were now lining up to offer praise. In Florida, for example, the state that once had banned his wiggle, Congressman A. S. Herlong asked Elvis to appear at a celebration sponsored by the De Leon Springs Chamber of Commerce.

This invitation came in the middle of April, as Elvis entered his third week of boot camp, and it was quickly rejected, not by Elvis or the Colonel but by the Army. "Private Presley is currently undergoing his initial cycle of training," the Army said. "It is contrary to Department of the Army policy to interrupt this important phase of his training except for compassionate or emergency reasons."

It also was becoming apparent by now that Elvis wasn't going to appear anywhere for the Army either. Sometime earlier, of course, there had been talk of Elvis's going into the Army's Special Services branch to sing his way through his tour of duty. The Army never made much of it publicly, but it was made abundantly clear that it would be flattered if Elvis marched to the same drummer heard by Eddie Fisher and Vic Damone when they served. They had been inducted during the Korean conflict and entertained the fighting troops. Damone even took on a special assignment to help recruit women for military service, recording a song called "The Girls Are Marching." It was thought by the Army brass that Elvis should serve in the same way—appearing in television commercials to boost enlistment, entertaining at military installations, selling a few bonds. At one point, much earlier, the Colonel even indicated some of this activity might be acceptable. But then he slammed the door.

The Colonel has never talked much about why he finally

said no to the Special Services. About all he's said publicly is that Elvis didn't want any special treatment, didn't want to take "the easy way out." Undoubtedly this was true. But the Colonel also knew this path served his own purposes, that if Elvis carried a rifle or drove a tank or marched for two years, rather than sang, the adult acceptance he was picking up would multiply vastly. It was, to put it simply, good for Elvis's image if he didn't sing.

"You can't imagine how much trouble the Colonel's decision caused," says someone then close to Elvis and who, because of a continuing association, asks to remain nameless. "It's never been printed, but the Colonel was fighting with the Army constantly. Even after Elvis had completed his advanced training and had been on the job driving a jeep in Germany, the brass kept after him, wanting him to do this, do that. One General in Germany wanted Elvis to sing at his daughter's birthday party and when Elvis said he didn't think he was allowed to do that, the General would have to talk with the Colonel, the General practically made it an order. The Colonel finally said Elvis would sing, but the General would have to invite every man in Elvis's unit to the party too. That ended that, but it wasn't easy on Elvis."

At the end of his eight weeks in boot camp the Army announced Elvis would be granted the usual two-week leave, then report back to Hood for another fourteen weeks of training, eight in advanced individual training as an armor crewman and six of unit training. It was also announced that in September he and 1400 other soldiers would be sent as replacements to the Third Armored Division in Germany.

Elvis may not have been on public display during this period, but it didn't mean his popularity was diminishing. If anything, the attention only increased.

Elvis wasn't in the Army a week when the *Phil Silvers*

Show offered a half-hour burlesque called "Rock and Roll Rookie," in which a look-alike actor named Tom Gilson played a guitar-picking sideburned draftee named Elvin Pelvin who owned eleven Cadillacs and a hound dog, while Silver, as Sergeant Bilko, sang "You're Nothing but a Raccoon" and "Brown Suede Combat Boots." As was noted in *Billboard:* "Gilson played it straight and with sympathy, thereby safeguarding the sponsor from the easily aroused wrath of you-know-who's fans."

(In New York, meanwhile, composers Lee Adams and Charles Strouse and writer Michael Stewart began writing *Bye Bye Birdie,* a Broadway musical whose story revolved around the induction of a rock 'n' roll singer named Conrad Birdie and the effect this had on Birdie's manager. It opened in 1960, shortly after Elvis's discharge, and ran for almost two years.)

The same week RCA released two more records—*Elvis' Golden Records,* what was to be the first in a series of his greatest hit albums, and his twenty-second single, "Wear My Ring Around Your Neck" backed by "Doncha' Think It's Time." By now the Colonel had made the fan clubs a highly profitable enterprise, and both songs were instant hits, with advance sales for each again topping the million mark.

And then in late May *King Creole* opened, just in time for Elvis to get back to Memphis on the leave that followed basic training and attend a preview with his parents.

His mother was not well, but in every other way it was a joyous homecoming. His girl friend, Anita Wood, who had visited him briefly in Texas, was there to join him in late-night roller-skating parties when Elvis again rented the Rainbow Rollerdrome, or to sit at home with him and watch television and talk. A couple of weeks later it would be reported that Elvis and Anita were engaged; both denied it, although Elvis had given her a diamond ring surrounded by eighteen sapphires. His fans continued to flock to the

Graceland gates, something Elvis always regarded as a little odd but assuring. And wonder of wonders, the critics greeted *King Creole* not with the sneers usually reserved for Elvis on screen but praise.

The *Hollywood Reporter*'s critic Jim Powers said the film made "extraordinary use of locations," called it exciting, said it dramatized juvenile delinquency rather than glorified or exploited it, and then said Elvis showed real promise. *Billboard* said it was Elvis's "best acting performance to date," taking special note of the scenes between Elvis and Carolyn Jones. Howard Thompson in the New York *Times* opened with this: "As the lad himself might say, cut my legs off and call me Shorty! Elvis Presley can act." And closed with "Acting is his assignment in this shrewdly upholstered showcase, and he does it."

Elvis was ecstatic. Friends say the reviews, especially that in the *Times,* made Elvis happier than they'd ever seen him before.

So it was in good spirits that he and some of his old buddies drove to Nashville on June 10 to record a few new songs. They returned to Memphis on the thirteenth to rent the Rainbow again and invite about thirty friends, Anita Wood among them, to join him in a farewell whirl. And then on Saturday he got into a red Lincoln convertible he had bought to celebrate and leisurely returned to Fort Hood.

Vernon and Gladys Presley followed less than a week later. Elvis, or perhaps the Colonel, had studied Army Regulations during the first eight weeks and it was determined Elvis could sleep off post if he had dependents living in the same area. Usually the word "dependent" covered wives and children, but in that Elvis's parents were dependent upon him for food, shelter and spending money, they qualified in the strict reading of the rule. So Elvis rented a three-bedroom trailer and then traded that for a three-bedroom house in the nearest town to the post, Killeen. The house was to remain in the custody of the Presley family for just two months, until the owners, an attorney and his wife, returned from their vacation. By which time, of course, Elvis was to be nearly finished with his advanced training and packing for Germany.

"Vernon and Gladys drove down last Wednesday in the black limousine," said Travis Smith, Elvis's uncle and gate-keeper at Graceland. "They said they'll stay with him as long as he's there. They just couldn't stand being away from him."

Travis also said the Presley family was talking about fol-lowing Elvis when he went to Germany too.

Some time later Elvis explained to a friend his real rea-son for moving off post. "Without taking anything away from Elvis's love of his parents," the friend says today, "it was essential that he should have a 'retreat' because, you understand, while he took all the guff that is Army issue, and knocked himself out to be just one of the guys, he was denied the one inalienable right that soldiers hold most dear —the right to bitch. Had he at any time complained about anything or anyone, some s.o.b. would have passed on the comments, and they would have been reported unfavorably by some angle-hunting reporter. So he just took whatever was handed out, and kept his mouth shut—at least until he was at home with his family."

July was ordinary. A twenty-four-year-old secretary in Washington sued Elvis for $5000, claiming she had suffered whiplash injuries while riding in a car that was struck from behind by one of Elvis's automobiles—in 1956! "Hard Headed Woman," a song from *King Creole,* replaced a novelty tune called "Purple People Eater" at the top of the charts. Elvis was clocked at ninety-five miles an hour in a sixty-mile zone in Fort Worth, trying to elude pursuing fans, and was given a ticket. Then he began advanced unit train-ing, his final classes before shipping out.

August was something else. That was when Elvis's world collapsed like a sand castle into the boiling sea.

His mother had not been well. It had been difficult for her to walk and to concentrate and to carry on a normal life. She had lost most of her enthusiasm and sprightliness. Elvis and his father decided she was too ill to remain in Killeen; she should return to Memphis and the family doctor. Which she did, with Elvis driving her to the train on Friday, August 8.

In Memphis doctors said she had hepatitis and she was given a private room at Methodist Hospital, one of the city's newest and most modern facilities. Hepatitis is an infection of the liver, one of the vital organs. In three days the doctors placed a call to Elvis in Texas. They said he should come home as quickly as possible.

Elvis obtained an emergency leave and went against his mother's wishes and boarded an airplane. He arrived in Memphis Tuesday night and went right to her bedside. The doctors said his presence improved her spirits tremendously but didn't much affect the odds. Her condition remained "serious."

All through the night Tuesday and all day Wednesday and Wednesday evening, Elvis and his father took turns sitting at the bedside. Sometimes Elvis sat with his pals, Alan Fortas, Lamar Fike, George Klein, his cousins. At three in the morning Thursday, Vernon was in the hospital room and Elvis was asleep at Graceland. Vernon said his wife began "suffering for breath." And then she died. Vernon called Elvis and told him what had happened.

The doctors later announced that Mrs. Presley had died of a heart attack.

A close friend of the Presley family's explains what happened. "Mrs. Presley loved white beans, corn bread and buttermilk," he says. "She was a half-a-dozen-eggs-and-a-stick-of-butter woman. She never got used to having money. Even when she was in Graceland, she bought twenty-five-cent bottles of shampoo and the smallest tubes of toothpaste available. That's not criticism. That's just the way she was, even when Elvis bought her Cadillacs.

"She tried very hard," says the family friend. "She really did. She wanted to be what she thought Elvis wanted her to be. She wanted to look good for Elvis, to be thin and attractive. But she was not supposed to be thin, and she stayed heavy, began to put on more weight. So she began to take pills. Diet pills. I guess they became a habit with her. And then she switched to alcohol.

"It was sad. Sometimes she couldn't even see across the room. She didn't even recognize me once, couldn't even see I was standing in the same room with her.

"All she wanted was to make Elvis proud. She just wanted him to be proud of her. And of course he *was* proud of her. But she kept on taking those pills, and drinking . . . and finally her big ol' heart gave out."

She was forty-six.

Funeral plans were made quickly. Vernon called James Blackwood to ask if the Blackwood Brothers would sing at the service, and when James said they were contracted to appear in North Carolina that evening, the Presleys chartered a plane to fly the gospel quartet back and forth. The Blackwoods had been one of Mrs. Presley's favorite spiritual groups, as well as the group Elvis once hoped to join, and it was important to have them present.

The service was held for four hundred invited guests. The Reverend James Hamill delivered the eulogy. The Blackwoods sang "Rock of Ages" and Mrs. Presley's favorite, "Precious Memories." Elvis stood next to his father crying. Outside in the Memphis street were three thousand fans, standing in prayerful silence.

From the funeral home the procession moved slowly to Forest Hill Cemetery, on Highway 51 south of Memphis in low rolling countryside three miles toward the city from Graceland. There wasn't much to distinguish Forest Hill from most other cemeteries, except it seemed somewhat better tended than many. Mrs. Presley was buried on a hillside several hundred yards back from the highway, near one of the asphalt roadways that wound through the property. Most of the markers were then, and are now, modest rectangular stones common to all cemeteries, but her monument was just that—an impressive ten-foot monument, with a life-sized marble statue of Jesus Christ standing before a cross, arms outstretched, two angels kneeling to the left and right at His feet. A standard-sized marker later would be placed about five feet in front of this, reading:

GLADYS SMITH PRESLEY
APRIL 25, 1912–AUG. 14, 1958
BELOVED WIFE OF
VERNON PRESLEY
AND MOTHER OF
ELVIS PRESLEY
SHE WAS THE SUNSHINE OF OUR HOME

There were sixty-five city policemen hired to handle the traffic and pedestrian problems at the service, as reporters, photographers and fans crushed forward, pushing rudely, taking in every sob and mumbled syllable.

"Oh, God," Elvis choked. "Oh, God, everything I have is gone . . ."

Elvis was given an extension on his emergency leave and remained in Memphis for another week.

On Sunday, August 24, he flew to Dallas, where he told newsmen who greeted him at Love Field that his father would be accompanying him to Germany. "One of the last things Mom said was that Dad and I should always be together," Elvis said. "I'll report back to Fort Hood in the morning. Wherever they send me, Dad will go too. Before I went home, I was scheduled to leave for Germany about the first of September. Mom and Dad and I often talked about going to Europe. I guess that's where we'll go now—the two of us." Friends then helped him load his luggage into a car and they drove off.

The remaining weeks at Fort Hood passed quickly as Elvis rapidly completed his training, and then he was shunted from line to line to line, from form to form to form, going through all that any soldier experiences in leaving any military post—return of equipment, final inspections, etc.—while preparing to go overseas. On September 19 he and his unit began the bumpy stop-and-go train ride to their port of embarkation, the Military Ocean Terminal in Brooklyn.

There was, however, a final damp hometown farewell—held when the train bearing Elvis and 340 other soldiers from Hood pulled into a switching yard in Memphis. There Elvis was greeted by about forty girls who had raced across town from Union Station when they learned the train would remain in the yards. He was permitted to speak to them and kiss a few goodbye. They were permitted to weep.

Then it was north and east, where Elvis was to be given still another farewell, this one from what seemed to be half the press of New York.

Elvis was an hour late in arriving and the newsmen began to get impatient. There were at least fifty photographers, moving back and forth and checking light meters. Reporters smoked cigarettes and looked at their watches and joked about coming all the way the hell out to Brooklyn for this. The Army was there in brassy attendance, flanked by Navy braid. The crew of the troopship *General Randal* was tending to final departure details. Colonel Parker was there, of course, along with Jean and Julian Aberbach and Freddie Bienstock from Hill and Range, and Steve Sholes heading up a large contingent from RCA. Among other reasons, RCA was there to record the press conference for eventual release as a commercial EP called *Elvis Sails*, a record that is still available and still selling. Adding even more confusion were the dozens who had not even the flimsiest reason for being present but came anyway, to get a glimpse of the celebrity who had caused all the no-interview rules to be ignored for the first time in the terminal's history.

Finally Elvis appeared, dressed in khakis and wearing a

garrison cap pulled down over but not hiding hair that had been bleached in the hot mid-Texas sun. He saw the photographers practically surrounding him and grinned, taking the nearest WAC in his arms. For five minutes there were cries of "One more, Elvis!" and "Grab the WAC again!" Then Irving Moss stepped forward to break it up. He represented the terminal command and said, "All right, give him a chance. If everybody will sit down, maybe Elvis will sing a song."

It was an absurd suggestion—Elvis had neither plans nor inclination to play or sing and there was no guitar around anyway—but it worked. And so the questions began.

What was it he wanted to do most when he got to Europe?

"The first place I want to go when I get a pass is Paris," he said. "I'd like to look up Brigitte Bardot."

(A day later, in an attempt to keep this angle going, wire-service men in Paris tracked Miss Bardot to get her reaction —which was that she was quite content with the singer-musician she already had, Sacha Distel. Then, of course, Elvis was pressed for his reaction to *that,* and he said what the hell, it was just an offhand remark, or words to that effect.)

Did he think his following had diminished in size or loyalty since he entered the Army?

"No, I'd say my fan mail has doubled. I've been getting around fifteen thousand fan letters a week and it's been driving them crazy down at Fort Hood." And then he added, looking at the Colonel, "Now they're sending them to the Colonel for answering."

Someone suggested rock 'n' roll might die and what would Elvis do then?

"I'd probably starve to death," he said. "If it ever did happen, and I don't think it would, I'd make a serious try to keep on top in the movies. That would be my best chance."

Was it true he was taking his family to Europe with him?

"My father and grandmother are following me to Germany in a few weeks. They'll be living in a house near the post where I'll be stationed. I guess we'll get one of those small German cars. I still have three Cadillacs and a Lincoln, but they stay home."

And his mother? The press was sorry about her death, but would Elvis make some comment now, in that he hadn't said anything since the funeral?

"I was an only child," he said. "She was very close, more than a mother. She was a friend who would let me talk to her any hour of the day or night if I had a problem. I would get mad sometimes when she wouldn't let me do something. But I found out she was right about almost everything. She would always try to slow me up if I ever thought I wanted to get married. She was right. It helped my career not to be married."

And from that, right into a question about Jerry Lee Lewis, who recently had been drummed out of England when it was learned he had married his thirteen-year-old cousin.

"He's a great artist," Elvis said diplomatically. "I'd rather not talk about his marriage, except that if he really loves her, I guess it's all right."

What kind of girl did Elvis want?

"Female, sir."

And so it went. A typical Elvis Presley press conference. There wasn't much hard news to come from it, nor was there any continuity in the questioning, but Elvis, of course, looked good. So long as he wasn't singing, and shaking, there wasn't an adult who could get mad at him.

He told them no, the guys in his unit hadn't been rough on him, but they had given him some unprintable nicknames. He mentioned a few of his favorite songs—"I'll Never Walk Alone," a hymn, among them. He held up a book he said he had been reading, *Poems That Touch the Heart*, and called it "wonderful stuff."

It was, all in all, a hell of a performance. If Billy Graham had been there, even he might have changed his mind about letting his daughter meet the boy.

"All right, you people," Irving Moss broke in. "That's gonna have to do it. Private Presley has a schedule to keep."

Then, with the Army band doing its best to make "Hound Dog" and "All Shook Up" sound as if they'd been written by John Philipps Sousa, the press departed and Elvis and approximately 1300 soldiers slowly moved toward Bremerhaven, Germany, where the whole thing would begin again.

Elvis was no stranger in Germany. His records sold briskly to German youth. His signature was worth three marks on the teenage autograph market, a signed picture equal to ten of his nearest local competitor, nineteen-year-old Peter Kraus, who admitted he took his style from Elvis's movies. There was even a magazine—*Bravo,* today one of the world's largest youth publications—started because of his popularity.

"Our bomb shelter generation revolted against the stiff, straight old ways," said Werner Goetze, a German disc jockey who at first broke Elvis's records on the air, but changed his mind when overruled by his listeners. "They threw away their lederhosen for blue jeans and started standing and walking like cowboys. They were bored with 'O Tannenbaum' and skipped 'Ach du lieber Augustin' to hear rock 'n' roll. Elvis Presley was just what they were looking for—an American Pied Piper to lead them to excitement."

Of course, not all Germany was thrilled about Elvis's prospective visit. Some, in fact, made it sound as if he would be as welcome as other American soldiers who had arrived in 1945, when Americans crossed the Rhine River in World War Two. Goetze hadn't just broken Elvis's records—he had called him "the whiner," "yowling boy" and "the lovesick stag." And Ferdinand Anton, a respected German archeologist, went on the Armed Forces Radio Network and said Elvis was a throwback to the Stone Age.

In a special report in The New York *Times Magazine* five

months before Elvis's arrival, the paper's Berlin correspond-
ent, Harry Gilroy, wrote, "Undoubtedly the liveliest youth
movement in Berlin and surrounding central Germany—
even allowing for the Communist, Socialist and Christian
Young People's organizations—is rock 'n' roll. Here, just
as in the United States, it looks like a route of Dionysus."
Gilroy then described the maniacal demand for blue jeans
(about all Elvis actually wore in his first films, which were
what the Germans saw).

It was, as the walls soon would proclaim in paint splashed
there by his German fans, *Elvis über alles!*

There were five hundred screaming teenagers waiting at
the dock in Bremerhaven on October 1, and Elvis was
spotted coming down the gangplank, even though he, like all
the others, was dressed in Army fatigues and carried a heavy
duffel bag. But only a few photographers got close enough
to take a picture. The Army had positioned a troop train
near the ship's unloading area and Elvis was rushed from
one to the other without so much as a single teenage kiss.
The train then sped to Elvis's permanent station in the rolling hills outside Friedberg, a village of 18,000 not far from
Frankfurt, in the Hesse section of central Germany. At
Friedberg Elvis's fans again were disappointed, as the train
passed right through the station where they'd gathered to
a siding inside the gates of the Army post.

The press reception was, essentially, a rerun of earlier
meetings, the only difference being that now there was an
international press corps, with the same old questions coming in half a dozen accents. For three days newsmen and
anxious feature writers were given reasonably free reign
over the post and were told to get everything they wanted
or else figure on doing without, because once the "open
house" ended October 5, Elvis and the post would be off
limits to civilians.

The press also was told that Elvis would be serving the

next sixteen months as a "scout" jeep driver. Originally he was to have joined the crew of a medium Patton tank. Why the change? No, said the Army, it wasn't special privilege or favoritism.

"The assignment of scout jeep driver is given to soldiers of above normal capability," said the post information officer. "The soldier must be able to work on his own, map-read and draw sketches, know tactics and recognize the enemy and enemy weapons."

Jeeps, and jeep drivers, may seem unimportant next to tanks and tank crews, but that wasn't the case, the Army said. Tanks and tank crews relied on jeeps and jeep drivers, and the information those in the jeeps obtained. So Elvis had been given more responsibility, not less. That's what the Army said.

By then, of course, Elvis's father and grandmother arrived and Elvis spent his first pass (issued just four days after his arrival) with them in a luxurious hotel, the Ritter's Park, in Bad Homburg, a resort spa a few miles from Friedberg. Thereafter, he spent all of his off-duty nights in the hotel or in another in nearby Bad Nauheim, another spa, until he and his father completed their house hunting. Whereupon Elvis moved his uniforms and gear out of the Army barracks permanently.

Again favoritism was charged and again the Army insisted everything was as it should be, that Elvis was soldiering by the numbers. Elvis was being permitted to live off post under the military sponsoring act, regulations governing a soldier's living with dependents and relatives.

Initially it was rumored that Elvis and his father were shopping for a castle, or at least a medieval mansion that would be large enough to accommodate a staff of secretaries as well as an occasional buddy from Memphis. Even when they took what obviously *wasn't* a castle or mansion, the rumors and criticism continued.

"That 'palace' was just an ordinary middle-class German

house," a family friend says today. "A bit larger than many, being two-storied, but by our standards hardly better than his old Memphis home on Alabama. And it was in a bad state of repair, which, Elvis told me, he had to pay for. Although he was paying an exorbitant rent, the landlady claimed that all the damage, which was obviously the wear and tear of the years, was caused by him and his fans. To avoid any unpleasantness or embarrassment to himself or the U.S., he paid, as the landlady had known he would do. It was a sort of blackmail that celebrities must often know, I suppose."

The house, with four bedrooms, was at Goethestrasse 14, and according to Red West, who later joined Elvis in Germany, it cost the Presleys eight hundred dollars a month, four or five times what a German national would have paid

His second month in Germany, Elvis joined the 32nd Tank Battalion in Friedberg on a convoy to the maneuvers area at Grafenwöhr, not far from the border separating Germany from Communist Czechoslovakia. During the exercises which lasted a couple of weeks, Elvis was tested on the location and observation of "enemy" positions, was instructed in map reading, and practiced rifle marksmanship.

Perhaps it was only coincidence that as soon as he approached the Iron Curtain the Communists began an anti-Elvis campaign. And perhaps it was because Elvis was in West Germany that the force of the bitter editorial siege came from East Berlin. In mid-December the official Communist Party newspaper, *Neues Deutschland*, published a picture of Elvis with a sixteen-year-old German girl he dated a couple of times, called him a "Cold War Weapon" and said that "Puffed up like a peacock, Presley, hooting like a ship warning buoy, is an advertisement for NATO in the West Zone." Another East German paper, *Young World*, criticized Elvis's voice—saying he had none—and lurched into some of the stilted copy that characterizes the Communist press "Those persons plotting an atomic war are making a fuss about Presley because they know youths dumb enough to become Presley fans are dumb enough to fight in the war."

Joseph Fleming of United Press International tried to explain the attack: "It appears that youths in Eastern Europe are expressing their distaste of the existing order in the only way they can. All free political expression is barred to them. Their press and radio are censored. All organizations except the church are run by the Communists. They are regimented in school, at work and in sports. Their only outlet is to wear their hair too long, use too much makeup, dance too wildly, and adopt as a symbol an American singer they are told they should despise—Elvis Presley. The Communists know this is a form of resistance and it has them worried."

The Soviet youth newspaper *Komsomolskaya Pravda* was warning that extreme Western styles paved the way for capitalist beliefs: "Although we want peaceful co-existence with the capitalist West, this does not rule out an ideological battle. We must oppose Western style and morality as a part of this battle." This was echoed by the publication of the Moscow Young Communist League, *Moskovsky Komsomolets*, whose editors said that tight pants and bootleg jazz— a reference to the Elvis songs still being recorded on discarded X-ray plates—could be the first step toward degradation and crime.

If anyone demanded proof, the Communists had it. The leader of a juvenile gang arrested in Halle, East Germany, was described as having gone wrong after buying several Presley records and hanging a signed picture of Elvis in his living room. And police in Leipzig were arresting members of another gang who, they said, had fallen under the influence of "NATO ideology" and had committed anti-state acts; the name of the gang, the police said, was the Elvis Presley Hound Dogs.

Knowing—or suspecting—a good thing when they read about one, State Department officials in the U. S. again asked if Elvis wouldn't like to entertain the troops and perhaps do a little propaganda work. The Colonel again said no.

It seems that almost every celebrity "dies" at least once in his public lifetime, and in January Elvis got his. He had, according to rumors and newspaper accounts, been killed in an automoble accident, his sports car demolished. He wasn't dead, of course. Not even hurt. He was alive and well and with Master Sergeant Ira Jones, checking the back roads in the area.

Elvis spent a lot of his time in that jeep, driving his sergeant around. If a "balloon went up" suddenly—Army talk for something unusual happening—and the tanks of his battalion had to move out on short notice, they'd have to know even the smallest facts about the condition of the roads. If West Germany were invaded, the scout jeeps would be leading the way to the battle lines.

Elvis's day began early, usually at five or five-thirty, in order to be at the post on time. Lamar Fike, who joined him by spring, usually was given the job of warming up the BMW as Elvis bolted a meager breakfast prepared by the family cook. By seven he was in the company area, and he didn't go home until five—or much later if the unit was re-turning from the field. It was a long day and generally an uninspiring one. Mostly he chauffeured his platoon sergeant around; wherever his sergeant—Jones, a happy but reticent Missourian—went, Elvis went. And the rest of the week it was just a matter of keeping things clean and operational to pass the rigid Saturday inspections.

Only things like mail call made Elvis's day exceptional. For him it meant as many as ten thousand letters a week, some of them addressed "Airman First Class Elvis Presley" or "Colonel Presley" or "General Presley," while others reached him marked "Elvis, U.S. Army" on them, and nothing more. To handle some of this, Elvis had hired a couple of secretaries in town, but most mail was sent to the Colonel's office in Madison.

The Colonel wasn't asleep in his trophy room during this

period. All through his Army years, although he didn't cut a record or appear anywhere, Elvis remained a highly commercial property which the Colonel represented quite masterfully. Elvis had been in Europe only a month when the Colonel told the papers in Nashville that Elvis earned $2 million in 1958, despite his being in the Army almost all that time. And he said he figured 1959 would be even better.

One of the problems facing the Colonel was the annoying fact there was so little unreleased material around. There were those few songs he cut in Nashville when he was on leave from Fort Hood, and that was about it. So the records had to be issued sparingly.

The first was the *Elvis Sails* EP. It sold far more copies than most novelty items, but didn't do nearly so well as some of the other EPs then available. The two from *King Creole*, for example, remained high on the EP record sales charts through most of 1959, making the records best-sellers for a period of more than eighteen months.

It was February when RCA released another album, *For LP Fans Only*. This was an unusual album, because all ten cuts on it were at least a year old, some of them nearly five years old. The most recent was "Playing for Keeps," which had been the B side of "Too Much," a hit during the winter of 1957. The tracks that had been around longest were four of the ten that originally had been released by Sun.

By late February there were no Elvis songs in *Billboard*'s Hot 100—the first time this had happened in nearly three years. In March RCA issued "A Fool Such as I" and "I Need Your Love Tonight," two otherwise anonymous songs that (according to RCA) earned Elvis his nineteenth consecutive million-selling record, and went to the number two and four chart positions, respectively.

Besides presiding over release of these records and seeing to it that royalty checks were received promptly and the records were promoted properly, Colonel Parker also made periodic announcements, just to keep Elvis's name in the news.

Not a difficult task, after all; all newsmen wanted was the slightest excuse for a story and they'd write one.

In March the Colonel said he was planning a "blockbuster-type welcome home party" for Elvis, a party that would be beamed via closed-circuit telecast to large auditoriums in a hundred cities. Elvis wasn't to be discharged for a year, but the news guys went for it, quoting the Colonel as comparing the party/telecast to a championship prize fight, and explaining that it was the only way for Elvis to satisfy all the requests he'd received for personal appearances.

Then in May Tom Diskin called the Nashville papers to say Private Presley had been signed by ABC-TV for a series of annual spectaculars to start after his discharge. Diskin said the contract had been negotiated with the network's president, Oliver Treyz, and that Elvis would be paid at least $100,000 per show.

Neither of these schemes was ever mentioned again.

In June the last of the unreleased material was pressed. This was "A Big Hunk o' Love" backed by "My Wish Came True." Like almost all Elvis records that had preceded it, it sold more than a million copies and went to number one.

On the first of June Elvis was promoted to specialist fourth class, which meant he was now being paid $135.30 a month. He celebrated in an Army hospital in Frankfurt, where he was treated for inflamed tonsils and a throat infection. Discharged a week later, he went on a two-week furlough to Paris, taking his buddy Cliff Gleaves along and checking into the expensive Prince of Wales hotel. While there, he visited the Lido, where he was dragged out of the audience onto the stage.

"For the first time in fifteen months," he said a day later to anxious newsmen, "there I was in front of an audience. Then it flew all over me, boy—sudden fear."

Said a room service waiter at the Prince of Wales: "The young ladies—such delights—are going in and out of Monsieur Presley's suite, in and out, like a door revolving."

Said Elvis to Art Buchwald: "It [Paris] reminds me of the life I used to live before I went into the service."

In July it was Steve Sholes's turn to talk about Elvis's continuing popularity. Elvis hadn't been on television in two and a half years, hadn't been seen in concert in over eighteen months, but "despite this long hiatus . . . Presley continues to sell in undiminished quantities." A glance at the record charts silenced any doubters. "A Big Hunk o' Love" remained in the top ten. The *King Creole* and *Love Me Tender* albums and EPs were selling again, thanks to renewed interest caused by the rerelease of the films as a summer double feature. And during the first week of August RCA issued another of its repackaged albums, *A Date with Elvis.* It was, of course, precisely what every young girl wanted.

This album was the second to include songs from his early days at Sun, all previously unavailable on an album, but now more than five years old. Others were three songs from *Jailhouse Rock,* one from *Love Me Tender,* and one previously unreleased country ballad. It was as if RCA had hit the bottom of the barrel. Not that the material wasn't good. It *was* good. It also was the end of it.

To make the package more appealing, several Elvis "extras" were added. The album sleeve doubled in size when opened, displaying a 1960 souvenir calendar (with Elvis's Army discharge date circled), there were four color photos on the cover at the top of the calendar, and inside there was a "complete picture story of Elvis's departure overseas" and a personal message from Elvis in Germany. The album went on the charts immediately.

"It's a tribute to his staying power that he continues on such a powerful level," said Sholes. "And we don't sell his records on a guarantee basis, you know."

What this last meant was when a record shopkeeper ordered five hundred (or however many) copies of Elvis's latest record, he couldn't return them if they didn't sell. This ran against general policy in the record business and only because

Elvis had such an exceptional sales history would retailers stand for it.

In August it was announced that Elvis's first film following his discharge would be—quite naturally—about a tank sergeant in the U.S. Army stationed in Germany, called *G. I. Blues*. The producer was Hal Wallis, Elvis's old friend from *King Creole* and *Loving You*, who went immediately to Frankfurt to begin shooting background scenes. For these he used tanks provided by the Third Armored Division, but he did not use Elvis.

"We prefer not to put him in front of cameras here," Wallis said. "We don't want any criticism and it might be misunderstood in some quarters. If we had asked, we could have had him."

This didn't halt the criticism, though. Paramount was offered cynical congratulations for not taking Specialist Fourth Class Presley from his jeep, but the same newspapers also asked how much it was costing the U.S. taxpayer to provide the tanks and tank crews.

Stan Brossette, a publicist who later would work with Elvis and the Colonel on ten pictures, tells a story about how anxiously Wallis had been awaiting Elvis's discharge: "He still had four or five pictures to do with Elvis and for two years he was counting the money he was going to put in the bank. Then when it got close to when Elvis was to return, the Colonel had one of those fake front pages made to say 'ELVIS RE-ENLISTS.' And in smaller letters underneath: 'Wallis Collapses.' He wrapped the page around Wallis's morning paper about two weeks before Elvis was to get out and put it on Wallis's front steps. So when Wallis came down for the paper that day—and he'd already begun shooting backgrounds, remember—and he saw that headline, he collapsed before he saw the smaller headline that said he had."

While Wallis was dodging criticism and directing the movement of tanks, Elvis was going into the first real record sales slump of his career back in the U. S. After "A Big Hunk o'

Love," there wasn't anything left on the Victor shelves, and after it slipped out of the Hot 100 in October, there was, and would be, nothing to replace it there for five months.

All RCA could do for the Christmas season was rerelease Elvis's Christmas album from the previous year and assemble still one more repackaged album, *50,000,000 Elvis Fans Can't Be Wrong, Elvis' Gold Records—Volume 2*. This contained ten songs, all previously released in 1958 and 1959 as singles. On the cover there were several pictures of Elvis in the $10,000 gold lamé diamond-studded suit the Colonel had ordered in 1956. It weighed about twenty pounds and Elvis hated it, and he wore it only to get the publicity it was created for.

Back in Germany it was business as usual. According to Elvis's sergeant, he "scrubbed, washed, greased, painted, marched, ran, carried his laundry and worried through inspections just as everyone else did." Sometimes Elvis would entertain his Army buddies informally, singing songs like "Danny Boy" and "I'll Take You Home Again Kathleen" rather than his record hits. The cookies continued to arrive from fans by the mail sackful. Elvis still went on maneuvers. He arduously practiced his karate, eventually winning a second degree black belt. And he and his father met their future wives—Priscilla Beaulieu (pronounced Bo-lew), then the fourteen-year-old daughter of an Air Force captain stationed in Wiesbaden, and Davada (Dee) Elliott, a Huntsville, Alabama, woman then married to an Army sergeant.

Often during the time Elvis was in Germany there were newspaper and magazine stories devoted to his Army girl friends. Within a few days of his arrival in Germany, in fact, he started dating a sixteen-year-old German girl and then went dining with a Berlin starlet named Vera Tschechowa. None of these, nor others, did he take too seriously. Only Priscilla seemed to occupy his thoughts for longer than a few weeks. He dated her for four months, until he was shipped

back to the U. S. Their dates were fairly ordinary—a movie,
a drive in his BMW (called the "Presley-Wagen" by the
German press), or a visit to his home.

There was another young girl in Elvis's life at this time,
who got absolutely *no* publicity, and yet she was living with
Elvis and his father and grandmother in the Presley house.
This was a young German girl—a child, really—whom Elvis
had "adopted" after he saw her father cruelly abusing her.
"She was was like a pet to him," says a friend. "He delighted
in her naïveté and responses to his generosity. He mentioned
bringing her to America with him if her father approved."
Her father did not approve.

By mid-January 1960 Elvis had been elevated to sergeant
and was commanding a three-man reconnaissance team for
the Third Armored Division's 32nd Scout Platoon. But not
for long, because it was announced that Elvis probably would
be discharged not in March as planned, but in February.
Quickly the media began to pump themselves up for the
welcome home.

Series of newspaper articles reviewing the past and pre-
viewing the future began running in newspapers from coast
to coast. A writer for one of the wire services even went so
far as to ask all the girls whom Elvis had dated in Hollywood
if they would consider dating him again. Most said they
would. A reporter from Louisville, Kentucky, had written
a light book about Elvis's Army career, *Operation Elvis*,
which was to be published the same month Elvis returned.
Fan magazines were announcing contests offering Elvis's
uniform as prizes. Two hundred prints of *Jailhouse Rock*,
which had grossed close to $4 million the first time around,
were rushed to movie theaters for an early March opening.
WNEW radio in New York spotlighted "The Return of Elvis
Presley" on its News Close-Up, calling the homecoming "a
musical, cultural and military phenomenon of our time,"
while other stations in other cities planned special programs
that took the appearance of Elvis marathons. Again there

was a rush of novelty songs, including "I'm Gonna Hang Up My Rifle" by Bobby Bare and "The King Is Coming Back" by Billy and Andy ("The king is coming back / Get your guitar off the rack / Trade your khaki for black slacks"). And although Elvis hadn't even recorded the songs yet, RCA ordered an initial pressing of one million copies of his first single, with plans to ship half that number within seventy-two hours of release. As for his first public appearance, this was not to be a special on ABC-TV or a closed-circuit TV concert as was announced in 1959 but a guest appearance on one of Frank Sinatra's shows, for which Elvis would be paid $125,000, more than any other guest performer in television's brief but expensive history.

The excitement was motivated honestly. Elvis *was* still the reigning monarch of the pop music charts, and it *was* a triumphant return to the U. S. Of course, as *Billboard* noted, Elvis hadn't really been away; during the time he'd been in the service he continued to sell a million or more records with every single release, a mark that was unprecedented, and it became abundantly clear even to his detractors that almost all alone he was responsible for shifting the course of popular music. During his absence much had happened. Jerry Lee Lewis had been banished by the prudish public and Little Richard had thrown his jewelry into an Australian river and gone into a seminary. Buddy Holly, Ritchie Valens and the Big Bopper were dead. Rock 'n' roll was reeling from a payola probe. The big album sellers in the winter of 1959–60 were Ricky Nelson, Fabian, Frankie Avalon and Bobby Darin—Elvis imitators. No one—absolutely no one—had come along during Elvis's tour of duty worthy of taking his throne.

There were other factors. His going into the Army at his peak merely left his fans drooling for more. His patriotism broadened his appeal so that not just teenagers liked him—and his record in the Army was impeccable. So he was praised by nearly everyone. Teenagers began queuing up for a record that hadn't been cut and the Mississippi legislature

passed a resolution saying he had become "a legend and inspiration to tens of millions of Americans and hence reaffirms
an historic American idea that success in our nation can still
be attained through individual initiative, hard work and
abiding faith in one's self and his creator."

During his next to last week in the Army Elvis gave his
only exclusive Army interview to Wally Beene, then a staff
writer with *Stars and Stripes,* now a public relations counselor
living on the flank of Beverly Hills. He remembers being impressed by Elvis's humility and that he still had his nail-biting
and foot-tapping habits, signs of nervous energy.

"Elvis talked about what it was like to go on maneuvers,"
Wally says today, "when it was the 'NATO forces' versus the
'aggressors.' Not only was Elvis pursued by a battery of civilian reporters and photographers, troops opposing Elvis's
unit were offered fifty dollars' reward and a thirty-day pass
if they captured Elvis. 'A GI from the Twenty-fourth Division almost nailed me,'" Wally quoted Elvis as saying. "'He
spotted me on the road and started to take me prisoner, but
about that time a string of our tanks rolled up behind him
and he ended up as the prisoner.'

"If Elvis ever wanted to go to the movies, Lamar would
have to drive the car around the block and Elvis would jump
over the back fence," Wally says. "The crowds out front were
that big. Once a girl threw a brick through a window in his
house when she was told it was too late to see Elvis. She had
knocked at the door and someone came out and said Elvis
was sleeping. After she threw the brick, Elvis came out and
lectured her. And then he gave her his autograph. Later they
put a sign on the door saying, 'Autographs between seven-
thirty and eight-thirty P.M.'

"There was a fierce loyalty the guys in his outfit had for
him," Wally says. "It was incredible how protective they felt
toward him. I think it was because they sensed he was a
regular fellow. He sat in the snow with them, ate the lousy
food, and the fact that he lived off post and commuted in a

fancy car didn't bother them. They lived in reflected glory to a certain degree. They had stories to tell back home: 'I was in the Army with Elvis Presley!' They were prepared to put the knock on him at first, but it reversed itself. In the end they were impressed by Elvis."

The day before Elvis left Germany, the Army staged a monstrous press conference. Elvis's old friend from Sun Records, Marion Keisker, now a captain in the Women's Air Force and assigned to Armed Forces Television in Germany, was there. It was the first time she had seen Elvis in more than two years.

"They were in a gym with all the klieg lights and tape recorders and thousands of people running around saying, 'At twelve-oh-two he will . . .' Ecccchhhh. I went to the other end to a bar where they were serving coffee. I looked up and there was a door just a few feet away. Suddenly it flies open and in steps Elvis in this ridiculous thing they had on him with red stripes and gold braid, an MP on either side. I said, 'Hi, hon.'

"He turned around and said, 'Marion! In Germany! And an officer! What do I do? Kiss you or salute you?'"

"I said, 'In that order.' And I flung myself on him.

"The PIO was enraged. He said he was going to report me, have me court-martialed. The PIO said, 'I certainly expected this sort of thing from some of the magazines, but not from a member of the Armed Forces.' He accused me of staging it. I said I was there officially, representing the Armed Forces Television station, of which I was the assistant manager. He said, 'Would you please leave.' I refused, of course.

"Finally Elvis got free and he came over and he said, 'Captain, you don't understand. You wouldn't even be having this thing today if it wasn't for this lady.'

"The Captain said, 'This WAF captain?'

"Elvis said, "Well, it's a long story, sir, but she wasn't always a WAF captain.'

"Through the rest of the press conference he was determined I wasn't going to get thrown out. So I stood there behind him and he kept reaching back to see that I was there."

The next day Priscilla went with Elvis to the Frankfurt airport. He kissed her goodbye and then with seventy-nine other GIs and their families he boarded a four-engine military air transport plane for the States.

The plane landed at McGuire Air Force Base in New Jersey, adjacent to Fort Dix, the Army post where he was to be discharged later that week. It was six-thirty A.M. and a snowstorm was approaching blizzard proportions as he stepped outside to bravely look into a twenty-five-mile-an-hour wind for five minutes, waving and smiling dutifully for cameramen. (The Colonel previously had asked *Life* magazine for $25,000 for the exclusive rights to photographs of Elvis's last days, and when *Life* declined, the Colonel invited everyone.) And then he was rushed to one of the post ballrooms for another press conference.

It was little different from all those which had preceded it in Elvis's life. Frank Sinatra's oldest daughter Nancy, then nineteen, was on hand to provide a little glamour, giving Elvis a box of dress shirts from her father. But the rest of the morning was predictable. The matter of his marriage-ability was covered half a dozen times, his hair and side-burns at least four or five times. He said he probably wouldn't grow the sideburns back—a statement that sent wire service reporters sprinting for the telephones. He said that he had brought back a couple of German guitars, that he liked "Dean Martin, Mr. Sinatra, Patti Page, Kitty Kallen and quite a few others," that he didn't have nineteen Army public relations men assigned to him in Germany—only one, a captain who represented the whole division—that if rock 'n' roll died out, which he didn't think would happen, he and a lot of other people would have to find something else to do. Asked if his superiors had chewed him out in the Army, he grinned and held up a Certificate of Achievement that recognized his "faithful duty and service, etc." This kept the photographers pushing and shouting for a good five minutes. Finally it came to a blessed end as someone quoted a lady reporter as saying Elvis was "the sexiest man I've ever seen," and what about that, El?

Elvis looked the questioner straight in the eye, grinned his lopsided grin and said, "Where is that young lady now?"

At Elvis's feet, sitting on the floor and chewing on a cigar, was Colonel Parker. Jean Aberbach, Steve Sholes, Tom Diskin, Freddie Bienstock and Bob Kotlowitz, a Victor publicist who would stay with Elvis the first six weeks, were standing to the left and right. Outside, in the blizzard, scratching on the windows and shouting pledges of undying love, were a couple of hundred teenagers. A sergeant went out to tell them to be quiet, but they wouldn't.

Two days later, on March 5, he was a civilian again, and as Tennessee Senator Estes Kefauver was inserting a tribute to Elvis in the Congressional Record, Elvis went to Memphis to rest.

With the Jordanaires in "Loving You," 1957

ABOVE: *Vince Everett and friends in "Jailhouse Rock," 1957;* BELOW: *Elvis poses somberly with his friends, Dewey Phillips and Nick Adams, 1957*

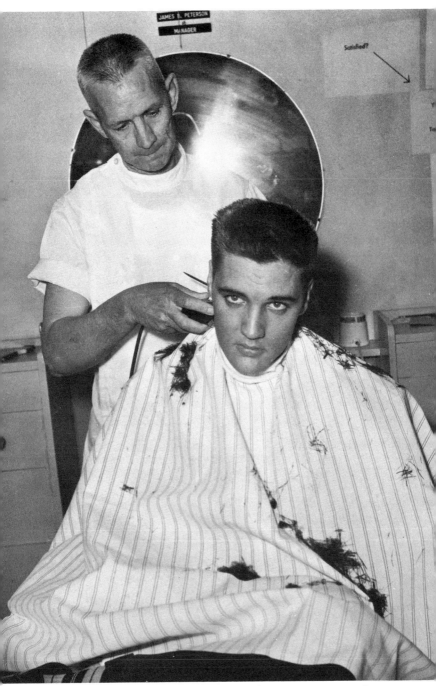

The Army haircut: "Hair today, gone tomorrow."

The Colonel (center) directs an Army fashion show

Waiting for news of his mother in a Memphis hospital, with (from left to right) Alan Fortas, Lamar Fike, George Klein, Billy Smith and Louis Harris, 1958

His mother's grave; nearby is a stone reading "She was the sunshine of our home"

On winter bivouac near the Iron Curtain in Germany shortly before his discharge, 1959

RIGHT: *A rare moment alone, at his Army post*

BELOW: *Back in uniform in 1960 with the Jordanaires in* G.I. Blues

-9-

HOMECOMING

THE TRIP TO MEMPHIS by train gave some indication of what the next few months would be like. At every stop —at Bristol, Virginia, in Johnson City and Knoxville, Tennessee, at Chattanooga—and at many stations between, day and night, there were hundreds of fans gathered with welcome-home signs. When he arrived in Memphis early Monday morning, the crowd was so large that police had to escort him to Graceland, where all up and down the highway more fans were gathered, causing a monstrous traffic jam. Gary Pepper, a Memphis boy Elvis's own age, held a sign aloft that said, "Welcome Home Elvis, The Tankers," the Tankers being a fan club he had organized in Elvis's absence. Gloria Martinez, twenty-one, and Sharlene Magee, nineteen, said they had kitchhiked in from Gary, Indiana. And Laura Driver, nineteen, from Brooklyn, said she had kissed Elvis at Fort Dix and flew to Memphis for another kiss, because she liked the first so much. The police car carrying Elvis whisked through the mob and disappeared up the sloping Graceland drive. No kisses. No autographs.

The first few days were spent calling friends, reassembling the old gang, putting several of the good ol' boys back on the payroll, lying around, looking at the house he hadn't seen in more than eighteen months, making plans for remodeling. Then on March 20 he and some of the boys drove to Nashville for the first recording session.

The Jordanaires were there, of course, and so were pianist Floyd Cramer, drummer Buddy Harmon and guitarist Hank Garland, all accomplished Nashville studio musicians who had played for Elvis previously and would make up the core of his Nashville band for several years more. Along with Scotty Moore and D. J. Fontana, naturally. The only one missing was Bill Black, who had formed his own group, the Bill Black Combo, and by then had had two hits, "Smokie" and "White Silver Sands." Among the songs recorded in that all-night session were "Stuck on You" and "Fame and Fortune," ballads for which there were more than a million orders even before Elvis opened his mouth.

The next day Elvis got on another train, this one for Miami Beach, where Frank Sinatra would be videotaping his show. "In every little town along the way the tracks were lined," says Scotty Moore. "Twenty-four hours a day. The whole trip. Photographers. Cameramen. Kids. I don't know where they came from." In some towns the Colonel had Elvis stand on the train's rear platform, as if he were running for President, and wave and sign a few autographs.

It was ironic that Elvis should make his return debut on Sinatra's show, for in 1957 Sinatra had said rock 'n' roll "is phony and false, and sung, written and played for the most part by cretinous goons." There was, however, a motive in his booking Elvis. This was the fourth and last Timex special for Sinatra; and the third broadcast, a Valentine's Day tribute starring Juliet Prowse, a South African dancer who'd dated Sinatra, had been only average in terms of audience response. In his final show Sinatra was determined to better that mark. Thus he had agreed to pay Elvis $125,000 for about six minutes' work. Said Sammy Cahn, who had long been one of Sinatra's best friends and top songwriters and was then serving as the show's executive producer: "You should make in a year what Frank is losing on this show.

But he wants to prove he can go big on TV." It was no secret that Sinatra was galled by the price the Colonel asked.

The show was to be taped at the Fontainebleau Hotel, where Sinatra was then closing a three-week engagement. Dean Martin was in town to open in the La Ronde Room after Sinatra closed and he along with Sammy Davis, Jr., Joey Bishop and Peter Lawford joined Frank on stage to repeat their entertaining "Summit Meeting" foolishness presented a month earlier in Las Vegas. And Mitch Miller was in town to conduct a mammoth sing-along show in the hotel's grand ballroom later that week. Perhaps never before in Miami's entertainment history had so many show business heavyweights gathered in one hotel at one time.

Still, much of the talk was about someone not a celebrity in the traditional sense but the manager of one of them: Colonel Tom Parker. The last time he and Elvis had been in Miami, when Elvis appeared at the Olympic in 1957, the Colonel had made a local name for himself by wearing a change apron and selling autographed Elvis photographs in the lobby. This time he called a meeting with three hundred members of Elvis's area fan clubs, a network of fanatical loyalty he used often and well. (At one point he signed up 250,000 five-dollar members, who received the usual packet of fan club material plus the next four Elvis singles —thereby racking up 250,000 sales *before* the records were pressed.) He told them how pleased he was they'd remained so faithful during Elvis's Army duty and gave them tickets to the show as a reward. And then the fans were released, to prowl the hotel hallways trying to break past the guards posted on Elvis's floor.

Elvis was in rehearsals, meantime, and showing considerable nervousness, along with the usual courtesy, calling his host "Mr. Sinatra." It was agreed that Elvis would wear a tuxedo and stand still while singing.

Despite the Colonel's efforts, it wasn't an all-Elvis crowd, of course. More than half the audience was composed of affluent middle-aged Sinatra fans. Which gave the press in attendance the angle they wanted. Here, after all, were idols from two generations, joined not only in television booking convenience but also in song. Elvis sang both sides of his new single and then sang one of Frank's big songs, "Witchcraft," after which Sinatra sang one of Elvis's, "Love Me Tender," with Elvis joining him in harmony. Eighteen years had passed since Sinatra's bobby-soxers swooned in the aisles of the Paramount Theater in New York, two had gone by since Elvis was causing riots. Now they were together. The audience came unglued.

A month later, on May 12, the "Welcome Elvis" special proved Frank had achieved what he wanted—he had become, for one hour, "big on TV." At least so far as numbers were concerned. Sinatra got a rating of 41.5, stomping all the competing shows. NBC's *Ernie Ford Show*, guest-starring Homer and Jethro and Johnny Cash, and *Groucho Marx* placed a distant second, sharing a 21.1 rating for the hour. CBS's *Markham*, a mystery starring Ray Milland, and a two-year-old rerun from *The Seven Lively Arts* series trailed, sharing a miserable 4.2.

Critically it was received less ecstatically. "The expected dynamite was, to put it politely, a bit overrated," said Ren Grevatt in *Billboard*. "The impression lingers . . . that Presley has much to learn before he can work in the same league with pros like Sinatra, Joey Bishop and especially Sammy Davis, Jr., who just about broke up the show with his chanting and impressions. Presley has a distracting habit which gives the impression he's never at ease. Let nobody touch his singing. That's fine as is. What he needs is a lot of coaching on how to stand and how to talk." Grevatt said it would be the Fontainebleau Hotel that would benefit most from the show. The New York *Times* was rougher. "The recent liberation from the Army of Elvis Presley may have been one of the most irritating events since the invention of

itching powder," John Shanley wrote. "While he was in the
service he lost his sideburns, drove a truck and apparently
behaved in an acceptable military manner. But now he is
free to perform in public again, as he did on last night's
'Frank Sinatra Show' on Channel 7. Accompanied by an
orchestra and the shrieks of a group of his frenzied young
admirers, he did several numbers including a duet with Mr.
Sinatra. Although Elvis became a sergeant in the Army, as
a singer he never left the awkward squad. There was nothing morally reprehensible about his performance, it was
merely awful."

Following the Sinatra special, Elvis returned to Nashville
for a recording session lasting twelve hours and during
which he recorded twelve songs, all of them released a week
later on an album called *Elvis Is Back*. The record was typi-
cally Elvis, a collection of songs with no particular theme,
no one direction. Some were ballads composed with Elvis's
soft warbling style in mind, others were rooted in the blues
or rock. There were a couple—"Soldier Boy" and "I Will Be
Home Again"—that smacked of exploitation, but none were
offensive. Many of Elvis's regular songwriters were represented—Stan Kesler, Jerry Leiber and Mike Stoller, Otis
Blackwell—along with two other respected blues writers,
Jesse Stone and Lowell Fulson. The fans greeted the album
the same way they'd greeted Elvis—ecstatically. Throughout the summer it was in the number two or three position,
kept out of number one by the Kingston Trio, and sales
passed the million-dollar mark.

Most of the songs Elvis was recording arrived with
Freddie Bienstock from New York, where most of the demonstration records were made. One of the producers of those
demos was Phil Spector, who has since produced records
for the Righteous Brothers, Ike and Tina Turner and the
Beatles and generally is regarded as the most eccentric and
creative producer in rock. "Elvis liked to hear things the

way they would be recorded, so you had to find somebody in New York who could imitate Elvis Presley," Phil says today. "All the songwriters would come to me and say, 'You make the demo for us, get a good drum sound, get a guitar sound, get a kid that really sounds like him, y'know?' There was a kid named David Hill who used to do a lot of Elvis's demos. Brian Hyland was another. P. J. Proby. A lot, I forget their names. People you'd call in, say, 'Sing like Elvis Presley.' And they'd do it. Then you stood a much better chance of getting Elvis to record it, because he always followed the demonstration records. If there was a lick or a riff that appealed to him, he wanted it in the record. In fact, many times—and this is not supposed to be known—many times he would use the demonstration track, the track that was cut in New York, and just sing over it. And that's what was released as Presley's new single. Far out, right?"

It didn't matter how the songs were recorded. "Stuck on You," like the records that preceded it and those that would follow, went to the top—arriving there *before* he'd had a chance to plug it on the Sinatra show. By then the Colonel was saying Elvis's TV price was $150,000. "I don't want Elvis to compete with his own movies," he said, referring specifically to *G.I. Blues,* then being filmed in Hollywood.

Elvis arrived in Hollywood in style—traveling with seven friends from Memphis and two new buddies from his Army days in a private railroad car that reportedly cost him nearly $2500 for the trip. He had the car parked on a siding and welcomed the press in a tuxedo and black suede shoes. And then he was driven to Paramount.

"Elvis is a natural for the movies," director Norman Taurog said at the time. "There is no stiffness with this boy. This is the most relaxed boy you could want. He reminds me of Crosby and Como. He is a good listener. When you have a good listener, you have a good actor."

G.I. Blues had as its hero Tulsa McLean, a tank gunner in

Germany, with longer-than-might-be-expected hair but no sideburns, who accepted a $300 bet that he couldn't break down the resistance of a standoffish night club dancer named Lili (Juliet Prowse). Elvis did his best to win the bet, and in the process, of course he won the girl. From that premise Elvis ambled through less than two hours of script, stopping often enough to sing eleven songs.

Visitors to the Paramount set during shooting included the wife and daughter of the Brazilian president, the king and queen of Nepal, the king and queen of Thailand, and princesses from Denmark, Norway and Sweden. Each claimed to be an avid Elvis fan.

On July 3 Vernon Presley was married to Dee Elliott, the woman he'd met in Germany. It was a private ceremony in the Huntsville, Alabama, home of her brother, Richard Neely, who served as the couple's best man. She recently had been divorced from her Army sergeant husband and had custody of their three sons, Billy, Ricky and David, all years younger than Elvis. The wedding was described publicly as "secret" and "sudden." Elvis did not attend.

That same week RCA released Elvis's second post-Army single, "It's Now or Never," a song that was based on the operatic "O Sole Mio" and once before had been adapted for contemporary use when Tony Martin sang "There's No Tomorrow." It was backed with "Mess of Blues" and both were credited with million-plus record sales, although it was "It's Now or Never" that occupied the number one spot for five weeks. Because it was a non-rocker, it was played on many more stations than were accustomed to playing Elvis records, a fact that must have been noticed by RCA and the Colonel, because the next single released was even further away from the rock 'n' roll beat.

This was "Are You Lonesome Tonight," a song that had been written in the 1920s by Dave Dreyer (who'd also written "Me and My Shadow"), when it was recorded by

Al Jolson. This wasn't even a song, but a recitation, one of those talky "ballads" that except for the secular country market went out with silent pictures. Still, it was even bigger than the previous hit, selling more than a million copies in the first week and prompting the largest flock of "answer records" in years. There was one version called "Who's Lonesome Tonight," in which a singer with the unlikely name of Redd Dogg called Elvis an idiot, one version of "Oh, How I Miss You Tonight" and four other versions of "Yes, I'm Lonesome Tonight."

Some people were saying Elvis was deserting rock 'n' roll. No one was contradicting them.

If there was any doubt, one only had to spend two dollars to see *G.I. Blues,* which was released simultaneously in more than five hundred theaters in October, or spend a few dollars more and get the sound-track recording. In the film Elvis not only worked with puppets but with small children. And although there were a few rockers in the "score," most of the songs sounded as if their roots were in Tin Pan Alley or 1940s Hollywood musicals rather than in country blues. Even "Blue Suede Shoes," reprised in the film, lacked the gutsy dynamism Elvis had given the song four years earlier.

"When they took the boy out of the country, they apparently took the country out of the boy," said Jim Powers in the *Hollywood Reporter.* "It is a subdued and changed Elvis Presley who has returned from military service in Germany to star in Hal Wallis' *G.I. Blues.*" Powers then described the film as a "fairly standard service farce," cast in the mold of *Sailor Beware* and a number of similar Hollywood comedy-musicals, and yawned his way to a close saying the picture would "have to depend on the loyalty of Presley fans to bail it out at the box office." And Bosley Crowther in the New York *Times* did little but marvel at how wholesome Elvis had become, saying he had honey in his veins instead of blood.

The critic from the *Hollywood Reporter* was somewhat off

target in his appraisal of the film's economic potential. *G.I. Blues* was one of Hollywood's box office champs, grossing $4.3 million in rentals in the U. S. and Canada alone, equal to the amount grossed by *Lost Weekend* or *The African Queen* or *Days of Wine and Roses*. But there wasn't much argument about the "new" Elvis. It was abundantly clear that the days of "Hound Dog" and *Jailhouse Rock* were past.

By the time *G.I. Blues* was released, Elvis was making a film at 20th Century-Fox. This one, released as *Flaming Star* following several name changes, gave Elvis his first "acting" role. In it he played a half-breed son of a Kiowa Indian (Dolores Del Rio in her first film role in several years) and a white rancher (John McIntire). They are caught in the middle of white-Indian warfare in West Texas in the 1870s, a conflict Elvis tries to resolve. Elvis, like his parents in the picture, dies—after singing only four songs.

Flaming Star was shot in forty-two days, mostly at the Fox studios in West Los Angeles, with some location filming on the sprawling Conejo Ranch in the nearby San Fernando Valley, the 8000-acre spread where much of television's *Rawhide* and *Wagon Train* were made. There were a few incidents. Eleven teenagers crashed the studio gates in the back of a rented laundry truck but got only as far as the Colonel's office. Elvis's buddy Red West chipped an elbow in a fight scene with Elvis. The Colonel put out a "family" of plaster RCA Victor dogs in the front yard of Elvis's dressing room/bungalow, one of which was promptly stolen. And there was an enormous bit of pulling and tugging over whether or not Elvis would wear brown contact lenses over his natural blue eyes. (He didn't.)

The film was rushed into release faster than any other opening nationwide just in time for the Christmas school holidays, a pattern that would become as much a part of the Colonel's policy in the release of future films as his reluctance to grant any interviews. The Colonel was processing thirty thousand Elvis Presley fan letters a month in 1960 (there were five thousand fan clubs worldwide) and he knew that many of these letter writers went to see Elvis's films time after time after time. Release timed to coincide with a school vacation would make it easier for these fans to attend the movies on weeknights as well as on weekends.

The Colonel seldom missed a bet.

From *Flaming Star* Elvis went into *Wild in the Country,* the last film he would make at 20th. Here he was a potential literary talent who had to overcome his rural beginnings, a lack of education and a personal history of violence. (He brains his brother, played by Red West, with a milking stool in the first scene.) Elvis also had to deal with a spiteful uncle (William Mims), whose ward he became, and his uncle's immature sex-crazed daughter (Tuesday Weld), along with the son of the town's richest citizen (Gary Lockwood). The rich kid hates Elvis, and before the picture ends, Elvis is accused of murdering him. There was even a suicide in the script for a while, but apparently that was considered too much for an Elvis audience to take, so the final scene was reshot so that a lady social worker (Hope Lange) who'd helped Elvis would not die by carbon monoxide but be saved by her smoldering-eyed hero. It was as if the gifted playwright Clifford Odets, who took credit for the script, had transferred Peyton Place from New England to Virginia.

Several records were released as the film was shot, including an album of spirituals and religious songs and some singles designed for the foreign market.

It was logical that Elvis would record an album of church songs and hymns because this was his favorite music. Gordon Stoker says Elvis and the Jordanaires and his friends and family often sang such songs for as long as six or eight hours at a stretch. Elvis himself once said he thought he knew every hymn ever written. Besides, the *Peace in the Valley* EP that

Elvis recorded in 1957 had been a consistent seller over the years. So the album *His Hand in Mine* was sort of a long-delayed follow-up. In it there were twelve songs, all featuring the Jordanaires and including several standards such as "Joshua Fit the Battle" and "Swing Down, Sweet Chariot," both of which Elvis arranged and adapted. The album was an excellent one, giving Elvis a chance to share the songs he liked to sing around the piano at home. It also showed how great a debt Elvis owed his favorite gospel groups.

Says Johnny Rivers, who had met Elvis by now and was joining him in occasional informal song: "One of his idols when he was young was a man named Jake Hess, who was the lead singer for the Statesmen Quartet. If you'll listen to some of their recordings, you'll hear some of that style that is now Elvis Presley's style, especially in his ballad-singing style. He was playing some of their records one day and he said, 'Now you know where I got my style from. Caught—a hundred million records too late.' It was really funny. I think he idolized Jake Hess. Jake and the Statesmen and the Blackwoods. He played all kinds of records, but mostly it was gospel music in those days."

His Hand in Mine—which pictured Elvis in a dark suit, dress shirt and tie, sitting at a white piano—never was what might be termed a smash hit, but sold briskly for almost a year, remaining on the charts long enough thereafter to qualify (eventually) as a gold record.

The other records released in the last months of 1960 were mostly from the *Elvis Is Back* and *G.I. Blues* albums, and none was issued in the U. S. From the first album, for instance, "The Girl of My Best Friend" was a hit in England; and from the movie sound track, "Wooden Heart" was the number one song in Germany, appearing on the charts under the German title "Muss I Denn Zum Stadtele Hinaus." In fact, "Wooden Heart," which was based on a 200-year-old German folk song and sung by Elvis partially in German, became a hit over much of Europe by February of the following year and finally, weeks after it was number one, was banned in the country where it got its start. Officially, Berlin radio stations prohibited play of the old student drinking song because it was uncomplimentary to German folk music; really, it was its popularity that caused the ban, as German record producers began to object to the intrusion of so many American records on the German market. The ban apparently had no effect on sales.

Nor did anything have any detrimental effect in 1961, no matter how much Elvis had changed. *Billboard* named "It's Now or Never" the vocal single of the year. The National Academy of Recording Arts and Sciences, the record industry's version of the Academy of Motion Picture Arts and Sciences, gave Elvis five Grammy nominations—three for "Are You Lonesome Tonight" and two for *G.I. Blues*. He had been awarded another row of gold records. Two motion pictures had been completed and released and a third was in preparation. (He would finish *Wild in the Country* after the holidays.) He had received the highest price ever paid a television guest star and his motion picture salary was moving toward the million-dollar mark.

What might have seemed ironic was that it was in this same year that attention was focused again on Elvis's beginnings in Tupelo. The superintendent of Tupelo's parks and recreation, John Tidwell, says that was the year concentrated work began on what is today the Elvis Presley Youth Center. Tidwell was a baseball scout for the Dodgers before he came to Tupelo the same year.

"We had the fourteen thousand dollars from the benefit Elvis did in fifty-seven, and that was enough to get started," he says today. "And then we solicited contributions, money or equipment. We asked local contractors to contribute machinery and men for one work day to level the land. From dawn to sunset there were tractors and bulldozers and construction people all over the area. One day and we had it started.

"We'd already moved the houses. There were very low-income people living in them when we bought them, half a dozen of these shotgun-style houses in a row. Where the recreation center is was a swamp, a tough one. The soil itself was the toughest I've ever seen. There were gullies and steep hills and washes. Eventually we had to add fertilizer to get grass to grow. And there was a snake-infested lake out back, which evidently had been a little cattle pond.

"I remember when we were filling in the swamp," he says. "A woman from Indiana came by to look at the birthplace, which was the only house we hadn't moved. At that time it was open, not padlocked like today, and she walked in and looked around. I didn't pay any attention to her at first, but after a considerable time passed and she didn't come out, I thought I'd best go after her. I found her standing in one of the two rooms, just crying and crying. I asked her what was wrong. 'He came from this,' she said. 'Yes, ma'am,' I said, 'but he got out.' "

On February 25 Elvis was in Memphis to headline two benefit shows in the city's 5500-seat Ellis Auditorium. The proceeds, along with those from a $100-a-plate luncheon at the Claridge Hotel, were to be divided among several local charities. The Colonel paid for ninety-eight tickets to the luncheon, pushing the take to $17,200. Among those there: Abe Lastfogel, the Colonel's good friend and head of the William Morris Agency and Elvis's personal agent; Jean Aberbach from Hill and Range; several RCA executives; Mayor Henry Loeb; Governor Buford Ellington; and the master of ceremonies, George Jessel.

Jessel also introduced Elvis at the afternoon and evening shows, which featured the Colonel's standard line-up of supporting acts—a singer, Gene Austin; a comedian, Dave Gardner, who became a close friend of Elvis's; and a juggling act, the Ashtons and Shirley. Playing behind Elvis were his old friends Scotty Moore and D. J. Fontana, with Floyd Cramer on piano and Boots Randolph on saxophone, and, of course, the Jordanaires. Elvis sang seventeen songs at the two shows, including his new single, "Surrender"—an updated version of "Sorrento"—and closed with the same song he'd used in all his early tours, "Hound Dog."

Says Scotty Moore: "We never ever really tried to top that song. Elvis felt 'Hound Dog' was the one they wanted and 'Hound Dog' was the one he gave 'em. And they always reacted the same way. If they weren't tore up by then—and of course they always were—why, 'Hound Dog' would just lay them out. He'd say, 'You ain' nothin' but a houn' dog,' and they'd just go to pieces. It'd be a riot every time."

There were nearly four thousand at the matinee, when tickets were three dollars, and more than five thousand at night, buying five-dollar tickets. Counting the luncheon, total receipts were nearly $55,000.

Elvis remained at home for the next week and then went to Nashville on March 8 for a non-singing appearance before a joint convention of both houses of the Tennessee State Legislature. He had been invited to attend the special session by Senator Lewis Taliaferro of Memphis, after legislators had passed a resolution paying tribute to Elvis for bringing so much fame (and although it wasn't mentioned, fortune) to Memphis and Tennessee, and for being so charitable.

Elvis made his entrance with the governor's daughter Ann on his arm and after an introduction that was so flowery it sounded like somebody reading Valentines, Elvis went to the podium. He looked at the politicians and their families before him and then at the hundreds of teenagers who had packed the two galleries above.

"Governor Buford Ellington, members of the legislature—and those who skipped school—good morning," he said, getting a big laugh at the reference to the hundreds of truants present. "I'm not permitted to sing, and I can't tell any funny stories like Tennessee Ernie Ford"—who had been there a week earlier—"but I can say sincerely that this is the finest honor I have ever received."

If that weren't enough to entrance the collected lawmakers,

Elvis then said, "People frequently want to know if I plan to settle down eventually in Hollywood. Now, I like to go out there to play [laughs] . . . er . . . er . . . work. But my home is in Memphis, Tennessee, and that's where it's gonna be." The place came apart. Elvis and the two buddies he'd driven to Nashville with returned to Memphis that afternoon.

Four days later Elvis went to Nashville again to record some more songs at the Victor studios.

And a week following that Elvis flew to Hawaii to his second public appearance of 1961 and his last until 1969. This was another benefit, to raise money for the Memorial Fund of the U.S.S. *Arizona,* the battleship that had been sunk by Japanese dive bombers almost twenty years earlier.

Says Minnie Pearl: "I was asked to be on the same show and I flew over with Elvis and his group. They'd had a big to-do in the Pan Am room that morning and Elvis, as always, was very kind to me. I've never had much conversation with him, because of the age difference, but he was always so courteous. We were on the plane and Jimmy Stewart was on the plane. Elvis had the stewardess ask Jimmy if he could speak to him for a minute. Jimmy and I talked about it later and said how much Elvis made us feel like grandparents."

She describes the arrival in Honolulu: "They held us in the plane until everybody got off. There were twenty-five hundred screaming women at the airport. Jimmy Stewart got off and they didn't even recognize him. They were pushed up against the fence. Elvis went along, shaking their hands. They lined the streets all the way to the hotel. They'd shout 'Elllllllvvvviiissss!'

"Tom Parker, who was with us, said to stay with Elvis. He wanted me in the pictures. We pulled up at the Hawaiian Village Hotel, which has a sort of lanai out front—the lobby isn't enclosed. There were five hundred women there and as we got out of the taxi, Elvis grabbed my arm and the women broke and mobbed us. I felt my feet going out from under me. My husband was behind me trying to get to me and he was screaming, 'Get out . . . get out!' I just knew I was gonna be killed. I never felt so close to death. You know, everyone wants to be number one, but that one experience was enough to convince me I don't want it."

The show was to be in the 4000-seat Bloch Arena in Pearl Harbor, not far from where the sunken battleship *Arizona* lay. Ticket prices were scaled for everyone, rising to a hundred dollars apiece for the ringside seats.

"Naturally all the generals and admirals came at the Colonel, trying to get to Elvis," says Ron Jacobs, one of Honolulu's leading disc jockeys, a position he held when Elvis last visited Hawaii for a concert in 1957. "And so the Colonel started snowing them about how important they were to the security of the world and how patriotic and so on, and if they'd line up, why he'd give them a little something from Elvis. So they lined up, all these guys in charge of the Pacific and parts west, and Parker went over to a trunk and carefully, almost secretly, pulled some tiny color pictures out and very stingily doled them out, one to each admiral and general.

"Later he showed me the inside of the trunk. It was full of eleven-by-fourteens in color, eight-by-tens in color, calendars, record catalogues, you name it. He told me he thought all the brass deserved was little pocket calendars.

"Then one of the admirals came to him asking for complimentary tickets and the Colonel said no—even if Presley's father came to the benefit he'd have to pay his way in, why even Elvis bought his ticket. Then the Colonel made sure the Negro chauffeur he'd been assigned was given two free tickets right up front next to all the brass."

It was true, Elvis *had* bought his own ticket to the show, the first of the hundred-dollar seats. Elvis and the Colonel also absorbed the cost of transporting and paying all the musicians and backup acts. They had read about the memorial committee's need for help in raising money and volunteered to stage the benefit only if every penny taken in at the box office actually went to the building fund. As a result, the committee received $47,000, to which Elvis and the Colonel personally added another $5,000.

As for the show itself, Elvis outdid himself. He sang nineteen songs, his longest show ever, and according to Gordon Stoker, at one point Elvis dropped to his knees and slid twenty feet to the front of the stage with the microphone in his hands, never missing a note. "We thought he was going right off the edge," says Gordon today. "Ray Walker [who'd replaced Hugh Jarrett as the Jordanaire's bass] was so surprised he didn't come in harmonically where he was supposed to. He just stood there with his mouth open, and nothing was coming out."

It was Elvis's farewell performance.

Elvis remained in Hawaii following the benefit to begin location shooting of his next film for Paramount, *Blue Hawaii*, another for Hal Wallis and Norman Taurog. This had him playing a rich man's son who returned from the service and much against his parents' wishes took a job with a tourist agency. Angela Lansbury played a convincing mother, Joan Blackman an appealing heroine and love interest, Nancy Walters an older woman seeking romance while vacationing in the islands. According to Ron Jacobs, the high points were the scenes involving the Colonel, none of which, sadly, were filmed.

"There had to be fifty-seven technicians and directors and script girls and makeup men and all the rest standing around with reflectors, waiting for the clouds to clear so the light would be just right for a matching shot," he says today. "Finally the sun comes out and they have twenty-six seconds to shoot. Elvis is ready. Everybody is ready. The director calls action and Parker comes out of the bushes, on camera, screaming for Hal Wallis. Wallis comes rushing up. The shot's been blown. He's furious, but he's trying to keep control, even if his face *is* purple. He asks Parker what's wrong and Parker says Elvis is wearing his own gold watch in the shot and that contract doesn't call for his providing wardrobe, but that's okay, so long as they come up with an additional $25,000 for the use of the watch.

"And the next day the Colonel has taken one of those aluminum tubes cigars come in and punched holes in it so it looks like a microphone, then run wires from that—wrapped with tire tape—into his hand-tooled valise, another wire from that into his ear, a pineapple in the valise for bulk, and he's walking around the lobby of the hotel interviewing people for what he says is the Pineapple Network.

"He's so weird," Jacobs says. "Why he even had me and Tom Moffatt [another local disc jockey] walking around the hotel lobby in huge floppy, fluffy snowman suits. He said we had to do it in order to become members of the Snowmen's League, so we did it, and then he refused to sign the membership card for five years. I love that weird sonofabitch."

Elvis apparently wasn't having so much fun. Minnie Pearl says she and her husband stayed at the Hawaiian Village for nearly a week following the concert and "the whole time we were there, Elvis never got out of his room except to work. They say he came down in the middle of the night to swim. He couldn't come down during the day. He had the penthouse suite on top of that thing there and we'd get out and act crazy, having the best time in the world, and we'd look up there and Elvis would be standing at the window, looking down at us."

-10-

THE
MEMPHIS MAFIA

ELVIS MAY HAVE BEEN LONELY, standing at the window of that Hawaiian hotel, but seldom was he alone. In the 1960s he had an impressive entourage, a group of seven to twelve—it varied—young men approximately his own age, all of whom were on salary, earning $150 to $250 a week. Most went wherever Elvis went and, except for two he met in the Army, all were from the Memphis area, so newsmen began calling them the "Memphis Mafia." It was the "Mafia" that gave Elvis—until he married—security, comfort and companionship.

There wasn't much news about Elvis during this period. One month he bought a $20,000 Rolls Royce with a built-in bar and four radio speakers, and that got about an inch of space, the same amount allotted to another story another month, when one of his salaried sidekicks, Red West, married Elvis's secretary, Pat Boyd. And when Elvis was sick with tonsillitis again, that warranted another inch.

His life had settled into a cushioned routine. There were "incidents," there were many things to remember or worry or laugh about. But the films and records and life style seemed fixed. So chronology lost much of its importance after the

Pearl Harbor benefit. Elvis wasn't on public display. For many it was as if he'd disappeared. "Disappearing" with him was the Memphis Mafia.

"We're talking about the roots," says Bill Bixby, who co-starred with Elvis in two films in the mid-sixties. "All those guys, if you stop and listen, they are the *sound* of his background. They are the feel of where he came from. They are old friends and base roots. Elvis is very comfortable because he keeps himself surrounded by pieces of his past."

There was Alan Fortas, the solid gregarious nephew of Abe Fortas who had been a scholarship football player at Vanderbilt University before he met Elvis. He had gone to work for him as a companion-bodyguard in 1958 during the filming of *King Creole,* had worked in construction while Elvis was in the Army and had returned to Elvis in 1960. Alan wears his thinning hair parted near his left ear. One of his proudest possessions is the transcript of Elvis's public school grades that was found in his father's junkyard after it was routinely discarded by the board of education. He wears on his left hand the diamond ring Elvis was wearing in 1957 when he slugged that guy in Toledo—a horseshoe of diamonds over a gold horse's head. Altogether, he was with Elvis eleven years.

"My job was I took care of his travel arrangements when we'd drive from Memphis to California," Alan says today. "I took care of making sure everything was ready for these trips. We'd go right out Route 66, never stop except to sleep in one of the Holiday Inns." Only once, Alan says, did they make a side trip, and that was just before Elvis married and they went eighty miles out of their way to see the Grand Canyon. "We'd just pile into the cars and drive, and they had to be ready. When you have a lot of cars, they break down. Not from use, but non-use. Tires go flat and batteries go dead. They get dirty. When it came time, I made sure they were ready to go.

"Another thing I did was if he wanted to buy a car, I'd see

what I could do—go down and deal on it. Elvis is just like anybody else or like I would be, when you get in a position to have them, when you love cars, you have them. He had quite a few of them, quite a few. Cadillacs, Continentals, convertibles, limousines, buses, pickup trucks, motorcycles, go-karts, sport cars, just about you name it."

Helping Alan watch over this fleet of vehicles was Sonny West, another Memphis boy and the best-looking of the bunch, a rugged sort of pretty boy who would leave Elvis to turn his looks into an acting career and then return to the payroll in 1970. He was a cousin of Red West.

A third member of the inner circle was Charlie Hodge, who was one of the two not from Memphis and who'd met Elvis in the Army in Germany. He had been one of the Foggy River Boys, singing behind Red Foley on Foley's ABC-TV show, *Ozark Jubilee*. It was music that brought him and Elvis together, and his contributions, once on salary, were his voice, sense of humor and almost puppylike worship of Elvis. His assignment was to supervise the musical aspects of Elvis's personal life and, when Elvis appeared in Las Vegas in 1969 and 1970, to play some backup guitar. He remains with Elvis today.

Helping Charlie with the music was Elvis's tall broad-shouldered high school friend, Bobby (Red) West. Red had gone into the Marines after the early touring with Elvis and had joined him again when Elvis was in Germany. Besides writing a couple of songs with his boss, Red was Elvis's movie fight "opponent," and off camera one of his karate partners. He left Elvis in 1968 to become a full-time songwriter and record producer back in Memphis, and his songs have been recorded by Pat Boone, Rick Nelson, Dino, Desi and Billy, and Elvis.

Elvis's cousins Gene and Billy Smith, who had grown up with him in Tupelo and had become a part of his entourage while he was recording for Sun, were short and dark and wiry and they favored wardrobe and hair styling that matched

Elvis's. Billy took care of Elvis's clothing, saw that it was clean and hung neatly, and helped him with his shopping. At Graceland the wardrobe at one point was a sixteen-by-twenty-foot room. Gene helped wherever he was needed but had little specific to do outside provide companionship.

Marty Lacker knew Elvis slightly during their high school days. Following two years in the Army, he worked in radio in Knoxville and New Orleans. He returned to Memphis and went to work for Elvis in 1960 and was the only married member of the group at that time. He is short, pudgy and, like Alan Fortas, wears his hair parted low over one ear. Until he left Elvis in 1967, he was Elvis's personal bookkeeper and secretary. Today he is a vice-president of one of the top recording studios in Memphis.

Joe Esposito was the other Mafia member Elvis met in the service and was the only Yankee in the group. He was from Chicago, had been schooled in accounting, and worked with Marty in keeping the books, handling payment of all personal bills, assisting with the driving, eventually becoming Elvis's number one man and serving as the buffer between Elvis and everyone else. He remains with Elvis today and his wife Joanie is Priscilla's closest friend.

Lamar Fike, who had joined Elvis in Germany, remained on the payroll throughout the early 1960s, later taking his family to Nashville, where today he heads the branch office of Hill and Range Songs. He returns to the Presley payroll, operating the lights, when Elvis appears in Las Vegas. He is a bulky graying man who, like Elvis, dyes his hair. His nickname is the "Great Speckled Bird."

Over the years there were many others—the monstrously huge ("larger than Orson Welles" is the way one acquaintance describes him) Ray Sitton, who was known as the "Chief" and today does character bits in Hollywood; Marvin (Gee Gee) Gamble, who served as Elvis's chauffeur and valet and whose wife Patsy was Elvis's cousin and secretary; Bitsy Mott, one of the early companions, a distant relation of the

Colonel's; Louis Harris, who became a television cameraman in Memphis when Elvis was in the Army; George Klein, who was president of Elvis's high school class and traveled with him during the hysterical fifties, leaving to become one of Memphis's top disc jockeys; Jimmy Kingsley, who joined Elvis after nine years as a judo and karate instructor in the Marines, and supervised stunt work for *The F.B.I.* television series; Cliff Gleaves, a former disc jockey from Memphis, now living in Florida; and Larry Geller, who served as Elvis's personal hair stylist, among them. Most of them stayed on the payroll for several years, but many came and went, some because they grew tired of being on twenty-four-hour call, others because they wanted to try acting or got married. "We had kind of a fast turnover," says Alan Fortas. "They'd quit, leave, come back. Some of the boys worked for Elvis three or four different times."

In 1970, Alan was the gusty, efficient manager of TJ's, a supper club in Memphis, and the man on the door was Richard Davis, a Memphis boy who quit his job on a highway survey team to go to work for Elvis in 1963, taking care of his clothes. He is as tall and thin as Alan is short and stocky, with fine blond hair slicked back at the sides. He left Elvis in 1968 to work as a movie extra and returned to Memphis in 1969, when his father died.

"I was with him seven years," Richard says today. "Seven days a week, twenty-four hours a day, three hundred and sixty-five days a year. Day and night. I know Elvis the man, not what you read in a movie magazine or some reporter writes in a newspaper. You can live ten lifetimes before you'll find another like him. He's got a heart of gold. He'll give you the shirt off his back. I love him. I haven't been with him in two years now, but I still love him."

Richard looks almost tearful. "I lived with him in Bel Air," he says. "I lived with him in Graceland. I used his credit cards. I got paid a salary. But it wasn't a boss-employee relationship. He was a friend. You don't get a job for him through an employment agency. The only way is if he trusts you enough, if he likes you, *he'll* ask *you.*"

"You want to know what kind of guy Elvis is?" Alan asks. "My father was sick and dying and I came to Memphis. Elvis said, 'You stay in Memphis and if it's two years, you pick up your paycheck every week and if you come back, you're fired. Go out to my house and pick up your check each week. Stay with your family.' I said it wasn't fair. He said, 'Stay.' And then he came to the hospital on Christmas and gave my father a gold pocket watch. He told me if there was anything I needed, don't hesitate."

And then Alan tells a story about the time he happened to mention he would like to go motorcycle riding with Elvis: "He said call the Triumph dealer, find out how much twelve motorcycles cost, put one in the name of everybody working for me. He's unreal. If you say you like his car, he may give it to you."

The stories go on and on. Rings, clothing and cars were exchanged. Elvis gave Marty Lacker two cars, another two (huge white Cadillacs) went to George Klein, and a fifth went to the president of one of his fan clubs. In one case Elvis paid for cosmetic surgery to help a friend's career. Elvis saw nothing unusual about this.

"I have no need of bodyguards," he once said, "but I have very specific uses for two highly trained certified public accountants, an expert transportation man to handle travel arrangements, make reservations, take care of luggage, etc., a wardrobe man and a confidential aide and a security man who will handle safety arrangements in large cities where crowds of people are involved. This is my corporation which travels with me at all times. More than that, all these members of my corporation are my friends."

"The boys were lovely," says Yvonne Craig, an actress who was in two films with Elvis, and dated him, in 1963. "They changed periodically, but all of them were polite. They're charming. They didn't swear around you, they pulled out your chair, there were six people lighting my cigarettes and asking me if I wanted a Pepsi. They were like brothers to him.

"You could tell they worked for him. Joe Esposito you could tell less. But there was a difference. When I say to my brother, 'When you get a minute, would you do such-and-such?' that's another tone of voice. They're pals, but they're always conscious of his likes and dislikes. Like, around Sinatra: Are his shoulders up? That means he's angry, or whatever. They're more conscious of his temperamental changes, however slight they may be, than your own brothers would be. He can be honking around with them, playing, and then say something in a slightly different tone and you know they work for him.

"He makes mention of this," says Yvonne. "When someone says something about the boys who hang around Elvis, Elvis says, 'They work for me.' Which is in defense of them. They *do* work and they're not hangers-on and they do earn a salary."

Even so, to hear the boys tell it today, much of the time was spent having fun. What Yvonne calls "honking around" often took on the appearance of a young boy's fantasy come true.

"There was one time," says Richard Davis, "we went to Beverly Hills and bought out three photo shops of all their flashbulbs, every bulb in all three stores, and then bought a half a dozen BB guns. We went back to the house, threw the flashbulbs in the swimming pool, where they floated, and then started shooting. Every time we hit one, it'd explode and sink. We did that three nights running. It took me two solid days to clean the pool after, but it was worth it.

"Another time, back in Memphis, I got the job of buying tractors. First I bought the little ones and graduated to the big diesels. We had the carpenter build a trailer that held fifteen or twenty people and we'd drive around Graceland as fast as we could, pulling that trailer full of people, see if we could throw everybody off. I think it was Billy Smith suggested we strap a saddle on the tractor, ride it like a horse. By now the yard behind the house looked like a field plowed by a drunk, all ruts and bumps. We'd take turns driving the tractor fast across the ruts, trying to buck each other off. We did that for several days.

"To us these things weren't crazy," Richard says today. "They were just new and different and fun. Elvis liked to try new things, liked to try everything once."

Of course there was some method to the madness. Hal Blaine, a drummer who worked most of Elvis's recording sessions in Hollywood, recognized the value of the horseplay. "We'd go anywhere from eight in the morning sometimes to four the next morning without letup," he says today. "And if Elvis seemed to get uptight at all, that was sort of their cue to start fun and games. Somebody'd come over and throw a karate punch at Elvis, he'd throw a kick back and pretty soon we're all drinking Cokes and he'd be telling stories about overseas. They went out and bought about a dozen of those butane lighters, cut the little nipple off the end, so when you opened it, it shot a tremendous flame. They used to chase each other around the studio with them. It was one of those things to keep Elvis loose. Everybody gets uptight sometimes and they'd been with him long enough to know the inflection of his voice on a particular matter. They knew it was time for fun and games."

And if they ever got tired of playing with one another, back in California there was always Scatter, the chimpanzee Elvis kept for a few years. Says Yvonne Craig: "Every time I saw Scatter he was dressed up like a person and he would sit at the bar and bang his glass until one of the guys filled it with bourbon. He would drink it down until he was tired of drinking, and then when he'd had enough, you could fill it up and he'd just dump it on the floor. He used to get loose and wander around Bel Air drunk and I think that's why they got rid of him. He was scaring too many of the neighbors."

(Although Elvis usually didn't consume anything harder than Pepsi and Nesbitt's orange soda, several of the boys did enjoy alcohol, and some of them spent so much time at the Red Velvet in Hollywood they had their own booth.)

And of course there were all the vehicles. Occasionally Elvis would get on his Harley-Davidson and lead a pack of Triumphs around the Bel Air hills—causing newsmen to call them "El's Angels" and the neighbors to call the police. Other times Elvis and the guys would go riding in the Cadillacs or the Rolls Royce. Going to the studio each day, the Cadillacs were driven nearly bumper to bumper. The real treat was to take the "Solid Gold Cadillac" for a spin.

Essentially, it was a 1960 Cadillac 75 limousine, one of the models that remained a favorite with Elvis for years afterward. He took it to George Barris in North Hollywood, then (as now) the top car customizer in the world. The top was lengthened and covered with a coarse-grain white pearl naugahyde material and the body was sprayed with forty coats of a specially prepared paint that included crushed diamonds and fish scales from the Orient. Nearly all the metal trim was plated with twenty-four-carat gold. There were gold records in the ceiling. Gold lamé drapes covered all the rear windows and the glass that separated the chauffeur from the passengers. There were dual gold flake telephones, one for the chauffeur who took incoming calls and announced the caller's name on the intercom. Within Elvis's reach were a gold vanity case with gold electric razor and gold hair clippers, an electric shoe buffer, a gold-plated television set, a phonograph, a multiplex amplifier, an AM-FM tuner with loudspeakers mounted under the front fenders, air conditioning, an electrical system for operating any household appliances, and a refrigerator that made a tray of ice cubes in exactly two minutes.

He bought a Dodge mobile home and then had a bus customized for the trips back to Memphis, where he still kept his mother's pink Cadillac locked away in a garage. And on nearby McKellar Lake there was a twenty-one-foot-long Century Coronado with a 325-horsepower Cadillac engine for water skiing.

They developed their own language. "They'd spend hours, days, thinking up lines to throw back and forth," says a close friend. "Things that didn't make any real sense. If there was a minor beef, somebody'd say, 'Big scene.' For a while they went through a period of 'I gotchers.' They'd say, 'I gotcher book. I gotcher message. I gotcher coat. I gotcher joke.' There were key words and phrases that only they understood.

"They'd bug him sometimes," the friend says. "He took his likes and dislikes out on them and they'd do everything but wipe his ass. He could say, 'Boy, it's a nice day,' and it might be raining out, but they'd start snapping their fingers and elaborating on how great the day was. There was one recording session, Lamar came up to him and said he thought the song Elvis had just sung was the greatest thing he'd ever heard. 'Ten million,' he said. Elvis said no. Lamar said, 'Five million. For sure—five million.' Elvis said no. Lamar said, 'Three. Three—easy.' Elvis said he didn't really like the song or the way he did it. And Lamar said, 'Now that you say so, it wasn't so good after all.' "

The boys lived with Elvis's moods—some brought on, apparently, by dieting. "He always had the weirdest eating habits I ever saw," says a friend. "Burnt bacon, olives, vegetable soup and peanut butter and banana sandwiches—that was about it. Sometimes he'd get on a jag of some kind, eating nothing but yogurt, but usually he didn't eat much at all. He could go through four recording sessions without eating. The rest of us would eat three meals and all he'd have was a bowl of soup and maybe a glass of milk. This was to keep his weight down. He'd run his movies and watch himself in a screening room, slumped way down in his seat, cringing, saying, 'No . . . no . . . too fat!' He worried about his weight all the time.

"He also worried about his hair. He went into seclusion. He

wouldn't be seen. People he loved would go to the Graceland gates and he wouldn't see them. If his hair wasn't right or his eyes weren't right, he'd hide. He was dyeing his hair black by now, but once he hadn't dyed it and he let it grow out. It was blond and he looked great. We said we thought it looked just great and he said he thought he'd leave it that way. Next time he saw him it was dyed double black.

"The temper was the hardest thing to take," the friend says. "One day he'd be the sweetest person in the world, the next day he'd burn holes in you with his eyes. It was hard on the guys. One time he fired every one of them, told them to get their asses back to Memphis, and they packed and left. By the time they'd got to the airport, Elvis changed his mind, so he had one of the boys paged and when he came to the phone, Elvis told them to get their asses back, they were on the payroll again."

It was the same temper that often caused the destruction of property. Back in 1957 he hurled an expensive guitar out of his hotel room into a hallway, splintering it. A visitor to one of his Bel Air homes tells a story about the time he demonstrated his reaction to a Lee Dorsey record by heaving a heavy glass ashtray through the front of the jukebox. Other friends say that over the years he has destroyed several television sets, that once when the lights didn't work properly on a bumper pool table, he took a pool cue and beat the table into pieces, and on at least two occasions, when his uncles strayed from the Graceland gate, Elvis ordered his limousine backed across the highway and driven at high speed *through* the gate.

The Mafia never complained.

Of course it was not without precedent for a celebrity to have a faithful entourage. Frank Sinatra, in fact, had two. One was formed in the late 1940s with songwriters Sammy Cahn and Jule Styne, his arranger and conductor Axel Stordahl, his manager Hank Sanicola and several song pluggers who generally served as "go-fers," the show business errand boys. The second clan—the rat pack—was formed rather more publicly in the 1950s with Dean Martin, Sammy Davis, Jr., Joey Bishop, Peter Lawford and others. Dozens more in entertainment have had similar groups, even if they were composed of just managers, publicists and office help: the conventional show biz claque. There were many Hollywood movie stars who had salaried companions. But most were like Sinatra's, somewhat remote; certainly they weren't members of a group that "lived in." Elvis's group lived in; they were, as Richard Davis says, on twenty-four-hour call, seven days a week, 365 days a year.

Alan Fortas says this presented unique problems: "All the guys stayed at the house and that was a big hassle. We had to find one that was big enough for all of us—five bedrooms at least. And most people do not like to rent to five, six, seven, ten, maybe a dozen boys, no matter who you are. Anybody has a house that size, they don't need the money so bad they're gonna take a chance of getting it tore up. It was tough finding a house with five, six bedrooms, four and five baths and a big den."

In 1960 Elvis and his boys did find a house, however, and moved from the Beverly Wilshire Hotel into a quasi-Oriental home at 565 Perugia Way in Bel Air. This was the first of three homes he rented in the expensive mountain community. It was built in a semicircle, one side fronting a small lushly planted drive-court, the other facing the Bel Air Country Club greens. In the center of the house was a garden, which the landlady had ripped out at Elvis's suggestion; Elvis thought a second den should go there, and he built a fireplace where a waterfall was.

Says Alan Fortas: "We had pool tables, all the pop records on the jukebox. We'd go to the record store ourselves, buy 'em, bring 'em back and put 'em on the jukebox. He listened to all kinds." The rest of the house remained as Elvis found it. It was furnished comfortably, but did little to project the tenant's personality.

The parties were something else again.

Ellen Pollon, who at ten had been standing outside the Knickerbocker Hotel as one of the "Hotel Hounds," was thirteen now and something of a regular visitor. "It was a very strange scene up there," she says today. "Nobody'd talk. All these guys he was in the Army with and some that were from Memphis. I never knew which were which. I could tell there was a pecking order, that much was evident. The girls would sit around and they'd ball this one or that one. They go to Lamar maybe and from that to Sonny and finally you'd get to Gene, who was Elvis's cousin, and from Gene you were supposed to get to Elvis, although it never worked out that way."

Says another girl who visited Elvis's Perugia Way home in 1962, when she was eighteen: "A friend of mine was going with one of the guys and she asked me to go to the house with her, and she explained the ground rules. She said if one of the guys took a fancy to me, I better take a fancy to him if I wanted to be invited back. And above all else, I had to be ladylike. So my girl friend asked for the one she was dating, he came to the door and invited us in. We were offered soft drinks and given the run of the house. I found Elvis in a back room, seated at the center of a horseshoe-shaped couch, feet up on the coffee table, captain's hat on his head, with half a dozen girls seated on the couch on each side of him."

"You could hear them plotting," says Ellen Pollon. "There were twenty or thirty there every time he had one of those parties, which really was a sort of open house. And the girls were always jockeying for position. Sitting on the couch, not too close, but close enough, within eye range. You'd see Elvis looking around and he'd look at a girl and she'd smile. Or if he looked as if he were *about* to look at a girl, she'd smile. As soon as he looked away again, she'd drop the smile. No one ever talked to each other. I went over to one girl to admire her boots and she wouldn't talk to me. Then I realized you can't talk to someone when they're working, and these girls were working.

"Most of the girls were in their twenties. Some were sixteen and I was the child in the group. Some of them were starlet types. Not the Tuesday Weld variety. More like Jana Lund. She was one of them. Supposed to be Elvis's girl friend. For a while anyway. You know the type—the ones who played the 'bad girls' in all the *Rock Rock Rock* movies. But they weren't in the movies, just that type.

"It was weird. We'd sit around watching television—that's what we did seventy-five per cent of the time—and nobody'd ever laugh at anything unless Elvis did. If Elvis laughed, everybody'd just roar. Not more than Elvis laughed, but just as much."

Other gatherings at the Presley manse were more relaxed, when Elvis had a date. "It was when I did *It Happened at the World's Fair* with him [in 1963] that Elvis asked me out—or in, as the case may be, because he doesn't go out," says Yvonne Craig. "It was odd, because I think Elvis actually did the asking. Usually Joe Esposito does the asking and if you say yes, Elvis makes the arrangements. But it was Joe who came to my door to escort me to the car, and there's Elvis sitting in his white gold-dusted mad Cadillac—this crazy-looking thing. He said very apologetically, 'I brought this because . . . uh . . . I thought you'd . . . might . . . want to see it.' And then he pushed all the buttons for me as Joe drove us to the house. We had dinner and we were the only two people sitting in his dining room and it was so quiet I could hear me chew. Then we went into the living room and all the henchmen were there with their dates watching television, so we went to his quarters. That was when I gave him a lecture. I said, 'Elvis, I have to tell you something. I think this is a dangerous move for you.' He said, 'What?' I said, 'Well, you're just lucky that I'm the way I am, because you have no idea, I mean you're living in Hollywood now, it's a terrible trap, if you're to take a girl alone back here to your quarters, she can say anything: rape, scream, carry on, and the court will say uh-huh, he did it. There'll be a lot of publicity and you'll be in trouble.' And he's sitting there saying, 'Yes, ma'am

. . . yes, ma'am . . . I'll certainly be careful about that.'

"I felt like a dummy the next day, but I did feel protective. He makes you feel that way. Elvis encourages a motherly interest. It isn't a weakness, it's just that he's so quiet and Southern and sweet."

Yvonne, who is an attractive bubbly brunette, says she dated Elvis again while they were co-starring in another film, *Kissin' Cousins*. This time she says he fell asleep on her.

"We were watching an old movie on television," she says today. "He fell asleep, so I turned out the lights, turned off the TV and tiptoed out of the room. I went to get Joe and said, 'Elvis is asleep, you better get him undressed and to bed and I've turned out all the lights.' So Joe says, 'You didn't turn out *all* the lights?' I said, 'Yeah, yeah . . . I'm not his mother.' Joe said, 'He likes to have one light on.' I said, 'Well, go turn one light on.' How was I supposed to know that? Anyway, so we walk out the front door and there's not one, but five Bel Air patrol cars—cops all over the lawn. Joe says to me, 'You didn't touch a button, did you?' I said, 'I touched every button in the room trying to get the lights to shut off.' What I'd done was call the Bel Air patrol. The next day Elvis said, 'I understand you had some trouble with the police last night.' He'd slept through the whole thing."

Elvis moved several times in the next few years, first leaving the house on Perugia Way for a much larger place at 1059 Bellagio Road. This was one of those cavernous Mediterranean-style homes that looked a part of 1920s Hollywood, with a marble entrance hall almost large enough for a basketball game and a bowling alley in the cellar. Red West says Elvis liked the mirrored master bedroom but thought the house was too much like a mausoleum, so everyone moved back to the Perugia Way place, where they remained for another two years. Then toward the end of 1965 Elvis leased a house at 10550 Rocca Place, on a winding dead-end street in Stone Canyon not far from the Bel Air Hotel. This was a low modern home with a large swimming pool and patio—with urns that Elvis had painted an electric blue—and a board fence that was easily and regularly climbed by fans. Elvis remained in this house through the first months of his marriage.

If he weren't making a movie, he'd race for Graceland, where he'd keep his boys up all night and sleep all day, when they ran errands. And every year he'd remodel the place, changing rooms or adding them.

A fifty-by-eighty-foot room was added to one wing, connecting the house with the pool, and at first this was used for his slot-car track, which he'd moved from one of the two large basement rooms. And then he got rid of the track and turned it into a trophy room, covering the walls with plaques and gold records, furnishing the room with dozens of *locked* trophy cases. (Sometimes fans sneaked in.) He added a full-size soda fountain to one of the dens, put a jukebox by the pool. He spent $40,000 expanding the kitchen and adding a sun porch adjacent to his bedroom above it. He put heavy wire mesh on all the windows for security, built a brick wall inset with stained glass windows around the pool for privacy. The color of the rugs and furnishings changed from blue to red to white. Behind the house he built another house, with offices for his father and the two secretaries he employed to handle some of the personal correspondence.

Altogether in 1965 there were ten employees—besides the secretaries, two daytime maids and one at night to assist his grandmother, three gatekeepers and two yard men. The maids doubled as cooks, and when Elvis was home with his retinue, the weekly grocery bill was more than $300.

Once, according to friends, he refused to leave his room; even his food was placed outside the door and if anyone had anything to say, he said it in notes shoved under the door.

Occasionally one of the guys would get a girl pregnant and Elvis would see that everything was taken care of.

His father and stepmother and stepbrothers had moved into a house of their own in the same neighborhood, but his aunt and grandmother continued to live in Graceland's east wing along with Priscilla Beaulieu.

Priscilla's father had written Elvis and his parents from Germany, asking if she could visit them during a vacation, and of course the Presleys said yes. They were then asked if they'd look after her as she finished high school. Again they said yes and (a Catholic) she was enrolled at Immaculate Conception High School in Memphis the last half of the year, graduating in June 1963, and after a time enrolled in the Patricia Stevens Finishing and Career School, studying modeling and dance. She lived at Graceland or with Vernon and Dee.

She and Elvis continued to see each other romantically during this period, but it was, according to friends, a fiery off-an-on relationship, as Elvis also dated most of his leading ladies in Hollywood. Priscilla joined her parents at Major Beaulieu's new post, Travis Air Force Base, near San Francisco, for instance, when Elvis joined Ann-Margret to make *Viva Las Vegas*. After she returned to Graceland, she increased the number of visits she made to Hollywood and often visited Elvis on the set.

Elvis made no public appearances during this period—1961 to 1967—but he hadn't abandoned music by any means. Of course there were the movie songs, but friends say they were becoming a drag for Elvis. What he really enjoyed, they say, were the informal sessions around the piano in the living room. In Memphis Elvis would reply upon his buddies and call in a few gospel singers he knew. In California he collected people like Johnny Rivers.

"We played football together in the park and he invited me up to his house and I hung out quite a bit," says Johnny today. "We played guitars and sang. My first hit record, 'Memphis,' which I didn't have until five years later, that was a thing he and I used to do together all the time. Whoever was in town was invited up. There was a standing invitation for some. Musicians from Nashville, local musicians. Roy Orbison came by once. I met one of the Everly brothers there. He'd worked with a lot of them. The Jordanaires would come by when they were in town. We did all kinds of music—a lot of Chuck Berry things, old Little Richard things, Fats Domino things, sort of the rock and roll standards.

"There were records scattered all around. New records. A lot of demos. He'd play them over and over to get a reaction. He collected records. Sometimes he'd go down and buy the whole Top Forty, or send somebody to Music City to get all the top albums and singles . . . along with a lot of spiritual things. Elvis loved music. Really loved it."

When there were no professional musicians and singers visiting, Elvis would round up some of his boys. Ellen Pollon was present at some of these sessions and says, "Elvis or Red would play the piano. Or Charlie. And Cliff would join them in singing. Together they looked like those guys who hung around drugstores and yelled at people. But they were singing gospel songs. The Statesmen Quartet and the Blackwood Brothers—Elvis would sing like them, and like the Ink Spots too. Those were the groups he liked. The only trouble was, he couldn't hit the low notes. He often said he wanted to be one of those black bass singers.

"I remember one time when one of his cousins was giving a colored newsboy outside the Beverly Wilshire Hotel a hard time and Elvis told his cousin to get the hell out of there—he really stuck up for the little colored kid. Another time one of his cousins was saying nigger-this and nigger-that, bitching about the Freedom Rides. I said I thought it was great that people would go down South, to risk their lives and all. He started the nigger-this and nigger-that, and I said I wished he wouldn't talk that way. I didn't want to antagonize him, because he was Elvis's cousin, after all, but he said their blood's different and they're dirty, and it was really getting

heavy. I said, 'Well, they're no dirtier than some white trash.'
That struck a chord and he really got mad. Then I called him
white trash and said I didn't care who heard me, meaning
Elvis. Then Elvis came into the room and told his cousin,
'Now, we're up North now and some people may not agree
with the way we think. Let's not talk politics. We're not down
home now.' And then he smiled at me. What he was doing
was cooling both of us out."

Johnny Rivers says he met Elvis playing football. This was
another activity that occupied Elvis's weekends; in fact, the
open houses and parties often were little more than an extension of the games.

At first the games were held at De Neve Park, a small tri-
angular plot of grass at the edge of Bel Air, near where
Beverly Glen Canyon runs into Sunset Boulevard. Later Elvis
and the boys were asked to take their games elsewhere; according to the canyon's neighborhood association, they were
tearing up the grass and causing a traffic hazard. This criticism came because, the way Dean Torrance tells it, a hell of
a crowd always gathered whenever Elvis played. Dean was
then half of the singing team, Jan and Dean.

"Jan and I sponsored teams for about six or seven years,"
he says today. "We had our own team. We used to practice
on Sundays and play weeknights in leagues. If there weren't
enough guys for two teams on Sunday to practice, and we
had enough for one team, we'd say, 'Hey, let's go up to the
canyon and play Elvis.'

"Trouble was, there were so many teams showing up, we
had to limit it to whoever scored two touchdowns was the
winner, and the loser was eliminated. Elvis would always win
and so his team played all day. They played well, but it also
seemed Elvis's team could run around trees and out into the
street, and if we came even close to those arbitrary lines,
they'd get out an engineer's sighting thing to see if we went
out of bounds. We'd object when they did it, but they always

said, 'Oh, it's all right to run around *that* tree.' And suddenly the game was over."

Dean says the games were a lot rougher than most touch games. There was no equipment worn, he says, the blocking was "good and crisp," and the players were fairly big. Elvis had Max Baer, Jr., on his team, and Ron Heller, who'd played ball at USC for two years, and Red West and Alan Fortas, both of whom had played football in colleges in Memphis.

"There was no reluctance to go after Elvis," Dean says. "Probably the opposite was true. So except for the flexible boundaries that seemed to work in their favor, Elvis won the games legitimately. We had to be a little cool. We couldn't go around blind-sighting somebody, or necktying them. But we didn't have any inhibitions about cleaning somebody out if we got a good shot. Elvis'd get wiped out right along with the rest of us."

After the game everybody'd go up to the house. The patterns were formed and set. It was time to begin the partying.

"When's the balloon go up?" someone would ask, using an expression left over from Elvis's Army days and referring to when some girl was scheduled to strip or Scatter would begin drinking or something else entertaining was planned.

"Goes up at ten o'clock."

At midnight Elvis would go to bed and some of the girls would stay until four or five, sitting there, wondering if he was coming back. He never did.

"It was like when you're stoned and nothing changes," says Ellen Pollon. "They could be dropping the atom bomb and you're inside Elvis's life and it doesn't matter. It just goes on and on. I think if I lived that way a week, I wouldn't know what day it was."

"He had created his own world," says Johnny Rivers. "He had to. There was nothing else for him to do."

-11-

THE MOVIES

FOR SEVEN YEARS ELVIS STAYED on his Bel Air and Memphis hilltops and horsed around with his Mafia, played football and rode motorcycles, dated pretty girls, drove around in amazing automobiles, stayed out of sight most of the time, worried about his weight and hair, cut records and made movies.

Mostly he made movies. From the spring of 1961 to the summer of 1968—the date of the videotaping of his first television special, which marked the beginning of his public return—Elvis starred in no less than twenty-one films, an average of three a year.

Near the beginning of this period was *Blue Hawaii*, the film made following the Pearl Harbor benefit. It was released for the Thanksgiving-Christmas holidays, and when it completed its run in five hundred or so theaters in the U. S. in early 1962, it had grossed $4.7 million, equal to *Gunfight at OK Corral* or *Pal Joey*, and was on *Variety's* list of all-time box office champions. The sound-track album became the fastest selling album of 1961 and occupied the top position on all album sales charts for much of 1962, eventually racking up more than $5 million in sales.

By the time this film was released, Elvis was the well-meaning but bumbling pride of a shiftless family of crackers living off the government in Florida in a film called *Fol-*

low That Dream. Arthur O'Connell played his father, Jack Kruschen and Simon Oakland a couple of inefficient mobsters trying to take advantage of our hero, Anne Helm his love interest, Joanna Moore a sexy but menacing welfare worker. Although Elvis was sympathetic enough in the role, the film did little to change the Hollywood hillbilly stereotype and little to advance his career, even though it was the first to take advantage of his natural flair for comedy.

No matter. No sooner was that in editing than Elvis had turned boxer to appear in a remake of the 1937 flick starring Wayne Morris, *Kid Galahad.* Elvis's karate training—by now he could split bricks—made the fight scenes credible enough, and Joan Blackman was there to listen to Elvis sing while the Kid's hard-drinking manager (Gig Young) tried to double-cross him, but the film needed more than that to put it many notches above the preceding one. The movie was, incidentally, the third in a row in which Elvis often appeared stripped to the waist, something producers apparently believed was an important plus.

Elvis's third movie role in 1962 was that of a charter boat captain in *Girls! Girls! Girls!* One of the writers was Edward Anhalt, who would, two years later, win an Oscar for scripting *Becket.* The picture had, oddly, only two girls in it, Stella Stevens and Laurel Goodwin. For the intellectuals Elvis spoke Chinese (to his sidekick, Benson Fong); and for the fans there were thirteen songs in the film and on the sound-track album, including another in the long line of title tunes by Jerry Leiber and Mike Stoller and the million-selling "Return to Sender," another by Otis Blackwell. The album was certified gold.

In 1963 Elvis made four musicals, the first taking him to Seattle for *It Happened at the World's Fair.* Now Elvis was a crop duster whose co-pilot and partner (Gary Lockwood) kept getting into gambling trouble. As for Elvis, he chased Yvonne Craig around a couch and then went after and—with the help of little Ginny Tui—landed Joan O'Brien, while singing ten new songs. One of them, "One Broken Heart for Sale," still another Otis Blackwell tune, sold the usual million-plus copies when it was released as a single.

Fun in Acapulco was a more substantial film, giving Elvis a solid story line about a trapeze artist (Elvis) afraid of heights following an accident in the States. In sunny Acapulco—and the scenery was terrific; this was something many of Elvis's films offered—he becomes a singing lifeguard who is followed around by a tiny Mexican boy (Larry Tomasin) and the usual flock of pretty girls, Ursula Andress and Elsa Cardenas among them. In the end, after warbling about a dozen songs, Elvis dives from a monstrous cliff, thereby dissolving his acrophobia and establishing himself as one hell of a gringo. There were no singles released from the film, but the sound-track album joined the others in gold on the wall in the den in Graceland.

The third film shot in 1963 was also shot on location, *Viva Las Vegas*. In this, one of his better musicals—and certainly his most successful, grossing $5.5 million in the U. S. alone—Elvis was a race car driver trying to raise money to buy a new engine for The Big Race. He also was competing with an Italian racing champion (Cesare Danova) for the attentions of a swimming pool manager and night club dancer (Ann-Margret). Before it was all over, and Elvis had won the race and the girl, the cast and crew visited every pictureque background within fifty miles of the Vegas strip and Elvis had sung several appealing songs, one a duet with Ann-Margret.

Social note: There was much made of the off-camera duet between Elvis and his redheaded leading lady in this picture, most of it a publicist's puffery. Ann-Margret even went so far as to say Elvis had given her an enormous bed. It was not true, yet when Elvis was asked he graciously said, "Anything the lady says, anything the lady says." And then he stopped seeing her.

Viva Las Vegas was followed by *Kissin' Cousins*, which was in many ways the archetypal Elvis Presley film and in others odd enough to warrant special mention. This was the first to be produced by Sam Katzman, known in Hollywood as the "King of the Quickies." He'd just completed *Hootenanny Hoot*, a revue that had showcased fourteen musical acts (Johnny Cash among them), in eight and a half days and was working on *Your Cheatin' Heart*, the story of the late Hank Williams, which starred George Hamilton and was shot in fifteen days. It was then that he met Colonel Parker. According to Gene Nelson, Katzman's director, Katzman allowed the Colonel to tell M-G-M how to distribute the Williams film, and it subsequently became one of the studio's biggest grossers. Then, Nelson says today, "over a cigar and a cup of coffee, Sam and the Colonel made a deal. The Colonel told Sam, 'Instead of making four-million-dollar pictures like we have been, we want to make a picture the way you do it.' "

"With me being a frugal producer, the Colonel figured we could save a few dollars," Katzman says today. "I saw a few of Elvis's pictures and some I liked, some I didn't. I knew Elvis at heart was a country boy, so I thought we better put him back in the woods, put him back in the country where he belonged. So I assigned a writer [Gerald Drayson Adams] to write an original story for him."

Later the script was rewritten appreciably by Gene Nelson, who says, "As we were writing it, when we came to a spot where a song was needed, we wrote down four to six suggested song titles and sent the scenes and titles to Freddie Bienstock in New York, who then sent them to his writers. And then we sent the script to the Colonel with a note: 'Before we send this to Elvis, we wanted you to see it.' The Colonel sent it back with his note: 'Thank you for the script, Gene. But if you want an opinion or evaluation of this script, it will cost you an additional $25,000.' "

Gene says the Colonel later explained, "We don't know how to make pictures. We have you for that. All we want is songs for an album."

The story was about as flimsy as most but offered the twist
of having Elvis in a dual role, playing an Air Force officer
trying to persuade a hillbilly family to allow a missile base
on their land, and also the part of his cousin, one of the
Smoky Mountaineers. Both characters—one brunet, the other
blond—danced and sang and, except for the hair of course,
sounded and looked exactly alike. As the hillbilly he again
had Arthur O'Connell as a father, Glenda Farrell as a mother
and Yvonne Craig and Pam Austin as sisters. In his role as
the officer he had Yvonne as his romantic lead.

In time the demonstration records began to arrive from
New York, three and four for each spot in the script, and
Nelson and Katzman began screening them. "We still hadn't
met Elvis," Gene says. "He had been busy on another film
and had gone back to Memphis for a rest when he finished
it. So we sent him the script and two demos for each spot.
We never heard from him but met him a few days later in
Nashville, where we were going to record."

They arrived in the middle of a snowstorm and reported
to the RCA studios, where Elvis signed a few autographs as
he walked through the gathered teenagers and then greeted
his friends the Jordanaires. The session began at nine in the
evening, and eight hours later every one of the nine songs
had been recorded. Elvis's performance was businesslike
professional, but matter-of-fact. There was no rock 'n' roll
in this collection of songs, just as there had been little or no
rock in the previous half-dozen films. And it was obvious to
those there, as well as to anyone except the most ardent fan
who listened to the album, that Elvis was practically throwing the songs away as he sang them. And then it was back
to Hollywood.

"Things got tense on *Kissin' Cousins* because of the tight
schedule," says Gene Nelson. "He'd never worked this way
before. The Colonel explained how he'd make more money
on the fifty per cent of profit deal he had [in addition to
$750,000 in salary] and I said it was like shooting a television

show and to pretend it was that instead of a film. Elvis went along.

"Nonetheless there were times when Sam leaned very, very hard. He was always on the set and I hadn't learned the patience and control I think I have now and I'd get uptight, and this upset Elvis. He came to me the last week and he said he didn't like to work this way, it wasn't worth it. He said he knew what pressure I was under and he volunteered to get sick or show up late if it would help. I thanked him and said to hang in—it was my problem, not his."

There were other problems too, not the least of which was the blond wig Elvis had to wear whenever he played the hillbilly cousin. "It was really trauma for him," says Yvonne Craig. "He didn't want to come out of the dressing room with the blond wig on. I figured other things were happening and said to Gene Nelson, 'What's the hangup this morning?' And Gene said, 'Well, it's a problem. Elvis feels that he looks odd in the blond wig and really he doesn't have the guts to get up and get out here yet. But don't anybody make any remarks like "Gee, you sure look funny with the blond wig on."' Elvis never said anything about the wig, except that he didn't care for it. But he dyes his hair. That's no secret, you know. And I thought, Could it have something to do with that?"

There also was an accident when the cast was on location for a week at Big Bear, a ski resort a couple of hours from Los Angeles. Glenda Farrell broke her neck during a scene when she was to flip Elvis from the porch of a house. Actually, Elvis flipped himself in the stunt and on the first take it worked perfectly. But on the second take she didn't let go and she went down, hitting her neck on a step. The rest of the picture she wore a brace until it was time to go on camera.

The final problem came in shooting the final scene, when Elvis and Lance LeGault, who was doubling him, were circling each other. "Marvelous Sam Katzman," says Yvonne

Craig. "Lance was supposed to stand with his back to the camera and as he moved, Elvis with black hair was moving up and as Lance made the turn, they were to lock off the camera and switch them, putting Elvis in a blond wig, Lance in a black wig. But somebody blew it and in the final scene you see Lance looking right into the camera. You could see it wasn't Elvis. Clearly. And Sam Katzman said, 'Nobody'll even know.' It was too expensive to shoot it again and that's the way it went into the theaters."

The film was completed two days late, but still in under two and a half weeks and at a total cost of $1.3 million, about a third to a fourth of what the likes of *Blue Hawaii* had cost. *Kissin' Cousins* apparently had all the right ingredients too, appealing to M-G-M so much the studio released it before *Viva Las Vegas*, in time for the Easter school holidays.

Elvis's first film in 1964 was *Roustabout*, which told the tired old tale about cold-hearted business types moving in to shut down a fumbling carnival. Elvis was a vagabond singer who fell in with Barbara Stanwyck, the show's owner, and then fell in love with Joan Freeman, daughter of Leif Erickson, the temperamental boss of the show. There was a blow-up caused by the romance, Elvis took his guitar to a rival show and then returned as the sheriff was moving in for foreclosure. Sue Ann Langdon was on hand as the female menace to the Presley-Freeman romance, there was a belly dancer—giving reason to unwrap a five-year-old classic by Leiber and Stoller, "Little Egypt," originally sung by the Coasters—and Elvis was permitted to ride a Honda around the dusty hillsides of Thousand Oaks, California, where the film was shot. None of the eleven songs was released as a single, but the sound-track album was another million-seller.*

* The only other noteworthy feature—in restrospect—was a scene that had two pretty girls taking an outdoor shower behind one of those board walls that cover from knee to neck. Billy Barty, a midget, came along to peek at the girls and then Elvis arrived to break up the resultant chaos. One of the girls was Raquel Welch, making a Hollywood debut she never talks about.

After *Roustabout* Elvis made *Girl Happy,* in which he was a night club entertainer who found love and reason to warble eleven new songs in Fort Lauderdale during the annual Easter college migration. The picture's producer, Joe Pasternak, previously had made *Where the Boys Are* in the Florida beach city and admits today that when he arrived with Elvis the city was less than thrilled, because his first film had "brought down ten times as many college boys and it almost wrecked the town." Elvis had three sidekicks in the movie backup band—Gary Crosby, Joby Baker and Jimmy Hawkins —and the girls he chased were Shelley Fabares and Mary Ann Mobley. The single released from the film was a typical mid-sixties dance number, "Do the Clam."

Elvis's third, and last, film for 1964 was *Tickle Me,* his first for Allied Artists, one of Hollywood's studios then staggering toward bankruptcy. It had Elvis playing a singing rodeo rider who got a job on an expensive dude ranch that apparently catered almost exclusively to voluptuous girls who spent most of their time in peekaboo bathing suits. The story line: Elvis and the girls (Jocelyn Lane, Julie Adams) go hunting for hidden treasure and find it. Said the New York *Times,* rightly: "This is the silliest, feeblest and dullest vehicle for the Memphis Wonder in a long time." Even so, the movie made a lot of money and Allied stepped away from bankruptcy court for another year.

Next came his second quickie for Sam Katzman, Elvis's first "costume" flick, *Harum Scarum,* a weak and muddled musical adventure that had Elvis running around some mythical Arab kingdom in robes and on dromedaries. The story had him playing an American movie star who was kidnaped during a sort of State Department tour in the Middle East. Mary Ann Mobley was the daughter of a king and somehow, following some foolishness involving political assassins and the like, everybody moved to Las Vegas, where Elvis entertained everybody. All Sam Katzman says about this one is "It didn't do so good as *Kissin' Cousins.*" The director,

Gene Nelson, believes Elvis never looked better, but says the script was "a bad choice." (At one point the Colonel suggested adding a talking camel, but no one was listening. It might have helped.) The film was shot in eighteen days, Elvis was paid a million dollars—and was owed the usual 50 per cent of profits—and it was released in several cities as part of a double feature with a witless Japanese horror film, *Ghidrah, the Three-Headed Monster.*

And then came *Frankie and Johnny,* a much-reworked version of the original story that had Elvis, a riverboat gambler, romancing Donna Douglas, who was then very big with fans of the *Beverly Hillbillies* television series. Nancy Novack played Nellie Bly in the film and for those who didn't see it, and remember the tragic ending in the popular legend, the United Artists studio had everybody happy and alive at the end. Adding to the musical farrago was the fact that Elvis and the cast performed the *real* story, with Frankie shooting Johnny after he started fooling around with Nellie, at one point in the script. It was a confusing film and not an especially entertaining one, although Elvis did look quite handsome and comfortable as a Southern gambler. "Even compared to some previous Presley turkeys," said the New York *Times,* "this one almost sheds feathers from the start."

And then came *Paradise, Hawaiian Style,* sort of a remake of *Blue Hawaii,* in which Elvis played an airline pilot whose inordinate interest in girls gets him in trouble with his boss, so he returns to Hawaii, where he convinces a buddy (James Shigeta) to set up a charter helicopter service. Suzanna Leigh was Elvis's girl friend and many of the scenes—dances and songs, primarily—were shot at the Polynesian Cultural Center on Oahu where Elvis's dressing room was a replica of a native royal palace from Hawaii's more primitive and natural past. The sound-track album of nine songs—plus one of the "bonus" tunes that were added to many sound-track LPs as filler—sold about as well as that of the preceding film —moderately, but profitably.

The pictures continued to appear, as regularly as the school holidays. In 1966 he made *Spinout,* his second with Joe Pasternak and sixth with director Norman Taurog. This was another one about fast cars and only slightly slower girls (Deborah Walley, Diane McBain, Shelley Fabares), plus a lot of fairly interesting rock 'n' roll. Each of the three girls used a different ploy to land Elvis—Shelley her dad's money, Diane a book she was writing, while Deborah was trying to get him to recognize her as something more than one of the four guys in his backup band. (He was a *singing* race car driver.) There were nine songs in the flick, and on the album there were three bonus songs, including "Tomorrow Is a Long Time," the only Bob Dylan song Elvis ever recorded.

Double Trouble was a little better, but not much. Elvis was a tuxedoed rock 'n' roll singer who was supposed to be in love with two girls at the same time—thus the title—an aggressive tease (Yvonne Romain) and a naïve English heiress (Annette Day). Elvis leaves for a tour of Europe and is followed by Miss Day, who is pursued by her murderous uncle and two bumbling but occasionally amusing hoodlums. There are also three bumbling foreign policemen in trench coats—played by former vaudevillians, the Wiere Brothers—and eight songs, one of them an updated "Old MacDonald's Farm."

The final film made in 1966 was *Easy Come, Easy Go,* in which Elvis played a Navy frogman searching for a sunken treasure ship. There were two girls—Dodie Marshall, a descendant of the treasure ship's captain, and Pat Priest—and three songs. Unfortunately, the only real moments of entertainment came when Elsa Lanchester appeared briefly as a wacky yoga cultist.

And then, just before he married in the spring of 1967, Elvis appeared in *Clambake* as the son of an oil millionaire who wanted to be loved—by Shelley Fabares—for himself and not his money. So he exchanges places with a Florida ski instructor (Will Hutchins) and wins a ski boat regatta, beating his rival in the film (Bill Bixby). Elvis acquitted himself in his usual competent manner—while singing seven songs—but the film was another in that long gray line of musical clinkers. Said the New York *Times:* "What do we see over his shoulder when the star drives Miss Fabares to the Miami airport and professes true love? Mountains, real Florida mountains."

Just as there were such easily recognizable commodities as "the Jerry Lewis movie" and "the beach party flick" (of which *Blue Hawaii* might be considered an antecedent) in the mid-sixties, there was something called "the Elvis Presley movie." They had, even by the time *Blue Hawaii* appeared in 1962, become so individualized—as predictable as the seasons, as pretty as postcards—they were a category unto themselves.

The plots seemed to be little more than thinly disguised vehicles designed to carry the star into a recording studio to produce another album of songs. Yvonne Craig calls the films operettas. "The philosophy seemed to be, Don't say it if you can sing it." The cast was composed of talented character personalities (Arthur O'Connell, Dolores Del Rio, Barbara Stanwyck and Gig Young) on one side and gaggles of attractive young people (Gary Lockwood, Bill Bixby, James Shigeta, and the bikini girls) on the other. Plus attractive locations and lots of shiny land, sea and air vehicles.

Essentially they were all fantasies, totally unrelated to reality, or to anything outside Elvis's world. Not even when twist number, "Rock-a-Hula Baby," was inserted at the last minute in *Blue Hawaii* or "Bossa Nova Baby" was shoe horned into *Fun in Acapulco* or "Do the Clam" was shoved into *Girl Happy,* all to capitalize on current musical or dance fads, did Elvis seem in touch.

A footnote: In 1965, as Elvis celebrated his thirtieth birthday, the number one song in the U. S. was "I Feel Fine," the fifth consecutive number one song for the Beatles. Later i

he year the Beatles visited Elvis at his Bel Air home, joining
him in an impromptu jam session, and although the Beatles
themselves say Elvis was what inspired them, Elvis didn't
have any number one songs from the spring of 1962 to the
winter of 1969.

The films were alike in another way—they were attacked
constantly, even by those who took part in them. As some of
the criticism was offered, however, so was an explanation.

Says Lance LeGault, the talented blues singer from Louisiana who doubled Elvis or plotted his choreography from 1960
through 1968: "We shot *Kissin' Cousins* in seventeen days
and I think that film was the turning point in Presley films as
far as shooting. Up until that time certain standards had been
maintained. But it seems to me from *Kissin' Cousins* [1963]
on we were always on short schedule. That's where we noticed
there was no rehearsal for all the numbers.

"Now I don't remember how long we were on *Viva Las
Vegas*," Lance says today, "but it seems it was ten or eleven
weeks. A long time. That was the picture just before *Kissin'
Cousins*. We weren't off a week or two weeks when—boom—
we jumped right back into *Kissin' Cousins*, which was shot
in seventeen days. From then on, once they realized they
could take this guy and do a film that quickly, we were on
quick pictures."

Lance is a tall, husky blond who met Elvis when he came
to a club where Lance was singing.

"He always had a thing—six o'clock, he was through. But
many times I stayed and worked with him late. On his own
time. Because we had the number to do the next morning and
there hadn't been time for him to learn it. More times than I
can tell you there was no lunch break. Because when everyone broke for lunch was an ideal time to use the stage, the
actual place where the scene was to be shot. And we'd rehearse all the lunch hour, except for the last ten or fifteen
minutes of it. That time he would use to get ready for the first
scene. Because he'd be wringing wet, his hair'd be messed up.

Because we'd worked thirty-five or forty minutes—hard! You know, Get this damn number cookin'. That's how the sched ules were set up. There'd be six or seven or eight songs to do where he had to move and there'd never be any time on the schedule for him to rehearse properly. It was a bear, man."

It was, apparently, largely a matter of attitude—the way the studios handled Elvis. "The first time I noticed it for rea was in *Roustabout*," Lance says. "Elvis rode a Honda in it Which is pretty silly, when you think about it, because Elvi rode Harleys. Always rode a big Harley. Yet in the film they put him on a 350 Honda. And this is a guy who's playing the part of a drifter whose only mode of transportation is hi bike. This is a guy who supposedly goes across country on a machine that's about right for the driveway, a 350 Honda.

"That's just a little, simple example. They never used Elvi to his full capacity in the situations in these films . . . in these songs that were given to him to do . . . never, never used the guy. I always had the feeling: Okay, here's a schedule and because it's Elvis we're gonna make so much money with the film regardless of whether he rides a Honda or he rides a Harley-Davidson, whether he sings a groovy tune like 'Don' Be Cruel' or 'All Shook Up,' where you had the real Elvis, a opposed to any piece of crap you want to name that he sang in the film. If you were there and saw it time after time . . . never counted up the films, but I think I did between twelve and fourteen, fifteen films, plus the NBC special . . . and kept seeing incident after incident after incident of taking somebody and treating him like it's good enough because it' Elvis and it's in *color*. And so we're gonna make two and a half times negative cost, plus another two and a half times . . y'see?"

Dozens of others agree, picking on the choice of director or the script or some other aspect of the films. Says a former studio executive who watched Elvis make more than a dozen films: "Directors usually handle Elvis with kid gloves. Ther was one picture that was thirty minutes late in starting, which is a lot of time when you're on location. They were late because Elvis wasn't there. And Elvis wasn't there because the director was afraid to send somebody to knock on Elvis's dressing room door. His best performances have been with gutsy directors, but there haven't been very many of them. They're afraid of alienating Elvis or the Colonel."

Says Gerald Drayson Adams, who wrote *Kissin' Cousins* and *Harum Scarum:* "There never were any story conferences. They consisted of money—first act, second act, third act money. And all were conducted by Colonel Parker."

"*Clambake* was one of the really, really awful ones," says Jack Good, the Englishman who had produced the *Shindig* television show before taking a small role in the picture. "There was a party after the film was completed, with Lance LeGault's band playing. And Elvis wouldn't sing. Slowly, Lance got him into a blues thing, 'Let It Roll.' And he was terrific. And I thought what a shame he doesn't do that sort of thing in the film."

Says Joe Pasternak: "Elvis should be given more meaty parts. He's thirty-five years old, he's a man, he's got guts, he's got strength, he's got charm. He would be a good actor. He should do more important pictures."

Many felt Elvis was talented. Even the hard-to-please Bosley Crowther of the New York *Times* had said, "This boy can act," about his portrayal in *King Creole,* recall. Others concurred. Don Siegel, the director of *Flaming Star,* said Elvis had switched from Little Richard to Stanislavsky, had become a Method actor who "jumps out at you from the screen." Yvonne Craig said she'd seen but one other actor more at ease while doing scenes, Spencer Tracy. Excusing some of his sadder efforts, even Hedda Hopper came to Elvis's defense, saying, so what if he wasn't a trained actor, neither was Gary Cooper; he learned on-camera too. Says Bill Bixby: "He is a performer, he is an actor. He is worth considerably more than people have given him credit for. Frank Sinatra once said the best singers are the best actors and I think he's absolutely right. He's a good example. When Frank decides to act, man, stand aside. Elvis Presley has the same kind of presence. There is a presence. That's the only word I can think of. They both have it and I am not making a comparison. When they take stage, they take stage. They are it." And Gene Nelson says, "He always could handle more than he ever took on."

Elvis apparently disagreed in 1963, when he said, "I've had intellectuals tell me that I've got to progress as an actor, explore new horizons, take on new challenges, all that routine. I'd like to progress. But I'm smart enough to realize that you can't bite off more than you can chew in this racket. You can't go beyond your limitations. They want me to try an artistic picture. That's fine. Maybe I can pull it off someday. But not now. I've done eleven pictures and they've all made money. A certain type of audience likes me. I entertain them with what I'm doing. I'd be a fool to tamper with that kind of success."

Perhaps so. But Elvis was being unduly modest and in a few years' time the audience, the success, changed. Gerald Drayson Adams says the Colonel once told him there were a quarter million dyed-in-the-wool Elvis Presley fans who'd see every picture three times, that Elvis transcended any material given him. This point is an important one. Elvis *did* transcend all the medium-to-lousy material he was assigned; when lines formed outside the theaters, those in the lines were there to see Elvis and no one or anything else. This had changed by 1966. Elvis had put on weight and his dyed hair was sprayed with so much lacquer you could bounce rocks off it and even the loyal fans who wrote for *Elvis Monthly*, a British publication, stopped going to the pictures. One called the films "animated puppet shows for not-overbright children." And Elvis began to wonder about the product he was turning out, first showing boredom and then occasional pique.

Red West, who continued to work as Elvis's stand-in, says today, "At first it was something new for him. After a while it got to be the same, a pickup from the last movie. It really got so he didn't enjoy doing them. At first he liked making movies, but when it didn't get any better . . . the scripts didn't get any better and the songs were all the same, it kinda got bogged down. Actually, some of the films he couldn't wait till they were through. Most of 'em. He liked *Wild in the Country* because there was a good story there. He liked *King Creole* and he liked *Flaming Star* and I can't think of too many more he enjoyed doing."

A dozen others say essentially the same thing—that Elvis began to abhor his films. Those present when Elvis cut songs for the movies say he'd wander over after listening to one of the demonstration records and say, "What can you do with a piece of shit like this?" But apparently he never said anything to the Colonel or the people at Hill and Range; according to friends, Elvis preferred to go along rather than fight with anyone. Gene Nelson says that after they'd finished *Harum Scarum,* Elvis came to him and said, "Maybe one day we'll do one right." And a former executive at M-G-M says that after Elvis had completed one of his pictures there, he approached the director and said, "Hey, there were some pretty funny things in this script. I'm gonna have to read it some day." He wasn't smiling.

Says Jack Good today: "I said to Elvis, 'Why do you keep making these rotten films? Why don't you do something really exciting, like *King Creole?*' He said he left all that to the Colonel, but that the Colonel promised something really exciting soon, real soon."

-12-
THE COLONEL [2]

THE FUNNY THING ABOUT IT was that while turning out so much pap, Elvis became the highest paid entertainer in history; as the quality of the films went down, Elvis's earnings went up, up, up, until they began to average out at between five and six million dollars a year. Other performers may have been wealthier—thanks largely to wise investment —but none was paid so much for performing. Elizabeth Taylor, Cary Grant and Audrey Hepburn were in the million-dollar-per-picture category, but Elvis stayed ahead because he was getting a million dollars *plus* 50 per cent of the profits, and for the better part of his career all the films were profitable.

"They don't need titles," said an M-G-M studio man who worked on five of them. "They could be numbered. They would still sell."

Elvis also contracted to do more pictures per year than any other superstar. The Grants and Taylors and Hepburns of the business insisted upon script approval and they were picky about what they'd do, but Elvis would amble (sing) through anything he was given, and few pictures were so complicated that they required more than five or six weeks to shoot, so Elvis did a lot of them.

A breakdown of his 1965 income:

—Salary for *Harum Scarum:* $1,000,000.

—Salary for *Frankie and Johnny:* $650,000. (This and other sums were under a million because of early contract dates.)

—Salary for *Paradise, Hawaiian Style:* $350,000.

—Percentage of profits from *Tickle Me:* $850,000.

—Percentage of profits from *Girl Happy:* $850,000.

—RCA record royalties: $1,125,000.

—Music publishing royalties: $400,000.

All of which came to more than $5 million and did not include income from non-performing activities such as royalties on Elvis Presley products still being carried by several large chains and mail-order businesses.

And if these figures weren't enough to impress, others were released the same year. It was when Elvis and the Colonel celebrated their tenth anniversary together that the Colonel said the seventeen films released to date (April 1965) had grossed between $125 and $135 million. Then, not to be outdone, RCA said Elvis had sold 100 million records valued at $150 million.

How did it happen? A look at what was titled *Colonel Parker's Special Promotion and Exploitation Campaign,* prepared for *Kissin' Cousins,* shows how this worked. Although it is only sixteen mimeographed pages long, it could be considered the definitive text in its field. Some of the bases the Colonel touched in the report, in the order given:

1. Every piece of outgoing mail from RCA and M-G-M and the Colonel's office carried literature about *Kissin' Cousins,* was rubber-stamped with a *"Kissin' Cousins* Is Coming" type of message, and carried an Elvis Presley pocket calendar.

2. Interviews were set with Elvis (rarely) and other cast and crew members (less rarely).

3. Photographs were taken whenever Elvis was visited on the set by celebrities.

4. A regular series of bulletins were issued to the leading fan clubs, with special attention paid to the hundred or so that offered their members fan club newsletters.

5. Radio spots employed the drawls of two of the Colonel's

favorite disc jockeys, Biff Collie and Squeakin' Deacon, and emphasized what the Colonel called "the fun and frolic of the hoedown and mountain folk humor."

6. The standard RCA tie-ins were planned—covering preparation and makeup of the album and singles to be released; scheduling of release (some of the dates had to be staggered so the album would appear in the stores the same week the film appeared in local theaters); preparation and distribution of streamers, display racks and other point-of-sale devices to be shipped to the 12,000 record dealers in the U. S. (all cross-promoting the film, of course).

7. Window displays were planned for lazy or unimaginative record store owners, along with disc jockey promotions and radio contests.

8. The M-G-M field men and the five hundred movie house managers, the RCA field men and the record retailers, all were told to get (a) friendly and (b) busy. They also were told how.

9. A special RCA campaign was launched: ELVIS MONTHS—APRIL AND MAY.

10. Just before *Kissin' Cousins* was released, press kits offering a wide assortment of pictures, feature stories, plot synopses, ads, etc., went to the Colonel's full list of columnists, wire service and newspaper writers. Wires and cables were sent to leading show business personalities, and personal contact was made with a list of disc jockeys and radio executives. "In short," the Colonel said in his report, "people in the trade were sensing that something was going on and they were watching with interest for the public reception."

11. Fan club presidents were written again and given means and materials with which to make everyone in their own communities and in the cities of all their members what the Colonel called "*Kissin' Cousins* minded." (Send the disc jockeys requests to play the title song, etc.)

"With the release of the picture and the first positive indications of a most enthusiastic public reception, these activities were continued and enlarged upon, carrying much the same excitement and interest of the election returns night," said the Colonel. "The bandwagon was starting to roll and everyone was being encouraged to get on board."

Before it was all over, the following promotional material had been distributed: 3,000,000 wallet-sized calendars; 15,000 *Kissin' Cousins* single-record streamers; 15,000 *Kissin' Cousins* album streamers; 5000 *Kissin' Cousins* lapel buttons for use in radio contests and distribution at record hops; 3000 eight-by-ten color photos; 1500 photo albums; 150,000 copies of "Kissin' Cousins" sheet music; 400 souvenir kits to writers; 1000 special promotional kits to exhibitors; and 15,000 fan club president kits, one to each club.

Says a former associate of the Colonel's who worked with him in promoting some of the movies: "What this all comes down to is the Colonel goes in ahead of Elvis and gets things stirred up. Elvis is catered to out of proportion to his size, when compared to anyone else of like or approximate stature."

This was the keystone to the Colonel's philosophy.

In 1963 Jon Hartmann was an aspiring actor who took a job in the mail room of the William Morris Agency, thinking it would give him invaluable contacts in terms of advancing a film career. The way he tells it today, Jon decided two weeks later to stick with the agency; the power thing involved in selling talent appealed to him. Six months after that he was given what was thought to be the "shit assignment" for William Morris employees—he was sent to join Colonel Parker's staff for two weeks. There he was to be the Colonel's "go-fer," to fetch him coffee on demand, to drive his car for him, to do whatever he asked. At the end of the two weeks the Colonel didn't so much as say thanks but said instead, "Why don't you come back on Monday?" It meant Jon had pleased the Colonel, and the way Jon looks at it now, everything he knows about show business, which is appreciable, he owes to the next six months. One of the first things he learned, he says today, was the manager's relationship with his client.

"The game of artist-manager is a very tricky game because the artist's manager, outside of the talent agency level, is a non sequitur," Jon says today. "He doesn't have a union. He is a manager only because he and the talent say he is. He doesn't have any other qualifications. It's a bastard art. His responsibilities can be whatever he determines they are. And the way I see it, the way the Colonel ran things, a good manager had to believe there were no rules or regulations—you can make your own rules so long as you can get away with it, and that's what makes a good manager.

"Once the Colonel saw what Elvis was, which was probably the first time he ever saw him, the Colonel probably was with Elvis constantly until Elvis was totally under the hypnotic control of his personality," Jon says. "Because a manager doesn't trust the artist. He's always afraid the artist is going to blow it. That's why he's the manager. And the Colonel only laid back on being Elvis's constant mentor, I would think, after Elvis's scene had sort of evolved into a position of safety, sociologically.

"What this is, is psychology at its highest level. What the Colonel is, is a superpsychologist to a superstar. He didn't see Elvis too often, but I don't think that Elvis would do anything without checking with the Colonel first."

Says one of the Colonel's friends: "He believes the artist should be able to live his life privately and he believes the personal manager should too. They seldom see each other outside work hours, maybe a couple or three times a year. I used to question that, but not any more. If you look at today's personal managers, the young ones, you see them living with the act and all that. Well, the relationships don't last very long. With Elvis and the Colonel, Elvis doesn't tell the Colonel how to run the business end and the Colonel doesn't tell Elvis how to sing. It works out pretty well."

And Ron Jacobs says, "Some people think the Colonel is a buffoon and that Presley is some kind of greasy puppet. It's just not true. It's a team, man—the best, most efficient team in America."

Spyros Skouras, former head of 20th Century-Fox, once tried to get Elvis to make a public appearance against the Colonel's advice. "If you can get Elvis to do it," the Colonel said, "you can *have* him." Elvis stayed home.

Says Jon Hartmann: "He made it totally easy on his client, y'see. Elvis floats on a cloud of adoration. He never witnesses any pressure. He just has to appear, that's all. He's totally free. He's freer than any other star. All the other stars are being called all the time for benefits and so on. Well, by the time I was with the Colonel, 1963 and 1964, it had been firmly established that Elvis did nothing. It was no to everything. No other star had, or has today, the freedom Elvis had."

Jon says the Colonel kept Elvis "loose" so subsequently Elvis would do anything he wanted him to. Jon says this may sound Machiavellian but isn't so nasty as it sounds, because most artists have no inkling how to operate a business and if the artist wants to be successful economically, he has to believe in a businessman as much as the businessman says he believes in the artist. And one of the keys to this arrangement is keeping the artist comfortable.

"The Colonel's comfort campaign includes having people next to Elvis who are the people he likes and who can keep other people away," Jon says. "That's why the Mafia was so close to him. That's why others couldn't get through. They weren't needed. Elvis had all the companionship he wanted."

Another thing Jon says he learned about was success and how it is assured through salesmanship.

"There's regional success and there's world success, and those are the two smaller kinds," Jon says. "Both of those are economic successes. There's another level of show business that transcends economic success. That's media success, media power. What Presley has, thanks to the Colonel, is the most media power he could possibly have.

"The Colonel doesn't sell Elvis to the public, dig? He sells

Elvis to the people who sell the public, and those are the media people—the television and motion picture personalities, the executives and businessmen who control the networks, the important radio people. It's like an endless trip for the Colonel. Elvis, as a product, always is in the state of being sold.

"He communicates with these people regularly and he draws on their energies, pulling them along with him. He makes it fun for them and that's why they go along. He makes them members of the Snowmen's League. He works one of his elaborate practical jokes. He sucks them in. I'll give you a small example. When the Colonel came into his office in the morning, there'd be a list of names on his desk. These were the people whose birthday it was that day. Most of them got a telegram: 'Happy birthday . . . from Elvis and the Colonel.' Somebody heavy he'd call to wish a happy birthday personally. On one occasion I suffered the indignity of having to stand in front of a microphone that was hooked into the telephone and sing happy birthday to a 20th Century-Fox executive, along with Irving, Grelun and Jim, the other guys in the office, in four-part harmony. I thought it was kinda rank, but I did it anyway, because I was into making it.

"The executives, or stars, or whoever, at the receiving end of this would think it was just terrific. They'd really be flattered. They'd get a big kick out of it. Most of them even felt they owed the Colonel something in return, which of course is what the Colonel had in mind to begin with. He'd sucked them in. Now they were on his team and the Colonel had them selling for him, selling Elvis to the public. It was amazing to watch. Every day the Colonel'd do something like this. And the team just kept getting bigger and bigger and bigger."

Jon mentioned the Snowmen's League. This preposterous organization occupied much of the Colonel's spare time over the years (dating back to the fifties) and its membership, in fact, formed a large part of the "team" Jon and others talk about. In the words of a slickly assembled booklet the Colonel distributes with a membership certificate and card to members, the organization was formed for those "skilled in evasiveness and ineptitude." The members—probably uncounted, according to the Colonel's friends—include dozens of the country's top executives and two, perhaps three, U.S. Presidents.

A classic piece of nonsense, its table of contents includes chapters on "Counteracting High Pressure Snowing: The Melt and Disappear Technique" and "Directional Snowing," which deals with "approach and departure simultaneously." Seven chapters were promised, none delivered—the following thirty-two pages were blank. But the story told in the back of the booklet is sufficient reason for making note of it. It tells how the Colonel thinks.

"In arranging and financing this report, our Chief Potentate, Colonel Tom Parker, first learned the unit cost per book. This cost, when buying a small number of books, seemed exorbitant in view of our financial state, which is less than negligible. However, by buying in larger quantities it was found that the unit cost per book became less and less. The Chief Potentate then increased the quantity ordered to the point where the unit cost went down to zero.

"This represented another problem, for to get the price down that low required a tremendous quantity of books. This meant a storage problem for the printer. However, the Chief Potentate agreed to allow the printer to cut back the order so that his savings on material and labor offset the cost of storage, thus permitting the printer to run these off at a reduced loss to himself for which he was very grateful."

What this was, was an example of something the Colonel recommended elsewhere in the pamphlet—the "snowman's willingness to see the other man's problems and show the greatest understanding without financial involvement." In other words, let someone else (RCA, M-G-M, William Morris) pick up the expensive overhead—the cost of office space, salaries, large mailings and the like.

According to members of the Snowmen's League—who say they would be "unsnowed" if it were known they talked—it cost nothing to get into the league, a thousand dollars to get out.

There are dozens of what seem to be apocryphal stories told about the Colonel, most of them told by the Colonel himself, but apparently most are true and most concern his own special means of making money for his boy. Any visitor to his suite of offices in the 1960s was treated to several.

Hubert Long, the Nashville talent manager who worked for the Colonel twenty years ago, remembers one: "When Elvis was going to do that film at the World's Fair, they were after him to do a personal appearance in a stadium that held thousands, and the Colonel was asking an enormous price. The Colonel said okay to everything and the promoter said okay to everything and then the promoter said, 'There's one thing we forgot, Colonel. This is outa-doors and what happens in the event of rain? Do we get another date?' The Colonel said, 'Wait a minute, you mean there's no roof on that building?' The promoter said, 'Oh no, it's a stadium.' The Colonel thought a minute and said, 'In the event of rain, we will have the concession to sell umbrellas.'"

An executive at 20th Century-Fox tells another: "The studio wanted Elvis to sing some additional songs in one of the films and the Colonel said it would cost the studio another $25,000. The man the Colonel was dealing with was aghast. He said absolutely not. Without blinking, the Colonel reached into his pocket, pulled out a pair of dice, tossed them on the man's desk and said, 'Tell you what—we'll roll the dice, double or nothing.'"

Other times when the Colonel got a call for Elvis to do something, he'd say the boy was tied up for the next three and a half years, but he'd be pleased to rent the gold lamé suit for the weekend for $5000. The gold Cadillac was leased to RCA and RCA put a man on staff full time to travel with the car, exhibiting it for charity. When asked if Elvis would do a walk-on on the *Joey Bishop Show*, the Colonel said yes, for $2500 and when the producer asked why so little, the Colonel said it would cost another $47,500 for Elvis to walk back off. And when a Beverly Hills publicity firm made a two-hour presentation, guaranteeing, among other things, the cover of *Life*, and the Colonel said how much money are we talking about, the agency thought he was asking their price, but what he was really asking was how much the agency was willing to pay for the honor of representing Elvis.

Even when the Colonel says no, he says it with a flair. When the Colonel says yes, however, some of the humor is lost in telling the story.

When the RCA contract expired some years ago and was renegotiated, for example, RCA executives complained to friends that the Colonel got everything but the dog in the company trademark. One friend says that, among other things, RCA agreed to press one million copies of each record, no matter what the record's quality or public interest in it—making it difficult if not impossible for distributors, who got the records whether they wanted them or not, to regulate their inventory in a normal businesslike fashion. While another friend quotes the Colonel as saying that RCA must print at least a million copies of the Elvis pocket calendar each year, distribute them without charge—and pay a royalty on each one of them for the use of Elvis's picture.

"I'd rather try and close a deal with the devil" is the appraisal attributed to Hal Wallis, who nonetheless made nine Elvis Presley pictures. Sam Katzman calls the Colonel "the biggest con artist in the world" and a critic describes him as "the toughest manager since Cardinal Richelieu." A former associate says, "Life is one big joke for the Colonel, as long as it's in his favor." While others quote the Colonel as once saying, "You don't have to be nice to people on the way up if you're not coming back down." Probably this last is not anything the Colonel would say, but even in apocrypha there seems to be more than a fleck of the truth.

However entertaining the stories, they don't sound terribly flattering, but Jon Hartmann is one of many who leaps to the Colonel's defense. "None of the Colonel's shit is evil," he says, "because even where he's laying it out heavy, he's giving those people something that they wouldn't get otherwise. He never takes anything unless he's giving something. He may have embarrassed me occasionally and made me angry, but sometimes he'd hand out hundred-dollar bills for no reason, or radios and records, and I regard the whole thing as an education. The Colonel understands people better than most men, y'dig? He knows how to give them what they want and get what he wants and make everybody happy.

"The only good deals are where everybody's happy. If anybody came out ahead of the other guy, then it wasn't a good deal. And the Colonel has a way of getting people to give him stuff, because he makes them feel he has it coming. It was never leverage used in an negative way. It was 'Look what I did for you, now what are you gonna do for me?' And the guy says, 'Anything you want, Colonel.' And the Colonel says, 'Okay, give me this and give me that.' Next day a crate of cigars or television sets or maybe a matched set of ponies arrives at the Colonel's office. And the guy who sent them *still*, somehow, thinks he owes the Colonel a favor."

Says another former associate: "The Colonel will get as much as he can contractually, but he's also the most honest man there is to deal with. Whatever he can get people to give up, he'll take. He'll say he wants an ashtray he sees on the desk of the guy he's dealing with and he'll say he wants the ashtray thrown into the deal, and if that ashtray isn't delivered on time, Elvis doesn't appear. It sounds small, but I'd take his word over anybody's. Whatever he says to anyone is it. He never goes back on his word."

At the time Jon Hartmann was the Colonel's flunky he reported to a suite of five incredibly cluttered rooms on the Paramount lot, one of the fringe benefits that came with the nine pictures Elvis made for Hal Wallis there. The office was to Parker and Presley, in terms of memorabilia, what the Smithsonian Institution is to America. Walls were covered with photographs of Elvis—from wallet-size to larger-than-life-size—and posters from his movies, in all languages. Another room was wallpapered floor to ceiling with autographed pictures of celebrities, from Charles de Gaulle to Bob Hope to Richard Nixon. In the kitchen there was a huge table for meetings and again the walls were covered—with gold records. In Parker's huge office itself there was an elephant's-foot trash basket and small elephants covered his desk. He was, and is, inordinately fond of elephants, ponies and midgets. There were enormous snowmen and teddy bears and bubble gum machines and neon displays, and on the wall behind his desk were dozens of framed certificates presented to the Colonel for his "non-artistic artistic help" in producing the predictable Elvis album art. (All album covers offered at least one large color photo and never—never—pictured anyone else or credited a record producer.) It was as if he'd never thrown anything away. Jon Hartmann says that when the Colonel moved from Paramount to M-G-M in 1964 he and the others on the staff had to do the moving, and it took weeks.

There was also a public address system in the office, with a horn on the Colonel's desk that squeaked. "He would call us by squeaking the horn and we'd all have to come running," Jon says today. "He'd squeak the horn into the p.a. or just squeak it until everybody was in there at attention. It was just a game we were playing. It was the Elvis Presley Game."

A chain of command had been established in the organization that ran the Elvis Game. The Colonel was the Colonel, and Tom Diskin, still with him after all these years, was the only other officer, perhaps equivalent to a lieutenant in rank. Says a former associate: "He's the one who's paid to do all the worrying." Says Jon: "Elvis has the Colonel to screen out all the unnecessary bullshit, to keep him isolated and comfortable . . . and the Colonel has Diskin. I would guess that the

Colonel only heard about ten per cent of the calls that came in and none of the minor problems. The Colonel speaks for Elvis and Tom Diskin speaks for the Colonel." Diskin, now in his mid-forties to fifties, has never married. He is reported to be a millionaire and has had at least one major operation for ulcers.

According to Jon, Jim O'Brien was next in line, serving as a kind of sergeant-at-arms. He was the Colonel's private secretary, what Jon calls an "efficient motherfucker who handled all the lower-level stuff." Like Diskin, he remains with the Colonel today.

Grelun Landon was a former press contact for Hill and Range. He next worked as a free lance publicist in Hollywood with the Colonel as one of his occasional clients, and then moved over as manager of West Coast public affairs for RCA. He was (and is) a genial, easygoing father of three who went along with more nonsense than most of his friends expected he would. He remains with RCA today and is an active member and sometime officer of the Country Music Association, but spends up to twenty hours a week with the Colonel.

Irving Schecter was another former mail-room boy from William Morris. He worked for the Colonel for four years, although the Morris Agency continued to pay his salary. Along with Jon, Irving was at the bottom of the totem pole and was, among other things, called upon to move the Colonel's belongings from one house in Palm Springs to another when, Jon says, they discovered Elvis's gold suit in the Colonel's closet and gleefully tried it on.

Every day at nine these six would report, and if the Colonel needed any more, he had only to call the Morris Agency or RCA or Paramount or M-G-M.

"Sometimes we'd draft some of the Memphis Mafia," says Jon. "Sometimes we'd pull them in to help with a special mailing. They hated that. If the Colonel put them to work, they thought that was the grossest bummer of all time, the worst part of their job working for Elvis."

The Colonel's office routine was a basic one, Jon says. If the Colonel wasn't there, as was the case on all Mondays and most Friday afternoons, when the Colonel went to Palm Springs, it was relaxed. If the Colonel was in town, "there was a state of tension until the Colonel left. And based on that tension, everybody was supposed to look busy even if they weren't busy. Like, O'Brien would wander around and say, 'Do something.' Y'know? So we'd feign working and go through bullshit changes, to make the Colonel happy, to play the Elvis Presley Game."

Still another former associate goes so far as to say, "The Colonel treats his office staff like shit, especially if there's anybody visiting. All it is, is 'Get the Colonel a cigar! Light Mr. So-and-So's cigarette. Do this! Do that!' And all the time he's winking at you." This same source says the willingness to comply is based on fear and that the fear stretches to the office the Colonel has maintained through the years in Madison. There, he says, the women who run the office (some of them Tom Diskin's sisters), who file, keep the Complete Elvis Presley Scrapbook, post checks, etc., are "so fearful the Colonel might put in an unannounced visit they keep all the pencils sharpened and the same length and everything in every drawer just so. Keep 'em crawling—that's the Colonel's philosophy."

Says another former associate: "When the Colonel was behind his desk, nobody relaxed. The M-G-M, the RCA, the Morris people who were there—every one of them was keyed up. The Colonel's a master at keeping people keyed up. There was one picture the Colonel walked onto the set and coughed. It wasn't intentional. He just coughed—once—and the stage went so quiet you'd-a thought it was the beginning of the world."

Says Ron Jacobs: "He used to carry a ballooning leather hand-tooled souvenir-of-Phoenix valise. And he'd walk into the Morris offices, where everybody was dressed in the dark suits, polished fingernails, everything very proper and cool and just the correct amount of hip and they're sitting around talking about Charlton Heston this morning four million dollars, right? And Parker walks in with his dishevel, socks down around his ankles, carrying that hand-tooled valise and every one of those guys just fall apart."

On the office directory in the lobby of the William Morris Agency in Beverly Hills there are just two names, that of the agency president, Abe Lastfogel, and that of Colonel Thomas Andrew Parker.

Jon Hartmann says he's afraid statements like these, and some he's made himself, make the Colonel seem like a heavy in some B movie. It wasn't really that horrible, he says today. Apparently looking back on it the way most men review their Army duty, he says there were a hell of a lot of laughs and a hell of a lot of genuine concern for the client.

There was the time a promoter entered the Colonel's office at Paramount and laid $50,000 in cash on the Colonel's desk to do a concert with Elvis, and the Colonel pushed the money back to him and said it wasn't enough. "It was policy," Jon says. "Elvis no longer did personal appearances. It wasn't projected as a temporary policy. It was, like, he'd done that part of his scene."

Other times the Colonel had everybody wearing jackets that had the name of Elvis's latest picture, *Girls! Girls! Girls!*, stitched all over the backs.

When someone approached the Colonel to write *his* life story, he said he was writing it himself (something he had been claiming since 1960) and calling it *How Much Does It Cost If It's Free?* He would, however, sell anyone an ad in the book, saying RCA already had taken the back cover for $25,000.

Jon says the Colonel liked to have him serve as chauffeur, driving him around in the beat-up old convertible Jon owned at the time. "The Colonel liked to sit in the back seat, with me at the wheel of this rotten old car, holes in the top and everything, and when we'd be passing through the gate and run into one of the studio executives, the Colonel would reach out through a rip in the top and shake hands, saying, 'Hello, how are you, how do you like my new car?'"

It wasn't all fun and games. "There was the fan club," says Jon, "and it was always serviced. At the time, it was run by the people in the Colonel's office in Madison. The Colonel was very much in tune with fan mail, making sure it was all answered, giving it personal attention, even when it was thousands of letters a day. He was so into this, making sure it was covered, he had arranged to have a mailbox in the mail rooms of the three other studios where Elvis had made pictures. Part of my scene was to go around once a week or so and collect that mail, package it and send it back to Madison."

It was also during this time, Jon says, that the Colonel made one of the biggest Elvis Christmas mailings in a history of Presley-inspired post office gluts. Not only did it carry the usual holiday wishes—to a million-plus recipients—on an eight-by-ten-inch card, it included an eight-by-ten Elvis Presley calendar, a small four-color chromatone postcard photograph, a mimeographed letter bringing all the recipients up to date on Elvis's activities, and one of those notched wooden sticks with a propeller on the end—when you rub a straight stick along the notches, the propeller spins—with the name of Elvis's latest movie, *Fun in Acapulco*, stamped on the side.

"Instead of feeding it down to the Paramount mail room a piece at a time, he waited until it was all done and then had us take it down all at once—ten trunks of the stuff—just to blow their minds in the mail room. That was the vibration the Colonel liked to project," Jon says. "He blew minds. His day consisted of getting everybody high on Elvis, whether it was the mail-room guys at Paramount or the head of 20th Century-Fox or one of his big-time Southern politicians. Everything he did, it was for Elvis."

The office routine seemed to change little after Jon left in 1964, eventually to serve as a ballroom operator and personal manager to several rock bands, including Canned Heat. The lower-level personnel changed periodically. Says Ron Jacobs: "Only Tom Diskin is on the Colonel's payroll. The others are paid by RCA or the studio or the Morris Agency. And they're assigned to him for life if he likes them."

Sometimes he called everyone together and did dramatic readings from the Hollywood trade papers. Says Stan Brossette, the M-G-M publicist: "He especially liked the gossip columns. When he read them, I couldn't breathe for laughing."

And often the Colonel helped others in the business. It was when Sonny and Cher had five records in the Hot 100 that he called their managers in to tell them—without charge, without tangible obligation—how to negotiate. Says one of the managers, Charlie Greene, "I'd been getting Sonny and Cher $2500 a night. After I left the Colonel's office I got on the phone and got them their first $10,000 gig."

He also talked several times with Brian Epstein, the Beatles' manager, providing guidance, especially regarding crowd security. So when the Beatles were sneaked through a mob of fans in a laundry truck and they took rooms in several hotels and Brian considered taking the Beatles through lying on couches that were covered with canvas, looking like so much furniture—it was because the Colonel had conceived and executed these same security measures in 1956 and 1957 when Elvis was touring the U. S.

"He has helped other acts countless times," says one of his closest associates. "He has to be involved and likes to be."

The Colonel was (and is) charitable in many ways. In Nashville Mrs. Jo Walker, executive director of the Country Music Association, says the first contributions to start the city's country and western music museum and hall of fame came from the Colonel and Elvis: checks for $1000 apiece. She says the Colonel, one of the fifty original lifetime members of the CMA, also provided an extensive and imaginative fund-raising campaign. Elsewhere in Nashville the Colonel's old friend and advance agent, Oscar Davis, was partially paralyzed by a stroke in 1963, and when his friends held a benefit party, the Colonel said rather than contribute anything then, he'd send Oscar a hundred dollars a month for life. Still elsewhere in the same city, Minnie Pearl says the Colonel has been sending her a big check each Christmas to be given to one of her pet charities, a home for unwed mothers. "He helps people," she says. "He hears of a widow who's gonna lose her home and he'll pick it up."

Once he was settled at M-G-M, the Colonel began staging what he called "moving drills." That meant if the Colonel ever encountered any friction from the studio, he could have every last eight-by-ten autographed picture, carved elephant and stuffed teddy bear packed in trunks and ready for a move to another studio in twenty minutes.

"Everybody ready to move?" the Colonel would shout.

"Yes, sah!" said someone back.

"Somebody grab the pitchas!"

"Yes, sah! Yes, sah!"

-13-

PRISCILLA

OVER THE YEARS, Elvis's name had been linked with those
of perhaps a hundred girls—some well known, some
not so well known, many of them his leading ladies. Almost
all the relationships, no matter how superficial and innocent
—as most apparently were, were heavily publicized, either
by an eager actress's press agent or the nosy fan magazines.
For years, from 1956 through the period when Elvis was
churning out so many films, the stories in these publications
were of the "Why Elvis and I Can't Marry Now by Anita
Wood" and "Why Troy's Women Prefer Elvis's Kisses" and
"The Night Ann-Margret Confessed to Roger Smith, 'I Can
Never Forget Elvis' " variety. Occasionally Priscilla Beaulieu
was mentioned, and in 1964 one fan magazine was insisting
that Elvis already had married her. It was an old question
asked often of eligible bachelors, and the press was quick
to jump on every shred of "evidence"—that she continued to
make Graceland home, that Elvis had stopped taking girls to
Memphis with him between movies, that they wore expensive,
matching rings, that in January 1967, when Elvis's sixteen-
year-old cousin Brenda Smith was hospitalized, she received
flowers with a card that was signed, "Love, Elvis and Priscilla." Still, it was apparent that most didn't take her too
seriously. She wasn't living alone in Graceland, certainly—

Elvis's aunt and grandmother were permanent residents—and besides, Elvis spent most of his time in Hollywood, dating Hollywood girls. Friends say Elvis enjoyed being a bachelor and they thought he'd never give it up, surely not for several more years.

On Sunday, April 30, the Colonel sent telegrams to his closest friends and associates: Abe Lastfogel, head of the William Morris Agency; Harry Brand, head of publicity at 20th; Grelun Landon and Harry Jenkins, both of RCA; Stan Brossette, the M-G-M publicist who'd worked with the Colonel on the past several pictures, among them.

"He asked us all to go to the airport and he told me to bring two photographers who could be trusted," says Stan Brossette today. "And at the airport we were asked to go to Las Vegas. Rona Barrett had been on the air saying Elvis was getting married in Palm Springs, but we didn't think that was right. Or we wouldn't have been going to Vegas. We thought that's why the Colonel wanted us, but we really didn't know. He didn't tell us and we didn't ask. We were just doing what he wanted done."

They were met in Las Vegas, taken to one of the city's smaller hotels and told to be in the lobby at seven the next morning, when cars would call for them. They were then bade a pleasant good night.

It was three o'clock the following morning when Elvis and Priscilla and four members of the wedding party arrived at the Las Vegas airport in a Lear jet. (The plane had come from Palm Springs.) Friends met them at the airport and drove them immediately to the Clark County courthouse, where Elvis paid fifteen dollars for the marriage license. There is no blood test, no waiting period in Las Vegas. Elvis said he was thirty-two, Priscilla said she was twenty-one. Both gave Memphis as their legal residence, both said it was a first marriage. They then were driven to the Aladdin Hotel on the Vegas Strip, where Elvis and Priscilla and their parents went off to separate suites to get ready, and the rest of the party saw to the catered breakfast that was to follow the wedding ceremony a few hours later. It was soon after that the newsmen began to arrive from downtown Las Vegas and Los Angeles—some of them diverted from Palm Springs.

"We were met at seven," says Stan, "and taken to the rear entrance of the Aladdin and put in separate rooms. Then we were told to meet the Colonel in the coffee shop. By now the hotel lobby was packed with press, but the Colonel wasn't talking. We had breakfast and then were returned to our rooms and told to call no one. Shortly after that he finally told us. I still don't know why the mystery. It was just something the Colonel did."

The double-ring ceremony began at 9:41 A.M. in the second-floor private suite of Milton Prell, the principal owner of the casino and hotel and a longtime friend of the Colonel's. It lasted eight minutes, was conducted by Nevada Supreme Court Judge David Zenoff and had Elvis and Priscilla promising to "love, honor, cherish and comfort." The word "obey" was not used. Elvis wore black tuxedo pants, a black brocaded coat and vest; Priscilla, a semi-fitted floor-length gown of white chiffon over satin with seed pearl and bugle bead trim on the bodice, a six-foot train, a double-tiered rhinestone crown and a full veil. She carried pink rosebuds on a white Bible and her ring had a three-carat diamond as the center stone, surrounded by twenty smaller diamonds.

Joe Esposito and Marty Lacker, the only two members of the Mafia present at the wedding, were dual best men; and Priscilla's only sister, Michelle (she had four brothers), was her maid of honor. Altogether there were but fourteen persons present.

If the ceremony was simple and traditional—forgetting for the moment the rather bizarre location; one would have expected a church in Memphis—what followed it was not. As soon as they said their "I do's" and kissed, they were escorted under guard to the Aladdin Room, where there was a five-foot-high six-tiered wedding cake decorated with pink and white frosting roses, and a breakfast for one hundred (including press, although the photographers had to leave their cameras outside) that reportedly cost $10,000.

Elvis and Priscilla and their families sat at a long head table, the guests at nine round tables, all covered with pink tablecloths. The food was served buffet style—although there were twenty waiters in white gloves serving champagne and tending to the smaller details—and included ham and eggs, Southern fried chicken, roast suckling pig, Clams Casino, fresh poached candied salmon, Eggs Minette and Oysters Rockefeller.

Circulating through the huge ballroom was a string trio playing romantic ballads, including "Love Me Tender."

Following breakfast there was a brief press conference. They were asked when they met and when Priscilla said it was in 1959, Elvis said, "About twenty years ago, I believe," and Priscilla said, "Yeah!" and it got a big laugh. They showed surprise that Priscilla was still in high school when Elvis was in the Army, seemed baffled by Priscilla's telling them she had been "traveling" since, and laughed again when Elvis said the ceremony seemed long.

Then the photographers made a rush, one shouting, "El, give her one more kiss on the cheek and slide over a bit, please. Big smile now—look happy!"

And Elvis said, "How can you look happy when you're scared? I'm a little bit nervous, you know. There's no way out of it. We appear calm, but Ed Sullivan didn't scare me this much."

"Why did you give up bachelorhood?" a reporter asked.

"Bachelorhood," Elvis said.

And then the Colonel jumped in and said, safely, "Can't give it up without gettin' married."

"Why did you wait this long to get married?"

"Well," he said, "I . . . I just thought . . . the life I was living was . . . too difficult, and I decided it would be best if I waited till I . . . I really knew for sure. And now I'm really sure."

Following that the photographers began calling orders

again, urging Elvis and Priscilla to shove cake into each other's mouth, and the Colonel called a merciful end to it.

Elvis and Priscilla went to their rooms, changed clothes, reappeared at two-thirty, got into a chauffeured Lincoln Continental and returned to Palm Springs for a four-day honeymoon in the great circular house that Elvis had leased. Then they flew to Memphis to spend some additional time at Graceland and on a nearby ranch Elvis had bought.

Elvis had purchased the 163-acre ranch near Walls, Mississippi, in February. He had become a familiar figure riding horses on the Graceland grounds and occasionally had gone riding at local stables, but neither seemed suitable; there wasn't room enough at Graceland, nor privacy anywhere else. So he paid $250,000 for a one-story one-bedroom board-and-brick residence, some cattle barns and the land, and immediately had it surrounded by an eight-foot cyclone fence.

The ranch, soon to be named the Circle G (for Graceland), was situated about four miles west of Highway 51 on Horn Lake Road, five miles south of his Memphis estate and just below the Mississippi state line. The land formerly had been used for growing cotton. In recent years it had been in pasture as a cattle ranch, and once Elvis took over—hiring a local cowhand to look after it—he bought some horses, cattle, tractors, trailers and trucks.

When Elvis and Priscilla returned to Los Angeles, shortly before Elvis was to begin work on his next film in June, Elvis faced two problems—resolving the turmoil within the Memphis Mafia caused by the sudden marriage, and finding a new home. The first was trickier than the last.

In a sense it was too late to soothe all the hurt feelings caused when Priscilla came between Elvis and his buddies. Although there isn't any one of them who will say anything publicly, it is no secret that some didn't care for Priscilla, that she didn't care for some of them, and that there were fights. And when only Marty Lacker and Joe Esposito were invited to witness the wedding ceremony, that cinched it for a few others.

Of course it was logical to expect Elvis wouldn't want a bunch of grab-assing menservants thumping around the living room once he'd selected a wife. Nor was it odd when Priscilla expected the payroll to be cut—and not for budgetary reasons. But that didn't halt the trumpeting and quarreling, and when it was all over, there were only two remaining on salary in California—Joe Esposito, who continued as Elvis's secretary-bookkeeper-confidant, and Richard Davis, who served as his valet and began working more closely with Elvis in his films. Alan Fortas stopped taking care of Elvis's cars and went to the Circle G Ranch to help with the livestock. The others either remained in Hollywood as extras and stunt men or returned to Memphis to go into the recording business. Marty Lacker became general manager of Pepper Records, for instance, and Red West eventually found himself on the staff of the American Recording Studios as a producer-songwriter. In time the size of the Presley household staff—not counting the usual maids and cooks—would increase to four or five again, but the Mafia was part of the past.

Elvis had promised his wife a new home and the one finally settled on was a huge multileveled house pitched on the topmost slope of a mountain in the Trousdale Estates, at 1174 Hillcrest Road. Trousdale was then one of the newest, and certainly one of the most expensive, of several sumptuous real estate developments undertaken in Southern California in the 1960s. The house originally had been built, on one of the choicest lots, for $169,000, but the next owner sank $200,000 into it, building in all the furniture and keeping workmen there for nearly eighteen months. It was in a California version of French Regency styling and had a huge pool, four cavernous bedrooms, half a dozen baths, a large living room with an adjoining bar decorated in black glass, and offered (when the smog cleared) a breathtaking sea-to-city view. There also was an expansive brick patio behind electrically operated gates—first metal, later wood—and another of Elvis's high storm fences. Additional privacy was provided by the stand of Tuscany cypress trees that lined the street. For a while Harry Karl and Debbie Reynolds lived up the street, and Hal Wallis owned the vacant lot next door, but most of his neighbors were industrialists, businessmen, doctors and developers. The house was only six years old when Elvis and Priscilla moved in and because the owner wanted to vacate immediately, he let Elvis have it for a song, $400,000.

Only Elvis's personal life and California mailing address changed during the first half of 1967. Everything else remained much the same, as the drooping film scripts and weak musical material continued to come his way.

Perhaps it was in the music that the story was most embarrassing, for it was in recording that Elvis got his start and generally was regarded as being strongest. When he married in May, he hadn't had a number one record in more than five years. And although many still had sold in excess of a million copies, several of *those* were songs recorded years earlier. The last million-selling record he received, for instance, was for sales of "Wooden Heart," but this was a song originally recorded in 1960 as a part of the *G.I. Blues* sound-track album, when it became a monstrous hit single in Europe—*and* it had been released in the U. S. not once, but twice, in 1964 and 1965. It was as if RCA was determined to make it a million-seller because Elvis was getting so few. The second most recent million-selling record was "Crying in the Chapel," released in April 1965, but recorded, according to Gordon Stoker, *before* Elvis went into the Army. He says legal problems kept it from being released sooner. Nearly all the other gold singles awarded from 1962 to 1965, when they stopped, were from the *Girls! Girls! Girls!, It Happened at the World's Fair, Fun in Acapulco, Kissin' Cousins* and *Viva Las Vegas* sound-track albums. Most were as bland as the movies.

Nor were things getting any better on the flicker front. Elvis reported for work in *Speedway* in June, and it was essentially the same as all the rest. In this picture he was a hotshot stock car driver from Charlotte, North Carolina (where some of the racing footage was filmed), who because of his manager's (Bill Bixby's) fondness for horse racing, owed the Internal Revenue Service $150,000. The IRS chief for the area (Gale Gordon) sent an undercover agent (Nancy Sinatra!) after Elvis and it was touch and go there for a while, but Elvis won the race, paid Uncle Sam with his winnings and got the girl. Of course the racing champ and the lady tax agent sang a few songs along the way, enough to fill up one side of an album.

Said the New York *Times:* "Music, youth and customs were much changed by Elvis Presley twelve years ago; from the twenty-six movies he has made since he sang 'Heartbreak Hotel,' you would never guess it."

Elvis was prankish by nature and his friends say the tedious film assignments only made him more capricious on the set. Says Jack Good of his experience in *Clambake:* "You could tell he was being bored out of his mind doing these pictures. That was the reason, I suppose, he was so ready to gag around a bit. Because what else was there to do? Nothing. Same old stuff. Elvis in boat. Elvis waving at girls. Elvis driving up. Elvis driving away. Elvis hitting somebody. Somebody hitting Elvis. That's about all it was, wasn't it? And Elvis sort of warbling away in that curious baritone voice. What a shame."

And so they joked. Says Red West of the same film, his last with Elvis: "It was the wildest we ever done. We'd get up on the rafters where they made the *Phantom of the Opera,* Richard and I and Billy, and we started out throwing water balloons down on the people, then it got to pies filled with shaving cream. Arthur Nadel, the director, came on the set one day with an ol' rain hat, coat and rubber boots. He said 'Roll 'em,' and somebody hit him with a water balloon. Another time, when somebody was supposed to come through a door, they put blood all over me like I'd been in a fight. They started the cameras and Elvis was acting his foot off when I come staggering in the door and fell down. He broke up."

Says Bill Bixby: "In *Clambake* they all had water pistols. You'd come around a corner and you'd get it. And then it was a small glass of water and the next thing you know it was a hose. I remember once when we were on a sound stage doing the water ski shots and it went from water pistols to buckets. It was all over the stage. If you were on the floor, you were in the fight. If not, get out. I don't know how long we stopped shooting, and afterward we had to get everything in one take so we wouldn't fall behind. And then in *Speedway* it was constantly cherry bombs. My dressing room door would fly open and in would come a cherry bomb and there I was in an eight-by-eight room with the door shut.

"It wasn't Elvis that threw the stuff most of the time," Bill says, "but you knew that the guys only did what pleased him, did things he inspired or suggested."

But the jokes are not the only thing Bill recalls. "First I found him to be a gentleman and then a gentle man," he says. "I found he could be sensitive to small issues. For someone of his stature there is very little for him to notice, y'know? He's so insulated by the people who surround him and by his own popularity. And yet Elvis will still find little things. He'll take the time to be very gentle with people. Especially with children. Little Victoria Meyerink . . . you know Elvis and I ended up in *Speedway* competing for her attention? It was a who-would-she-marry kind of thing. The fact that you can perform with a child doesn't mean you're going to act with that child in the same way personally, and Elvis did. And he certainly didn't have to.

"At that time I knew how much Elvis wanted a baby. When I was doing that picture, Elvis had gotten married, snuck off as it were. It was very, very private. But after it was announced, he talked an awful lot on the set about how much he wanted a baby."

Elvis had good reason to be talking about babies, and

wanting one, because Priscilla was pregnant by then, something Elvis announced in July. "We really hadn't planned to have a baby this soon," he said. "But less than a month after we were married [and before Elvis started *Speedway*] Priscilla came back from the doctor in Memphis and told my father and me the good news. I was so shocked I didn't think I could move for a while. Then it began to dawn on me that this is what marriage is all about."

As for the Colonel, who always had something to say, he said he already had a contract drawn up "for the new Presley singer."

The news had been withheld for six weeks, Elvis told a writer at the time, because they weren't sure. "We'd been back there [Memphis] a while when Priscilla went to the doctor and he made a test and told her the results were positive. Isn't that right? Isn't it positive? Or is it negative? Anyway, he told her it looked as though she were pregnant but he couldn't be absolutely sure, because an early test isn't always accurate. The excitement of the wedding and all might have affected the results. She went back to the doctor for another test and that one was positive too. Still she wasn't sure. She went to the doctor a third time and he told her, 'You've flunked this test three times. You're pregnant.'"

Says Bill Bixby: "After he found out, he was ecstatic. Elvis was happier than I had seen him." Bill says Elvis always wore his wedding ring, right up to a take, then put it into his pocket, replacing it afterward. "He seemed totally content," Bill says. "I remember him whistling and humming. He was thinner and everything seemed to be falling into place."

It was just before Elvis went into his second film of the year, in September, that he used his fists again. It was on a Sunday, September 17, in Memphis, when a former yardman at Graceland went to Vernon's house (he and his family had moved out of Graceland) to see about getting his job back. Vernon told him the job wasn't open, that he had

known it was a temporary job for four months only, while
the regular man, a Negro, was sick. The yardman, Troy Ivy,
said he thought it was "pretty raw" to give a Negro his job,
and left, according to Vernon, after threatening both Elvis
and his father.

About a half hour later Ivy appeared at the Graceland
gates and, according to Elvis's report to the sheriff, the man
was "drunk, belligerent, arrogant, cursing loudly and he took
a swing at me." The way Elvis told it, Ivy missed and Elvis
responded, knocking the man to the ground with one punch.

And then Elvis returned to California for *Stay Away, Joe,*
a film in which Elvis played a shabby Navajo Indian brave
who returned from the rodeo circuit to his Arizona reservation with twenty heifers and a bull he had promoted from
his Congressman. The idea was that if Elvis and his Indian
father (Burgess Meredith) were successful in raising cattle,
the U.S. government would help the whole reservation. Of
course Elvis barbecued the bull and sold the cows to buy
some plumbing and other home improvements and then, for
good measure, started chasing the girl friends of his fellow
braves.

"I look at my old movies and I can pick up on my mistakes," Elvis said at the time. "There's a lot I'd like to change.
I want to grow up on the screen. When I see my old movies,
something is always happening to me, someone's always telling me what to do. Girls are chasing me. Bad guys are after
me. Now I'm getting away from that. In this picture I'm a
kind of sharp Navajo, a wheeler-dealer who's always promoting something. It's a more grown-up character—part Hud,
part Alfie. He's a man, not a boy, and he's out looking for
women, not just waiting for them to stumble over him.

"In most of my pictures I'm singing in every other scene
but in this one I do only three songs and I get to do a lot more
acting. There isn't a guitar in the whole picture."

When the company was on location, outside Cottonwood

Arizona, Douglas Laurence, the producer, says a huge bull moved and ruined a shot that was otherwise acceptable, so the shot had to be made again. Laurence says Elvis walked over to the bull and punched it on the forehead, stunning it.

Elvis completed the picture in November, about the same time *Clambake* was released to the usual mixed reviews, and returned home to Memphis to supervise an auction scheduled for November 5 on his ranch. Among the thousand or so items put on the block: a battered guitar, a hundred doors and a blue bathtub taken from Graceland in a recent remodeling, several pairs of boxing gloves, two catcher's mitts and, pointedly, five house trailers that Elvis had bought to house the members of the Mafia when they stayed at the ranch. Although not all the stuff sold was Elvis's—he'd agreed to let neighboring farmers add their excess equipment—the possibility that Elvis was selling *anything* he owned so enthralled his fans that several thousand turned out. And the auctioneer reported at day's end he had collected more than $100,000.

This was, by now, the sum that Elvis was giving to charity each year. Even back in the hysterical 1950s Elvis was—like the Colonel—a charitable man, usually giving rings and cars away. Although sometimes he was more imaginative, as when he contributed a trunkful of teddy bears to be auctioned by the National Foundation for Infantile Paralysis and gave a kangaroo he'd received from an Australian fan to the Memphis zoo. Then in 1961 he headlined a benefit show for Memphis charities at the city auditorium. Since then Elvis has contributed money rather than do any more benefits, always matching, and often exceeding, the sum he would have raised by singing. The two local newspapers, the *Commercial Appeal* and the *Press-Scimitar,* supervised a massive collection each Christmas and usually Elvis or his father took the checks down personally. Almost always each check was made out for $1000 and often there were more than a hundred of them. They went to, among others, church building funds, the YWCA, the Boy Scouts, Baptist and Catholic children's homes, Goodwill Industries, the Salvation Army, the Memphis Heart Association, a home for incurables, homes for the aged, the Muscular Dystrophy Association, Jewish community centers, day nurseries and schools for retarded children.

Nor were the Christmas checks the end of it. In 1964 he bought the yacht President Roosevelt used during World War Two, the *Potomac,* for $55,000 and, following a comedy of errors that had the March of Dimes and the Coast Guard Auxiliary in Miami refusing it, gave it to St. Jude's Hospital in Memphis. In Hollywood in 1965 he gave $50,000 to the Motion Picture Relief Fund and a year later pledged 2 per cent of his salary for one picture to the same fund—which brought his total contributions to the hospital and home for failing movie people to $240,000. And he still was giving cars as gifts, the way some people buy flowers.

"These are the stories he doesn't like told," says one of his friends. "He's given away more than a million dollars the past ten years and he doesn't like to talk about it and he doesn't like other people to talk about it."

His philanthropic activities were not totally secret, of course; when Vernon or Elvis walked into the Memphis newspaper offices with a fistful of $1000 checks every Christmas, it was not the sort of thing the press easily overlooked. So the city tried to respond by naming something after him.

Over the years various Memphis agencies and bureaucrats had nominated nearly a dozen buildings, parks and roads— even the Lauderdale Courts—to carry the Presley name. At one point Mayor William Ingram took it upon himself to rename the Mid South Coliseum the Elvis Presley Coliseum, but even that was overruled when a city commissioner said Park Commission policy provided that buildings be named only for the deceased. Elvis's friends say he didn't care whether they named anything after him or not, but he sometimes wished they'd make up their damned minds.

Elvis was showing himself to be a religious man too, even

if he had long ago given up attending church services. An album of spiritual songs RCA had released in March, *How Great Thou Art,* was played on nearly 350 radio stations in fifty states, without commercials, paid for by Elvis and the Colonel. (The album won a Grammy the following year for Best Sacred Performance.) And for Christmas the stunt was repeated, this time including some of Elvis's earlier Christmas songs and more than 2000 radio stations were used.

Over the years Elvis had received so many awards he had no trouble filling the fifty-foot trophy room in Graceland's south wing. Most of these had come for his (1) Americanism, (2) charity, (3) humanity, or (4) all the above. The only negative note was in winning the Sour Apple Award (along with Natalie Wood) for being least cooperative with the Hollywood press corps.

He was a millionaire possessed of unfailing politeness and an unimpeachable love of God, mother and country, and had a beautiful, gracious Southern *pregnant* wife.

He began appearing on the best-dressed lists.

Album titles of the movie period: *Something for Everybody* (1961), *Elvis for Everyone* (1965).

Even Hedda Hopper, who slapped Elvis around verbally in the fifties, loved him in the sixties, devoting several Sunday columns to saying how swell a fella he'd become.

Says a movie executive who worked closely with the Presley camp for several years: "The Colonel didn't want Elvis to come out sounding like Jesus. It's pretty bland. But everybody assumed that's what the Colonel wanted, and that's exactly what he sounded like, and maybe that's what he had become."

Elvis Presley once may have represented some sort of threat to the American Way, but now he was a part of the Establishment—the All American Boy. Compared to Elvis, Jack Armstrong was a Communist.

-14-

CHANGES

ELVIS REMAINED AT GRACELAND all during January 1968, Priscilla's last month of pregnancy, and at eight-thirty the morning of February 1 Elvis and Priscilla got into a blue 1968 Cadillac driven by Charlie Hodge and were taken to Baptist Memorial Hospital. They were followed by a black Cadillac carrying Richard Davis and Jerry Schilling, with Joe Esposito at the wheel. The second car was a reserve vehicle, in the unlikely event Elvis's car should break down.

Within half an hour Priscilla had been admitted and two uniformed but unarmed off-duty city policemen were stationed at the entrance to the maternity ward. Elvis was then taken to the doctors' lounge to wait, where he was joined by Joe, Charlie, Jerry and Richard, and later by Patsy and Gee Gee Gamble, Marty Lacker, Jerry Schilling's wife, Lamar Fike and George Klein, and finally Vernon and Dee, whose telephone had been out of order and therefore were among the last to be notified.

Outside the hospital, reporters were swarming all over the steps.

Eight hours later, at 5:01 P.M., the child was born, weighing six pounds fifteen ounces, and named Lisa Marie, a name Elvis and Priscilla said they picked from a baby book, although the Colonel's wife's name is Marie. Vernon and Dee were dispatched to tell the reporters the news. Elvis sent one of the boys for cigars, called his grandmother, who was bed-ridden with a broken hip at Graceland, tried to reach the Beaulieus in California, and then went to see his daughter.

It had been nine months to the day since he and Priscilla were wed.

The guards remained on duty outside Priscilla's room the four days she stayed there, keeping hundreds of fans away. Priscilla, meanwhile, had a closed circuit television set placed nearby, giving her a round-the-clock view of the hospital nursery. Downstairs at the switchboard the calls came in from all over the world. At Graceland thousands of cards and hundreds of pink booties and dolls and blankets and dresses arrived.

One day after Priscilla and the baby returned to Grace-land, Elvis's closest Hollywood friend, Nick Adams, was dead. Nick had toured with Elvis in the fifties, and later, when Nick found parts hard to get, Elvis paid some of his bills.

Elvis's first film in 1968, started a few weeks after Lisa Marie was born, was *Live a Little, Love a Little,* another bit of fluff from the M-G-M mattress. In it Elvis was a photog-rapher with two bosses, the publisher of a *Playboy*-type magazine (Don Porter) and a high-fashion advertising exec-utive (Rudy Vallee!). It was, vaguely, based on Dan Green-burg's novel *Kiss My Firm but Pliant Lips* and was shot for the most part in an authentically garish estate that seemed much like those in Trousdale. And Vernon had a bit part but no lines.

At first glance it seemed the pattern was unbroken. But there had been a shift of direction—made when Elvis did *Stay Away, Joe.* It was in that film the dialogue implied Joan Blondell had been an "older woman" in Elvis's life and he was, besides that, actually seen romping (if clothed) on a bed with Quentin Dean, a teenager. In *Live a little, Love a Little* the script included several "dammits" and one "how the hell" and had Elvis rising from a bed recently shared with Michele Carey, the shapely starlet who pursued him through most of the movie.

Not too many months before an M-G-M executive was quoted as saying, "He has never made a dirty picture. They never go to bed in a Presley picture."

"I don't think I'm changing my image," Elvis told a writer at the time. "I think you have to mature a little bit."

No matter what he said, his image *was* changing and in the next picture, *Charro*, filmed in the summer of 1968, Elvis abandoned several more "trademarks." Usually in his films Elvis was given a nice wardrobe, but in this one, a western, he wore the same greasy leather pants throughout. He also appeared in the film unshaven, looking much like the former outlaw type he was supposed to be. In the story, he was asked to find his old gang, then being sought for stealing the gold and silver cannon that fired the last shot in the Mexican revolution. Not only was his face partially hidden in the scruffy beginning of a beard, his hair was covered by a hat. Nor were there any pretty girls in bikinis. And he didn't sing one song; he didn't even hum.

"A different kind of role . . . a different kind of man" was the way the advertising read.

In the next picture, capriciously titled *The Trouble with Girls (And How to Get into It)*, Elvis was the manager of a Chautauqua troupe that gets mixed up in the affairs of one of the towns it visits. Elvis does get into some "trouble" with girls (Marlyn Mason and Nicole Jaffe), but nothing to warrant the film's title. In fact, Elvis didn't even appear in the picture until halfway through. It was a bad film, even if Vincent Price and John Carradine had bit parts, and Elvis sang a couple of songs and looked great in long wide sideburns and an ice cream suit and hat. But there was a nod toward the new image. It came when Elvis was massaging

Marlyn Mason's shoulders and suggested they continue their conversation in bed.

Something else happened in 1968 to change the Presley image more than any cinematic propositions could. It had been announced by the Colonel in January that NBC-TV would finance and produce a one-hour special to be broadcast during the Christmas holidays and later would finance and produce a motion picture as well—a combination making it possible for the Colonel to keep the salary near the million-dollar level. Elvis's films had been dropping in popularity, and profit, lately and unless the Colonel agreed to do a film *and* a special, probably the million-dollar figure would not have been met anywhere in Hollywood. Whether or not the move was forced, however, it was one of the most astute made by the Colonel in years. It initiated what afterward was to be called Elvis's "comeback."

Steve Binder had produced and directed a Petula Clark special—during which there was an incident over guest star Harry Belafonte touching Petula on the arm—when he got the call to serve in the same categories for Elvis. At the time, his partner was Bones Howe, the record producer who'd worked with Elvis in the late 1950s and early 1960s, and it was understood he would supervise the music on the show. The call came from Bob Finkel, who had produced the *Jerry Lewis Show* for ABC and who was to be executive producer in title, the vice-president in charge of keeping Colonel Parker amused in fact.

"The way I felt about it," says Steve today, "was I felt very, very strongly that the television special was Elvis's moment of truth. If he did another M-G-M movie on the special, he would wipe out his career and he would be known only as that phenomenon who came along in the fifties, shook his hips and had a great manager. On the reverse side, if he could do a special and prove he was still number one, he could have a whole rejuvenation thing going."

"And," says Bones, "we both felt that if we could create an atmosphere of making Elvis feel he's part of the special, that he was creating the special himself—the same way he was organically involved in producing his own records in the old days, before the movies—then we would have a great special. People would really see Elvis Presley, not what the Colonel wanted them to see."

Both Steve and Bones seemed miffed at the Colonel in retrospect. They say he had his ideas of what the special should be like and he wasn't moving: Elvis would come out, say "Good evening, ladies and gentlemen," sing twenty-six Christmas songs, say "Merry Christmas and good night." Steve and Bones felt this would be disastrous and said Elvis should talk more and perhaps sing only *one* Christmas song. The Colonel then referred to a special Easter program he'd promoted, the broadcast of one of Elvis's religious albums which, according to the Colonel, drew "millions of letters," and he said the television special, scheduled for broadcast the evening of December 3, would follow the same format.

"I in no way wanted to do a Christmas show full of Christmas songs," says Steve. "I wanted to leave that to the Andy Williamses and the Perry Comos, the people who you know do weekly television and sing Christmas songs at Christmastime. The one thing I knew that I wanted was Elvis to say something—let the world in on that great, great secret, find out what kind of a man he really was."

For weeks it went back and forth, and even when the conceptual differences were settled and it was agreed Elvis would sing only one holiday song, there were other problems. Elvis's friend Billy Strange, who had done the music for *Speedway* and *The Trouble with Girls*, was fired as the show's musical director and replaced by Billy Goldenberg, who previously had worked with Steve but at first was convinced he had nothing in common musically with Elvis. Steve wanted some new songs written and talked about Elvis singing songs already recorded by other singers, and the Colonel insisted Elvis sing only material *he* published. There was a battle over whether there'd be a sound-track album and if so, who would pay for it. Elvis normally paid for all his sessions, providing RCA with a completed master tape, but in this instance NBC paid for the sessions and *then* the Colonel claimed the tape was theirs. NBC had its own huge orchestra and objected when Steve and Bones said they wanted to hire extra musicians, people Elvis knew. Sponsor repressatives from Singer worried about (Steve's words) "offending the little ladies in the Singer Sewing Centers across the country."

The show was to tell the story of a young man leaving home and what happens when he enters the outside world. "The first thing the boy does," says Steve, "he walks into a whorehouse. It did not say whorehouse. There was no suggestion that he was physically going to take one of the girls and go to bed. In fact, it was pointed up that the girl he zeroes in on is Purity, the girl with no experience, and before the moment of truth, the place is raided and he's back on the road to his next adventure. That scene was taken out in editing. It happens to have been the best scene I've ever been responsible for. If I didn't say I was doing a bordello sequence, and said I was doing a number with twenty girls and Elvis, there would have been no fuss. I made an error and said what I was doing. It was that special moment in the show. People would have remembered it for years. At the same time, of course, Dean Martin can play with a girl's boobs on the air and people say it's great clean American fun."

And then Steve decided to take out the one Christmas song, confronting the Colonel with his decision with Elvis present. "The Colonel was furious," says Steve, who was being called "Bindel" by the Colonel now. "He said Elvis *wanted* to do a Christmas song and so we were going to *do* a Christmas song. Elvis was just sitting there, head hanging down, and the Colonel said, 'Isn't that right, Elvis?' Elvis just nodded, and when the Colonel left, he looked up and said, 'That's all right . . . we'll take it out.'

"With all his hollering and threats and the rest of it, the

Colonel let the show be done. He's a sly old fox. He is the wizard in *The Wizard of Oz*. He *is* Frank Morgan, the guy behind the big black velour with lots of gadgets and neon signs lighting up and all, and he's putting on the whole world. So there were showdowns. Everything was meetings. If a microphone was placed six inches to the left and it was supposed to be six inches to the right, there was a meeting to discuss it."

The meetings with Elvis were more relaxed—so relaxed, in fact, Billy Goldenberg says, he was convinced the time to tape the show would come and they'd still be sitting around telling stories and plunking guitars. The first several of these were held in an office Steve and Bones shared on the Sunset Strip.

"When I sat down with Elvis," Steve says, "I wanted to find out where he was at musically, because a lot of people who are said to be part of today can never really get past yesterday. I said to Elvis, 'Would you do all the songs you have done in the past again?' He said 'Certain ones I would do, a lot of them I would never do again.' I said, 'If I brought you "MacArthur Park" today and nobody had touched it yet, would you record it?' He said yes. I knew we were home free. If Elvis would think of 'MacArthur Park' for himself, I knew he wanted to be part of what's happening right now."

Elvis always arrived with an entourage. "Always at least Joe Esposito and one or two others," says Bones. "Lots of times Tom Diskin came. And we'd sit around in director's chairs, play records, talk. There were tons of those little Dutch cigars for Elvis. Lots of Pepsi."

One day, Steve says, he asked Elvis what would happen if they walked out on the Strip. Elvis seemed apprehensive, but he said he was willing to find out. "So we did it," says Steve. "Four o'clock in the afternoon and there we were, standing outside the Classic Cat [a topless bar]—Elvis, Joe Esposito and me. We stood there to the point of embarrassment. Kids were bumping into us and saying 'excuse me' or not even saying that. Elvis started talking louder than normal, trying to be recognized or noticed or something. But nothing happened. Nothing. Zero."

Finally the meetings ended, with several ideas down on paper, and Steve went to the Colonel to say he was having Billy Goldenberg start writing music for the show.

"The one thing I've always felt about Elvis is that there was something very raw and basically sexual and mean," says Billy. "There's a cruelty involved, there's a meanness, there's a basic sadistic quality about what he does, which is attractive. You know the story *In Cold Blood?* I've always felt Elvis could very well play one of those guys, that he is that kind of person. Most of Elvis's movies have shown him as the nice guy, the hero, but really that is not where he shines best. He's excited by certain kinds of violent things. The karate is just one example. It's all over him. I thought, if there was a way we could get this feeling in the music . . ."

Billy also tells a story about sometimes finding Elvis alone in a studio playing Beethoven's "Moonlight Sonata." "He'd get to a certain point and he'd not know how to do it and I'd show him the chord and he'd do it over and over again until he got it. And then some of the guys would come in and he'd stop, as if it were a sign of some weakness."

With the musical direction formed, there were two other decisions made that gave the show much of its subsequent power. The first came as a suggestion from Bill Belew, the costume designer, that Elvis wear a black leather suit. Elvis never had worn leather before—that was Gene Vincent's trip —but Bill thought he had, and it was approved. He also designed a gold lamé tuxedo reminiscent of Elvis's gold suit of the 1950s, but at the last minute Elvis refused to wear it. The other decision was Steve's, and that was to assemble a number of the guys from Elvis's present and past—Lance LeGault, Scotty Moore, D. J. Fontana, Alan Fortas— and to surround Elvis with these guys during rehearsals and, perhaps, during a part of the show itself. The Jordanaires were asked, but the invitation came so late, they'd already committed themselves to thirteen studio sessions that week in Nashville. The idea was to keep Elvis comfortable during rehearsals and to see if the interaction between Elvis and his friends could be translated into program content. Says Steve: "I thought it would be an excellent way to get Elvis talking, sitting there with the guys he knew, but it was an experiment only. We weren't really sure what would happen."

"A whole week we were there," says Scotty today. "We did our rehearsing at night, if you would call it rehearsing. What it amounted to was we'd set up the guitars in the dressing room and everybody'd set back and start yakking. Just bangin' around. It was like old times. First somebody'd think back on a good story on the other one, tell it, then maybe sing a couple of songs."

The sessions in Elvis's dressing room lasted four and five hours and audiotapes reveal them to be as spirited as they were directionless. There was a lot of laughter, with lines about executive producers and waitresses and people standing naked in windows, and Elvis sang and sang and sang. Many of the songs, like the people around him, were from his past: "Love Me," "When My Blue Moon Turns to Gold Again," "Are You Lonesome Tonight," "I Got a Woman."

By now the recording sessions largely had been completed. The days were long, beginning at noon and usually running until after midnight. With musicians Elvis knew—including some of the best studio rhythm men in Hollywood: Hal Blaine on drums, Don Randi on piano and organ, Tommy Tedesco and Mike Deasy on guitars, Larry Knectal on bass—Elvis remained quite comfortable.

"It was like a live performance," says Bones. "I gave him a hand mike and when he sang he performed. He didn't just stand there. He worked out—complete with twists and turns and knee drops."

There was one more battle to be fought—over how the show would end.

"I wanted Elvis to say in his good night something about who he was," says Steve. "He could say, 'Peace . . . good will toward men,' anything he wanted. And the Colonel would have no part of it. He still wanted Elvis to sing 'Silent Night' or some other Christmas song, and say good night, and I kept saying everybody does a Christmas song at the end of their show and when Elvis ends that show, it's got to blow everybody's mind. So I got Earl Brown, who was my choral director, and I took him aside and said, 'We're under the gun now and I want you to go home tonight and write me the greatest song you ever wrote to close the show.' And I explained what I wanted Elvis to say. Next morning at seven o'clock Earl woke me up and said, 'I've got it.' I rushed to the studio and Earl played for me 'If I Can Dream.'"

Steve took the song to Bob Finkel, who said the Colonel would "blow his stack." So Steve next went directly to Elvis, took him into a quiet room with a piano, and once again Earl played and sang "If I Can Dream." The song was, essentially, a plea for peace and understanding—key lines were "If I can dream of a better land / Where all my brothers walk hand in hand"—certainly not a message alien to a show planned for December broadcast. But it did represent another shift in direction for Elvis, a move toward making the personal—social—statement Steve was looking for.

"After Earl played it, Elvis said to play it again," Steve says. "Earl played it six times for Elvis and Elvis sat there. And then he said, 'I'll do it, I'll do it.' Unbeknownst to us the Colonel was saying at that very moment to Finkel and Tom Sarnoff and all the rest, 'Over my dead body will Elvis sing an original song'—right there in the next room. So now I open the door and say Elvis has a new song for the end of the show. I couldn't have said a worse thing. But nobody wanted another confrontation. And Elvis had already said yes. So they said, 'Let's hear it.' And before it had been played all the way through, one of the guys from RCA, Norm Racusin, had the title registered in one of Elvis's publishing companies."

All during this time, of course, the Colonel was up to his usual tricks—some of them expensive enough, Steve says, to warrant his having a special slush fund in the show budget to cover them.

"It was a sideshow with the Colonel carrying on with Finkel," says Bones. "The Colonel would say, 'Finkel, give me twenty dollars.' Finkel isn't about to *not* give the Colonel twenty dollars, so he reaches into his pocket and peels a twenty from his gold Florentine money clip. The Colonel puts it on the table and says, 'I'm thinking of a number between one and ten. What's the number?' Finkel says, 'Four.' The Colonel says, 'Wrong number. Seven.' And he puts the twenty in his pocket. So now Finkel is sucked into the game called Honesty. The Colonel says, 'It's called Honesty, Finkel. I got to be honest with you. Give me another twenty and tell me what number.' Of course Finkel wins a couple of times. But the Colonel took Finkel for about six hundred dollars in Honesty money before the special was over. The Colonel has tremendous insight to people's personalities. He knew somehow that Finkel's weak spot was money."

Another time, Bones says, the Colonel pulled a trick on Finkel he said he normally reserved for freeloaders who came around looking for favors. "The Colonel had this incredibly delicious champagne and offered Finkel a glass. And Finkel expresssed genuine enthusiasm. So the Colonel said, 'Really like that champagne, huh, Finkel? I gotta see you get some.' And two days later there's a full case waiting for him at home. Finkel chills it and tells his wife the Colonel has given him a case of the best champagne he's ever tasted. They light candles, do the whole bit, and they sit down to have a glass before dinner and it's water. Every bottle in the case is filled with water."

Still another time the Colonel came to rehearsals dressed as Robert E. Lee. By now Finkel had begun to join the fun, so he rented a seventeenth-century admiral's costume. And then the Colonel put the two William Morris agents assigned to him in royal guardsmen's uniforms and had them stand at attention outside his dressing room for two days. And Finkel was supposed to top that.

The show was to be taped the last week of June, so on the twenty-seventh, a Tuesday night, Elvis held a press conference that coincided with the visit to NBC's Burbank studios by forty-five television editors from all across the country.

"He gets uptight at press conferences because they're nothing but dumb questions," says Steve, who sat to one side of Elvis. (Steve and Finkel were wearing neck scarves identical to the one Elvis wore.) "He hated it, but I think he got great satisfaction out of it, really being on top of it. He's really bright. He doesn't have to be defended on that. His first instincts are normally right. I was amazed by his sense of humor, his being able to laugh at himself. Every time he'd get ready to answer a question, he'd have a funny way of tapping me on the leg as if to say, 'Watch me put the guy on with this one.' And then he'd turn it around on himself—saying he was doing the special before he got too old, things like that."

The production numbers were taped first. And in some of these the supporting cast was monstrous, with dancers and singers all over the place. (At a get-acquainted party held at the start of rehearsals there were so many people—thirty-six dancers, thirty-five musicians, a total of eighty performers in the "Guitar Man" opening alone—everyone wore name tags, including Elvis: "Hello! My Name Is Elvis. What's Yours?") In one number there were several wardrobe changes for Elvis. In another his name in lights formed a background twenty feet high.

The day of the live videotaping, before an audience, Elvis was not so sure of himself. "He was really frightened," says Bones. "He sat in makeup sweating. He said, 'I haven't been in front of those people in eight years.' He said, 'What am I gonna do if they don't like me? What if they laugh at me?'"

"Of course he'd performed on movie sets," says Scotty, "and sometimes there's three, four hundred people there, but that's different."

"That's right," says D. J. "Those people are working, they're paid to laugh and scream. But those people out there in the studio were real live people, man."

The ticket holders—including Diskin and his family, who had to wait with all the rest—filed into the NBC studio and took seats on bleachers arranged around three sides of a fifteen-by-fifteen-foot white stage rimmed in red. At the last minute the Colonel suggested the prettiest girls in the audience be moved close to the stage, even to sit on the edge of it.

"That was a stroke of genius on his part," says Bones. " 'Get them close to Elvis,' he said. The Colonel was moving around the crowd like a carnival barker, picking the faces he wanted, saying, 'Who here really loves Elvis?'

"So Elvis finally came out in that leather suit, all his guys were there on the fourth side of the stage, and when he reached for that hand mike, his hand was actually shaking. You could see it on the camera. But then he started singing and it was all over. He was terrific."

He had been introduced by a Los Angeles disc jockey. Lance LeGault had memorized every song, every camera cut, every move Elvis had in this show, and he was seated to Elvis's right, with a tambourine. Charlie Hodge was there with a guitar, along with Scotty Moore. Alan and Lamar and the others were there too, laughing, talking, feeding Elvis lines and reacting to those he contributed himself. The songs came naturally and forcefully, including dozens of the early hits: "That's All Right [Mama]," "Blue Suede Shoes," "Heartbreak Hotel," "Love Me," "Are You Lonesome Tonight," "Lawdy, Miss Clawdy" and, pleasing the Colonel, "Blue Christmas."

And they talked—about the time the crowd destroyed D. J.'s drums and when Elvis was censored at the Pan Pacific

Auditorium in Los Angeles. They shouted, whistled, and echoed one of Elvis's favorite expressions: "Mah boy, mah boy!" Charlie remembered the time when a girl got into the house and got on the intercom and said, "I'm in the house, where's Elvis?" Elvis came right back: "I told her, I said, 'If you're lookin' for trouble . . . you came to the right place . . .'"

It was like the evening sessions in the dressing room, only now Elvis was performing—moving across the stage as some sweaty, sexy fertility god, hair the color of India ink, black leather shining in the strong spotlights.

"He was so frightened when he went out and so with it once he got there," says Bones, "he was shot when it was over. He came off the stage, we practically had to carry him off. While we were slapping each other on the back. It was like we'd won a football game."

Altogether, counting both audiences, Steve taped nearly four hours of this. Most of it was thrown on the floor and in the edited show, ready three months later in September, the "live" segment was under a half hour long. But it opened the show and was the most impressive part of it. The "experiment" had worked.

"After it was all over," Steve says, "Elvis asked me what I thought as far as the future was concerned. I said, 'Elvis, my real, real feeling is that I don't know if you'll do any great things you want to do. Maybe the bed has been made already, maybe this'll be just a little fresh air you'll experience for a month. Maybe you'll go back to making another twenty-five of those movies.' He said, 'No, no, I won't. I'm going to do things now.'"

The show was broadcast Tuesday night at nine o'clock, December 3, opposite *Red Skelton* and *Doris Day* on CBS, and *It Takes a Thief* and *N.Y.P.D.* on ABC, swamping everyone, and was followed by a Brigitte Bardot special that gave NBC the evening. The same week, the sound-track album was released. Elvis had gone back into the studio after the show to recut the vocal to "Memories," but the rest was as it had been prerecorded for the production numbers and sung live for the sections with an audience. Both the special and the album were received favorably.

"There is something magical about watching a man who has lost himself find his way back home," said Jon Landau in *Eye* magazine. "He sang with the kind of power people no longer expect from rock 'n' roll singers. He moved his body with a lack of pretension and effort that must have made Jim Morrison green with envy. And while most of the songs were ten or twelve years old, he performed them as freshly as though they were written yesterday."

"It wasn't the old Elvis, trading on the nostalgia of early rock and obsolete Ed Sullivan censorship," said the writer in *Record World,* "it was a modish performer, virile and humorous and vibrating with the nervousness of the times."

The New York *Times* said that Elvis "helped bring the pop world from illusion to reality" and called Elvis "charismatic."

Two other Elvis stories appeared in the same December 4 edition of the New York *Times.* One reported that readers of the *New Musical Express,* England's top music paper, had voted Elvis the number one male vocalist of the year. And Mike Jahn quoted Tom Diskin in an interview as saying Elvis's movie income was dropping noticeably enough for the Colonel to consider some personal appearances.

"For the time that goes into it," Diskin told Jahn, "it's more profitable for him to appear in public. It takes Elvis fifteen weeks to make a movie, on the average. If he appears for ten weeks, one concert a week at $100,000 each, he can do much better."

Diskin said Elvis had two more films to do, but that they were "keeping open" the possibility of a concert tour in eight or nine months. Such a tour, he said, would take that long to plan properly and, besides, it would be better to wait until summer, so concerts could be staged comfortably in baseball parks, then thought to be the only locations where $100,000 a night could be guaranteed.

Elvis himself said in 1968, "I'm planning a lot of changes. You can't go on doing the same thing year after year. It's been a long time since I've done anything professionally except make movies and cut albums. From now on I don't think I'd like to do as many pictures as I've done—almost three a year. Before too long I'm going to make some personal appearance tours. I'll probably start out here in this country and after that, play some concerts abroad, probably starting in Europe. I want to see some places I've never seen before. I miss the personal contact with audiences."

Already Elvis was making changes—in becoming a father, in taking somewhat meatier and more adult movie parts, and in returning to television. There was another noticeable shift in 1968 and that was in his recordings. There were several besides the sound-track albums. There was a grab bag of left-overs called *Elvis Sings Flaming Star and Others*, an album released by Singer to promote the special, and Volume 4 of the *Elvis' Gold Records* series, which contained twelve songs released over an eight-year period, only three of which actually sold a million copies.

But if these albums were disappointments, most of the singles released in 1968 were not, beginning in January with a gutty foot-stomping version of Jerry Reed's "Guitar Man." For those looking for meaning in song lyrics, this one seemed precisely right for Elvis: "I've come a long way from the car wash / Got to where I said I'd get / Now that I'm here I know for sure / I really ain't got there yet / So I think I'll start all over / Sling my gi-tar over my back / Gonna get myself back on the track / Ain't never, never gonna come back."

The back side of this single was "High Heel Sneakers," a hit for Stevie Wonder. Although it too carried much of the power of the "old Presley," only "Guitar Man" appeared on the charts, peaking at a disappointing forty-three.

In March Elvis released another of Jerry Reed's country rockers, "U.S. Male" and this one went to twenty-eight, with the flip side, the title song from *Stay Away, Joe*, selling well enough to appear farther down in the sixty-seven position. This was followed by three others—"You'll Never Walk Alone" for the Easter season, "Your Time Hasn't Come Yet, Baby" and "A Little Less Conversation"—none of which went any higher than sixty-three.

But then in October, nearly a full two months before the television special was aired, RCA released "If I Can Dream." By December it had reached the number twelve position in *Billboard*, his highest position in five years. "If I Can Dream" also gave Elvis his first million-selling single in more than three years.

And then in January 1969 Elvis walked into a recording studio in Memphis for the first time since he had left Sun fourteen years earlier. To many it meant that Elvis had gone "home."

Chips Moman and his American Recording Studio in Memphis were in the middle of a long winning streak, although you couldn't tell it by looking at the facilities. The cluttered orange-and-black studio, a converted dairy, was in a state of continual breakdown and repair. The offices were next door over a restaurant, with the only entrance at the top of a rickety fire escape. And both were in one of the city's poorest, blackest neighborhoods. The boulevard that ran past the studio may be named for Danny Thomas and many top recording stars may have recorded here, but the glamour of Hollywood was far away.

Still, when Elvis entered the studio January 13, Chips, one of the owners, was as a producer-engineer working his way through what would be a string of ninety-seven chart records in a period of just twenty-eight months. A group Chips found and recorded, the Box Tops, accounted for several, and some others were by Dionne Warwick, Joe Tex, Wilson Pickett, Joe Simon, the late Roy Hamilton, Neil Diamond and Merilee Rush. Chips says there had been so many hits, not because the funky studio had any special "sound"—as many claimed—

but because the house band was so good. It was this backup group, he says, and the experience every man in the band had, that attracted Elvis.

"Elvis knew what was coming out of here," Chips says today. "I had met him, but that's all. I'd been around Memphis a long time. So he must-a come here for the musicians, because they play on all the sessions. They're under contract to us. They're part of the organization, part of the family."

The musicians were Memphis musicians, some of whom Elvis had known for years, even if he hadn't worked with them. Reggie Young and Bobby Emmons, a guitarist and organist, had been in the late Bill Black's combo. Gene Chrisman, the drummer, had been with Jerry Lee Lewis. Bobby Wood was a piano player who'd had a few small hits of his own. Mike Leech was a bassist who'd worked in local clubs for several years. And helping Chips with production was one of the top guitarists and bassists in the country, Tommy Cogbill. For the sessions with Elvis, Chips added some brass—Wayne Jackson, Ed Logan, Bob Taylor—and brought in part of the string section of the Memphis Symphony Orchestra, along with several backup singers, including Ronnie Milsap, a white blues singer Chips produced for Scepter Records. The names weren't well known outside Memphis, but the sound was.

Elvis booked the studio for ten days and had laryngitis four of them. But with sessions beginning at eight at night and running until dawn, he still cut thirty-six songs, enough material to fill two albums—*From Elvis in Memphis,* released in May, and half of the *Memphis / Vegas* set released in October—account for some miscellaneous singles, and still have songs left over. It was, flatly and unequivocally, Elvis's most productive recording session ever. It also made it abundantly clear that the days of the "Fort Lauderdale Chamber of Commerce" and "No Room to Rhumba in a Sports Car" movie sound-track songs were over.

There were unadorned country songs such as "Long Black

Limousine," which told the story of a hearse bringing a girl
friend home, and Eddy Arnold's composition "I'll Hold You
in My Heart (Till I Can Hold You in My Arms)." There were
raunchy blues songs: "Power of My Love" and "After Loving
You." There were lush ballads, Neil Diamond's "And the
Green Grass Won't Pay No Mind" and Burt Bacharach's "Any
Day Now," as well as John Hartford's modern country classic,
"Gentle on My Mind." And there were some more songs by
Mac Davis, a young Texan who says he was moved to write
his first song after seeing Elvis perform in Lubbock in 1954.

Elvis had recorded three of Mac's songs already—"A Little
Less Conversation," "Memories" and "Charro," the last two
to be released in March—and was working with Billy Strange
when Chips called for material.

"Chips said he wanted some country songs," says Mac today. "I didn't know what he meant, so we sent a tape with
seventeen of my songs on it. The first two songs on the tape
were 'In the Ghetto' and 'Don't Cry, Daddy.'"

Mac says he had played "Don't Cry, Daddy" at Elvis's
house months earlier and that Elvis's reaction was that he
wanted to do it sometime because it made him think of his
mother. And "Ghetto," he says, had been rejected by Bill
Medley, who "thought he'd already done enough protest-type
material."

After the session, Elvis and Priscilla went to Aspen, Colorado, for a month's vacation, and Elvis learned to ski.

The movie *Charro* was released in March and only a few
critics seemed to believe Elvis's first non-musical represented
much of an improvement. The title song, backed with "Memories" from the television special, barely limped into the top
forty. In April two more singles were released—Elvis's annual
Easter record, pairing the title songs from his two religious
albums, *His Hand in Mine* and *How Great Thou Art*, and
the "protest song" that Bill Medley had rejected. For Elvis it
exploded.

"In the Ghetto" told the story of a child born in the ghetto a child who was "gonna be an angry young man sometime" and learn how to steal and fight. The child grew up, bought a gun and got killed in a robbery attempt, the world looked the other way and next day another child was born in the ghetto. Many seemed stunned when Elvis released the song, but they shouldn't have been. It was really a logical extension of "If I Can Dream." Still, disc jockeys who had in the post-Beatle post-Dylan days become somewhat "hipper than thou" as regards Elvis, began to play *this* record more than any Presley record of recent years. And it went to number three, selling a million and a half copies, fast.

Coincidentally, as "In the Ghetto" was becoming a hit, Elvis was in Hollywood, making a film (his thirty-first) about a ghetto. This was an improbable property called *Change of Habit*, taking its title from the fact that Elvis, playing a doctor working in the slums, falls in love with one of his nurses, who is, unbeknownst to him, a nun. If that premise wasn't enough to boggle the minds of Presley fans, what the three screenwriters did with it proved more than adequate. Elvis's nurse-nun-love interest, played by Mary Tyler Moore, was but one of three nuns who had changed to street clothes to work in the ghetto, and each had her moment—Miss Moore when a speech defective being treated in Elvis's clinic tried to rape her, Jane Elliott when she was forced to slug a cheating grocer, and Barbara McNair when she confronted some of the local black militants. But it all worked out in the end. Elvis asked his nurse-nun-love interest to marry him, and although it wasn't spelled out, the viewer was left with the impression she was going to leave the order and do so. Elvis sang three songs in the film and was sporting a new hair style, longer and bushier.

After this Elvis and Priscilla went to Honolulu with Patsy and Gee Gee for two weeks.

At the end of May Elvis was back in Memphis to supervise the transfer of the horses from his Mississippi ranch to Graceland. During his vacation his father, who handles some of

Elvis's financial matters, had sold the ranch to D. L. McClel lan. McClellan paid $440,100 for the Circle G and said he was going to turn it into a country club, with a clubhouse, a miniature golf course and swimming pool.

Once the horses were at Graceland, kept in stables behind the main house, Elvis began riding across the grounds with Priscilla almost every day. In fact Elvis's visits home to Mem phis now followed a rigid but comfortable pattern. Elvis would rise from bed in the afternoon, go for a swim in his pool, eat breakfast, and at five-thirty or six ride down to the front gate to sign autographs and talk with visiting fans. Oc casionally, when the crowds got so unwieldy as to cause the state police to send cruisers to sort out traffic, Elvis had the gates opened, so everyone could come in. Then maybe some of the guys would come over for some pool or television, until midnight, when Elvis's Midnight Movies began at one of two theaters downtown.

The Midnight Movies had become a tradition. "It's what Elvis did after he stopped renting the Rollerdrome and the amusement parks," says Alan Fortas, who soon was to leave the Presley employ, now that the ranch had been sold. "Paul Shafer at the Malco Theater set it up for him. Every night Elvis wants to see movies, Mr. Shafer reserves the Malco from midnight on, however late Elvis wants it, and gets the pic tures Elvis asks for. Usually they're all the latest movies whatever's current. And he'd go down there with as many friends as'd be around, plus others who knew about it, fan club presidents and so on—maybe as many as forty or fifty peo ple some nights. And we'd run the pictures one right after the other all night. They sit there sometimes from eleven o'clock midnight, to five o'clock, maybe six in the morning. Watching movies. Every night. Every night is generalizing purty good but you'd be safe saying five nights a week. Believe me. He still does that. He just loves movies. He's a very avid movie fan."

Some of the films Elvis watched weren't current, but slightly older movies that he liked especially. *Goldfinger* was one. Other times at the Malco, and occasionally at the Memphian or on the sixteen-millimeter camera in the Graceland den, he'd have one of his own films run. But never *Jailhouse Rock*, because his leading lady, Judy Tyler, was killed in an accident while on her honeymoon the week following the film's completion. And never *Loving You*, in which his mother appeared, sitting in the audience in one scene. So that when he went back to work, he'd usually seen another thirty or forty films.

This time back on the job it was something new for Elvis. On July 5 he left Graceland for Los Angeles to begin rehearsals for what was to be his first public appearance in over eight years.

ABOVE: *In* Kissin' Cousins, *with and without the blond wig, 1964*

In his second role as an Indian, in Stay Away, Joe, *1968*

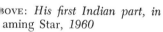

ABOVE: *His first Indian part, in* Flaming Star, *1960*

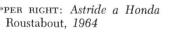

UPPER RIGHT: *Astride a Honda in* Roustabout, *1964*

RIGHT: *An unshaven gunslinger in his first nonmusical role,* Charro, *1969*

ABOVE: *Sharing a bed with Michelle Carey in* Live a Little, Love a Little, *1968;* BELOW: *Sharing a ride wtih Dodie Marshall in* Easy Come, Easy Go, *1967*

Sharing a break with his pals Jerry Schilling, Richard Davis and Max Baer

At his wedding to Priscilla Beaulieu, Las Vegas, May 1, 1967

OPPOSITE: *Nine months later in Memphis—Charlie Hodge over Priscilla's right shoulder and Vernon over Elvis's left shoulder—leaving the hospital with Lisa Marie*

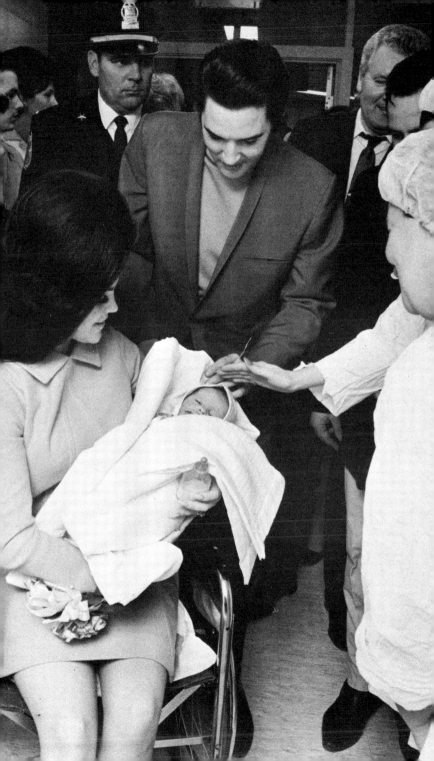

ABOVE: *From the "live" segment of the NBC TV special, 1968*

OPPOSITE: *In rehearsal at M-G-M for* That's the Way It Is, *1970*

At the International Hotel, Las Vegas, 1970

Las Vegas—"I can't help falling in love with you . . ."

-15-

LAS VEGAS

"I GOT TIRED OF SINGING to the guys I beat up in the motion pictures," Elvis said the night he opened in Las Vegas.

So, months earlier, the Colonel had gone to work, negotiating a contract with the International Hotel, a thirty-story building that was to be the largest hotel (1519 rooms) in Las Vegas but then was still under construction. It was, on completion, the first major Las Vegas hotel built off the Strip. It cost $60 million, and at 346 feet was the tallest building in Nevada. It had the world's largest casino, and in the middle of its eight-and-a-half-acre rooftop recreation area was a swimming pool that held 350,000 gallons of water, the largest man-made body of water in the state, aside from Lake Mead. It had 240 miles of carpeting, more than 2500 employees (who were to be paid $25 million the first year), an eighteen-hole golf course, a convention hall that seated 5000, six major dining areas (not counting the Showroom Internationale, which seated 2000 and was to be Elvis's showcase for a month), a thousand slot machines and a computer-operated reservation desk.

It seemed a suitable place for Elvis to use for his public return.

The Colonel made his deal with Bill Miller, the massive, white-haired talent booker who had been the first to gamble then-unbelievable salaries on Red Skelton, Ray Bolger, Donald O'Connor and other stars who hadn't performed publicly in years, and then was the first to bring in the fleshy spectaculars. He was in semiretirement in the Caribbean when he was asked to book the International, to go after the names that would fill a showroom twice the capacity of any other in town.

Miller doesn't talk about the deals he makes, but when Barbra Streisand opened the Showroom on July 2, it was generally known that her manager had made a complicated million-dollar stock and capital deal for four years. Nick Naff, the International's publicity head, says the original deal with Elvis was for five years, one engagement a year, on an option basis. "But contracts like that don't mean much to the Colonel," Nick says today. "The Colonel likes to do it one show at a time." It is believed that Elvis was promised a million dollars too. And so that the Colonel could say he got more than Miss Streisand, the Presley-Parker forces were given more "extras," such as rooms and transportation.

Then it was time to assemble the show. The Colonel hired Sammy Shore, a noisy, hardworking comic who depends upon smoky barroom humor and creates nothing new on stage, working instead with prepared material. Elvis picked the backup singers and found someone to organize the band. The male vocalists he selected were the Imperials, a quartet that had backed Elvis on the *Spinout* album and one of his religious LPs, *How Great Thou Art*. (Again the Jordanaires had been asked, but they felt they couldn't afford to leave Nashville for that long; Gordon Stoker calls this one of the biggest disappointments in his life.) The four girls were the Sweet Inspirations, then under contract to Atlantic Records. And the bandleader was James Burton, one of the best and most popular of studio guitarists in Los Angeles.

"First I got a call from Tom Diskin," James says today, "asking if I'd be interested in putting a group together. I said yes and then I got a call from Memphis. It was Joe Esposito on the line and I'd never heard of Joe Esposito and all he said was, 'There's somebody here wants to talk to you.' And Elvis said hello. We talked, kicked it around, and after about forty mintes, I felt I knew what he wanted."

What Elvis wanted, James says, was a rock 'n' roll band, and the four men he hired were, if not always the first asked, among the best available.

James's roots, like Elvis's, were in country rock. He grew up in Shreveport and remembers seeing Elvis on the *Louisiana Hayride* Saturday nights. The first record he played on, when he was fifteen, was Dale Hawkins's "Suzie Q," in 1957. He then went to Hollywood to make an exploitation film with country singer Bob Luman (*Carnival Rock*) and there met Ricky Nelson, who asked him to join his band, which he did soon thereafter. He even moved in with Ricky and his brother David and their parents Ozzie and Harriet for a year. The past several years he had done almost nothing but studio work, always turning down tours and personal appearances. He once refused three months with Bob Dylan because the money didn't match studio work. He recently bought a big home in the Toluca Lake section of Los Angeles, not far from Bob Hope's old place. He prefers his 1949 Cadillac over his other half dozen cars, is married and has two children.

Jerry Scheff, the blond mustachioed bassist, was raised in northern California, spent four years in the Navy band playing string bass and tuba, then traveled for two years with what he calls "two-bit, small-time Dixieland and lounge groups," finally coming to Los Angeles to become a studio musician after his instruments and clothes were burned in a Palm Springs night club where he'd been working. Four years as a studio man came next, with six months out in 1969 touring as one of Delaney and Bonnie's friends. He's married and has two children.

Ronnie Tutt, the bearded drummer, was another of Delaney and Bonnie's friends and is from Dallas, where he was a bass singer and sometime percussionist for a company that produces commercial jingles. He was moving his wife and six children to Los Angeles when he got the call to audition for Elvis's band and, in effect, stopped in Vegas for a month en route to California. When not appearing with Elvis, he is another busy studio musician.

Larry Muhoberac, who backed Elvis on piano, organ and electric piano, had gotten the call to join the band from Tom Diskin, who remembered him from ten years of working with Elvis off and on—dating back to when Larry was the youthful musical director of the benefit show Elvis did in Memphis in 1961. Larry also had played with the Woody Herman, Hal McIntyre and Ralph Flanagan bands and served as an executive in the jingle factory Ronnie worked in. Larry was raised in New Orleans, is married and has four children. He is a studio musician now.

The only member of the band who couldn't be tagged a studio musician was John Wilkinson, who is essentially a vocalist, signed, like Elvis, to RCA Victor. His producer is Rick Jarrard, who is José Feliciano's producer. He provided what James Burton calls "basic rhythm guitar" and like most others in the band, although none of them was miked, added some backup harmony.

Serving as an ex-officio member and combo factotum, and playing acoustic guitar, was Elvis's buddy from his Army days, Charlie Hodge.

The boys had a lot in common. They were, most of them, Southern, or were rooted firmly in the basic country and blues traditions from which Elvis had come. (Elvis says country music probably was a bigger influence on him than rhythm and blues, but not by much.) In fact, every one of them names Elvis as a major reason they are in the business. They were somewhat older than many of their contemporaries—in their late twenties to early thirties—and possessed a certain reserve, a maturity that matched Elvis's. They were, most of them, family men: settled.

First Elvis rehearsed with his band for two weeks in Los

Angeles, playing and singing more than a hundred songs, picking twenty or so that he would use as the core of the show, including nearly a dozen of his old hits, the rest more recent songs, with a small selection of songs made known by other vocalists. He worked on the "choreography," which because he never really choreographed anything in the traditional sense, meant there were some karatelike moves he wanted to incorporate. And then he took the band to Vegas, where they rehearsed another two weeks with the Imperials and the Sweet Inspirations and finally with the hotel's twenty-five-piece orchestra.

One of the members of the band, Larry Muhoberac, would be replaced for the next Vegas engagements by Glenn D. Hardin, who says, "Elvis likes to rehearse himself, and he likes to hang around guys and sing. So he don't rehearse just the songs he's gonna do. He likes to rehearse anything anybody can name. If you take off playin' 'Stagger Lee,' he enjoys that and he'll just sing it, man, for about an hour and a half. He gets a big kick outa that. And by doin' that, when you get on stage with him, you feel like you done ever' song in the world. 'Cause he may just jump inta one of them one night. He feels very comfortable. I think he's figured all that out: He can bust inta anything he wants to and the band'll be able to play it."

When rehearsals were finished, Elvis had lost fifteen pounds and he had never looked better.

"We were opening a new hotel," says Nick Naff, "and we read all the signs. We figured Barbra Streisand was the hottest entertainment property in the world. She'd just won an Oscar, she had three pictures going, her name was fantastic. And Elvis was an unknown stage property. We weren't sure. We knew he'd be a draw, but my God . . ."

"With Streisand," says Glenn D. Hardin, "they couldn't keep the sumbitch full. But with Elvis it was full, full, full. Elvis was the magic word."

The fans had come from Europe and Australia. Hotel employees were taking calls from all over the country from people begging for reservations that no longer existed. The opening week was sold out and the rest of the month nearly so.

Still, no one was taking risks. There had been something of a "rock revival" going on in the last months of 1968 and much of 1969—a popular reaction to the overintellectualization of rock music that had set Dion, Rick Nelson, Little Richard, Bill Haley, Fats Domino, Carl Perkins, Chuck Berry and others striding along the comeback trail. Elvis had been getting some promising press as well, thanks in part to improved record material and the television special, but also because of the renewed interest in rock's roots.* Elvis had even been praised at length and often in the underground press, which surprised even the sage ol' Colonel. So it was agreed that no reporter, whether he represented the New York *Times* or the Los Angeles *Free Press*, couldn't attend the opening if he wanted to. To make it easier, Kirk Kerkorian, the hotel's owner, made available his private plane, reportedly the first DC-9 in private ownership, remodeled to accommodate twenty luxuriously.

"Who could turn down such an offer?" asked Robert Christgau in *The Village Voice*.

The Showroom Internationale was a masterpiece in ostentation, a monstrous multileveled restaurant and balcony that seated two thousand nearly comfortably and offered as part of the décor a phony Roman colonnade, some larger-than-life-size figures in Louis XIV velvet and lace, paintings of Greek ruins which made a travesty of artistic perspective, and hanging precariously above all this, some scattered cupid-like angels. The menu offered a narrow but gout-inducing selection of wines and foods that began with Fonds d'Arti-

---

* About midway through Elvis's month-long engagement, on August 17, the NBC television special was re-run. Because of the seasonal difference, "Blue Christmas" was replaced with "Tiger Man." Again it attracted an exceptional viewing audience.

chauts Farcis Walewska and closed with Savarin Glacé Napoléon.

Finally a disembodied voice: "Ladies and gentlemen, welcome to the International Hotel and the Elvis Presley show with Sammy Shore, the Sweet Inspirations and the Imperials."

The gold lamé curtain rose, tucking itself away in the ceiling, to reveal the Bobby Morris orchestra in tuxedos, the four Sweet Inspirations bopping toward the audience, looking much like a road show version of the Supremes, singing show tunes. Sammy Shore came next. He knew the invitation-only crowd was there to see Elvis and he aimed some of his material that way: "The Colonel came up to me and said, 'I like your kind of humor.' I said, 'Why, thank you. I like your chicken.' And the Colonel said, 'You do? Well, lick my fingers.'" And then he said, "Youth is wasted on the young. Give us what the kids got and you know what you'd have? A lot of old people with pimples."

As Sammy was keeping the older folks laughing—boring or antagonizing the younger ones—Elvis stood in the wings. He was drumming his fingers against his thighs nervously. He watched Sammy, probably not seeing or hearing him, then disappeared farther backstage to talk to one of the boys positioned there for security, then he reappeared again, still drumming his fingers.

Sammy closed with a routine that used evangelism as its base, blue humor and a lot of tambourine-banging as its means of delivery, and got off. The curtain fell, there was a frantic moment rolling out the piano and drum kit and getting set, musicians and singers scuttling back and forth, stagehands moving microphones, and then the curtain went up again.

The band was pounding out a rolling, thunderous "Baby, I Don't Care" rhythm and without a word from the disembodied voice, Elvis sauntered to center stage, grabbed the microphone from its stand, hit a pose from the fifties—legs braced, knees snapping almost imperceptibly—and before he could begin the show that he had pushed through three full-dress rehearsals that afternoon, the audience stopped him cold. Just as he was to begin his first song, he was hit in the face with a roar. He looked. All two thousand people were on their feet, pounding their hands together and whistling, many of them standing on their chairs and screaming. And he hadn't even opened his mouth.

Finally the ovation subsided, the band picked up the beat and Elvis hit the pose again: "Waaaaaaaal, it's one for the money . . ."

The leg snapped.

"Two for the show . . ."

The leg snapped again, and he thumped his acoustic guitar.

"Three to get ready, now go cat go . . ."

It was as if the audience had fallen through a time warp, leaving the sixties for the fifties, appearing somewhere on the biting edge of memory that went with high school and the beginnings of rock 'n' roll. It was a shortened version of "Blue Suede Shoes," lasting only a minute and a half, and as the audience was applauding, Elvis walked to his right, toward Charlie Hodge, who handed him a glass of water.

"During the show you'll see I drink a lot of wa-wa," he said, using his daughter's word for water. "That's because the desert air is very dry and it affects my throat. I've also got some Gatorade. It's supposed to act twelve times faster than water." He held the bottle aloft. "Looks as if it's been used already to me . . . but if it aids my gator . . ."

The comment was made offhandedly in the familiar sluring drawl that had come out of Mississippi and gone through so many movies, emerging nearly fifteen years later as the voice of a relaxed yet polished performer. Backstage the boys were laughing at the joke. "Gatorade . . . used already . . . whew!" Haw haw haw.

Elvis went into his second song, "I Got a Woman," and then, almost as an afterthought, something he'd forgotten, he said, "Good evening, ladies and gentlemen. Welcome to the big, freaky International Hotel, with those weirdo dolls on the walls, and those funky angels on the ceiling . . . and, man, you ain't seen nothin' until you've seen a funky angel."

The next song was "Love Me Tender" and this was for the fans. Elvis spotted a pretty girl near the edge of the stage and knelt down and kissed her. He kissed a second, and a third, and a fourth, working his way along the stage. Still singing.

And from that right into a medley of his early hits—"Jailhouse Rock," "Don't Be Cruel," "Heartbreak Hotel" and "All Shook Up." Here and there the lyrics were altered slightly, as if Elvis was playing with the songs, not regarding them so seriously as perhaps he did in the 1950s.

Then, mock serious, he said, "This is the only song I could think of that really expresses my feelings toward the audience."

He sang "Hound Dog."

It was just the way it had been in the fifties, when "Hound Dog" was the song he used to *close* his shows. The same gutty power was there, along with just a shade of parody. Elvis was singing the song because he enjoyed it and because he thought it funny. Later in the month he would tell the audience, as he went to get some water, "When I drink wa-wa, just say to each other, 'Is that him, is that him? I thought he was bigger than that.'" Elvis knew there was something that was bigger than reality involved: the image. And Elvis was ready to laugh at it.

The next song was "Memories."

After which he looked at the floor and spotted the letters "B.S." in marker pen. "It says 'B.S.' here," he told his audience. "Do you think they're trying to tell me something?" There was scattered laughter. "Oh . . . maybe it stands for Barbra Streisand." There was a roar of laughter.

Right into "My Babe," an up-tempo song that had been a hit for the Righteous Brothers.

Then "I Can't Stop Loving You."

The audience was reacting—creating and distributing energy in massive waves—and Elvis was reacting to that. His voice was deeper, richer, more sensual then it was in ten years of soggy films, guttier even than nostalgia gave it credit for being before the soggy films began. And behind and all around it was the tight, basic yet soulful rhythm of James Burton and his good ol' boys, and the scaling, precisely timed harmony of the Imperials and the Sweet Inspirations, filling in every musical crack, building a melodic yet roughhouse wall of sound.

"I'd like to do my latest release," he said, catching his breath and drinking some Gatorade. "It's been a big seller for me." And then he added modestly, "Something I really needed."

"In the Ghetto."

And from that right into the song he said would be his next single, "Suspicious Minds." Elvis was forty minutes into his show and the audience was in disarray. Bouffants were tilting, neckties askew. People were sweating. Women were wriggling on the edge of their seats, debating whether or not to make a dash for it. Elvis was wearing a modified karate suit, tied at the waist and slashed down the front, all black. With all that black, black hair covering the tops of his ears, shaggy, almost Beatle-length, the lean features of his face, and the moves—the legs spreading, stretching, actually *vibrating* —it was enough to make any female itch. All that was needed was a final push.

A six-minute version of "Suspicious Minds" provided it. In this, a heavy production number utilizing the full orchestra, Elvis told the story of getting "caught in a trap," loving a girl and knowing it couldn't go on—with suspicious minds. He also turned the stage into a karate mat, kicking and slashing and tumbling like a man fighting his way out of the most in-credible Western brawl ever devised in Hollywood. Never missing a note.

There was another standing ovation.

Elvis was panting now, gulping for air, trying to swallow more Gatorade. And grinning.

"Yesterday," he sang, "all my troubles seemed so far away . . ." It had come full circle. Elvis, who had been the inspiration for the Beatles, now was singing a Beatles song. And then he sang a second one, "Hey Jude." Not the entire song. Just the title and the rhythm sounds ("Na na na na nanana na . . ."), over and over again. If before, the showroom resembled an orgy scene, or at least a pentecostal revival at fever pitch, now it was a giant sing-along.

As Elvis finished the next song, "Johnny B. Goode," an old Chuck Berry hit, many were calling requests. Elvis nodded his thanks but went on, diving into one of his earliest songs, "Mystery Train," which ran directly (same rhythm line) into "Tiger Man."

"I'm the king of the jungle," Elvis sang, "they call me Tiger Man . . ."

He closed with "What'd I Say" and two thousand people were on their feet. Elvis bowed and left and came back and sang the song he intended to close with anyway, the song he has since closed every show with, "Can't Help Falling in Love."

The thunder continued as Elvis moved through the good wishes and glad hands backstage, heading for his dressing room to change for a press conference the Colonel had arranged.

"Why have you waited so long to perform live again?" the first reporter asked.

"We had to finish up the movie commitments we had before I could start on this. I missed the live contact with an audience. It was getting harder and harder to sing to a camera all day long."

"Will you do more live shows?"

"I sure hope so. I want to. I would like to play all over the world. Yes, Britain of course is included. I chose to play Las Vegas because it is a place people come to from all over."

"Are you tired of your present type of movie?"

"Yes, I want to change the type of script I have been doing."

"Do you feel it was a mistake to do so many movie sound-track albums?"

"I think so. When you do ten songs in a movie, they can't all be good songs. Anyway, I got tired of singing to turtles."

It was as if the press wanted Elvis to recant. The same question kept coming at him.

"What kind of scripts would you like to do?"

"Something with meaning. I couldn't dig always playing the guy who'd get into a fight, beat the guy up, and in the next shot sing to him."

And finally the reporters moved on. "Did you enjoy performing live again?" one asked.

Elvis said he had been nervous that he didn't feel relaxed until after "Love Me Tender." He dodged a question about his salary, looking toward the Colonel, who was wearing a long white laboratory jacket covered with the words ELVIS IN PERSON. He admitted he dyed his hair but said it was only because he'd always done it for the movies. And he joked.

"How do you like the role of being a father?"

"I like it."

"Do you plan to add to your family?"

"I'll let you know."

"How does your wife feel about you being a sex symbol again?"

"We're planning to add to our family."

The critics were ecstatic. "Elvis Retains Touch in Return to Stage," *Billboard* headlined, pointedly placing the review on its country music page, where Elvis first appeared exactly fifteen years earlier. Said David Dalton in *Rolling Stone:* "Elvis was supernatural, his own resurrection . . ." Ellen Willis in *The New Yorker* said that if Elvis continued to perform, and "Suspicious Minds" was as big as it should be, he again would have a significant impact on popular music.

Variety called him a superstar, said he was "immediately affable . . . very much in command of the entire scene," while proving himself to be one of the most powerful acts in Vegas history. "There are several unbelievable things about Elvis," said *Newsweek*, "but the most incredible is his staying power in a world where meteoric careers fade like shooting stars." And on and on and on. The reviews couldn't have been better if the Colonel had written them himself.

As the month wore on—two shows a night, seven days a week—Elvis relaxed more. Friends say he had been extremely nervous opening night, quoting him as saying he wasn't sure he could "cut it" any more. They say he also was aware that many of those coming to see him were doing so because they figured Elvis was some kind of freak, pushed on stage once each decade now, and that it was a bizarre curiosity rather than an interest in him or his music that attracted them. But from the first night, it became absolutely clear that Elvis would do more than serve as a contemporary version of the two-headed cow, or any other act in a sideshow.

Elvis changed the songs each night. Seldom, if ever, were the same ones sung in the same order. Sometimes he sang a Bee Gees song, "Words," other times the eight-year-old Del Shannon smash, "Runaway," or a song that was one of the first really popular rhythm and blues hits, "Money Honey," or some of his own early hits ("Love Me," "Loving You," "That's All Right [Mama]") or some that he'd recorded recently in Memphis. But usually the songs were familiar. And always "Suspicious Minds"—released two weeks later—was the one that caused the greatest excitement.

He added a mini-autobiography that sometimes rambled so much he sounded stoned: "Like to tell you a little about myself. I started out . . . in childhood. I started out when I was in high school, went into a record company one day, made a record and when the record came out a lot of people liked it and you could hear folks around town saying, 'Is he is he?' and I'm going 'Am I am I?' . . . whew [out of breath]

. . . Elvis deterioratin' at the Showroom Internationale in Las Vegas . . . where was I? . . . oh, anyway, made a record, got kinda big in my home town, few people got to know who I was, that's w-u-z, was. See, so I started down in the wuz . . . ah shucks, what I mean to tell you is I was playin' around these night clubs, alleys and things. Did that for about a year and a half, then I ran into Colonel Sanders . . . Parker, Parker . . . and he arranged to get me some [blows nose] Kleenex . . . he arranged to get me . . . whew, I'm tellin' you . . . shot to hell, this boy can't even finish a sentence straight . . . anyway there was a lot of controversy at that time about my movin' around on stage so I . . . cleared my throat again, looked at my watch and ring and the guy said . . . the guy said? . . . the guy said nothin' . . . I'm the guy! I'm telling you, you better get this together, boy, or this is gonna be the last time they let you up on a stage.

"So, as I said, I went up to New York, did the Jackie Gleason show three times . . . whew, sure has been a long time . . . anyway, did that couple of times . . . had pretty long hair for that time, and I tell you it got pretty weird. They used to see me comin' down the street and they'd say, 'Hot dang, let's get him, he's a squirrel, get him, he just come down outa the trees.' Well, anyway, did the Ed Sullivan show. They just shot me from the waist up. Ed's standing there in the wings sayin', 'Sumbitch! Sumbitch!' I didn't know what he was sayin' so I'd say, 'Thank you very much, Mr. Sullivan.'

"Next thing they dressed me up in a tuxedo and had me singin' to a dog on a stool. You know I'm singin' to this dog and the dog is goin' 'Whhhoooaaaugh!' and I'm goin' 'Whhhooo-aaaugh!' Then I got into the movies—*King Creole, Jailhouse Rock, Love Me Tender, Loving You,* loving her . . . so I done four movies and I was feeling pretty good with myself, had a pair of sunglasses and was sittin' there in my Cadillac going, 'I'm a movie star, hot damn!' and the driver's goin', 'Whew, watch that squirrel, man, he's just outta the trees.' I was livin' it up purty good there for a while and then I got drafted, and shafted and ever'thing else. One thing I found out, though, is that guys really miss their parents in the Army, they're always goin' around callin' each other 'Mother.' When I got out I did a few more movies, and a few more movies, and I got into a rut, you know there's this big rut just the other side of Hollywood Boulevard . . . POW! . . . you know they let me do my thing here for a while and then they put me away for another nine years . . ."

Elvis, who had—according to the myth—never said more than "yes, sir" or "yes, ma'am," couldn't shut up. It boggled the mind.

Elvis amused himself—as well as his audience—in many ways. He mopped sweat on borrowed napkins, once even blew his nose, and returned them to their ecstatic owners. He changed a word in "Yesterday" so he sang, "Suddenly, I'm not half the *stud* I used to be." He walked over during a song and goosed one of the Sweet Inspirations. He introduced Charlie Hodge as Kate Smith. And the kisses became as much a part of the performance as "Suspicious Minds" and karate chops. One night, when one of the women said she wanted seconds, he practically lifted her off her feet, bit her playfully and threw her back to her husband. But most nights the fans attacked him. Maria Luisa Davies, who had come from Liverpool with her sister Gladys, talks proudly of her own "Las Vegas debut."

"I hopped onto a chair, onto our table and onto the stage," she said in an eleven-page report she distributed to other fans. "Elvis was singing in the middle of the stage. When he saw me standing there, he walked over towards me, still singing. He came straight over to me and I flung my arms around him and gave him a gigantic hug. The audience let out a tremendous roar. Gladys said, 'I just saw Elvis's face come over your shoulder' and while he was imprisoned, she ruffled his hair and can report it is as soft as silk. It wasn't greased or 'dressed' in any way. Well we knew that, but it is nice to be able to say I know because I touched him. I let Elvis go and the next thing I knew was that Mr. Diskin was hovering near and he helped me step down onto the table and my chair, and the floor again. As Elvis was returning to the center of the stage again, someone ran on from the side. Elvis had his back to her and didn't know she was there until she pounded on him, spun him around and kissed him hard. She just hung on."

Once during all the kissing, Priscilla ventured forward. Elvis kissed her along with the others and said, "Don't I know you?"

At the end of the month-long run, the hotel announced that Elvis had attracted 101,500 customers, far more than Barbra Streisand had, and more than anyone else would.

The night after he closed, Elvis went to Nancy Sinatra's opening in the same showroom—with Mac Davis on the show with her—and backstage gave her the printing plates from the ad he had taken out in the local newspaper advertising her show. He then flew to Los Angeles and from there went to Palm Springs to relax for three weeks, flying to Graceland on September 23. And then, before leaving in October for three weeks in Honolulu and two more in Nassau with Priscilla, Patsy and Gee Gee, he spent two days in Nashville, re-recording most of the vocals for what would be released in November as the first of his "live" Vegas albums.

In the late autumn and winter months, as Elvis vacationed, the product continued to pour out. By now "Suspicious Minds" had gone to the top of the record charts, giving Elvis his first number one record in nearly seven years, since "Good Luck Charm" in 1962. It was followed by "Don't Cry, Daddy," the weeper Mac Davis had written more than a year earlier and which Elvis had recorded in Memphis in January. It went to number six and was, like "Suspicious Minds," certified a million-seller.

And then in December Elvis's thirty-first movie, *Change of Habit,* was released. Because of the enthusiasm over his

Las Vegas appearances and renewed interest in his recordings, the film was practically—and kindly—overlooked. And
where it was noticed, it was criticized sharply or laughed at,
a ghost from Elvis's past.

Elvis was back at Graceland for Christmas, resuming the
Midnight Movies and spending some of his days planning
the annual New Year's Eve party he'd been hosting the past
few years. This year it was to be at T.J.'s, the supper and music
club managed by Elvis's old buddy Alan Fortas. (Richard
Davis was on the door.) Lamar Fike and his wife Nora came
down from Nashville. Joe and Joanie Esposito were there, of
course, along with Patsy and Gee Gee Gamble, Red and Pat
West, Sonny West and his date, and Charlie Hodge. Other
guests included Gary Pepper, one of his biggest fans, and
several of the city's top musicians. Ronnie Milsap, who'd
been making the club home base the past six months, performed and was joined by some of the people Elvis had
worked with earlier, Chips Moman, Tommy Cogbill, Reggie
Young. Even Mark James, who'd written "Suspicious Minds,"
got up and sang. It was, according to those there, a swell
party.

Five days later Elvis returned to Los Angeles to begin
rehearsals for his second Las Vegas performance.

When it was announced Elvis would return to the International Hotel in January 1970, some said it was too soon,
that he should have waited a year as suggested in the original
contract. They said the winter engagement would only dis-
appoint those who recalled so vividly his return from "re-
tirement." To go back in only five months, and to do so during
the slack season, would be a mistake. But by mid-January, a
week before opening, all but seven days of the twenty-nine
had been sold out—nearly four thousand seats a night—and
hotel and reservation clerks had been instructed to say
Showroom reservations could be made only by guests staying
in the hotel. This wasn't a move to prop up sagging occu-

pancy but to give guests first crack at seeing Elvis, as is Las Vegas custom.

"Elvis changes the entire metabolism of the hotel," says Nick Naff. "And he is singularly significant in one regard: there is constant occupancy. Tom Jones, they fly in, see the show, fly out again. Elvis has such a following, so many fans, for him they fly in, check in and stay two weeks, going to every show."

Most of the changes in the show were minor. Glenn D. Hardin took Larry Muhoberac's place at the piano and organ and began arranging some of Elvis's material, giving the hotel orchestra a more noticeable role in the show. Ronnie Tutt had gone to work for Andy Williams and was replaced on drums by Bob Lanning. Elvis's wardrobe was somewhat flashier, with the addition of a couple of dozen macramé belts hung with semiprecious stones. The only major change was in the selection of songs.

Elvis had decided, wisely, that for his August performances he would concentrate on his own hits, songs that were immediately recognizable as his—perfect for a return. The second time around much of the emphasis was shifted to songs made popular by other vocalists. So on opening night, a Monday, January 26, after he'd sung "All Shook Up" and "That's All Right [Mama]," Elvis said he wanted to sing songs not his own. He glanced at Dean Martin, seated in the booth next to that occupied by his family, and mimicked him: "Everybody needs somebody . . ." and then—bang!—into a version of "Proud Mary" that came on with the power of a trainload of gospel singers. (The Sweet Inspirations and the Imperials were back, along with the predictable Sammy Shore.) And later in the show he sang "Walk a Mile in My Shoes," "Sweet Caroline" and "Polk Salad Annie"—hits in the past year for Creedence Clearwater Revival, Joe South, Neil Diamond and Tony Joe White, respectively. The rest of the songs were from his own catalogue, but the manner in which he sang these four—strongly, dramatically—made them the most memorable. Put simply, when Elvis sang them, it was difficult to recall the originals.

He had just sung "Sweet Caroline" and his hair, longer than in August, covering his ears, was mussed and damp. He was wearing a white jump suit slashed to the sternum, fitted closely at the waist and knees and belted. The macramé belt and collar, knotted by a dancer friend of Bill Belew, Elvis's costume designer from the television special, fairly dripped jewels. Even his fingers seemed more encrusted and studded than ever, with displays of gold and diamonds so massive he could have ransomed a king with either hand. He looked at the audience, glanced at his backup band.

"Let's go down to Loozy-anna," he said.

The band played the familiar opening to a recent hit. "Some of y'all never been down South too much," Elvis said, the heavy rhythmic bass line continuing behind him. "I wanna tell you a little story so you'll unnerstan' what I'm talking about. Down there we have a plant that grows out in the woods and the fields, and it looks sompin' like a turnip green. Ever'body calls it polk salad."

He paused.

"That's *polk* . . ."

He bumped his hip.

"salad!"

The familiar hip. The movement that was Elvis's in 1954 at the Overton Park Shell in Memphis when he sang "Good Rockin' Tonight" and made it so difficult for Webb Pierce to follow him remained Elvis's in 1970, just as it had the first time he'd come to Vegas. And then he took "Polk Salad Annie" and made *it* his. If "Suspicious Minds" was the high point of his August show—and it inarguably was—"Polk Salad Annie" took the honors this time.

Following that, Elvis introduced the song that would be his next million-selling single, a ballad, "Kentucky Rain." He sang "Suspicious Minds," with a half a dozen karate kicks, some amazing leg stretches and several knee drops. And then he went into his regular closer, "Can't Help Falling in Love." After which Elvis dropped to one knee, holding one arm aloft in something that seemed a cross between a black power salute (in white on white) and the classic gladiator's pose. And the gold lamé curtain fell.

Out front the entire audience was on its feet, causing the crystal chandeliers above to swing noticeably from the force of the stormy applause, piercing whistles and shouts.

"I've never seen anything like it," said Emilio, the maitre d' at the International and an eighteen-year veteran of Vegas showrooms. "The phones ring all day and people begin lining up at ten A.M. for reservations. The response is stronger than last summer."

Elvis seemed more relaxed, even when the flu and a persistent cough hung on for the final two weeks of the engagement. Often he would be hit with what those around him called the "sillies," sometimes laughing all the way through a show. Several times he toyed with women, teasing them. He'd unzip part of his jump suit, quickly zip it up again, and grin devilishly. Other nights his frenzied movements would cause the macramé belt to work its way around him until the ends were hanging down in front, whereupon Elvis would notice them, look embarrassed, grin, and with a quick movement swivel the sash ends to the side again and wink.

"He likes to put on an audience," says Glenn D. Hardin. "He likes to have some fun."

And nearly every night women threw either their room keys or themselves—and occasionally their underwear—toward the stage in fantasy sacrifice.

"He'd play a few tricks on the orchestra too," says Glenn D. "They'd be right in the middle of an orchestrated thing and he'd suddenly skip a verse. On purpose. He's got a thing about gettin' locked in—got to do this verse, that verse—and he'll take a notion he don't wanna do that tonight and so he'll skip one, leavin' them up there playin' somethin' where he ain't.

"He didn't do it very much, but if he gets a little bit bugged or somethin's not suitin' him, he'll just kinda drop that show completely and move on in a different direction and start really wingin' it. He threw a few surprises on us.

"He a strict showman and he really grooves on what he's gonna do. And he really pays attention to how to pace his songs and he really checks their reaction. He'll adjust that show right down the middle the first four or five nights. You can tell there's somethin' really buggin' him because he can't keep it movin' like he really wants to. But, boy, when he gets it set, you can tell it too. He's happy and he really lets fly.

"He really gets it on," says Glenn D. "I really enjoy it. You play hardaway and you ain't gonna outdo Elvis. I mean you do anything you wanna do and it won't attract any attention in your corner. Which is really fun—to go to a gig with that in mind. Do it. And he'll be out there takin' care of it all."

There were three songs during the month that took Elvis to the piano. He played and sang the raucous Lloyd Price hit, "Lawdy, Miss Clawdy," and for two other slower songs he merely played: "Blueberry Hill" and "Old Shep."

Elvis closed February 24, a day later than originally scheduled. The members of the band drove their cars to Los Angeles and flew back to Vegas on the twenty-sixth, boarded Kirk Kerkorian's DC-9 with Elvis and the singers and flew to Houston. It was there, in the Astrodome, that Elvis was to perform six times, the featured attraction of the annual Houston Livestock Show and Rodeo.

Like the International Hotel, the Astrodome was a logical choice, even if the acoustics in a baseball park—enclosed or not—always leave much to be desired. It was, like the hotel, a monument constructed of superlatives. For the three evening performances—there also were to be three matinees—the field was lighted by three hundred foot-candles, one-third more than had been used before. There were 44,500 armchairs, sufficient number for over a hundred movie theaters.

The temperature was a constant seventy-two, a one-mile-an-hour breeze provided circulation, and a smoke detector checked visability and pollution, feeding information to a weather station computer in the roof, the first system of its type ever developed. Some of the box seats—which are leased for five years for $15,000 a year—were seven stories above the playing field. The eighteen-story Shamrock Hilton Hotel could be positioned in the middle of the field and not touch the dome or its walls. Even Billy Graham, presumably an expert on magnitude, was impressed, pronouncing the Astrodome "one of the great wonders of the world."

"The Astrodome was a purty crummy gig," says Glenn D. Hardin. "The Astrodome is just a big ol' giant terrible place to play. We rehearsed there for a minute to see how it was gonna sound one night and Elvis told ever'body, 'This is gonna be rather atrocious, so don't fight it, go ahead and play.' So we did. We just rolled out there on a trailer each night to do our number, and then split.

"They had wires and networks that run out in the field and the cowboys would just hook the trailer to a jeep. They'd dim the lights, they'd roll us out there and plug us in, and they'd put Elvis in a brand new red jeep with white seats. He'd ride all around and ever'body'd freak and he'd get on the trailer and bust inta 'Blue Suede Shoes.' You could hear the echoes bouncing all over the place. It definitely wasn't made for any serious giggin' inside. So he'd just sing it, knowin' it was terrible, and we'd go home."

Even when Elvis had engineers flown in from Los Angeles and Las Vegas to work on the sound system, it never was what it should have been.

However unfortunate the booking aesthetically, in other ways it made sense. Economically, of course, it was sound. Elvis was guaranteed $100,000 a show, plus a percentage of the box office. Because he broke so many records—playing to 207,494, nearly doubling the Vegas figure in one-tenth the number of appearances—he walked away with a reported

$1.2 million. Glenn D. says one of the reasons the Colonel agreed to the concerts was to pick up enough money to cover the cost of paying everyone for the month in Vegas and certainly this figure was adequate. (The sidemen do not talk about salary, but Hal Blaine says he turned away $10,000 for the month.)

Another reason for the Astrodome was its location, for it had been in East Texas that Elvis got one of his first big pushes in 1954 and 1955; it was here that the early fans had been thickest, and Elvis genuinely wanted to return to them.

A final reason was the price of admission. Tickets had been scaled down to a dollar, so even the poorer fan could get in.

The engagement was important largely because it marked Elvis's first appearance outside Vegas, which some took to mean a tour—or at least several other concerts—might be forthcoming. Otherwise it wasn't so extraordinary. Elvis held a short press conference; Priscilla flew in, partially dispelling rumors that she and Elvis had separated; and the security was what it always was—massive and airtight. Before Elvis returned to Los Angeles he had collected another box of awards for his trophy room—five gold records, a gold deputy sheriff's badge (the Colonel got one too), a Stetson, and a King Midas Rolex watch that was valued at $2500 and looked as if it had been carved from a solid bar of gold and shaped to Elvis's wrist.

It appeared the Colonel had topped himself in March, when it was announced that Elvis would do a nationwide closed circuit television show that would bring him the largest sum—a million-dollar guarantee—ever paid an entertainer for a single performance. Elvis was to appear in the 5000-seat Las Vegas Convention Center a few days before opening again at the International Hotel next door, and the concert was to be broadcast simultaneously to 275 cities, with a potential audience of (that magic figure again) one million. Of course the idea was the Colonel's but he called two young

Los Angeles concert promoters to implement it: Jim Riss-miller, a tall, lean, bespectacled former William Morris agent, and Steve Wolf, his shorter, darker, more garrulous partner, who had a background in television. They both were in their middle twenties but had been promoting concerts for three years, presenting nearly everyone from Bob Hope to the Rolling Stones.

The way they tell the story, they had been after Elvis for a fifteen-city tour, and when Tom Diskin told them no, they presented an offer for one concert at the Anaheim Stadium, home of the Angels baseball team. This time Diskin told them to be at the Colonel's Palm Springs home the following Saturday.

As soon as they arrived, the Colonel, dressed in a turquoise T-shirt and a cap, glasses pitched at the end of his nose, took them to the bedroom he'd converted into an office. It was, like his office at M-G-M in Culver City, cluttered with photographs and mementos. Occasionally one of the Parker cats came in, or the housekeeper arrived with cookies and milk. "It was," says Steve, "very folksy."

The meeting was equally casual. "We were going through our speech and he was going through his press clippings," says Jim. "He was reading, saying three hundred thousand this, four hundred thousand that, and passing the clippings to us as we talked. The more he showed us, the more excited we were getting. And after we got through talking ourselves blue about Anaheim, he said he wasn't interested. He told us he owed the International to keep Elvis out of the area. And then he said what he wanted to do was a closed circuit show. He knew we had tried to set one up with the Rolling Stones and that, plus our Anaheim offer, made him think of us. We said okay, let's talk."

"We were prepared to negotiate," says Steve. "But the Colonel gave us the deal he had in mind and that was it, take it or leave it. We were to give Elvis a million. He also said he wanted us to pay costs of producing the show—musicians, singers and so on—approximately a hundred thousand more. It was fair deal, everybody would have made money, but he threw it out so fast we had to keep asking him over and over and he kept saying, 'I told you boys—now for the last time, this is the deal.' He really hits you. He doesn't sit back and let it sink in. You're almost sorry you asked."

Rissmiller and Wolf, who call themselves Concert Associates, went to their bosses, Filmways, with the deal they'd made, and the Filmways people "fell off their chairs. The scale was so large," says Steve. "The logistics of the thing were staggering."

A second meeting was called, during which Steve and Jim gave the Colonel a check for $110,000 representing one-tenth of the guarantee, the deposit the Colonel had asked. "The condition was we wouldn't get the money back if it fell through," says Steve. Those present at this meeting, all crammed into the same small bedroom office, included Diskin, the Colonel's secretary Jim O'Brien, George Parkhill of RCA, Steve and Jim of course, and two nervous Filmways executives.

At ten o'clock in the morning, less than a week later, when Steve and Jim entered their Beverly Hills offices, they were told the Colonel wanted to see them at eleven-thirty. This was for a meeting with Irving Kahn, president of TelePrompTer, the company that would provide the closed circuit equipment. The cast was otherwise the same, with the addition of Joe Esposito and a William Morris mail-room clerk who was responsible that day for serving the fried chicken, hot dogs and hard-boiled eggs. The meeting was held in the Colonel's M-G-M office kitchen, "the cookhouse."

Apparently much of the meeting passed with Parker and Kahn, a flamboyant former press agent with 20th Century-Fox, flattering each other. Then when they began to talk business, Kahn made a huge undertaking monstrous by suggesting the show also be sent to Japan and Europe by Telstar. Steve and Jim confess today to being somewhat bewildered by talk *that* big, but they agreed generally to everything that was discussed. And it was understood there would be future meetings.

"When Irving Kahn left," says Steve, "the Colonel told us what we'd done wrong in the negotiating. He also told us where he thought Kahn's strengths and weaknesses were. He wasn't telling us what to do, but he kept saying, 'If I were you . . .' And when he says that, that's when you get the pencil out."

The Colonel additionally made it clear that advertising for the concert and broadcast would *not* read "Concert Associates Presents Elvis." He said, "Let's get it straight who we're promoting here—Elvis or you." He told them when they advertised for local promoters in the two hundred-plus cities not to accept any collect calls "because if they can't pay for the call, you don't want them." This, the Colonel said, would eliminate 90 per cent of the dead wood. And when they said they'd make an announcement in April, he said they had the date right, but *he* would do the announcing. "I'll have the boy there and we'll do it right," they quote the Colonel as saying.

Then on March 19, the story was given considerable space in the Los Angeles *Times*. The writer, Robert Hilburn, had the facts correct and gave what appeared to be a logical reason for the Colonel to concoct the scheme: "To maintain his image as 'King,' Presley needs 'super engagements.' By appearing in Las Vegas' biggest showroom and in the Astrodome, he had just that. But what else was there." Answer: " . . . the closed circuit package is a first for the entertainment field. It is a match, both financially and in artistic prestige, for the Las Vegas and Houston engagements. In fact, it would, if ticket sales match expectations, exceed them both."

But that was the last ever heard of the project. Steve Wolf and Jim Rissmiller duck the question when asked, but it is apparent *they* broke the story and the Colonel reportedly was purple with rage. Besides, fairly good sources say Filmways made some additional demands not accepted by the Colonel. In any case, says Steve, "It kept being tabled and finally it was tabled past the date when there was sufficient time to organize. There were some phone calls, but there never was another meeting."

The Colonel did return the $110,000, however.

At the same time this was going on, the Colonel was negotiating with the people at the International. All the kitchen workers had gone on strike in Las Vegas in March and the hotels were empty. Nick Naff at the International says there was a meeting of all the hotel administrators to determine what might be done to bring the business back as quickly as possible, once the strike ended. Nick says it was unanimously agreed that the personality who could get the action going in Vegas fastest was Elvis, and the International was asked if it would try to get Elvis back for a week or ten days. Nick says a deal was made with the Colonel all right, but the strike ended sooner than they thought and it was impossible to assemble the show so quickly. Others contend the act already booked into the International, the Gene Kelly show, refused to be bumped for the ten-day period. And so Elvis did not return to Vegas until August, as scheduled.

In May another single was released, "The Wonder of You," a highly orchestrated arrangement of a highly commercial song included in his next album, *On Stage,* released in June. The album included many of the songs Elvis had sung that were not his own—"Sweet Caroline," "Polk Salad Annie," "Proud Mary," "Walk a Mile in My Shoes," "Runaway" and "Yesterday," the last two from his first Vegas appearance and not from February as was indicated on the album cover. Like its predecessor, *On Stage* contained some of Elvis's ad lib comment ("Honey, I've already kissed you . . . you've had it"); but probably unlike any other album in history, it did not have his name printed anywhere on either side of the album sleeve—a fact that did not detract from sales.

It had been more than a year since Elvis finished his last film, *Change of Habit,* fulfilling all his commitments. Of course the Colonel had been made some offers during this time, but the terms dictated by him did not seem especially appetizing. Steve Binder, who had produced and directed the television special, went to the Colonel's friend, Abe Lastfogel, the president of the William Morris Agency, with one idea. This was for Elvis to participate as host and interviewer-narrator of a filmed history of rock 'n' roll. According to Steve, Lastfogel quoted the Colonel as wanting: a million dollars for ten weeks of Elvis's time (and if the picture wasn't finished then, too bad!), plus 50 per cent of profits; 25 per cent of the television sale on top of 10 per cent for television distribution; total cost of picture not to exceed two million dollars; no shooting after six o'clock or on weekends; no work the last two weeks in December or the first two in January. Steve says he values the letter, but he lost interest in the project after reading it.

And then it was announced that Elvis would star in a documentary film about himself. It would be called *Elvis* and was to be shot in rehearsal and on stage at the International in August.

The morning of the day Elvis opened his third month-long appearance at the International, the Colonel was supervising the decoration of the building's entrance, watching half a dozen men climb ladders and hang hundreds of little colored flags on strings. The flags said it was an "Elvis Summer Festival" and they gave the entrance to the huge hotel the look of a used-car lot.

Inside, on the carpeted steps leading to the casino, stood a pretty blonde hawking Elvis Presley photographs (one dol-

lar) and picture books (a dollar and a half), and beyond her
every dealer and pit boss was wearing an Elvis Presley scarf
(three-fifty, available at the hotel's gift shops) and a white
Styrofoam skimmer with a colorful band that once again pro-
claimed the month an "Elvis Summer Festival."

Elsewhere in the hotel—in the six restaurants, by the
bay-sized pool, in the half-dozen bars, in the youth (baby-
sitting) hostel—were hung posters and autographed pictures
and scarves and banners and flags. Outside the Showroom entrance the hotel's professional decorator was stapling this
stuff to everything that wasn't moving.

At the reservation desk there was a line thirty feet long,
and an attractive redhead was telling the day's three hun-
dredth caller (her estimate) that no, there wasn't any room
at the inn—every one of the hotel's rooms was full. (Herb
Alpert was told he could bunk in with record producer Lou
Adler or go somewhere else.) The Showroom itself was reported sold out for two shows a night, seven nights a week
for nearly the entire engagement.

Two of Elvis's big fans, Bob and Nancy, were there to get
married in a chapel near the hotel. Sue and Cricket were
there too, but wherever Elvis is, they are. The girl from Chicago, the one who'd bitten Elvis on the neck in February
during a performance, was back. On the elevators were
dozens more, trying to get past the guards on the thirteenth
floor, where Elvis was staying in the sumptuous Crown Suite.
Still more fans wandered aimlessly through the casino, wearing I LIKE ELVIS buttons, seeking a familiar face—a fan from
England or Australia met there the last time Elvis was in Las
Vegas; one of Elvis's hired hands, who often played black
jack and cruised the casino for girls; or, prize of prizes, Elvis's
dad, Vernon, who liked to play the nickel slots; or Colonel
Tom, who regularly dropped hundreds at roulette.

Giving the scene a final bizarre touch was a forty-man
camera crew from M-G-M, there to continue shooting for the
documentary the Colonel wanted in the theaters by Thanks-

giving. So regularly were they in the casino—interviewing the
bell captains, the dealers, the maitre d', the bartenders, the
change girls, the chefs, the fans—that the gamblers paid them
no mind, even if they *were* hauling and shoving huge Pana-
vision cameras between the rows of slot machines.

"What's all that?" said a woman with pendulous breasts,
dressed in a halter and Bermuda shorts.

"They're making a TV about Elvis," said her husband.

"Oh," said the woman. "Gimme another five, will ya, hon?
I wanna play the quarter machines."

It had begun a week earlier, as Eddy Arnold entered his
final week in the Showroom. It was then the film crew arrived
with the Colonel and some of his staff, followed by Elvis and
his boys and the five-man backup band. Each day thereafter
the name Elvis was heard more and more.

Already the filming had begun, back in Los Angeles, as
Elvis started rehearsals at an M-G-M rehearsal hall and the
documentary's Oscar-winning director, Denis Sanders, visited
some of southern California's top Elvis fans.

"What we're trying to do," said Denis, once he arrived in
Vegas, "is capture Elvis the entertainer, from the point of
view of the fans, the hotel and the audience."

He explained that about half the film—fifty minutes to an
hour—would be edited from Elvis's first five performances in
the Showroom, the rest would be in scene and interview.
Scenes like Bob and Nancy Neal's wedding—in three takes,
incidentally—and interviews like those with hotel employees
and the members of the *Hair* cast.

Some scenes filmed with the cast that was appearing in the
hotel's theater were deemed too far out for inclusion in the
film. They began with someone mentioning one of Elvis's
M-G-M films, *Harum Scarum,* and saying what a horror it
was, and built to where a black actor improvised a scene,
playing Elvis as an illiterate learning how to talk.

"What I'm shooting is a musical documentary," said Denis, "and I'm not just talking about the concert segments. Everything in the film will be musical. Just as Elvis, or any other performer, alternates fast numbers with slower numbers, say, or creates moods, so will I. We'll have a sad scene, a happy scene, another sad scene, and so on. Other elements will be constructed like in a ballad when you hit the instrumental break, we'll maybe cut to a face in the audience and from that cut to the same face getting married."

If this sounded not at all like the predictable Elvis Presley flick, it was because Denis Sanders was not the predictable Elvis Presley director. He came to the project with an astonishing—for an Elvis film—background. His six-hour documentary for National Educational Television, *Trial: City and County of Denver vs. Lauron R. Watson,* won the 1970 *Saturday Review* television award and the 1970 Cannes Film Festival prize for the best news film. He wrote the ninety-minute television special *The Day Lincoln Was Shot;* directed segments of television's *Naked City, Route 66, Alcoa Premiere* and *The Defenders,* as well as several features, including *Shock Treatment* and *One Man's Way;* wrote the screen adaptation of Norman Mailer's *The Naked and the Dead.* His *Czechoslovakia, 1968* won the Academy Award for best documentary in 1969. His motion picture short *A Time Out of War,* which he wrote, produced and directed, also won an Academy Award, in 1954.

Denis says he doesn't know why he was called to direct the Elvis film. He'd never even met the Colonel or Elvis and the only contact he'd had with M-G-M was in 1959, when he was kicked off the lot after working just two weeks as director of *The Subterraneans.* At that time, he says today, M-G-M said he was turning Jack Kerouac's story into an "immoral film."

However unsuitable Denis seemed to be on the surface, probably he was the perfect choice. Elvis's films hadn't been making the fortunes claimed, and it was logical that with his return to personal appearances there should have been a concurrent shift in the film direction. Making a documentary—

as opposed to another cream-puff musical—was a means of realizing this shift. Making a *good* documentary cinched it.

Budget for the film was between $1 million and $1.3 million, surprisingly little of which went to Elvis. Denis gets no more specific than to say half the budget covered all the "above the line," or creative, costs. Normally Elvis got a million dollars, so this apparently meant Elvis had taken a cut.

It had been an unusual week for Elvis in many ways.

When the Colonel arrived in Las Vegas, trailing a staff of attendants from RCA, M-G-M and the Morris Agency, he took an entire wing on the fourth floor, where he posted a round-the-clock uniformed guard who allowed no one admission but was instructed to give all visitors an Elvis Presley postcard and an Elvis Presley calendar or record catalogue. The Colonel then had his staff decorate the hallway—covering one wall with a gigantic Elvis movie poster, the other with banners and flags, stacking the Styrofoam hats five feet high outside the doors.

Meetings were held daily, during which minions were given assignments, or perhaps did little more than chat with the Colonel's wife back in Palm Springs on the telephone.

"Say hello to Stan," the Colonel'd say to his wife, Marie, handing the phone to Stan Brossette, whom the Colonel persisted in calling "Brickett."

"Hello, how are you feeling today?" Stan would say. "How are Chrissie and Midnight?" (The Parker cats.) "Yes, ma'am, everything sure is going okay. Yes, ma'am. Here's the Colonel now."

And the Colonel, who called his wife two and three times daily, would tell her what he had for breakfast.

As the days passed, the activity increased. The Colonel was in a room the hotel had converted into a paneled office —unprecedented for a manager anywhere. Now the Colonel had a permanent "Las Vegas office." Across the street the Landmark Hotel had been booked solid with the overflow from the International. In the gift shops there were no more scarves or "Elvis Summer Festival" hats. Someone said this was planned by the Colonel, who knew that if there weren't enough to go around, the demand would be greater when he allowed a few more to be put on display. The hotel's security force had been augmented by 50 per cent—to provide Elvis and the Colonel with twenty-four-hour guards, give Elvis two guards to walk him from the dressing room to the Show-room, and post one guard outside every door leading back-stage. Security was so tight by opening day, even Stan Brossette was having his calls screened. Whenever anyone or-dered something from room service, with their order came an RCA catalogue of all Elvis's records and tapes, two eight-by-ten black-and-white photographs, two color eight-by-tens (six or seven years old and showing Elvis with blue hair), and an Elvis Presley pocket calendar.

In the casino bars could be seen the people from Elvis's past, coming to pay semiannual homage to the man they knew in the good old days. George Klein, who was president of Elvis's senior class at Humes High in Memphis in 1953, was there, talking with mountainous Lamar Fike, who was buying a drink for Jim Kingsley, the Memphis newspaperman who'd grown up in Tupelo about the same time Elvis did and since had prided himself on being "the newspaperman closest to Elvis."

And the Colonel was giving Denis *his* last-minute instruc-vations: Dwayne Hickman, Juliet Prowse, Sid Caesar, Xavier Cugat, Herb Alpert, Slappy White, Dale Robertson, George Hamilton, Jack Benny, Jane Morgan, Jackie Cooper, Sammy Davis, Jr., Sonny Liston, Cary Grant.

And Denis Sanders was giving his forty-man crew final in-structions before taking eight cameras into the Showroom, five of them to remain rolling throughout the hour-long show.

An the Colonel was giving Denis *his* last-minute instruc-tions. "Now don't you go winning no Oscar with this pitcha," he said, "because we don't have no tuxedos to wear to the celebration."

-16-

THE FANS

MRS. VIRGINIA COONS WELCOMED the visitors to her modest Redondo Beach, California, home. With her in the living room were her daughters, Elaine, sixteen, and Nancy, twelve. Her husband, Arthur, a lathe operator, was out for the evening and her son, David, fourteen, was playing in the neighborhood.

"Usually we watch films first," she said, almost before everyone had exchanged names and found seats. She nodded toward an eight-millimeter projector at one end of the small room and as her son entered asked him to put the screen in place in front of the televison set. On nearly every piece of furniture in the room was a framed picture of Elvis.

"We're quite proud of these films," he said. "This one was shot by a friend."

Suddenly the room went black and the first of the home movies in color began with a shaky shot of Elvis's Trousdale gate. The gate swung open and a huge black limousine drove out, Joe Esposito at the wheel, Elvis seated next to him. The scene lasted under a minute and was followed by another that had the same limousine coming back. Now it was the end of the day and Elvis was returning from work at the studio, Mrs. Coons explained. This scene lasted a bit longer, as Elvis had Joe stop the car long enough for him to sign a few autographs for the fans clustered outside his home. And then the car disappeared through the gate. The next scene showed the limousine coming back out again. It was another day—at least Elvis had changed his clothes—and with a wave Elvis was gone. This lasted under thirty seconds. Then there was another return home at the end of the day, and once more Elvis signed a few autographs.

With the sputtering sound of film whirling loose on the reel, the first movie ended.

"This next one's more exciting," said Mrs. Coons. "It was taken by a fan when Elvis was in Houston. I'm afraid it's all out of focus, though."

The second film began.

Halfway around the world, in England, Rex Martin, the president of the Gloucestershire branch of the Official Elvis Presley Fan Club of Great Britain and the Commonwealth, was preparing a list of tape recordings he had for exchange or sale. Some of the items:

ELVIS ON THE FRANK SINATRA TV SHOW 1960. LIVE! about 6 min. Starts "It's very nice to go travelling" into: FAME & FORTUNE; STUCK ON YOU: Quality good! $1.50

ELVIS / SINATRA SHOW EXTRAS: about 5 min. RARE. El & Frank joke around on stage. Then Frank sings a line of LOVE ME TENDER, & El sings a line of Frank's hit song "WITCHCRAFT" alternating between the 2. At the end they both duet together on the ending of LOVE ME TENDER. (Fantastic tape!) $2

ELVIS ON THE ED SULLIVAN TV SHOW. "LIVE" 1957 about 6 minutes. Talks & Sings HOUND DOG: Then a medley of LOVE ME TENDER / HEARTBREAK HOTEL / HOUND DOG / PEACE IN THE VALLEY / LOVE ME / & TOO MUCH. Quality fair only. $1.50

ANNETTE DAY Talks about Meeting ELVIS: and filming with him for Double Trouble + a USA interview with Annette & a short scene from Double Trouble. 50¢

VANCOUVER RADIO SHOW ON ELVIS: Includes 1956 interview talking about people who called him ELVIS THE PELVIS: 1957 VANCOUVER

PRESS CONFERENCE about 12 minutes: Talking about how he got started, his first Memphis show: Touring, making films & TV shows. Col. Parker etc. etc. Very interesting stuff. $2

In Portland, Oregon, a college senior named Carl Obermeier was hastily filling orders for bumper stickers imprinted ELVIS MASTER OF ROCK 'N' ROLL (fifty cents), blue T-shirts with white letters that boast I'M AN ELVIS FAN (three dollars, plus twenty-five cents mailing), pencils with FOREVER KING ELVIS cut on the sides (six for a quarter), combs that say I'M AN ELVIS FAN CLUB MEMBER (six, in assorted colors, for a dollar), and a wide range of rubber stamps for the fan to cover his or her correspondence with messages such as MUSIC THAT WILL BE NEW TOMORROW, OUR ELVIS IS SINGING TODAY! and YES, I'M AN ELVIS FAN AND PROUD OF IT! Carl says business is good.

As long as there have been heroes and heroines there have been fans, and the Elvis Presley fan probably is in many ways like all who came before. He or she contributes dependable career support, usually economic, less often emotional. Certainly most of Elvis's fans are those who buy his records, perhaps seen an occasional movie, and if convenient see him in concert, and let it go at that. But however important this large amorphous mass of followers may be, it is the *avid* fan who has contributed so much to the myth. This is the fan who makes it abundantly clear that the word's origin is in "fanatic."

It is difficult to say how many there are. Colonel Parker's office claimed there were upward of three thousand fan clubs in 1970, although the figure probably was inflated and many were marginal operations with limited memberships. Still, Carl Obermeier says he has 750 members in his "Hound Dogs" Elvis Fan Club ("A 100% Elvis Organization"); and Sean Shaver, the twenty-seven-year-old photographer who is president of the "El's Angels" E.P.F.C. in Kansas City, claims a roster of 950 in twenty-five countries. In Germany the International Elvis Presley Club Göttingen—whose ad-

dress was printed on the record sleeve of a recent single released in Germany—has nearly three thousand members. In
England, where Elvis fans have a crusading zeal not even
surpassed by vegetarians, Seventh Day Adventists and, currently, women's libertarians, the Elvis Presley Fan Club of
Great Britain and the Commonwealth boasts four thousand
members and once mustered no less than a hundred thousand
signatures on a petition to get Elvis to do a concert there.
(The Colonel was reported impressed but unmoved.) Certainly there are a sizable number of fans, more perhaps than
are attracted to any other single personality. (The Beatles
may have had more fan club members in 1964–66, but where
are they today?) Perhaps the Colonel was correct when he
said there were a quarter of a million he could count on.

It is, of course, the Colonel who has cultivated the fandom,
regarding the clubs as the money in the bank they represent.
The letters he sends the club presidents may be mimeographed, but they're full of news and come often; and RCA
is instructed to send enough calendars, photographs and record catalogues for all the members. Whenever Elvis fans
gather in convention, as they do in many parts of the world,
the Colonel sends a telegram. Even more care is directed toward those with newsletters, magazines and bulletins, of
which there are, apparently, several hundred.

One of them is *The King's Scepter,* official organ of the
Kissin' Cousins International E.P.F.C. It is headquartered in
Spokane and lists Elvis Presley as honorary president; Judy
Palmer, president; club song, "Kissin' Cousins"; club colors,
royal blue and gold; club dues, two dollars a year. In recent
years it has run between two and six letter-sized pages, all
crammed almost to the borders with record reviews, effusive
praise of Elvis's Las Vegas shows, plugs for other fan clubs,
shorter news and gossip notes, and a number of nicely repro-
duced photographs. Judy signs her periodic report "Elove."

About half the size and considerably more commercial is
the slender bimonthly publication that serves the "El's Angels"

E.P.F.C. In part this is because the club's president and newsletter editor, Sean Shaver, also runs the Elvis Presley Record Club of America, through which members can buy any of Elvis's records, new or old, at discounted prices. Sean also peddles sheet music and other memorabilia, and signs the newsletter "Till next time, Keep Elvis King."

A more ambitious journal was the last assembled and distributed to special friends of the Elvis Presley Fan Club of Southern California—club motto: "Perpetrators Perpetuating Presley Platters"—whose joint chiefs, Linda Webster and Nancy Ambrose, lived in Mar Vista. This publication, stapled inside a manila file folder, reprinted articles from several metropolitan newspapers and one national magazine, and included five radio request forms, a letter from "Colonel Parker's Office," a section devoted to a disc jockey in Chicago who had stuck with Elvis through the years, a special report written by Virginia Coons, a Xerox copy of an Elvis movie ad, two color and two black-and-white photographs, four calendars from four different years, two different Easter cards and—for the collector—one bubble-gum card from 1956.

Clearly, the most professional of the American Elvis publications does not represent a club but is, rather, a monthly five-and-a-half-by-eight-inch magazine run on a break-even or just slightly profitable basis. This is Rocky Barra's *Strictly Elvis,* which Rocky edits in his Livonia, Michigan, home. It is now in its fourth year and costs six dollars for twelve issues. Like others in the field, it publishes articles written by fans and carries the texts of press conferences and rare interviews, most of them from the 1950s. Excellent graphics are the *Strictly Elvis* high point. And Rocky is himself a rock singer, bearing a marked resemblance to his idol.

Many of Elvis's fans resemble him, or try to. Some are teenagers like Steve Miller, a junior in a Spokane high school. He says it was in 1960, when he was eight, that he first heard one of Elvis's records. "When I played the record I flipped," he says. "I thought, Man, I gotta look into this Elvis guy! So straight to the drugstore I went and bought a teen book with Elvis stuff and I read up on him. I bought a bunch more Elvis records and ditched my Ricky Nelson ones. I cut out a lot of Elvis pictures and plastered them on my wall and then I put my hair up in a pompadour just like Elvis. My friend Dave Kirkingburg and I would get our Elvis records together and imitate him hours on end. The first movie Dave and I saw was *Loving You*. After the movie Dave and I went all over the place grinning like Elvis. We also tried to talk like him. The main Elvis habit I copied—and I still do it—was putting my shirt collar up." And several older Elvis fans, including a twenty-five-year-old California dentist, are the hit of private parties they give when they stand in front of their record players pantomiming to Elvis songs. Says a friend of the dentist: "For that moment, as long as he is pretending to be Elvis, he *is* Elvis."

It is a religious fervor many of the fans manifest in trying to explain how they feel about Elvis. Says Julie Montgomery, a twenty-three-year-old student from Polson, Montana: "Since October 1955 so many of my experiences, dreams—not day-dreams but sleep dreams—and memories involve Elvis that they'd fill a book. I've had no control over and have not at-tempted to control these experiences. I believe that there are powers and forces working to pull me toward Elvis. These forces are so strong that at this point in my life I couldn't pull away from Elvis if I desired to do so." Irene Feola, who is twenty-seven and a housewife and mother of two from Carmel, New York, is another in whose dreams Elvis has been cast in the starring role. "I have to tell you about a dream that came true one year ago," she says. "I flew to Las Vegas to see Elvis at the International. Me! I left Sunday, August tenth, and stayed with a girl friend that lives there. I saw him Monday and Tuesday night. But you wouldn't believe this. I had front-row seats and I kissed him! He stood in front of me and I called him. He looked at me and walked over and bent down and whispered that I was sweet and then he kissed me on the lips. Every time I talk about it now I wish I were there. No one will ever understand how I feel. I love him! He has given me happiness and excitement in my life that will never die. This is my dream come true. Elvis kissed me! For that moment, it was just me." What does Mr. Feola say? His wife says he understands.

The fans sew the names of Elvis's movies on their skirts and shirts, the names of the characters he's played on their bedspreads.

They save their money for pilgrimages to Graceland and Tupelo, where they shoot up dozens of rolls of film, mostly of the gates, houses and each other.

They send request cards to radio stations—often using the cards provided by the fan clubs, an idea of the Colonel's—to insure broadcast of Elvis's records, and then vote, and vote often, in all readership or audience surveys to insure Elvis his usual number one position.

They inundate Elvis and Priscilla—whom they seem to love rather stoically—with Christmas, birthday and anniversary gifts, send dolls and clothing by the truckload to Lisa Marie, pile fresh flowers on Elvis's mother's grave, and mail get-well cards when anyone is sick.

They write letters to one another, sign them "Elvisly yours" and "Proud 4 Presley," and cover the envelopes with stickers and rubber-stamped messages or stamps showing Elvis's face.

They track Elvis relentlessly, hoping to get a snapshot and have the picture duplicated by the score to trade for other almost identical snapshots taken by other fans, all of which they keep in huge scrapbooks along with newspaper clippings, postcards, calendars and the buckets of promotional literature mailed by RCA and the Colonel each year. One fan boasts sixty-two scrapbooks, another thirty thousand photographs.

They collect anything they can get their hands on—taking leaves from the Tupelo trees, grass from the Graceland lawn, bricks from the Trousdale patio. A thirty-one-year-old cashier in Honolulu has some of the sand Elvis walked on. Several have glasses he drank from in Vegas—preserving the water in bottles—and napkins stained by his sweat. One fan in Australia claims even to have some garbage taken from one of Elvis's trash cans. When asked what she had in her Elvis collection, a girl named Mary, who lives in Cleveland, said, "Everything except for the real thing. And oh, what I could do with the real thing." Mary is thirteen.

They decorate entire rooms, creating Elvis environments, covering the walls of bedrooms as completely as the Colonel has covered his office walls. A teenaged fan in Indio, California, has a photograph in the glove compartment of her car, another laminated in plastic so it won't get wet when she takes it into the shower. "I sleep under an acre of Elvis photos," says a twenty-year-old typist from Miami, "and the record player never stops."

They join clubs the way aspiring public office holders join civic organizations. Many clubs take their names from one of Elvis's songs or films. Besides those mentioned, there's the Ready Teddy E.P.F.C. (in Quebec), the Stuck on You Forever Elvis Fan Club (West Malaysia), The Blue Hawaiians E.P.F.C. (Beverly Hills), the Love Me Tender E.P.F.C. (Monroe, Louisiana) and the Sound of Elvis Fan Club of Australasia, whose members call themselves Roustabouts. Others describe the members' collective state of mind: the Forever Faithful E.P.F.C. (Mount Holly, New Jersey) and the For Ever for Elvis Fan Club (with branches in Miami, Memphis, Mexico City, Australia and Brazil). The list goes on and on. There are clubs in every major city in the U. S., where any traveling fan is sure to have a place to stay the night.

Some fans even name their children for Elvis. Stephen Toli, a twenty-eight-year-old construction worker from Somerville, Massachusetts, is one of these. Steve and his wife are among the most active and prolific American fans, members of nearly a dozen clubs and correspondents for several British fan publications. Says Steve: "I have a boy four years old named Stephen Elvis. And my other son, who is two years old, is named Lonnie Glen—Lonnie from *Tickle Me* and Glen from *Wild in the Country*."

When Elvis was hit with a paternity suit in 1970, several fans called the Colonel's office, and although they said they didn't believe the charge for a minute, they wanted to adopt the baby.

Being an Elvis Presley fan is not inexpensive. Glenn D. Hardin, Elvis's pianist in Las Vegas, tells one story: "There was this little ol' girl from Chicago and her father was a lawyer. We did about sixty shows and she made forty-five of them. She sat in the same seat twice a night. She told me in the bar her pop paid eighty bucks a night for that, for tips and all. Like, they gave them eighty bucks a night and she got that chair. She was a groovy little girl. Her father took a bunch of us out to dinner one night. The boys in the band. It was a thing like: If my little girl likes Elvis, we'll take the band to dinner; if we can't get Elvis, we'll do the next best thing."

Most fans don't have rich poppas, however, and are like Judy Palmer, the twenty-two-year-old president of the Kissin' Cousins E.P.F.C. in Spokane. "I've been very lucky and have met Elvis and seen him several times," she says. "I spent a month in Memphis, February 1968. Then I was part of the audience at Elvis's live TV special tapings in Burbank in June 1968. I saw him at his Los Angeles home last April 1969 and have seen six shows, each trip to Vegas, August 1969 and February 1970. I imagine that from this list of travels you'll assume I'm a millionairess. I work as an assistant manager at a photo-camera shop and make two dollars an hour. But I spend all my vacations in Elvis country."

On that salary, she says, it is difficult for her to cover club operating expenses. "I get from thirty-five to fifty letters a week," she says, "and the majority of them don't enclose a stamp for reply. I spend about twenty dollars a month on postage, plus another twenty dollars every two or three months to mail the newsletters. And the newsletters themselves cost another forty dollars or so. It's costly having a club, but I enjoy it, so I feel it's worth the money I put into it. It's fun to share Elvis with other fans."

By far the biggest Elvis spenders are two fans who divide their time between Memphis and Los Angeles. Sue Wiegert, who is twenty-four, with a college degree, and Cricket Mendell, who is twenty-one, are the dynamic duo of Elvis fandom; they are, almost all of every day, within sighing distance of Elvis. This means that when Elvis is in Los Angeles the girls begin each day outside his house, wave to him as his limousine appears and then lead the car to the studio, where they will wait until it is time to escort him home again. If Elvis flies to Memphis, Sue and Cricket point their Dodge Dart in that direction and get there as fast as possible. If he goes on location, or to Las Vegas, or Houston, or anywhere else they can drive, that's where they go too. When Elvis is at the International, they go to every show, charging everything to their credit cards.

Occasionally the girls do take jobs, of course, working as temporary secretaries in whichever city they're in so they can make the payments on the credit-card charges, pay for food and rent. But most of the time their vocation is Elvis, their avocation more of the same. As a consequence, the apartments they have shared, and continue to share, in both cities are less than sumptuous, usually containing little more than a bed and a record player. Often they sleep in the car

Cricket, a plain little blonde with a lot of energy and girlish enthusiasm, became an "Elfan" in Canton, Ohio, where by 1963 she had joined upward of thirty fan clubs and, figuring she could do as well, formed her own, the Elvisites. The club motto is "King Elvis Reigns Supreme." Sue is a brunette less garrulous than her partner. She first saw Elvis on one of the Sullivan shows in 1956, finished college at her mother' insistence and after forming *her* own fan club, Blue Hawaiian for Elvis, started hanging on the Graceland gate. That's where the two girls met in 1967. They've been inseparable since.

Sue and Cricket are reluctant to talk with writers these days, fearing what they call—without using the word—"exploitation." They permitted themselves to be interviewed for an article in *West* magazine the summer of 1970 and began threatening lawsuits even before the story appeared. Asked why, they said they were afraid Elvis would think they were paid for the interview, that they were taking advantage of their friendship (that was the word—friendship) with Elvis.

If Sue and Cricket are the champs of Presleymania, England is where most of the runners-up live. In Great Britain there are Elvis fans in sufficient number and heat to support a slick newsstand magazine devoted to him, *Elvis Monthly*. In its sixty-four pages are many familiar features—record raves, assorted discographies and other statistical compilations, letters to the editor, a personal testimonial titled "Discovering Elvis" (usually carrying the conviction and verve normally found only in a fresh religious convert), columns of gossip and news, and occasional poems. There are monthly reports from Memphis on what Elvis has been doing day to day, provided by Gary Pepper, whose father works the Graceland gate; a column of club news edited by Albert Hand, a printer who founded the International Elvis Presley Appreciation Society; dozens of photographs; and a few advertisements such as "The Jordanaires Sweater—from the Jordanaires' own ladies' dress / sweater shop in Nashville. Usual Price: twenty-five dollars. For Elvis fans: a fifteen-dollar international money order." *Elvis Monthly* also is responsible for an *Elvis Special* yearbook and offers badges, records, notepaper and envelopes.

It was on this five-by-seven-inch magazine that the *Beatles Monthly* was based, but while *Elvis Monthly* is now in its eleventh year, the Beatles publication folded in 1969, after five.

Most important function of the *Monthly* is communication,

for it is through this publication that most of the biggest Elvis "do's" are supported, planned and announced. (Title of a recent article: "Presley Parties Pack Power.") In honor of Elvis and Priscilla's third wedding anniversay, for example, Maureen Fricker planned an all-day celebration party that promised screenings of *Roustabout, Follow That Dream* and selected short subjects including three Warner Pathé news films, one of them of Elvis's wedding. Additionally there was a "Question Half Hour" and a "Discussion Half Hour." Tickets: 18/- (about two dollars), including tea, biscuits and assorted sandwiches.

A larger Elvis "do" is the annual Elvis convention, now in its sixth year, organized by the *Monthly*, and usually held in London, but in 1970 all over Europe. "Fans travelling on the eight-day Elvis fans' holiday will be treated to an Elvis Party in Brussels, when films of Elvis' Las Vegas engagement, taken by a fan will be shown," said Todd Slaughter, president of Britain's Official Elvis Presley Fan Club in a recent issue. "In Holland, two feature films are planned, and when fans move on to Koblenz, the German Fan Club promises a screening of the Elvis Presley NBC-TV Show. And don't forget, in addition to the Convention [in Luxembourg], we are hoping to arrange with a Luxembourg cinema for the screening of *Live a Little, Love a Little* and *Charro*." It was enough to make any Elvis fan drool with anticipation.

The organization is fantastic. Says Maria Luisa Davies, the club's branch leader in Liverpool: "What happens here is that the country is divided into areas which have an area leader. It is my job to keep in touch with the members who live in the locality, answer their queries—to save Todd from being snowed under with questions—to organize trips to other towns to see Elvis films, etc. Because we are such a small country we can get about meeting other members. I think it is the spirit of companionship and the wonderful feeling of being of one accord which makes these events so successful."

Many of the European events take their cue from Elvis's

philanthropy and are used as a vehicle to raise money for some charity, in England usually for guide dogs for the blind.

Elvis Monthly is not the only Elvis publication in Europe. In Italy there is the *Elvis Times*, a full-sized newspaper published monthly, half in English, half in Italian. In Holland a fan, Hans Langbroek, spent ten years researching—largely by mail—Elvis's early life and published an attractive and generally quite accurate if highly personal and chatty biography that takes Elvis through 1955, *The Hillbilly Cat*. And in England and Ireland there are dozens of regularly issued newsletters and fan magazines.

It is unfair to generalize about what the "average" Elvis fan(atic) is like in terms of background, age, occupation and so on. But polls have been taken, one of them by *Elvis Monthly*, and fragmentary pictures are formed. In England, apparently, nearly half the *Monthly* readership is between nineteen and twenty-two, with the young men claiming a slight edge in numbers over the young women, the rest fairly equally divided between under-eighteens and over-twenty-threes. Clerks, white-collar workers and professions (43 per cent) placed well ahead of factory workers and tradesmen (30 per cent) and students and housewives (22 per cent). In the U. S. there seem to be two essential types of fans, differentiated largely by age, with twenty serving as a boundary. The older fans remember Elvis from the 1950s; those twenty and under became fans during his post-Army days.* Clearly two-thirds of all fan club members are in their teens or younger, not a surprising finding except that it leaves one-third twenty or older, a large number of them in their late twenties and early thirties. Females have the edge in the U. S., but for all fans the education level is—compared to England—low, closer to the national average. Although college registration has more than

---

* Apparently the only survey taken is my own, with distribution of three thousand questionnaires being handled by some of the fan clubs themselves. Some of the material in this chapter is based on information from those questionnaires.

doubled in the past twenty-five years, the median education level for white Americans is short of a high school diploma, while only about 20 per cent of the U.S. work force is professional or proprietorship, the rest being sales people, laborers, farmers and the like. Discounting for the moment the students, it is, generally, from the lower to middle economic classes—those who work rather than think for a living—that Elvis gets his most vigorous fans. There are, for example, an astonishing number of IBM keypunch operators, with factory assemblers and clerks following.

Of course many fans are teenagers going through the normal stages of hero worship. There is nothing odd about that. But many—the most zealous—do show character traits of interest to psychologists. These are the ones who are so possessive and so paranoid they deny Elvis human frailty. Thus they write obscene and threatening letters to anyone who attacks him or so much as criticizes a film or performance. Similarly, when a critic reviews Elvis favorably, he is flooded by letters and cards of thanks. And when stories of trouble between Elvis and Priscilla persist, if the fans believe them at all (which is doubtful), they are convinced it's Priscilla's, not Elvis's, fault. And as for all the bad films and weak sound-track recordings, they were the Colonel's doing; said the *Elvis Monthly*, noting that 44 per cent disapproved of the Colonel's policies: "A defeat of Elvis's management even after 1969's successes is a startling condemnation of the 1963/7 policy. Had this question been asked in 1967 the noes would have numbered at least 75%."

Psychologists say this exaggerated adoration often is a reflection of some identity crisis within the fan, that he (or she) is often so poor or so unpopular among his peers he must select someone glamorous through whom to live his life vicariously. Said one psychologist: "By affixing himself to an established star and devoting so much time to worshiping that star, in Elvis's case collecting scrapbooks and photographs and so on, he can develop—at least in his own mind—a *rela-*

tionship with the star, which by itself seems to be enough to make that individual 'better' than the peer group that rejects him. It is an old insecurity, self-treated in an old and generally harmless fashion."

But just why Elvis attracts so many of these people remains a mystery. Perhaps it is because they're made to feel so welcome.

Whoever they are, and whatever their motivations, the "Elfans" are fascinating creatures, upon whose backs much of the Elvis success story rests.

In Hollywood, Ann Moses, the pretty twenty-three-year-old editor of *Tiger Beat,* a newsstand magazine for teenagers, was trying to convince her publisher that her readers really do want more Elvis features, that it wasn't just her own prejudices. She, like most Elvis fan "leaders," has a better education than many—with two years of college—and also like many others says she became an Elvis fan through her husband. "I think being an Elvis fan is like being in love," she says. "You can't explain *why,* or *how,* it happened, but that feeling is just there and unmistakable."

In Morningside, Maryland, Bill Kaval, a twenty-seven-year-old police officer with three small children, was working on one of his discographies and film lists. Bill corresponds with fans over much of the world (England, Japan, Italy), is a member of several fan clubs, believes he has one of "the most complete Elvis Presley collections in the world" and is one of the more serious students and statisticians of the Presley phenomenon.

In Chicago, Lana Kotenko, twenty-two, entered her office for the filing and typing assignments that provide money for periodic visits to Memphis and Las Vegas. She is an attractive girl who covers much of her clothing with Elvis pictures and slogans. "Is he ever beautiful and sexy!" she exclaims. "And when he saw me with all my Elvis buttons and an Elvis blouse which I wore, he just couldn't believe his eyes. And I was so nervous I started crying." It was Lana, friends say,

who later bit Elvis on the neck during one of his performances in Las Vegas.

("I think Elvis is genuinely amazed by some of his fans,"
says Stan Brossette. "I've seen looks in his eye that say, 'Man,
you're weird.' I mean, how could he take it all seriously after
all these years?")

And in Redondo Beach, Mrs. Virginia Coons was threading
another Elvis film on her projector. Mrs. Coons, one of the
truly big collectors, has approximately 25,000 photographs of
Elvis in her collection and as she brings them out, book after
book after book, she likes to comment on how Elvis stands
with his right foot turned just so; it is obvious she has studied
these pictures countless times.

"There," she said, patting the projector and reaching for
the light switch. "This was one taken from the balcony at the
International."

The film lasted only a few minutes and then Mrs. Coons
ran it backward.

-17-

NOW

I THINK HE HAS IT in his mind he wants to work about twice a year," says Glenn D. Hardin. " 'Cause he's done all them run-all-over-the-country type things. The International's kinda a nice place. It's an easy way to do a gig. The money's decent. It's a good crowd. He likes to work out a little bit. He seems purty pleased. He wouldn't go back if he didn't. He don't need the money. I don't think he wants no full-time gig."

Once he'd completed this third month at the hotel in 1970, Elvis did go back on the road, with six performances in six days, in Phoenix, Detroit, St. Louis, Miami, Tampa and Mobile. And probably in the year or two following he will make his first appearances in Europe. But these are not the bone-breaking personal appearance tours of his Sun Records days, when he slept in the back of Scotty's Moore's Chevy or drove non-stop from West Texas to Shreveport to fulfill his *Louisiana Hayride* commitment. These are tours he can do in a week. One or two of those a year, plus the Vegas engagement, isn't enough to weary a man, or disallow the vacation time in Hawaii he likes.

There is no accurate way to determine Elvis's annual income, but estimates are possible. For his two months in Las Vegas, best sources say his salary is in the $1 million neighborhood (plus all the extra rooms and so on); other estimates double that. And any other personal appearances can be figured at a minimum of $100,000 or a sizable percentage of the box office, whichever is largest, for each performance.

Besides his performance income there is that which comes from record sales. The royalty figures are a closely guarded secret, but it can be assumed they exceed the big-company average, which is about five cents for each single sold, twenty-five to thirty cents for each album. In that Elvis has a production deal with RCA—meaning he provides RCA with a mixed and edited tape, paying all cost of producing it—it can just as safely be assumed that royalties are *much, much* higher than the average. The Colonel wants to be second to no one. So record royalties—based on four singles and three albums a year, most of them gold, which is not unreasonable—would account for at least another $1 million, perhaps a lot more.

Music publishing royalties add more. He continues to hold controlling interest in his own two companies, Elvis Presley Music (now including the American Division of Elvis Presley Music, formerly American Music) and Gladys Music. Hill and Range also has purchased other companies, including two of Marty Robbins's old firms, Marty's Music (including "El Paso") and Marizona Music. Freddie Bienstock, an officer in Gladys and Hill and Range, says Elvis now owns more than two thousand songs. Income from this: probably $500,000.

Miscellaneous income, such as that from an occasional film, plus his share of the sale of earlier films to television, the odd licensing agreements and so on, could add another $500,000, or more, depending on the number of films.

Total: between $3 million and $5 million.

Strangely, Elvis apparently gets to keep relatively little of it. Unlike many successful entertainment personalities, Elvis has never hidden behind paper corporations and holding companies or taken advantage of complicated capital gains deals and other tax dodges. He has not invested heavily in oil and cattle, and only minimally in real estate. There is no Elvis "empire," not in the traditional sense. Friends close to Elvis and the Colonel say this is because they honestly don't mind paying huge amounts to the government.

"He has a man come down from Washington every year to handle Elvis's taxes," says one of the Colonel's Nashville friends. "The Internal Revenue Service has been making out Elvis's and the Colonel's tax forms for years. The Colonel says he doesn't want any mistakes made, doesn't want to have happen to Elvis what happened to Joe Louis, getting wiped out for ten years of back taxes."

Elvis himself once echoed the Colonel: "I'd rather pay my taxes than worry about them. I don't want to wake up one of these days to find I owe the government more money than I have. Anyway, there seems to be enough left."

Elvis is, in many ways, a lot brighter than most think. Nearly everyone who's spent some time with him mentions this—and it is not entirely because, as they admit, they thought he'd intellectually conform to the hillbilly roles he so often played in his movies.

"Elvis has a very curious mind," says Bill Bixby, who is probably one of the brighter, more articulate young actors today. "We'd sit around and shoot the breeze about so many things. He really wants to know. He gets passions about things. He gives reason to believe his intellectual curiosity is rather broad, and there are many things he wants to know about and understand. He gets passionately involved in his discussions when he finds he has a willing audience who is sincerely interested in what he's talking about and isn't just paying him lip service."

Yvonne Craig, who reads political and sociological textbooks for kicks, says that when she dated Elvis he was on a medical jag, that he was reading several medical books at the time.

"He is fascinated by words," says Stan Brossette. "He'll ask what a word means: 'Say it again . . . can you use it this way . . that way?' Others would let them go by, pretending they know. His mind is so fine, so sharp, he could have been anything he wanted."

Stan says Elvis has four memorable characteristics: (1) his sensitivity and politeness, (2) his curiosity and instinct: his mind, (3) his boundless energy, and (4) his sense of humor. Explaining the last, he tells what is probably the best Elvis Presley story of all: "I never even met Elvis the first Presley picture I was publicist for. And then I just *met* him on the second. And then I *spoke* to him on the third. It was a gradual process and so when I had to go to him for the first time to request permission to bring a visitor on the set, I was less than sure of myself. It was a princess from somewhere or other and I made a speech to Elvis about how big a fan she was: 'She has all your records and she's seen every one of your pictures three times and she says if she doesn't meet you, her trip to America will have been a total waste.' I must have talked for a full three minutes, and Elvis just stood there listening. When I finished, his lip curled a little, he looked right at me and said, 'Does she fuck?' "

Elvis remains close to his family, and few new friends have entered the inner circle in years. His father and stepmother (he calls her Dee) and three stepbrothers, now in their teens, live in a modest but comfortable four-bedroom house in the development that flanks Graceland, where his aunt, Delta Mae Biggs, and his paternal grandmother, Minnie Presley, continue as year-round residents. One of his uncles, Travis Smith, was partially paralyzed by a stroke a few years ago; but another uncle, Vester Presley, the favorite of the fans, remains on the Graceland gate. And the names on his personal payroll—though some change from season to season—remain as familiar as brothers' names. As this is writtten, Joe Esposito, Charlie Hodge and Sonny West have been joined again by Richard Davis.

"Hollywood is full of actors and actresses who think they are close to Elvis," says Stan Brossette, "but they're not. Elvis may be reasonably close during shooting, and these people expect the relationship to continue, and it doesn't. The only exception is Shelley Fabares, who wouldn't even do interviews when she was doing a picture with Elvis. She didn't want to be asked about him. They see each other. But she's the only one. And there are no actors."

Elvis seems to enjoy meeting people and his manner is such that he puts even the most nervous at ease—excepting some dumb-struck fans, of course. Occasionally he seems even to take a liking to one of these strangers, asking him to come up to his suite at the International for an hour or so, sometimes (but rarely) asking him home to dinner when in Los Angeles. But it's not often. And even when it does happen, it does not mean, however much the stranger wants it, that Elvis is his pal and confidant.

"Elvis has his own friends—the boys—and no matter how cold it sounds, he doesn't need any new ones," says someone who once was a part of the group. "He's never really alone, unless he takes the Harley out for a ride sometimes or orders everybody out of the house. Most times he's constantly surrounded. That's what we were for. That's part of it, anyway. We were—are—his friends."

"I don't think he thinks of his life as isolated," says Stan Brossette. "He's never been to Disneyland and there are things he feels he can't do, but I don't think he'd want to change it any. I think he enjoys it. I never get the impression of sadness or loneliness, and when you see someone often over a period of five years, you get impressions."

Usually the guys go with him everywhere, unless Priscilla is along. If Elvis goes to the house he leases in Palm Springs not far from the Colonel's house for a weekend away from Priscilla, he'll take Richard and Sonny—both bachelors in 1970—and perhaps one or two others with him. Usually it will be a quiet weekend, motorcycle riding in the desert, swimming in the pool, playing Monopoly and Scrabble—Elvis's favorite games—and giggling at the all-night weather on television after the movies have gone off. When he travels with Priscilla—and they do not spend all their time together— usually Joe Esposito and his wife Joanie are along, now that Gee Gee and Patsy have left.

Priscilla has changed over the years. No longer is she the naïve teenager with lots of curls and baby fat that Elvis met in Germany. She doesn't even resemble her. She is far more attractive now, wearing her long straight hair dyed nearly as dark as Elvis's, dressing in modish mini-dresses. (Friends say Elvis at one point preferred more modest clothing and her hair back-combed high on her head.) She is quite slender, from periodic but strenuous dance instruction.

"She is very sharp, very intelligent, very aware of his whims," says Johnny Rivers. "She knows how to keep him happy and when to leave him alone. She really knows him. When I was talking with her in Las Vegas, she told me, 'I just come up two or three times while he's working here. I don't stay here and bug him. I just know he has to do his thing and be alone at certain times.' It's a mature attitude to take. It's the only way she could have a successful marriage with him."

Says Stan Brossette: "She carries off being Mrs. Presley with considerable grace."

The Colonel is remarkably homespun, once you cut through the elaborate jokes and hard-nosed bargaining. All of his often hokey, usually ostentatious ways do have a common, or ordinary, base. The apartment he keeps at the Wilshire Comstock, not far from Beverly Hills, is in direct contrast to his office. "The home is bare," says Ron Jacobs. "It's nice, but it's bare. There's no stuff. It might be a dentist's home." The Colonel isn't in this apartment much, usually spending at least half the week in Palm Springs. And his wife Marie, whom he often calls "Miz Parker" or "Miz 'Rie," stays in Palm Springs nearly always.

"She doesn't come into town except every two years or so

for a wedding or a funeral," says Stan Brossette. "Her big thing is raising money for her church. She's tough, she knows how to keep the Colonel in line, but she's a lamb, really. And they really do groove on each other. Miz Parker is the big thing in his life—much bigger than Elvis. They're like child-hood sweethearts on a honeymoon."

The Palm Springs home is quite comfortable, but not espe-cially showy. It has three bedrooms, a den, a living room-dining room combination, and a pool with indoor-outdoor carpeting. There are three or four expensive pieces of elec-tronic equipment, like home video units, but they're there only because they arrived as birthday presents from his friends.

"The Colonel has all kinds of friends," says Stan, "includ-ing the Abe Lastfogels and the Kirk Kerkorians, who are gonna send more than a bottle of booze, which wouldn't be appreciated anyway. So every time June 26 rolls around, the stuff starts coming in. The most expensive cigars Dunhill makes, in crates the size of a desk. TV sets. You name it. And what he really enjoys is getting a gag—an ashtray you wind up and it walks across the desk, something like that."

When the Colonel finishes work for the day, he does not talk about Elvis. Except for the well-decorated extra bed-room he uses as an office, the only sign of Elvis in the Palm Springs house is a single autographed portrait. At Wednes-day night dinners with a small circle of friends at the Hill-crest Country Club in Los Angeles, Elvis is not discussed, even if nearly everyone present devotes much of his time to promoting or selling Elvis. At parties Elvis's name is never mentioned.

"Two of the Colonel's good friends," says Stan, "are his plumber and his wife."

The Colonel and Elvis don't really see each other much, meeting only when it is necessary or so casually—introducing a fan backstage at the International—it seems not at all. They socialize rarely, perhaps once a year. One visitor to the Colonel's office says the Colonel admitted in the summer of 1969 that he hadn't heard the last three Elvis albums or seen the last four Elvis movies. Yet the relationship remains close.

"Think about the personalities who have meant as much as Elvis in terms of mass appeal," says Ron Jacobs. "There's Valentino, Sinatra, Elvis and the Beatles. And Parker and Elvis are tied up in so tight a knot, you cannot think of one without the other."

It is as if, back in 1955, when Elvis and the Colonel first shook hands, the Colonel told Elvis, "You stay talented and sexy and I'll make amazing deals that'll make us both rich as rajahs." Elvis has stayed talented and sexy, the Colonel has made amazing deals, and both are *richer* than rajahs today.

Scotty Moore, D. J. Fontana and Neal Matthews, one of the Jordanaires, were talking about how much confidence they thought Elvis had in the early days.

"It's hard to say how confident he was," Scotty said. "I think he had confidence the minute he walked on stage. But I don't see how he could have had any inkling he was gonna be as big a star as he was. He had a goal—"

Neal interrupted. "I don't think he thought that far ahead."

Scotty said, "It happened so fast. I don't think even today he realizes what he's done."

"That's right," said D. J. "I don't think he really realizes it."

APPENDIXES

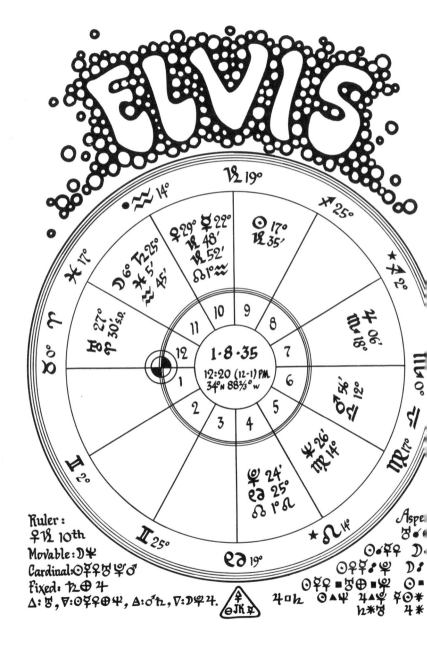

–A–

SUN IN CAPRICORN

GENERAL COMMENTS: The overall picture is schizoid. He is a curious mixture of the insensitive and the sentimental, capable of extreme emotional intensity and also of a corresponding coldness. When he's on, he's on all the way. When he's off, it's better to just let him be until his tune comes around again. An idealist who consciously expects to be hurt, he attempts in every way possible to protect himself from being hurt nonetheless. He has his own motives, could be called exceptionally selfish—but there is an impersonality about his selfishness, a naïveté or lack of comprehension that things could be any other way. He is very much a force of nature.

There are many basic conflicts. He's terribly suspicious, but he's also extremely gullible. His vision of the world is an idealist's vision and the honesty he seeks is based on that vision, so when someone's honesty doesn't match his, instead of realizing that everyone's different, he tends to think that the person is fooling him or himself. He's probably one of those people who are always a little bit outraged at the way people are as opposed to the way they *should be.* His view of the world is pretty narrow, rigid, opinionated, eccentric. He will change his opinions, but he doesn't like to change them for anyone else. I imagine his life is that of a pleasant dictator.

He is given to wild outbursts of temper. He tends to get morbid fantasies about how people are treating him and get angry. There is a tendency to fire and rehire people, to have erratic relationships with the people he works with.

He is also capable of giving, suddenly giving something beautiful, although it is easier for him to give things than himself. There is a lot of sentiment. He does not like to feel uncomfortable and he does not like to know others are uncomfortable; he really wants to make sure that people he cares about are all right. He is capable of being very kindly, of being suddenly taken on a trip and going into it all the way, of becoming totally involved. But his external involvements don't last very long; he tends to snap in and out of them.

He is the type who is very possessive if he thinks he is being threatened. He can be used by people and he fears being used by people, therefore he alternates moods: good-natured one day, in a black mood of melancholia the next.

He is a lot shyer than he would like to be. He needs people around him all the time, finding some kind of back-to-the-womb security in them. And he needs approval so much he probably is willing to take it from people he doesn't personally respect. He really needs flattery. He needs to be reassured.

He reacts violently to criticism, even from people close to him yet he is a perfectionist and his own harshest critic.

He is very conscious of his physical appearance. He probably gets worried if he notices a blemish, but he wouldn't like to appear unmanly about it. His tastes are unusual; he would tend to be more flashy than not—but conventionally flashy. He would also notice women's appearances. He would really dislike women to wear certain things. He can be quick to criticize bluntly, yet he is able to bowl people over with his charm.

He doesn't like to think of injustice being done, but he is only interested in what is right in front of him, so he is somewhat indifferent; he is not the great humanitarian he would like to think he is. A lot of things he does he does to fulfill a kind of little script he has written in his head about himself. He keeps a lot of true interests secret just out of a feeling that they're his and why should they be anybody else's.

Politically he seems to be indifferent and he reacts only when he feels it personally and then he is capable of being a violent revolutionary. He is capable of going along like a conservative, and suddenly something will outrage him and he will react like a Yippie. If you are on the right side and can demonstrate to him you are on the right side, you've got a good ally.

He is not one to let frustration eat at him. His endurance is good and he overcomes frustration by fighting through, and he is patient so long as he gets little satisfactions along the way.

He's got a shifting quantity of possessions, in that things can go in and go out of his life very rapidly—including money. Although he may not understand it technically, he likes quality—especially pretty, well-made things.

He probably likes some sort of slapstick humor. Freaky things will strike him. He can be very funny at times, have 'em rolling, but he takes himself seriously; there is a time to have fun and a time not to have fun.

He is very romantic. He has a romanticized self image. He swashbuckles to himself. He would like to James Bond it up. He would like to save the world in the sense of being somebody's hero. If you take the tone of a John O'Hara novel, something like *Appointment in Samarra,* and transfer it to Memphis, it probably would have something of the tone of the life he leads, although you would have to take out a lot of the intellectualization and put in a little hogfat or something.

EMOTIONAL / SEXUAL: Emotional maturity is a long, slow thing for him. He began to approach it in the last few years. There is something of the unawakened adolescent here. It takes him a long time to admit to love or feelings—even to himself—but once he does, it takes him a very long time to change them. He does a lot of superficial stuff, but his deepest feelings are very slow and steady, very traditional, very solid.

He was exposed to some traumatic, violent incidents as a child, which scarred him, so it is difficult for him to develop natural tenderness. The violence also directs his relationship with love and pain. It makes him something of a sado-masochist. He wants to be an apple pie boy, but he also has the urge to be stomped on. He really wants to idolize womanhood, but there is a Victorian fascination with wicked women. He dislikes mature or older women, prefers the young girls and the mother images. He has very strong sex drives, but a lot of his sexual energy is sublimated in his work. Sex is important mainly as a physical need. He is also hung up on ritual and fetishes.

FAMILY: He is almost fanatical about his family and home life, with the mother serving as the strong influence. He probably goes on melancholy trips; when she was alive, his mother predisposed him to melancholia. In fact, there is some indication his mother was a secret dipsomaniac. There is a sense of excessively emotional, weeping melodrama.

He probably didn't marry for so long because he felt so exposed and he couldn't commit himself, or he held secret morbid doubts of his own adequacy. There is a limitation in fatherhood, which means he may not be able to have other children, or there will be some trouble with the child he has, or perhaps he has a secret child; there is a sorrow in fatherhood. There is some secret involving incest or intermarriage. He is the type who will enjoy children most when they are out of infancy, when they are young enough that they won't be threatening but old enough to learn. He may adopt kids, support many kids not his own.

MENTAL: The mind and the emotions are tied in very strongly. He is instinctive almost totally. He has the capacity to pick up facts, but he reacts on an instinctive level entirely. He is much more intuitive than intellectual. I think he has some clairvoyant gift, operating for about half a second, which may be why he knows how to handle people. There is a feeling of knowing what is going to happen in a few minutes or seconds. His guesses will be good, so long as he's not emotionally involved. Even then they're not bad if he takes them first-hand, without rationalization.

PHYSICAL: He has tremendous physical energy, mostly nervous energy. It is mostly the excitation he gets from people. It is why he wants people around him, so he may draw energy from them. He has tremendous phsyical tolerance; he can survive just about anything. But there is some kind of nervous or glandular condition that doctors don't understand very well, and his ability to digest and assimilate is not all that great. He should not eat much meat or heavy Southern cooking. He should not smoke. If he gets interested in diet, he'll become fanatical about it, probably urging everyone around him to eat the same foods. Alcohol is a poison to him and his attraction to "speed" is dangerous to his liver and kidneys.

CAREER: Taurus is his rising sign, ruling music, which explains why he has a beautiful voice—that melodious, almost cowlike quality. His appreciation for stringed instruments and for the interweaving of sounds is highly developed. He probably likes to go off and practice by himself. Technically, he's really together.

But he could just as easily have been a carpenter, racing driver (land, air or sea) or mechanic, cocaine dealer or diplomat. He has an extremely good sense of public relations. He has evangelical gifts. He could, and may, become a great preacher in the Billy Graham tradition, or a politician. He is an instrument that a lot of people can work out on; he is a mass catalyst; he can pick up and transmit energy.

His financial judgment is not good at all. He tends to excess, which indicates other people somehow give him perspective. He is very lucky in partnerships, secret deals and strange arrangements. There is one special friend who is also a father figure and/or a mother figure, but the relationship with his real father is not at *all* positive.

His nerves get snarled unless he has something to do all the time. There are sudden enthusiasms and dislikes. He wants to do things *right now*, change horses in midstream, but usually only around old friends or in controlled circumstances. He keeps his cool with strangers. He is good in emergencies or stress situations as long as he can both lead and keep an adviser around.

He is a very hard worker, a perfectionist who seldom finds any lasting satisfaction.

He can do just about anything he wants to, and he has not reached his career peak.

FORECAST 1971–72: The key phrases are pressure from other people, investments mushrooming and dying strangely.

Early to mid-1971 his relationship with the Colonel or some other important business partner will radically alter in some way related to handling of assets and creative decisions. There is excellent support for stable personal and long-term interests and the home. But there will be unforeseen legal difficulties and the loss of a friend or family member. There will be continuing great power and support from past fans and attachments, making it possible that some religious or political conversion will come between March and September 1971, causing him to expend huge sums on some hidden or private quest. He may emerge as a powerful political figure in a few years, with an emphasis on conservation and individualism.

Caution in all travel is advised. He should avoid flying as much as possible. Periods centered in May 1971 and September and October 1971 are difficult for travel by air and sea. Lungs and nervous system are vulnerable at this time. He should avoid alcohol and all artificial stimulants and depressants like the plague through most of 1971 and the first part of 1972.

There will be many new friends and in some way socially a change. But either his marriage, a child or secret family obligation, or the fruit of a business partnership may go sour on him. There will be a very heavy period of mental and emotional coming of age in his thirty-seventh year (1972). He is going to surprise everybody, completely change or re-create his public image before the mid-1970s are over. He has a period of terrific strain in his home life in late 1975. He may become someone almost alien to his carefully built up "roots."

It is possible that he will get on the ecology bandwagon and sponsor some unique system of pollution reduction or reforestation. He has an energy pattern in his chart that makes him a very powerful force for whatever side he's on, and also makes it very hard to guess what side that will be. Potentially, there is a plentiful source for good. The testing and strain in 1971–72 will be the key to his direction for some time.

Prepared by Antonia Lamb
Los Angeles, 1970

DISCOGRAPHY

The records released through December 31, 1970, are listed here by label number and title, date of release and highest position reached on *Billboard*'s most important national sales charts, the Honor Roll of Hits and Top 100 until 1958, the Hot 100 since then. Other symbols: * means RCA claims a million or more sales; ** means RCA claims a million or more sales for both sides of the single; G means the Record Industry Association of America (RIAA) has presented a gold record, certifying a million or more copies sold in the case of singles and EPs, $1 million or more in retail sales for albums. RCA reports worldwide sales and the RIAA only national sales.

45 and 78 rpm singles released by Sun Records

1. **SUN 209**   August 1954
   "That's All Right [Mama]" / "Blue Moon of Kentucky"

2. **SUN 210**   October 1954
   "Good Rockin' Tonight" / "I Don't Care if the Sun Don't Shine"

3. **SUN 215**   January 1955
   "Milkcow Blues Boogie" / "You're a Heartbreaker"

4. **SUN 217**   May 1955
   "I'm Left, You're Right, She's Gone" / "Baby, Let's Play House"

5. **SUN 223**   August 1955
   "Mystery Train" / "I Forgot to Remember to Forget"

45 and 78 rpm singles released by RCA Victor

NOTE: Nearly all the early singles have been re-issued and given new release numbers. The numbers here are the original ones.

1. **RCA 6357**   November 1955
   "Mystery Train" / "I Forgot to Remember to Forget"

2. **RCA 6380**   November 1955
   "That's All Right [Mama]" / "Blue Moon of Kentucky"

3. **RCA 6381**   November 1955
   "Good Rockin' Tonight" / "I Don't Care if the Sun Don't Shine"

4. **RCA 6382**   November 1955
   "Milkcow Blues Boogie" / "You're a Heartbreaker"

5. **RCA 6383**   November 1955
   "I'm Left, You're Right, She's Gone" / "Baby, Let's Play House"

6. **RCA 6420**   January 1956 (1) (23) °°
   "Heartbreak Hotel" / "I Was the One"

7. **RCA 6540**   May 1956 (3) (31) °
   "I Want You, I Need You, I Love You" / "My Baby Left Me"

8. **RCA 6604**   July 1956 (1) (1) °°
   "Hound Dog" / "Don't Be Cruel"

9. **RCA 6636**   September 1956
   "Blue Suede Shoes" / "Tutti Frutti"

10. **RCA 6637**   September 1956
    "I'm Counting on You" / "I Got a Woman"

11. **RCA 6638**   September 1956
    "I'll Never Let You Go" / "I'm Gonna Sit Right Down and Cry Over You"

12. **RCA 6639**   September 1956
    "Tryin' to Get to You" / "I Love You Because"

13. **RCA 6640**   September 1956
    "Blue Moon" / "Just Because"

14. **RCA 6641**   September 1956
    "Money Honey" / "One-Sided Love Affair"

15. **RCA 6642**   September 1956
    "Shake, Rattle and Roll" / "Lawdy, Miss Clawdy"

16. **RCA 6643**   September 1956 (1) (27) °°
    "Love Me Tender" / "Any Way You Want Me"

17. **RCA 6800**   January 1957 (1) (34) °°
    "Too Much" / "Playing for Keeps"

18. **RCA 6870**   March 1957 (1) (58) °°
    "All Shook Up" / "That's When Your Heartaches Begin"

19. **RCA 7000**   June 1957 (1) (28) °°
    "Teddy Bear" / "Loving You"

20. **RCA 7035**   September 1957 (1) (27) °°
    "Jailhouse Rock" / "Treat Me Nice"

21. **RCA 7150**   December 1957 (1) (8) °°
    "Don't" / "I Beg of You"

22. **RCA 7240**   April 1958 (3) (21) °
    "Wear My Ring Around Your Neck" / "Doncha' Think It's Time"

23. RCA 7280   June 1958 (2) (28) ° G
   "Hard Headed Woman" / "Don't Ask Me Why"

Along with most other companies, RCA Victor discontinued the 78 rpm record in 1958, and the following are 45 rpm singles

24. RCA 7410   October 1958 (8) (4) °
   "I Got Stung" / "One Night"

25. RCA 7506   March 1959 (2) (4) °
   "A Fool Such As I" / "I Need Your Love Tonight"

26. RCA 7600   June 1959 (1) (12) °
   "A Big Hunk o' Love" / "My Wish Came True"

27. RCA 7740   March 1960 (1) (17) °
   "Stuck on You" / "Fame and Fortune"

28. RCA 7777   July 1960 (1) (32) ° °
   "It's Now or Never" / "A Mess of Blues"

29. RCA 7810   November 1960 (1) (20) ° °
   "Are You Lonesome Tonight" / "I Gotta Know"

30. RCA 7850   February 1961 (1) (32) °
   "Surrender" / "Lonely Man"

31. RCA 7880   May 1961 (5) (26) °
   "I Feel So Bad" / "Wild in the Country"

32. RCA 7908   August 1961 (5) (4) °
   "Little Sister" / "His Latest Flame"

33. RCA 7968   November 1961 (2) (23) ° ° G
   "Can't Help Falling in Love" / "Rock-a-Hula Baby"

34. RCA 7992   February 1962 (1) (31) ° °
   "Good Luck Charm" / "Anything That's Part of You"

35. RCA 8041   July 1962 (5) (55) °
   "She's Not You" / "Just Tell Her Jim Said Hello"

36. RCA 8100   October 1962 (2) (99) ° °
   "Return to Sender" / "Where Do You Come From"

37. RCA 8134   January 1963 (11) (53) °
   "One Broken Heart for Sale" / "They Remind Me Too Much of You"

38. RCA 8188   June 1963 (3) °
   "(You're the) Devil in Disguise" / "Please Don't Drag that String Around"

39. RCA 8243   October 1963 (8) (32) °
   "Bossa Nova Baby" / "Witchcraft"

40. RCA 8307   October 1963 (12) (29) °
   "Kissin' Cousins" / "It Hurts Me"

41. **RCA 0639**   **April 1964 (34)**
"Kiss Me Quick" / "Suspicion"

42. **RCA 8360**   **April 1964 (29) (21)** °
"Viva Las Vegas" / "What'd I Say"

43. **RCA 8400**   **July 1964 (16)**
"Such a Night" / "Never Ending"

44. **RCA 8440**   **September 1964 (16) (12)** °
"Ain't That Loving You, Baby" / "Ask Me"

45. **RCA 0720**   **November 1964**
"Blue Christmas" / "Wooden Heart"

46. **RCA 8500**   **March 1965 (21)**
"Do the Clam" / "You'll Be Gone"

47. **RCA 0643**   **April 1965 (3)** °
"Crying in the Chapel" / "I Believe in the Man in the Sky"

48. **RCA 8585**   **May 1965 (11) (55)**
"(Such an) Easy Question" / "It Feels So Right"

49. **RCA 8657**   **August 1965 (11)**
"I'm Yours" / "(It's a) Long Lonely Highway"

50. **RCA 0650**   **October 1965 (14)** °
"Puppet on a String" / "Wooden Heart"
NOTE: This is the second time "Wooden Heart" was on a single and the million-seller claimed is for this song.

51. **RCA 0647**   **November 1965**
"Blue Christmas" / "Santa Claus Is Back in Town"

52. **RCA 8740**   **January 1966 (33) (95)**
"Tell Me Why" / "Blue River"

53. **RCA 0651**   **February 1966**
"Joshua Fit the Battle" / "Known Only to Him"

54. **RCA 0652**   **February 1966**
"Milky White Way" / "Swing Down Sweet Chariot"

55. **RCA 8780**   **March 1966 (25) (45)**
"Frankie and Johnny" / "Please Don't Stop Loving Me"

56. **RCA 8870**   **June 1966 (19)**
"Love Letters" / "Come What May"

57. **RCA 8941**   **October 1966 (40) (41)**
"Spinout" / "All That I Am"

58. **RCA 8950**   **November 1966**
"If Every Day Was Like Christmas" / "How Would You Like to Be"

59. **RCA 9056**   **January 1967 (33)**
"Indescribably Blue" / "Fools Fall in Love"

60. **RCA 9115** May 1967 (63) (92)
"Long Legged Girl (with the Short Dress On)" / "That's Someone You Never Forget"

61. **RCA 9287** August 1967 (56) (78)
"There's Always Me" / "Judy"

62. **RCA 9341** September 1967 (38) (44)
"Big Boss Man" / "You Don't Know Me"

63. **RCA 9425** January 1968 (43)
"Guitar Man" / "High Heel Sneakers"

64. **RCA 9465** March 1968 (28) (67)
"U.S. Male" / "Stay Away, Joe"

65. **RCA 9600** April 1968 (90)
"You'll Never Walk Alone" / "We Call on Him"

66. **RCA 9547** May 1968 (71) (72)
"Let Yourself Go" / "Your Time Hasn't Come Yet, Baby"

67. **RCA 9610** September 1968 (63) (95)
"A Little Less Conversation" / "Almost in Love"

68. **RCA 9670** October 1968 (12) °
"If I Can Dream" / "Edge of Reality"

69. **RCA 9731** March 1969 (35)
"Memories" / "Charro"

70. **RCA 0130** April 1969
"How Great Thou Art" / "His Hand in Mine"

71. **RCA 9741** April 1969 (3) ° G
"In the Ghetto" / "Any Day Now"

72. **RCA 9747** June 1969 (35)
"Clean Up Your Own Back Yard" / "The Fair Is Moving On"

73. **RCA 9764** August 1969 (1) ° G
"Suspicious Minds" / "You'll Think of Me"

74. **RCA 9768** November 1969 (6) (6) ° G
"Don't Cry, Daddy" / "Rubberneckin'"

75. **RCA 9791** January 1970 (16) °
"Kentucky Rain" / "My Little Friend"

76. **RCA 9835** May 1970 (9) (9) ° G
"The Wonder of You" / "Mama Liked the Roses"

77. **RCA 9873** July 1970 (32) (32)
"I've Lost You" / "The Next Step Is Love"

78. **RCA 9916** October 1970 (11) (11)
"You Don't Have to Say You Love Me" / "Patch It Up"

33 1/3 rpm extended play (EP) albums released by RCA Victor

1. **RCA LPC 128**   January 1961 (14) °
   Elvis By Request: Flaming Star
   "Flaming Star," "Summer Kisses, Winter Tears," "Are You Lonesome Tonight," "It's Now or Never"

45 rpm extended play (EP) albums released by RCA Victor

NOTE: EP charts were not begun until 1957, and chart positions noted for records released in 1956 indicate positions reached as long as two years later

1. **RCA EPA 747**   1956
   Elvis Presley, Vol. 1
   "Blue Suede Shoes," "I'm Counting on You," "I Got a Woman," "One-Sided Love Affair"

2. **RCA EPA 1254**   1956
   Elvis Presley, Vol. 2
   "Tutti Frutti," "Tryin' to Get to You," "I'm Gonna Sit Right Down and Cry," "I'll Never Let You Go"

3. **RCA EPA 821**   1956 (5)
   Heartbreak Hotel
   "Heartbreak Hotel," "I Was the One," "I Forgot to Remember to Forget," "Money Honey"

4. **RCA EPA 830**   1956 (6)
   Elvis Presley
   "Shake, Rattle and Roll," "I Love You Because," "Blue Moon," "Lawdy, Miss Clawdy"

5. **RCA EPA 940**   1956
   The Real Elvis
   "Don't Be Cruel," "I Want You, I Need You, I Love You," "Hound Dog," "My Baby Left Me"

6. **RCA EPA 965**   1956
   Any Way You Want Me
   "Any Way You Want Me," "I'm Left, You're Right, She's Gone," "I Don't Care If the Sun Don't Shine," "Mystery Train"

7. **RCA EPA 4006**   1956 (10)
   Love Me Tender
   "Love Me Tender," "Let Me Be," "Poor Boy," "We're Gonna Move"

8. **RCA EPA 992**   1956 (4) G
   Elvis, Vol. 1
   "Rip It Up," "Love Me," "When My Blue Moon Turns to Gold Again," "Paralyzed"

9. **RCA EPA 993**   1956
   Elvis, Vol. 2
   "So Glad You're Mine," "Old Shep," "Ready Teddy," "Anyplace Is Paradise"

10. **RCA EPA 994**   1957
    Strictly Elvis
    "Long Tall Sally," "First in Line," "How Do You Think I Feel," "How's
    the World Treating You"

11. **RCA EPA 1-1515**   1957 (1)
    Loving You, Vol. 1
    "Loving You," "Party," "Teddy Bear," "True Love"

12. **RCA EPA 2-1515**   1957 (4)
    Loving You, Vol. 2
    "Lonesome Cowboy," "Hot Dog," "Mean Woman Blues," "Got a Lot o'
    Livin' to Do"

13. **RCA EPA 4041**   1957 (2)
    Just for You
    "I Need You So," "Have I Told You Lately That I Love You," "Blue-
    berry Hill," "Is It So Strange"

14. **RCA EPA 4054**   1957 (3)
    Peace in the Valley
    "Peace in the Valley," "It Is No Secret," "I Believe," "Take My Hand,
    Precious Lord"

15. **RCA EPA 4108**   1957 (2)
    Elvis Sings Christmas Songs
    "Santa Bring My Baby Back," "Blue Christmas," "Santa Claus Is Back in
    Town," "I'll Be Home for Christmas"

16. **RCA EPA 4114**   1957 (1) ° G
    Jailhouse Rock
    "Jailhouse Rock," "Young and Beautiful," "I Want to Be Free," "Don't
    Leave Me Now," "Baby, I Don't Care"

17. **RCA EPA 4319**   1958 (1)
    King Creole, Vol. 1
    "King Creole," "New Orleans," "As Long As I Have You," "Lover Doll"

18. **RCA EPA 4321**   1958 (1)
    King Creole, Vol. 2
    "Trouble," "Young Dreams," "Crawfish," "Dixieland Rock"

19. **RCA EPA 4325**   1958
    Elvis Sails
    Excerpts from the press interview with Elvis at the Brooklyn Army
    Terminal, September 22, 1958

20. **RCA EPA 4340**   1958
    Christmas with Elvis
    "White Christmas," "Here Comes Santa Claus," "O Little Town of
    Bethlehem," "Silent Night"

21. **RCA EPA 5088**   1959
    A Touch of Gold, Vol. 1
    "Hard Headed Woman," "Good Rockin' Tonight," "Don't," "I Beg of
    You"

22. **RCA EPA 5101** 1959
A Touch of Gold, Vol. 2
"Wear My Ring Around Your Neck," "Treat Me Nice," "One Night," "That's All Right [Mama]"

23. **RCA EPA 5141** 1960
A Touch of Gold, Vol. 3
"Blue Moon of Kentucky," "All Shook Up," "Don't Ask Me Why," "Too Much"

24. **RCA EPA 4368** 1962 (15 in Hot 100)
Follow That Dream
"Follow That Dream," "What a Wonderful Life," "Angel," "I'm Not the Marrying Kind"

25. **RCA EPA 4371** 1962 (30 in Hot 100)
Kid Galahad
"This Is Living," "I Got Lucky," "A Whistling Tune," "King of the Whole Wide World," "Riding the Rainbow," "Home Is Where the Heart Is"

26. **RCA EPA 4382** 1964 (92 in Hot 100)
Viva Las Vegas
"If You Think I Don't Need You," "I Need Somebody to Lean On," "C'mon Everybody," "Tomorrow and Forever"

27. **RCA EPA 4383** 1965 (70 in Hot 100)
Tickle Me
"I Feel That I've Known You Forever," "Slowly But Surely," "Night Rider," "Dirty, Dirty Feeling," "Put the Blame on Me"

28. **RCA EPA 4387** 1967
Easy Come, Easy Go
"Easy Come, Easy Go," "The Love Machine," "Yoga Is As Yoga Does," "You Gotta Stop," "Sing, You Children," "I'll Take Love"

33 1/3 rpm albums released by RCA Victor

1. **RCA LSP 1254** April 1956 (1) ° G
Elvis Presley
"Blue Suede Shoes," "I'm Counting on You," "I Got a Woman," "One-Sided Love Affair," "I Love You Because," "Just Because," "Tutti Frutti," "Tryin' to Get to You," "I'm Gonna Sit Right Down and Cry," "I'll Never Let You Go," "Blue Moon," "Money Honey"

2. **RCA LSP 1382** October 1956 (1) ° G
Elvis
"Rip It Up," "Love Me," "When My Blue Moon Turns to Gold Again," "Long Tall Sally," "First in Line," "Paralyzed," "So Glad You're Mine," "Old Shep," "Ready Teddy," "Anyplace Is Paradise," "How's the World Treating You," "How Do You Think I Feel"

3. **RCA LSP 1515**   July 1957 (1) ° G
Loving You
From the film: "Mean Woman Blues," "Teddy Bear," "Loving You," "Got a Lot o' Lovin' to Do," "Lonesome Cowboy," "Hot Dog," "Party" Bonus Songs: "Blueberry Hill," "True Love," "Don't Leave Me Now," "Have I Told You Lately That I Love You," "I Need You So"

4. **RCA LSP 1035**   November 1957 (1) ° G
Elvis' Christmas Album
"Santa Claus Is Back in Town," "White Christmas," "Here Comes Santa Claus," "I'll Be Home for Christmas," "Blue Christmas," "Santa Bring My Baby Back," "O Little Town of Bethlehem," "Silent Night," "Peace in the Valley," "I Believe," "Take My Hand, Precious Lord," "It Is No Secret"

5. **RCA LSP 1707**   March 1958 (3) ° G
Elvis' Golden Records
"Hound Dog," "Loving You," "All Shook Up," "Heartbreak Hotel," "Jailhouse Rock," "Love Me," "Too Much," "Don't Be Cruel," "That's When Your Heartaches Begin," "Teddy Bear," "Love Me Tender," "Treat Me Nice," "Any Way You Want Me," "I Want You, I Need You, I Love You"

6. **RCA LSP 1884**   August 1958 (2) °
King Creole
"King Creole," "As Long As I Have You," "Hard Headed Woman," "Trouble," "Dixieland Rock," "Don't Ask Me Why," "Lover Doll," "Crawfish," "Young Dreams," "Steadfast, Loyal and True," "New Orleans"

7. **RCA LSP 1990**   February 1959 (23)
For LP Fans Only
"That's All Right," "Lawdy, Miss Clawdy," "Mystery Train," "Poor Boy," "Playing for Keeps," "My Baby Left Me," "I Was the One," "Shake, Rattle and Roll," "You're a Heartbreaker," "I'm Left, You're Right, She's Gone"

8. **RCA LSP 2011**   August 1959 (32)
A Date with Elvis
"Blue Moon of Kentucky," "Young and Beautiful," "Baby, I Don't Care," "Milkcow Blues Boogie," "Baby, Let's Play House," "Good Rockin' Tonight," "Is It So Strange," "We're Gonna Move," "I Want to Be Free," "I Forgot to Remember to Forget"

9. **RCA LSP 2075**   December 1959 (31) ° G
50,000,000 Elvis Fans Can't Be Wrong, Elvis' Gold Records, Vol. 2
"A Fool Such As I," "I Need Your Love Tonight," "Wear My Ring Around Your Neck," "Doncha' Think It's Time," "I Beg of You," "A Big Hunk o' Love," "Don't," "My Wish Came True," "One Night," "I Got Stung"

10. **RCA LSP 2231**   **April 1960 (2)** °
Elvis Is Back
"Fever," "Girl Next Door Went A-Walking," "Soldier Boy," "Make Me Know It," "I Will Be Home Again," "Reconsider, Baby," "It Feels So Right," "Like a Baby," "The Girl of My Best Friend," "Thrill of Your Love," "Such a Night," "Dirty, Dirty Feeling"

11. **RCA LSP 2256**   **October 1960 (1)** ° G
G.I. Blues
"Tonight Is So Right for Love," "What's She Really Like," "Frankfort Special," "Wooden Heart," "G.I. Blues," "Pocketful of Rainbows," "Shoppin' Around," "Big Boots," "Didja' Ever," "Blue Suede Shoes," "Doin' the Best I Can"

12. **RCA LSP 2328**   **December 1960 (87)** ° G
His Hand in Mine
"His Hand in Mine," "I'm Gonna Walk Dem Golden Stairs," "In My Father's House," "Milky White Way," "Known Only to Him," "I Believe in the Man in the Sky," "Joshua Fit the Battle," "Jesus Knows What I Need," "Swing Down, Sweet Chariot," "Mansion over the Hilltop," "If We Never Meet Again," "Working on the Building"

13. **RCA LSP 2370**   **June 1961 (1)** °
Something for Everybody
The Ballad Side: "There's Always Me," "Give Me the Right," "It's a Sin," "Sentimental Me," "Starting Today," "Gently," The Rhythm Side: "I'm Comin' Home," "In Your Arms," "Put the Blame on Me," "Judy," "I Want You with Me" Also: "I Slipped, I Stumbled, I Fell" (from *Wild in the Country*)

14. **RCA LSP 2436**   **October 1961 (1)** ° G
Blue Hawaii
"Blue Hawaii," "Almost Always True," "Aloha Oe," "No More," "Can't Help Falling in Love," "Rock-a-Hula Baby," "Moonlight Swim," "Ku-u-i-po," "Ito Eats," "Slicin' Sand," "Hawaiian Sunset," "Beach Boy Blues," "Island of Love," "Hawaiian Wedding Song"

15. **RCA LSP 2523**   **June 1962 (4)**
Pot Luck
"Kiss Me Quick," "Just for Old Times' Sake," "Gonna Get Back Home Somehow," "Easy Question," "Steppin' Out of Line" (from *Blue Hawaii*), "I'm Yours," "Something Blue," "Suspicion," "I Feel That I've Known You Forever," "Night Rider," "Fountain of Love," "That's Someone You Never Forget"

16. **RCA LSP 2621**   **November 1962 (3)** ° G
Girls! Girls! Girls!
"Girls! Girls! Girls!" "I Don't Wanna Be Tied," "Where Do You Come From," "I Don't Want To," "We'll Be Together," "A Boy Like Me, a Girl Like You," "Earth Boy," "Return to Sender," "Because of Love," "Thanks to the Rolling Sea," "Song of the Shrimp," "The Walls Have Ears," "We're Coming in Loaded"

17. RCA LSP 2697   March 1963 (4)
It Happened at the World's Fair
"Beyond the Bend," "Relax," "Take Me to the Fair," "They Remind Me
Too Much of You," "One Broken Heart for Sale," "I'm Falling in Love
Tonight," "Cotton Candy Land," "A World of Our Own," "How Would
You Like to Be," "Happy Ending"

18. RCA LSP 2765   September 1963 (4) ° G
Elvis' Golden Records, Vol. 3
"It's Now or Never," "Stuck on You," "Fame and Fortune," "I Gotta
Know," "Surrender," "I Feel So Bad," "Are You Lonesome Tonight,"
"His Latest Flame," "Little Sister," "Good Luck Charm," "Anything
That's Part of You," "She's Not You"

19. RCA LSP 2756   November 1963 (3) °
Fun in Acapulco
"Fun in Acapulco," "Vino, Dinero y Amor," "Mexico," "El Toro," "Mar-
guerita," "The Bullfighter Was a Lady," "No Room to Rhumba in a
Sports Car," "I Think I'm Gonna Like It Here," "Bossa Nova Baby,"
"You Can't Say No in Acapulco," "Guadalajara" Bonus Songs: "Love
Me Tonight," "Slowly But Surely"

20. RCA LSP 2894   March 1964 (6)
Kissin' Cousins
"Kissin' Cousins," "Smokey Mountain Boy," "There's Gold in the Moun-
tains," "One Boy, Two Little Girls," "Catchin' On Fast," "Tender Feel-
ing," "Anyone," "Barefoot Ballad," "Once Is Enough," "Kissin' Cousins"
Also: "Echoes of Love," "Long, Lonely Highway"

21. RCA LSP 2999   October 1964 (1) °
Roustabout
"Roustabout," "Little Egypt," "Poison Ivy League," "Hard Knocks,"
"It's a Wonderful World," "Big Love, Big Heartache," "One-Track
Heart," "It's Carnival Time," "Carny Town," "There's a Brand New
Day on the Horizon," "Wheels on My Heels"

22. RCA LSP 3338   April 1965 (8)
Girl Happy
"Girl Happy," "Spring Fever," "Fort Lauderdale Chamber of Com-
merce," "Startin' Tonight," "Wolf Call," "Do Not Disturb," "Cross My
Heart and Hope to Die," "The Meanest Girl in Town," "Do the Clam,"
"Puppet on a String," "I've Got to Find My Baby" Bonus Song: "You'll
Be Gone"

23. RCA LSP 3450   July 1965 (10)
Elvis for Everyone
"Your Cheatin' Heart," "Summer Kisses, Winter Tears," "Finders Keepers,
Losers Weepers," "In My Way" (from *Wild in the Country*), "Tomor-
row Night," "Memphis, Tennessee," "For the Millionth and the Last
Time," "Forget Me Never" (from *Wild in the Country*), "Sound Ad-
vice" (from *Follow That Dream*), "Santa Lucia" (From *Viva Las
Vegas*), "I Met Her Today," "When It Rains, It Really Pours"

24. RCA LSP 3468 October 1965 (8)
Harum Scarum

"Harem Holiday," "My Desert Serenade," "Go East—Young Man," "Mirage," "Kismet," "Shake That Tambourine," "Hey Little Girl," "Golden Coins," "So Close, Yet So Far" Bonus Songs: "Animal Instinct," "Wisdom of the Ages"

25. RCA LSP 3553 April 1966 (20)
Frankie and Johnny

"Frankie and Johnny," "Come Along," "Petunia, the Gardener's Daughter," "Chesay," "What Every Woman Lives For," "Look Out, Broadway," "Beginner's Luck," "Down by the Riverside" and "When the Saints Go Marching In" (medley), "Shout It Out," "Hard Luck," "Please Don't Stop Loving Me," "Everybody Come Aboard"

26. RCA LSP 3643 June 1966 (15)
Paradise, Hawaiian Style

"Paradise, Hawaiian Style," "Queenie Wahine's Papaya," "Scratch My Back," "Drums of the Islands," "Datin'," "A Dog's Life," "House of Sand," "Stop Where You Are," "This Is My Heaven" Bonus Song: "Sand Castles"

27. RCA LSP 3702 October 1966 (18)
Spinout

"Stop, Look and Listen," "Adam and Evil," "All That I Am," "Never Say Yes," "Am I Ready," "Beach Shack," "Spinout," "Smorgasbord," "I'll Be Back" Bonus Songs: "Tomorrow Is a Long Time," "Down in the Alley," "I'll Remember You"

28. RCA LSP 3758 March 1967 (18) ° G
How Great Thou Art

"How Great Thou Art," "In the Garden," "Somebody Bigger Than You and I," "Farther Along," "Stand by Me," "Without Him," "So High," "Where Could I Go But to the Lord," "By and By," "If the Lord Wasn't Walking by My Side," "Run On," "Where No One Stands Alone," "Crying in the Chapel"

29. RCA LSP 3787 June 1967 (47)
Double Trouble

"Double Trouble," "Baby, If You'll Give Me All of Your Love," "Could I Fall in Love," "Long Legged Girl," "City by Night," "Old MacDonald," "I Love Only One Girl," "There Is So Much World to See" Bonus Songs: "It Won't Be Long," "Never Ending," "Blue River," "What Now, What Next, Where To"

30. RCA LSP 3893 November 1967 (40)
Clambake

"Clambake," "Who Needs Money," "A House That Has Everything," "Confidence," "Hey, Hey, Hey," "You Don't Know Me," "The Girl I Never Loved" Bonus Songs: "Guitar Man," "How Can You Lose What You Never Had," "Big Boss Man," "Singing Tree," "Just Call Me Lonesome"

31. **RCA LSP 3921** February 1968 (33)
Elvis' Gold Records, Vol. 4
"Love Letters," "Witchcraft," "It Hurts Me," "What'd I Say," "Please Don't Drag That String Around," "Indescribably Blue," "You're the Devil in Disguise," "Lonely Man," "A Mess of Blues," "Ask Me," "Ain't That Loving You, Baby," "Just Tell Her Jim Said Hello"

32. **RCA LSP 3989** June 1968 (82)
Speedway
"Speedway," "There Ain't Nothing Like a Song" (with Nancy Sinatra), "Your Time Hasn't Come Yet, Baby," "Who Are You," "He's Your Uncle, Not Your Dad," "Let Yourself Go," "Your Groovy Self" (with Nancy Sinatra) Bonus Songs: "Five Sleepy Heads," "Western Union," "Mine," "Goin' Home," "Suppose"

33. **RCA PRS 279** November 1968
Elvis Singing Flaming Star and Others
"Flaming Star (from *Flaming Star*), "Wonderful World" (from *Live a Little, Love a Little*), "Night Life," "All I Needed Was the Rain," "Too Much Monkey Business," "Yellow Rose of Texas" and "The Eyes of Texas" (medley), "She's a Machine," "Do the Vega," "Tiger Man" (recorded live at NBC for the *Elvis* special, for which this album was released through Singer Sewing Centers)

34. **RCA LPM 4088** December 1968 (8) ° G
Elvis (TV Special)
"Trouble" and "Guitar Man," "Lawdy, Miss Clawdy" and "Baby, What You Want Me to Do," *Dialogue*, Medley: "Heartbreak Hotel," "Hound Dog," "All Shook Up," "Can't Help Falling In Love," "Jailhouse Rock," *Dialogue*, "Love Me Tender," *Dialogue*, "Where Could I Go But to the Lord," "Up Above My Head" and "Saved," *Dialogue*, "Blue Christmas," *Dialogue*, "One Night," "Memories," Medley: "Nothingville," *Dialogue*, "Big Boss Man," "Guitar Man," "Little Egypt," "Trouble," "Guitar Man," "If I Can Dream"

35. **RCA LSP 4155** May 1969 (13) ° G
From Elvis in Memphis
"Wearin' That Loved On Look," "Only the Strong Survive," "I'll Hold You in My Heart," "Long Black Limousine," "It Keeps Right on A-Hurtin'," "I'm Movin' On," "Power of My Love," "Gentle on My Mind," "After Loving You," "True Love Travels on a Gravel Road," "Any Day Now," "In the Ghetto"-

36. **RCA LSP 6020** November 1969 (12) ° G
From Memphis to Vegas / From Vegas to Memphis (2-record set)
"Blue Suede Shoes," "Johnny B. Goode," "All Shook Up," "Are You Lonesome Tonight," "Hound Dog," "I Can't Stop Loving You," "My Babe," "Mystery Train" and "Tiger Man" (medley), "Words," "In the Ghetto," "Suspicious Minds," "Can't Help Falling in Love," "Inherit the Wind," "This Is the Story," "Stranger in My Own Home Town," "A Little Bit of Green," "And the Grass Won't Pay No Mind," "Do You Know Who I Am," "From a Jack to a King," "The Fair's Moving On," "You'll Think of Me," "Without Love"

37. **RCA LSP 4362**   May 1970 (13)
    On Stage: February, 1970
    "See See Rider," "Release Me," "Sweet Caroline," "Runaway," "The
    Wonder of You," "Polk Salad Annie," "Yesterday," "Proud Mary," "Walk
    a Mile in My Shoes," "Let It Be Me"

38. **RCA LPM 6401**   August 1970 (45)
    Worldwide 50 Gold Award Hits, Vol. 1
    "Heartbreak Hotel," "I Was the One," "I Want You, I Need You, I Love
    You," "Don't Be Cruel," "Hound Dog," "Love Me Tender," "Any Way
    You Want Me," "Too Much," "Playing for Keeps," "All Shook Up,"
    "That's When Your Heartaches Begin," "Loving You," "Teddy Bear,"
    "Jailhouse Rock," "Treat Me Nice," "I Beg of You," "Don't," "Wear My
    Ring Around Your Neck," "Hard Headed Woman," "I Got Stung," "A
    Fool Such As I," "A Big Hunk o' Love," "Stuck on You," "A Mess of
    Blues," "It's Now or Never," "I Gotta Know," "Are You Lonesome To-
    night," "Surrender," "I Feel So Bad," "Little Sister," "Can't Help Falling
    in Love," "Rock-a-Hula Baby," "Anything That's Part of You," "Good
    Luck Charm," "She's Not You," "Return to Sender," "Where Do You
    Come From," "One Broken Heart for Sale," "Devil in Disguise," "Bossa
    Nova Baby," "Kissin' Cousins," "Viva Las Vegas," "Ain't That Loving
    You, Baby," "Wooden Heart," "Crying in the Chapel," "If I Can
    Dream," "In the Ghetto," "Suspicious Minds," "Don't Cry, Daddy,"
    "Kentucky Rain" Plus: Excerpts from *Elvis Sails*

39. **RCA LSP 4429**   November 1970 (183)
    Back In Memphis
    "Inherit the Wind," "This Is the Story," "Stranger in My Own Home
    Town," "A Little Bit of Green," "The Grass Won't Pay No Mind," "Do
    You Know Who I Am," "From a Jack to a King," "The Fair's Moving
    On," "You'll Think of Me," "Without Love." (NOTE: If this list looks
    familiar, it is because it matches the list of songs on one of the two discs
    released one year earlier as *From Memphis to Vegas / From Vegas to
    Memphis*. It is incredible that RCA would attempt to market the same
    material. The *Billboard* charts show the scheme was only moderately
    successful.)

40. **RCA LSP 4445**   December 1970 (21)
    Elvis: That's the Way It Is
    "I Just Can't Help Believin'," "Twenty Days and Twenty Nights," "How
    the Web Was Woven," "Patch It Up," "Mary in the Morning," "You
    Don't Have to Say You Love Me," "You've Lost That Lovin' Feeling,"
    "I've Lost You," "Just Pretend," "Stranger in the Crowd," "The Next
    Step Is Love," "Bridge Over Troubled Water." (NOTE: Only "I just
    Can't Help Believin'" is from the film soundtrack; all the others are
    studio cuts.)

*33 1/3 rpm albums released by RCA Victor on their low-priced Camden
subsidiary*

1. **RCA CAS 2304**   April 1969 (96)
   Elvis Sings Flaming Star
   A rerelease of the Singer album originally issued November 1968

2. RCA CAS 2408 April 1970 (105)
Let's Be Friends
"Stay Away, Joe" (from *Stay Away Joe*), "If I'm a Fool," "Let's Be Friends," "Let's Forget About the Stars," "Mama" (from *Girls! Girls! Girls!*), "I'll Be There," "Almost" (from *The Trouble With Girls*), "Change of Habit" (from *Change of Habit*), "Have a Happy" (from *Change of Habit*)

3. RCA CAL 2428 November 1970
Elvis' Christmas Album
"Blue Chistmas," "Silent Night," "White Christmas," "Santa Claus Is Back in Town," "I'll Be Home for Christmas," "If Every Day Was Like Christmas," "Here Comes Santa Claus," "O Little Town of Bethlehem," "Santa Bring My Baby Back," "Mama Liked the Roses." (NOTE: All except "If Every Day Was Like Christmas" and "Mama Liked the Roses" are from the RCA Christmas album first issued in 1957.)

4. RCA CAS 2440 November 1970 (65)
Almost in Love
"Almost in Love" (from *Live a Little, Love a Little*), "Long Legged Girl" (from *Double Trouble*), "Edge of Reality" (from *Live a Little . . .*), "My Little Friend," "A Little Less Conversation" (from *Live a Little . . .*), "Rubberneckin'," (from *Change of Habit*), "Clean Up Your Own Back Yard" (from *The Trouble With Girls*), "U.S. Male," "Charro" (from *Charro*), "Stay Away, Joe" (from *Stay Away, Joe*)

Records offering otherwise unavailable material, released without authorization for collectors and the "bootleg" or "pirate" trade; all appeared in 1970

1. *Please Release Me* (33⅓ rpm album) "Fame and Fortune" and "Stuck on You" (from Frank Sinatra TV special), "Teddy Bear" and "Got a Lot o' Livin' to Do" (from *Loving You*), "Treat Me Nice" and "Jailhouse Rock" (from *Jailhouse Rock*), "A Cane and High Starched Collar" (from *Flaming Star*), "The Lady Loves Me" (duet with Ann-Margret from *Viva Las Vegas*), "C'mon Everybody" (from *Viva Las Vegas*), "Dominique" (from *Stay Away, Joe*), "Baby, What Do You Want Me to Do" (guitar instrumental from Elvis TV special), interviews from 1956-57.

2. "My Baby Is Gone" / "Baby, Let's Play House" (45 rpm single released with *Please Release Me;* "My Baby Is Gone" is a slow version of "I'm Left, You're Right, She's Gone," from an unreleased Sun tape)

3. *Untitled* (45 rpm extended play [EP] album) "My Baby Is Gone," "Jailhouse Rock" (instrumental theme from *Jailhouse Rock*), "A Cane and High Starched Collar" (from *Flaming Star*), "Love Me Tender" / "Heartbreak Hotel" / "Hound Dog" / "Peace in the Valley" / "Love Me" (medley from Ed Sullivan Show, 1957), "Got a Lot o' Livin' to Do" (from *Loving You*)

4. *The Hillbilly Cat Lives at the International Hotel* (2-record set) "That's All Right [Mama]," "I Got a Woman," "Tiger Man," "Love Me Tender," "I've Lost You," "I Just Can't Help Believin'," "You've Lost That Loving Feeling," "Polk Salad Annie," "Johnny B. Goode," "The Wonder of You," "Heartbreak Hotel," "Blue Suede Shoes," "Whole Lotta Shaking Going On," "Hound Dog," "One Night," "Bridge Over Troubled Water" "Suspicious Minds," "Can't Help Falling in Love" (with dialogue, from a performance recorded in August 1970), "I Got a Woman," "Hound Dog," "Polk Salad Annie," "Heartbreak Hotel," "One Night," "When the Snow Is on the Roses" (from another show during same engagement)

–C–

THE FILMS

The films are listed chronologically, according to release date.

1. *Love Me Tender* (20th Century-Fox) November 1956
2. *Loving You* (Paramount) July 1957
3. *Jailhouse Rock* (Metro-Goldwyn-Mayer) October 1957
4. *King Creole* (Paramount) May 1958
5. *G.I. Blues* (Paramount) October 1960
6. *Flaming Star* (20th Century-Fox) December 1960
7. *Wild in the Country* (20th Century-Fox) June 1961
8. *Blue Hawaii* (Paramount) November 1961
9. *Follow That Dream* (United Artists) March 1962
10. *Kid Galahad* (United Artists) July 1962
11. *Girls! Girls! Girls!* (Paramount) November 1962
12. *It Happened at the World's Fair* (Metro-Goldwyn-Mayer) April 1963
13. *Fun in Acapulco* (Paramount) November 1963
14. *Kissin' Cousins* (Metro-Goldwyn-Mayer) March 1964 .
15. *Viva Las Vegas* (Metro-Goldwyn-Mayer) May 1964
16. *Roustabout* (Paramount) November 1964
17. *Girl Happy* (Metro-Goldwyn-Mayer) January 1965
18. *Tickle Me* (Allied Artists) September 1965
19. *Harum Scarum* (Metro-Goldwyn-Mayer) October 1965
20. *Frankie and Johnny* (United Artists) March 1966
21. *Paradise, Hawaiian Style* (Paramount) June 1966
22. *Spinout* (Metro-Goldwyn-Mayer) October 1966
23. *Easy Come, Easy Go* (Paramount) March 1967
24. *Double Trouble* (Metro-Goldwyn-Mayer) April 1967
25. *Clambake* (United Artists) October 1967
26. *Stay Away, Joe* (Metro-Goldwyn-Mayer) March 1968
27. *Speedway* (Metro-Goldwyn-Mayer) May 1968

28. *Live a Little, Love a Little* (Metro-Goldwyn-Mayer) October 1968
29. *Charro* (National General Corporation) March 1969
30. *The Trouble with Girls* (Metro-Goldwyn-Mayer) May 1969
31. *Change of Habit* (NBC-Universal) October 1969
32. *Elvis: That's the Way It Is* (Metro-Goldwyn-Mayer) November 1970

–D–

ACKNOWLEDGMENTS

There were more than a thousand sources: dozens of books, plus all the articles in all the magazines, with special thanks to the offices (and the files) of *Billboard* and *The Hollywood Reporter,* plus all the newspapers, with the most help coming from the files of the New York *Times* (1956–70), the Los Angeles *Times* (1956–70), the Nashville *Tennessean* (1956–70), the Memphis *Press-Scimitar* (1954–70) and the *Daily Journal* in Tupelo (1930–70). Thanks, too, to the Tupelo Public Library and the Library of the Academy of Motion Picture Arts and Sciences in Hollywood.

All these sources probably had mistakes in them. So did some, and perhaps all, of the following. They are the warm and cooperative people who gave their time and granted interviews.

In Tupelo: Mayor James Ballard, Mr. and Mrs. J. C. Grimes, Mrs. Faye Harris, Mrs. Tressie Miller, the Reverend Eugene Moffat, Buck Presley, Hershell Presley, J. M. (Ikey) Savery and John Tidwell.

In Memphis: Mrs. Ruby Black, James Blackwood, Stanley Booth, T. C. Brindley, Ray Brown, Richard Davis, Buzzie Forbess, Mrs. Elgie Forbess, Alan Fortas, Arthur Groom, Edwin Howard, W. J. Huettel, Bob Johnson, Stan Kesler, James Kingsley, Jerry Lee Lewis, Marion Keisker MacInnes, Elsie Marmann, Chips Moman, Herbie Omell, Gary and Mr. and Mrs. Sterling G. Pepper, Sam Phillips, Tom Phillips, Vester Presley, Mrs. Jane Richardson, Mildred Scrivener, Willie Smith, James and Gladys Tipler and Bobby (Red) West.

In Nashville: Roy Acuff, Jack Clement, Oscar Davis, D. J. Fontana, Jack Hurst, Juanita Jones, the Jordanaires (Gordon Stoker, Neal Matthews, Hoyt Hawkins, Ray Walker), Scotty Moore, Bob and Helen Neal, Minnie Pearl, Webb Pierce, Cecil Scaife, Dolores Watson Siegenthaler, Mrs. Jo Walker, Bill Williams and Happy Wilson.

In Shreveport: Frank Page.

In New York: Fred Bienstock, Otis Blackwell, David Dalton, Ahmet Ertegun, Jerry Leiber, Mort Shuman and Mike Stoller.

In Los Angeles: Gerald Drayson Adams, Steve Allen, Wally Beene, Bill Belew, Steve Binder, Bill Bixby, Robert (Bumps) Blackwell, Hal Blaine, Dudley Brooks, Stan Brossette, Walter Burrell, James Burton, Mrs. Virginia Coons, Yvonne Craig, Ken Darby, Mac Davis, Dolores (Dee) Fuller, Billy Goldenberg, Jack Good, Charles Greene, Glenn D. Hardin, Jon Hartmann, Bones Howe, Ron Jacobs, Pete Johnson, Sam Katzman, Antonia Lamb, Lance LeGault, Larry Muhoberac, Gene Nelson, Rick Nelson, Bill O'Hallaren, Johnny Otis, Joe Pasternak, Little Richard Penniman, Ellen Pollon, Jim Rissmiller, Johnny Rivers, Denis Sanders, Jerry Scheff, Phil Spector, Cliffie Stone, Dean Torrance, Moe Weise, Ben Weisman, John Wilson and Steve Wolf.

In Las Vegas: The employees and officers of the International Hotel.

Thanks also to the dozens more who talked off the record or asked not to be quoted. As is usual with such sources, if there seemed to be an ax to grind, the information was discounted.

And all the fans, especially Bill Kaval, who helped with the discography, and Rex Martin, for providing so many rare audio tapes.

Photos courtesy of the Gilloon Agency, United Press International, Lillian Foscue Vann, 20th Century-Fox Film Corporation, Paramount Pictures Corporation, Metro-Goldwyn-Mayer Studios, National General Corporation, National Broadcasting Company, U.S. Army.

Thanks to Jerry Kay for the astro chart on page 422.

And finally, thanks to Jann Wenner and *Rolling Stone,* for the impetus and continued support.